THE SUNDAY TIMES
COOK'S
COMPANION

Edited by
Shona Crawford Poole and Richard Girling

EBURY PRESS
LONDON

First published in 1993

1 3 5 7 9 10 8 6 4 2

First published in the United Kingdom in 1993 by Ebury Press
Random House, 20 Vauxhall Bridge Road, London SW1V 2SA

Random House Australia (Pty) Limited
20 Alfred Street, Milsons Point, Sydney,
New South Wales 2061, Australia

Random House New Zealand Limited
18 Poland Road, Glenfield,
Auckland 10, New Zealand

Random House South Africa (Pty) Limited
PO Box 337, Bergvlei, South Africa

Random House UK Limited Reg. No. 954009

Editor: Susan Fleming
Designer: Sara Kidd
Illustrations: Coral Mula
Photographs: Graham Kirk and Charlie Stebbings

A CIP catalogue record for this book
is available from the British Library

ISBN 0 09 178170 1

Typeset by Textype Typesetters, Cambridge
Printed and bound in Great Britain by Butler & Tanner Ltd, Frome and London

CONTENTS

INTRODUCTION

'**T**he good cook,' says Anton Mosimann, 'is an eternal apprentice.' There could be no clearer exposition of the spirit in which this book has been written. Being a good cook is as much a matter of attitude as it is of experience. No-one need ever be a *bad* cook. Even the novice, if he or she accepts good advice, can begin by cooking simple things *well*.

It is not easy to associate the exquisite creations of Raymond Blanc with the robust, one-pot dishes of the farmhouse kitchen. Yet the association is one that M.Blanc himself cherishes and cannot forget. In cookery, as in art, simplicity is the surest sign of perfection: good, seasonal ingredients that taste of themselves; harmonious combinations of texture and flavour. By the Blanc canon, good food may as easily be a dish of perfectly cooked new potatoes as of wild mushrooms stuffed with chicken mousse. There are peaks, he says, and there are plains. Not better or worse, but just different; and it is important to enjoy them both.

The aim of *The Sunday Times Cook's Companion* is to range across this entire, vast culinary landscape, to the advantage of every kind of cook from the never-boiled-an-egg beginner to Raymond Blanc himself. 'It is,' said an American friend, 'a *mother* of a book.' And so, in the best possible sense of the word, it is.

Even in France, the womb of culinary invention, standards have been seen to slip. *Le Fast Food* doesn't stop at the Channel; neither does the industrial production of 'convenience' foods, with all their temptations to cut corners, save time, accept what you're given. There was a time in England – a time which lasted well into the last century – when mothers would bequeath to daughters their kitchen books: meticulously kept, handwritten descriptions of recipes, rules of hygiene, household remedies. Later they handed on their copies of that tradition's final and most grandiose flourish, the works of Mrs Isabella Beeton.

It all seems as remote now as the pony and trap. What is handed down today often goes little further than the wisdom of the tin-opener and the key to the deep freeze. Whole generations are growing up who have never understood – because they have never experienced – the true delight of creating good simple food from fresh raw ingredients. If they do attempt to cook 'well', it is too often with an eye for novelty, being seduced by 7 over-coloured recipe books into piling one flavour on top of another with little or no understanding of what they are doing, or why they are doing it.

The *Cook's Companion* brings the art of cooking back to where it belongs: into the domestic kitchen. Above all, it addresses itself to *understanding*. From the most basic things (lid on or lid off when you boil cabbage? why?) to the most sophisticated, it lays out the theory with the same simple clarity as it describes the practice. Learning to cook is like learning to play the piano. You can serve up good tunes from day one, and it is easy to deceive. But only with the basics in place, the scales and the harmonies, can you know which tunes are worth attempting, and how to adapt and extemporise upon them.

The book is clearly set out with separate sections on all the major groups of ingredients; all the important culinary techniques. These are the work of Shona Crawford Poole, distinguished traveller and former food editor of *The Times*. The recipes used to illustrate the sections in themselves add up to a formidable culinary repertoire, though in a sense this is not the point.

The word *Companion* is well chosen. The book is prescriptive only in the sense of setting out what will and will not work in terms of chemistry and physics. It offers some guidance on taste, and there are six distinguished cooks – Anton Mosimann and Raymond Blanc among them – to explain the essentials of their favourite cuisines, but in the end its most important offering is freedom.

Freedom to make informed choices; freedom to develop your own distinctive style; freedom from blandness; freedom from mystique. Here are all the things your mother *would* have told you, if only she had known. And here, on a plate, is the most important ingredient in any cook's repertoire – the confidence that comes from knowing exactly what you are doing.

A mother of a book indeed.

Richard Girling, May 1993

PART ONE
TECHNIQUES

CHAPTER I

BOILING, POACHING AND STEAMING

BOILING

The action of boiling is unmistakable. At a temperature of 100°C (212°F), water bubbles vigorously and steam rises from the turbulent surface. Everyone recognises it and can measure it without resort to a thermometer. It is the first cooking method with which most people become acquainted. As boiling water does not get any hotter for boiling longer (it just evaporates), cooking food in water is one of the easiest of all culinary processes to control.

It is simple, but not *that* simple. The temperature at which water boils can be raised by increasing the atmospheric pressure, as in a pressure cooker, or by adding other ingredients – sugar, for example. The temperature of sugar syrup will rise to about 150°C (300°F) before it begins to colour and caramelise as the water content boils away.

Water's boiling point can also be reduced. The standard boiling temperature of 100°C (212°F) assumes normal atmospheric pressure at sea level. The average rate at which temperature drops with altitude is about 1°C (2°F) for every 1,000 feet climbed. This is why chalet girls working in high Alpine ski resorts cook soft-boiled eggs for 6 or more minutes, and why no airline can make a decent cup of tea after take-off in a cabin pressurised to about 8,000 feet.

It is not only the *temperature* of boiling which is inconstant. The very meaning of the word can change from one recipe to another. Green vegetables are one of the few foods for which the instruction to boil may be taken literally. For appearance's sake at least, they are best cooked at a full, rolling boil from start to finish. Boiled potatoes are better cooked at a very slightly lower temperature to stop them breaking up, and boiled beef is simmered, not boiled.

Speed is an essential factor in preserving colour and flavour (see Chart). The larger the volume of boiling water, the less heat will be lost when you add the vegetables to it.

Chlorophyll, the green colour in leaves and stalks, peas and beans, contains an atom of magnesium which is de-stabilised by heat. When the cooking water is acid, the loose magnesium is usurped by hydrogen which turns the vegetables a drab, dull green colour. Hence the no-lids rule. Volatile acids in the steam will condense on the cover and fall back into the cooking water, increasing the acidity.

In alkaline cooking water the magnesium is replaced by metal ions such as copper or zinc. Alkaline conditions created by the addition of soda have the double disadvantage of accelerating the breakdown of the cell walls, causing mushiness and allowing in copper ions which are poisonous in repeated doses.

There is a trade-off between preserving the colour and taste of green vegetables and preserving their vitamins. Some people prefer to use small quantities of water, or to steam vegetables, on the grounds that fewer of the water-soluble vitamins B and C will be lost in cooking. Such losses are unquantifiable outside the laboratory, and are partially offset by the increased speed of cooking in larger volumes of water.

PRESERVING THE COLOUR OF GREEN VEGETABLES

- **Do** boil small quantities of vegetables in large quantities of water.
- **Do** cook them as briefly as possible, while still to your taste.
- **Do** test them frequently for doneness.
- **Do** choose small, tender vegetables whenever possible, or cut them into similar-sized pieces which can be cooked quickly.

- **Don't** cover the pan, especially for the first few minutes of cooking time.
- **Don't** add soda. It does preserve colour but it spoils taste and texture.
- **Don't** add a copper coin or cook in an untinned copper pan. Both are dangerous.

Mediterranean Fish Soup

SERVES 6–8

'Bring to the boil' is the most common instruction in cookery books, but recipes which call for continuous boiling are relatively rare. Bouillabaisse, and the smooth but equally rufous Mediterranean fish soups, are among the few. Here boiling is used to fuse the oil and water into a stable union so that there will not be blobs of fat floating in the plate. Chinese cooks exploit the same action to make deliberately cloudy 'cream' stocks which take added flavour from the chicken or duck fat suspended in them.

The recipe given here is the *soupe de poissons* of waterfront cafés from Corsica to the Côte d'Azur. With its traditional accompaniments of *rouille*, a chilli-spiced and garlic-laden version of mayonnaise, plus croûtons and grated cheese, it is a meal in itself. This is not *haute cuisine* but a practical soup evolved to use the least marketable of the fisherman's catch – little, bony fish and those with unattractive faces or oddly coloured flesh.

Its character depends on using three or four varieties (but not oily fish such as herring), including heads and tails. A *mouli-légumes* (see page 303) is best for puréeing.

For the soup

2kg (4½lb) fish, including at least one whole fish and a piece of conger eel
120ml (4fl oz) olive oil
2 leeks, white part only, finely sliced
1 large onion, finely chopped
2 cloves garlic, finely chopped
1 bulb Florence fennel, finely sliced
2 ripe red peppers, de-seeded and finely chopped
225g (8oz) ripe tomatoes, roughly chopped
Bouquet garni *(see page 261)* of parsley, thyme, bay leaf and orange zest
55g (2oz) dry white breadcrumbs
2 tablespoons tomato paste
Pinch of saffron
6 tablespoons pastis (Pernod or Ricard).
Freshly ground black pepper

For the rouille

2–6 cloves garlic, peeled
1 egg yolk
2 teaspoons cayenne pepper
Salt (½ teaspoon initially, then to taste)
150ml (¼ pint) fruity olive oil

For the garnish

2 half-baked half-baguette French loaves
110g (4oz) Beaufort, Comté or Gruyère cheese, finely grated

Wash and gut the fish and scrape off any very large scales (see page 226). Cut it into large pieces, keeping the heads, tails and fins on.

Heat the oil in a large, heavy-based pot and add the leeks and onion. Soften the onion without browning it. Add the garlic, fennel, peppers, tomatoes and fish, and about 2.75 litres (5 pints) of cold water. Bring quickly to the boil and add the *bouquet*, breadcrumbs, tomato paste and saffron. Cook the soup, uncovered, at a soft, rolling boil for about 20 minutes. Discard the *bouquet*.

The easiest way to turn this fearsome brew into a smooth, bone-free soup is to work it through a *mouli-légumes* fitted with its finest disc. Alternatively, briefly process or liquidise the soup before sieving it. Discard bones and bits.

Reheat the soup and season it with the *pastis* and black pepper. Without a slug of aniseed-flavoured *pastis* the soup will taste good, but not typically Mediterranean.

11

Rouille can be made in a processor or by hand. Put the garlic in the processor and chop finely. Add the egg yolk, cayenne, salt and 1 tablespoon of oil and process for a few moments before adding the oil in a thin, steady stream while the machine is running. The sauce is ready when it is thick and glossy.

To make it by hand, crush the garlic in a pestle or bowl, and work in the egg yolk, cayenne and salt. Once it is a smooth paste, begin incorporating the oil, a few drops at a time to begin with, then beating in a thin, steady stream.

For the croûtons, cut the half-baked bread in 1cm (½in) slices and dry them in a hot oven until they are very lightly coloured. Serve the soup very hot and allow each diner to spread croûtons with *rouille* and a sprinkling of cheese before floating them across its surface.

BLANCHING

To blanch is to plunge an ingredient briefly into rapidly boiling water. How briefly depends on what is being blanched. It is done for a variety of reasons – preparing some fruits and vegetables for freezing, or for further cooking by other methods, or for firming up offal such as sweetbreads so that they can be handled more easily. Meat or poultry which is to be cooked by boiling is sometimes blanched to precipitate scum before being cooked in fresh water. Blanching is also used to loosen the skins of soft fruits such as tomatoes and plums so that they can be peeled.

POACHING AND SIMMERING

Poaching and simmering are less precise cooking instructions than boiling and can indicate a range of temperatures from a degree or two below boiling point to very much lower, say 96–98°C (205–209°F) down to 82–87°C (180–189°F). Which is why, since few cooks stand with thermometers in their pans, many different expressions have been employed to indicate poaching's subtleties. The great Escoffier said: 'However nonsensical it may sound, the best possible definition of a poaching is a boiling that does not boil.' This has the merit of covering the placidly bubbling liquid that is just below boiling, to the cooler, barely shivering liquid that is at the correct temperature for cooking delicate recipes like *quenelles* (see Glossary).

The term poaching indicates that the food is to be cooked in water or stock at a temperature below boiling point. Simmering embraces a similar temperature range but a wider variety of liquids, including thickened sauces and gravies. Thus the terms poaching and simmering are sometimes, but not always, interchangeable.

Modern taste demands that fish and chicken should not be overcooked, and common sense that it should be sufficiently well cooked not to pose a health risk. Food poisoning caused by salmonella bacteria in poultry and, less frequently, in eggs, has been the cook's main worry in recent years. Public health advice tends to the crude, as in 'ensure chicken is well cooked all through'. However, this need not spell culinary disaster to the careful cook with an accurate thermometer.

A temperature of 70°C (160°), held for at least 2 minutes, is sufficient to kill salmonella bacteria. So poaching a tender young chicken breast at 82–87°C (180–189°F) is safe provided the heat reaches right through it and that it is maintained with reasonable accuracy.

Poule au Pot

SERVES 4–6

The classic poached chicken dish, *poule au pot* is a relic from cauldron cooking over open fires, when an old farmyard fowl could be sent whole to the table, stuffed for extra flavour, tender after several hours of gentle cooking, and surrounded by vegetables cooked in the same pot. Preceded by a plate of the cooking broth poured over a slice of dried bread or toast and sprinkled with cheese, it is a one-pot meal that can be made on a single gas ring.

A free-range roasting chicken or capon is more succulent than an older boiling fowl, but cannot match it for flavour. In this recipe, using chicken stock (see page 76) as the poaching liquid makes a worthwhile difference. A further refinement is

A classic poule au pot

to cook a fresh batch of vegetables with the chicken for the last 40 minutes of its cooking time. The first batch can be discarded.

For the stuffing
55g (2oz) fresh white breadcrumbs
6 tablespoons milk
110g (4oz) pork sausagemeat
2 tablespoons chopped parsley
1 large egg
salt and freshly ground black pepper

For the pot
2.3kg (5lb) boiling chicken, dressed weight
2 tablespoons clarified butter (see page 239)
450g (1lb) carrots, scraped
450g (1lb) small white turnips, trimmed
450g (1lb) onions, peeled
Bouquet garni (see page 261) of celery, bay
     leaf, thyme and lemon zest

For the stuffing, soak the breadcrumbs in the milk and squeeze them dry in your hands. Mix together the soaked breadcrumbs, sausagemeat, parsley and egg, and season well. Check the stuffing for seasoning by frying a teaspoonful then tasting it. Stuff the chicken under the skin of the breast (see page 220). Truss the bird securely (see page 218).

Choose a heavy pot large enough to hold the chicken and all the vegetables. Melt the clarified butter or dripping and brown the chicken lightly all over, taking care when turning it not to pierce the skin. Add the vegetables and bouquet garni. Cover them all with cold stock or water and bring the pot slowly to the boil. Immediately reduce the heat to a slow, steady simmer with bubbles rising unhurriedly but continually to the surface. Skim the surface thoroughly. Cook the chicken, with or without a lid depending on which method best helps maintain a steady simmer, for about 3 hours for a boiler, 2 hours for a roaster.

Carefully lift the chicken and vegetables from the broth on to a warm serving dish and keep warm. Discard the bouquet garni. Check the seasoning of the broth, and reserve 600ml (1 pint) to make a velouté sauce (see page 78).

Carve (see the illustrations on page 35) and serve the chicken and vegetables. Pass round the sauce separately.

POACHING A WHOLE SALMON
If you have never cooked one before, the possibility of ruining such an expensive fish can be intimidating. Poaching is the reliable answer. It is a virtually foolproof way of cooking a whole fish to succulent perfection. You can use it to cook a salmon of any weight from 2.3kg (5lb) upwards without any adjustment to the cooking time, provided that the fish and the fish-kettle are of reasonably compatible size. The only problems with timing are when to buy and when to cook the fish if it is too big for the fridge. Remember that a large fish may take up to 12 hours to cool completely, and that fish keeps better cooked than raw. Allow about 110g–170g (4oz–6oz) each.

Clean the fish, leaving on its head and tail. Set it on the rack of a fish-kettle and lower it into the pan. Use a measuring jug to add enough cold water – or court bouillon (see page 77) – to cover the fish. Then add 1 tablespoon of salt for every 600ml (1 pint) of water. Bring slowly to the boil, and boil for 1 minute only. Immediately remove the kettle from the heat and cover it tightly – with foil as well as the lid if it is loose-fitting. Stand the pan in a cool place and leave until tepid. Lift out the fish and allow to cool before skinning it.

The fish-kettle is important. It not only allows you to lay out the fish straight and submerged in the poaching liquid, but the rack allows you to lift out the fragile cooked fish afterwards without any risk of damage.

A PERFECT POACHED EGG
A neatly poached egg is a lovesome thing and a surprisingly rare one. First look to your eggs. They must be fresh, new-laid ideally, but certainly no more than a week old (see page 243). Forget swirling the water which is a technique designed to improve the appearance of old eggs. Forget egg-poaching pans with a small depression for each egg. The eggs will be steamed, not poached in these. And forget adding vinegar to the poaching water. Its astringency spoils both taste and texture.

Note: Egg-white sets at 60°C (140°F) and the yolk at 70°C (160°F). Salmonella bacteria are rendered harmless by being held at a temperature of 70°C (160°F) for at least 2 minutes. So runny yolks are not without some risk.

Choose a wide, shallow pan with a lid. A heavy sauté pan which retains its heat and will hold at least 5cm (2in) depth of water is ideal. (A wide casserole may be a better choice.)

Bring the water, unsalted, to the boil and take it off the heat. Immediately add the eggs, breaking them carefully into the water to retain their shape. The eggs could be broken into individual cups and slid into the boiling water. Cover the pan and leave the eggs to poach undisturbed until the whites are opaque.

Use a flat-bladed, perforated fish slice to lift the eggs out of the water. Trim off the ragged edges – there will be plenty of white sitting plumply round the yolks if the eggs were really fresh – and serve immediately.

If the poached eggs are to be incorporated in another dish they should be transferred into cold water and left in it until needed.

STEAMING

Steaming is all the rage and, as food fashions go, it has more good sense going for it than most. Cooking in the steam heat that rises from boiling water in a covered pan is a slower and gentler process than boiling. Fewer vitamins and minerals are lost, and it uses no fat. It can be a very fuel-efficient method (in Chinese restaurants you will often see a whole stack of steamer baskets in a wok over a single gas flame), and it is aesthetically pleasing too. Steaming is an unscummy process which leaves food looking recognisably like itself. It is a particularly good method for the fragile flesh of fish, which is easily overcooked.

Steam is not noticeably hotter than the boiling water it rises from, about 100°C (212°F) give or take a bit for altitude and even big weather systems. It imparts its heat to the food suspended in it, then condenses back into the liquid below, to be reheated and rise as steam again.

Usually the liquid is simply water, although it may be flavoured with wine and vegetables as in a *court bouillon* (see page 77), or may contain aromatics to scent the food with fragrant vapours.

Most saucepan ranges include matching, stacking steamer pans with flat, perforated bases. Chinese bamboo steamer baskets are inexpensive, as are expanding metal steamer baskets with perforated 'petals' which open and close to fit pans of many sizes. A big steamer can be improvised with a rack standing in a baking tin under a foil lid, or with a drum sieve over a large pot.

Strictly speaking, fish cooked between two plates over a pan of hot water is not really steamed at all. But this time-honoured method of cooking a single serving with a minimum of fuss fits more neatly here than anywhere else. It works best for pieces of fish which are of a fairly even thickness, for fillets and for flat fish. A piece which is very thick in the middle and thin at the edges can be flattened by placing it between two sheets of plastic wrap and hitting it quite gently with a cook's mallet or rolling pin.

Season the fish with salt and pepper and place between two plates with plain edges which fit well together. Rest the plates over a pan of fast-boiling water for 10–15 minutes or until the fish loses its translucence. When it is cooked the flesh will be opaque but still have a pearly sheen. Test the thickest part to see if it is done. Use the point of a knife to push apart the flakes of flesh and check that the centre too is opaque.

PRESSURE-COOKING

Just as water boils at a lower temperature up a mountain, so it boils at a higher temperature when pressure is increased, down a coalmine, for example. Increasing the pressure, and therefore the temperature at which water boils, is the principle used in pressure-cooking to reduce cooking times. It is a method which achieves savings in fuel and nutrients as well as in time. It is particularly good for root vegetables, and for pre-cooking fruit and vegetables for preserves.

The main disadvantage of pressure-cooking is that because the pan must be sealed until cooking is complete, the cook cannot see, taste or test the contents without interrupting the process, first cooling the pan and reducing the pressure. Pressure-cookers vary in design and users should follow the manufacturer's instructions with care.

15

The Cooking of China

by YAN-KIT SO

Chinese food is as distinctive in appearance, with its mosaics of morsels, as it is in smell and in its intensely savoury tastes. The whole structure of a Chinese meal is different.

Yan-Kit So, food writer and broadcaster

I nstead of the typically western combination of starter, main course and pudding, the day-to-day Chinese meal consists of rice (or noodles and steamed bread) and a number of dishes to be shared by the diners, who eat with chopsticks rather than cutlery.

It traces its origins back to more than a thousand years before the Christian era. As soon as Chinese history began, and dynastic records were written, food became a subject worthy of study. These early written records, detailing the dietary habits of the kings and nobles of the Zhou (Chou) dynasty, the longest in history, from the 11th century to 221 BC, show that the patterns of Chinese cuisine had already begun to evolve.

The imperial kitchen, staffed by more than two thousand people whose duties were clearly defined, reflected the high prior-ity the Zhou kings gave to food. As well as providing for daily necessities it played an important role in sacrificial rituals and banquets. Hundreds of different chefs specialised in meat, fish and seafood, vegetables, fruits and grain foods, assisted by their *sous-chefs* and *commis*.

Thus was the tradition forged for the later dynasties to follow. Not least among these was the most recent, the Qing (AD 1644–1911), which, after the fashion of its predecessor the Ming (AD 1368–1644), ran its imperial kitchen on a grand scale. When the Qing dynasty ended, many of the chefs from the palace joined restaurants in Peking where they continued to exert their influence. In Peking today, the government-endorsed restaurant, Fang Shan, originally set up in 1925 by erstwhile Qing court chefs to continue the legacy of court dishes, thrives on the revival of what is known as Qing Palace Cuisine, attracting both Chinese and foreign tourists alike.

The range of ingredients used

during the Zhou period was already vast and carnivorous, at least for the upper classes and the aristocracy. Among the ancient texts that contain references to food, none has as rich a stock as the *Liji* (*Li Ch'i*) or the Book of Rites, which sets out the rules of propriety, rituals and ceremonials for the court and its subjects. While one and all, 'from the princes down to the common people, without distinction of degree' ate 'soup and boiled grain', the upper classes had a wide range of meats, if not for every day, then at least for special occasions: roast and minced beef, roast mutton, roast pork, lamb, minced fish, dog, muntjac, pheasant, hare, quail and partridge etc. A sucking pig, roasted or stewed, was popular for a sacrifice or a banquet. For those not blessed with noble birth, growing old was an advantage, for the elderly were respected by the kings who granted them the privilege of eating meat and other good food.

For the nourishment of the elders, a range of complicated dishes, referred to in *Liji* as 'Eight Delicacies', were specially prepared. As some of the earliest recipes known, they show how elaborate Chinese cookery methods had already become.

The idea of serving eight 'delicacies', or delicious dishes, has endured. Whenever the Chinese have a banquet, which can be a formal or festive occasion or just an excuse for family and friends to get together and have a feast, the menu very often includes eight dishes.

Chinese tastebuds recognise five tastes – salty, sweet, sour, bitter and peppery-hot – and every Chinese cook, professional or amateur, must practise the mixing and blending of them.

Crisp Lettuce with Spicy Fermented Bean Curd

This tenet was put in writing in the 3rd century BC by a colourful and wealthy politician, Lu Buwei, who attributed it to Yi Yin, the chef who had become prime minister more than a thousand years previously. In discourse with his king on the quest for the root of all tastes, Yi Yin articulated the theory which ever since has been ingrained in the Chinese psyche:

'As for the matter of harmonious blending, one must make use of the sweet, sour, bitter, pungent and salty. But which tastes one adds first or later, and how much or how little, the balance is very subtle, for each produces its own effect. The transformation which occurs in the *ding* [cauldron] is wonderful and delicate. The mouth cannot express it in words, nor can the mind illuminate its meaning. It is like the subtlety of archery and horsemanship, the difference between *yin* and *yang* and the changes of the four seasons. Thus the dishes last for a long time yet are not spoiled; they are cooked yet not ragged, sweet yet not cloying, sour yet not acid, salty yet not severely so, peppery-hot yet not burning, mild yet not insipid and rich yet not greasy.'

At a first glance these words may seem to deepen the mystique of Chinese cookery, yet

17

they are actually very down to earth. In a modern Chinese kitchen, the two fundamental preparatory techniques everyone has to grasp are the cutting of ingredients into various sizes, followed by the mixing of flavours.

Consider for example a piece of meat – say beef, chicken or pork. It is usually cut into thick or thin slices, large or small cubes, or coarsely or finely minced. Then condiments such as salt, soy sauce, sugar, ground pepper and rice wine are added to interact with the flavour of the meat. How many, and how much, of these you add is the essential craft of harmonious blending.

The same principles can be applied to a sweet and sour sauce: the proportion of the three basic flavours, salt, sugar and vinegar, is vital to the resulting taste of the sauce, if it is not to be either cloying or too acidic.

Another ancient concept, already established by the 3rd century BC, is *yin* and *yang*. It is the Taoist perspective of the cosmic order: a dualist philosophical belief that the universe is held by two fundamental and natural forces. *Yang* is represented by the sun, heaven, light, strength, positiveness, heat, summer and man. *Yin* by the moon, earth, darkness, weakness, negativeness, cold, winter and woman. They may be in opposition to each other, yet the two forces are symbiotic. When *yin* and *yang* are in perfect balance, harmony will reign.

In the same way, the theory goes, the human body is regulated by cooling and heating elements. Healthy well-being depends on keeping in check the alternating dominance of one element – *yin* or *yang* – over the

other, striving to maintain a harmonious balance between the two. Yet some people, of both sexes, are physiologically more prone to one element than the other. Their healthy state depends on adjusting the balance.

The Chinese believe that each food ingredient has either *yin* (cooling), *yang* (heating), or neutral properties, and that there is a direct correlation between the properties of the food you eat and the *yin-yang* balance in your body. If you are by nature more of a heating per-

> *When you consider the myriad dishes in the Chinese cuisine, it is remarkable how few condiments, herbs and spices are used to create them.*

son, then eating *yang* food can only exacerbate the condition. *Yin* food on the other hand will help redress the balance. Season and weather also play their part. Heating food eaten in winter reduces the *yin*; cooling food in summer counters the heat.

The rules of *yin* and *yang* are based on empirical rather than scientific rules and never completely agreed upon, but the majority of meats such as beef, lamb, venison, chicken, goose and pigeon are said to be *yang* or heating foods, though duck is *yin* and pork neutral. Among aquatic foods, prawn, lobster, carp, octopus, squid and eel are *yang*; crab, oyster and clam are *yin;* and most fish, especially freshwater species, are neutral.

Herbs and vegetables such as ginger, garlic, spring onion, coriander, chilli pepper, pepper

and celery are *yang*; beansprout, green bean and spinach are *yin*, while most Chinese vegetables of the brassica family – *bak choi*, *choi sum*, Chinese leaf and mustard greens – are neutral. The protein-laden bean curd, the Chinese alternative to dairy products, is neutral, as is rice.

In terms of cookery methods, frying, stir-frying and deep-frying are *yang*; steaming and boiling are *yin*; stewing is neutral.

Despite all this, it is not true that the Chinese will refer to a *yin-yang* chart before cooking their daily food or ordering in a restaurant, though many will reject a particular dish because it is too heating or too cooling. Most people take a relaxed attitude. Many joke about *yang* foods having aphrodisiac qualities – hence the penchant for shark's fin, abalone, deer tendon and the like. On the whole, 'balance' and 'harmony' are the key words by which they benefit from their awareness of the *yin-yang* concept.

As the time-honoured formula of a Chinese meal is rice accompanied by a few other dishes, a commonsense approach to menu selection – choosing a variety of meat, seafood, fish and vegetables – is the common recipe for good health. As it happens, the usual mix of cooking methods – boiling (the rice), stir-frying (the vegetables and/or meat) and steaming (the fish) – also contributes to the natural balance.

The absence of dairy products, saturated fats conducive to heart disease, is a blessing. Instead, the Chinese have given the world its most health-giving food – *doufu*, or bean curd, which is at once cholesterol-free and protein-rich. For a thousand years it has been a staple in the diet of the Chinese, rich and poor, vegetarians and carnivores alike. Vegetables, rich in minerals, vitamins, calcium and to a certain extent oestrogen, are also important. The fact that Chinese people eat more vegetables than westerners is often given as the reason why the Chinese seem to suffer less from coronary heart disease. Lard used to be the preferred fat for making dishes rich and flavourful, but in modern Chinese cuisine it has been replaced by the much more healthy, nutty-flavoured peanut oil as the medium for stir-frying and deep-frying. Stir-fried vegetables are famous for their freshness, and for keeping their vitamins intact. Even Chinese deep-fried foods, which feature prominently on restaurant menus, are light rather than encased in heavy batters sodden with grease.

When you consider the myriad dishes in the Chinese cuisine, it is remarkable how few condiments, herbs and spices are used to create them. The basics are salt, soy sauce, sugar, vinegar, white or black ground pepper and cooking oil, preferably peanut, or corn and other vegetable oil. Add rice wine and fresh ginger, garlic and spring onion – the Chinese trinity – and you are ready to stir-fry. Augment these with star anise, Sichuan peppercorns, dried chillies, fermented black beans, fresh coriander, fresh chilli and sesame oil, and the range of dishes within your grasp extends to all four corners of China.

Without doubt, no other cuisine in the world places the same kind of emphasis on texture. The Chinese palate is very partial to crispness, a vital quality it looks for not just in vegetables and deep-fried foods but also in

meat, crustacea and pasta. 'Crisp' and 'tough' are two quite different things, however, especially when it comes to vegetables. These must be cooked just enough for their 'rank rawness' to be dissipated, while their innate fragrance is brought out.

Crispness is not the only texture the Chinese are keen on. They enjoy ingredients velvetly tender or smoothly gelatinous, satinly slippery or simultaneously bouncy and slippery. This makes them great enthusiasts for chewing chicken and duck feet,

Chinese tastebuds recognise five tastes – salty, sweet, sour, bitter and peppery-hot – and every Chinese cook, professional or amateur, must practise the mixing and blending of them.

sucking fish heads and fish fins, munching strips of edible jellyfish – not to mention shark's fins.

Variation and contrast in texture is sought not just between the different dishes in a meal, but also between the ingredients in a single dish. Nowhere is this better illustrated than in the case of crunchy vegetables stir-fried with slices of tender meat, the basic combination of so many everyday dishes. My recipe for duck breast with pickled cucumber and pineapple (see page 22) is a more sophisticated example, in which flavours and textures both blend and contrast.

Not surprisingly, Chinese cookery methods have much in

common with other cuisines – boiling, simmering, braising, stewing and roasting, for instance. But there are two methods, both distinctively Chinese, which have exerted the most far-reaching influences on other national cuisines, especially in the 20th century. If one is to cook Chinese dishes at all, then one must grasp the nettle of these two techniques – steaming and stir-frying.

STEAMING

This is one of the oldest of all Chinese cookery methods, dating as far back as four thousand years, yet it has maintained its popularity second only to stir-frying. It preserves the natural juices from the ingredients (they are used in the accompanying sauce), while all the innate tastes and goodness remain intact.

A direct descendant of early vessels is used in modern Chinese kitchens – the metal steamer, made of aluminium or stainless steel. Round in shape, it consists of a deep base container (to hold a large quantity of water), two fitted steaming containers with perforated bottoms, one on top of the other, and a fitted lid. The base container is half filled with water and brought to a rolling boil. Then you place the food to be steamed either directly on to the perforated surface of a container, or in a slope-sided heatproof dish inside the container. Put on the lid, and turn up and maintain the heat to ensure that plenty of steam rises from the boiling water and circulates inside the container to cook the food.

In place of metal steaming containers you can use specially-made bamboo baskets with slotted bottoms. These are fine as long as you find the right size to fit snugly to the base container. A bamboo fitted lid is ideal because it absorbs most of the condensation.

Or you can do what many Chinese families do, and rig up a simple steamer using a wok. Sit the wok on its ring on top of the burner. Place a stand (a metal trivet or other supporting rack) in the centre of the wok. Put the food to be steamed in a heat-proof dish (it should have shallow sloping sides so that the juices are retained when the food is cooked, thus preserving its goodness and taste), then place the dish on the stand. Fill the wok with boiling water, but not so much that the bubbling water will come into contact with the dish. Put the lid on the wok, then turn up and maintain the heat to ensure that plenty of steam rises and circulates to cook the food.

With this simple steamer, the Chinese can steam not only fish but even a whole duck (though this, needless to say, needs much more time). Even if you don't have a wok, all is not lost. Use a large saucepan instead.

STIR-FRYING

This is both the most popular and the most sophisticated of Chinese cookery methods. Ever since the 19th century, when the whole world began to hear about and taste Chinese food, stir-frying has created such a frisson that chefs of different backgrounds and nationalities now vie with each other in their skill with the wok.

Stir-frying is a much more recent technique than steaming, made possible only with the development of the iron wok.

Even though there are archaeological relics of the earliest pots, their evolution into pre-sent-day woks – thin-sided, hemispherical pans with broad rims and two looped handles – is not well understood. What is generally accepted is that by the Song dynasty (AD 960–1279) stir-fried dishes had become a vogue, and the repair of cast-iron woks was a service offered in market places.

As the wok took hold, Chinese cuisine came of age. It has never looked back; rather, it has gone from strength to strength, and in the 20th century has been basking in the pride of international recognition. During the last few decades, as the popularity of the wok has spread by leaps and bounds throughout the world, cast iron has given way to the lighter and non-breakable version made of carbon iron.

Woks vary in size. For twenty years I have used two, each with a 35cm (14in) rim diameter and two looped handles on opposite sides. Many woks have single long handles; this kind is more suitable for the type of stoves which have holes and flames underneath. As gas allows instant control of the flame, it is the most suitable and convenient fuel to use.

The technique of stir-frying is described as a sequence of steps, but the action must be continuous and uninterrupted. To begin, put the wok on the strongest burner in the range. Heat the wok over the highest heat until you see smoke rising from the sides, quite a lot of it. This usually takes no more than 20 seconds.

Next, *arouse the wok*. Add a small amount of oil, say 2-4 tablespoons, hold the wok by one handle and swirl the oil around to cover as much of the sides as possible. This both heats the oil evenly and creates a wide cooking area for the ingredients.

Add a small quantity of the condiments (usually ginger, garlic and spring onion but not necessarily all three of them), already cut or sliced, and let them sizzle in the oil. All at once the aroma will hit the nostrils, and you know that – to use the Chinese kitchen jargon – the wok has been 'aroused'.

Quickly stir-fry the food. Before the condiments get burned, add the main ingredient. This will be ready cut up, and often will have been marinated. Wasting no time, slip the wok slide down along the curve to the bottom and start turning and flipping the food – the classic stir-frying action.

Instead of just stir-frying, restaurant chefs, mostly men endowed with sinewy arms, will pick up the wok in one hand and toss the ingredients in the air. Either way, the action results in even cooking, and allows the heat to seal in the juices of every single morsel. If it is a simple vegetable stir-fry, you must take care not to lose the crunchy crispness: scoop the pieces on to a serving plate as soon as they are ready. With meat or fish, however, the procedure goes on a little longer.

Now splash in the wine. Holding a bottle of rice wine – Shaoxing, for instance – and with one finger partially closing the top, splash in along the sides of the wok a small amount, say 1 tablespoon. The wine will sizzle, enhancing the fragrance and quickening the cooking. When the sizzling subsides, reduce the heat to medium or low, lest the food gets overcooked or dried, and continue to turn and stir the pieces until they are just done.

Lastly, add the simple sauce.

Steamed Plaice Fillets

This will usually consist of a few tablespoonfuls of stock, some seasoning and a little thickening agent. Pour it into the wok and continue to stir briskly, drawing in the pieces until the sauce coating them is cooked and thickened.

The stir-fried dish, redolent of the wok's fragrance, is ready to be enjoyed. It may have taken all these words to describe the procedure, but the cooking time, from start to finish, is no more than 3–4 minutes.

Because the cooking time is so short and the movement is continuous, it is vital to have everything ready and to hand. Be sure to check your list of ingredients, and then line them up within reach, in order of use.

Another mistake is to crowd the ingredients all at once into the wok. If a meat ingredient is to be accompanied by one or two ancillary ingredients, more often than not the latter have to be stir-fried separately before they are added at the last moment.

People always want to know how to prepare a new wok for its first use. Chinese folklore insists that a newly-wed couple should 'initiate' their wok with some symbolic rituals.

If you prefer practicality to ritual, this is what you do. Gently scour the wok and wash with mild detergent; then use a cloth or kitchen paper to apply a thin film of cooking oil over both sides. After cooking with it, wash it with mild detergent and water. Dry it and rub over a thin film of oil to prevent it from rusting – especially if you don't intend to use it every day. With use over a period of time, a dark patina will gradually build up, and you won't have to rub oil after every use.

Duck Breast with Pickled Cucumber and Pineapple

Serves 4 with 2 other dishes

In early summer in the south of China when the new roots of ginger, tender and crisp and free of tough fibres, appear in the market, people like to cook duck breast with pickled ginger. As tender ginger is virtually unobtainable in the west, however, I have substituted cucumber.

1 cucumber, about 450g (1lb)
2 duck breast fillets (Barbary or English), 400–425g (14–15oz)
1 medium ripe and sweet pineapple, about 340g (12oz)
5 tablespoons peanut or corn oil
6 spring onions, trimmed and cut into 2.5–5cm (1–2in) sections, white and green parts separated
2 large cloves garlic, thinly sliced
12–16 very thin slices of peeled ginger
1 tablespoon Shaoxing (Shaohsing) rice wine or medium dry sherry
Small bunch of coriander leaves, trimmed and patted dry
1–1½ tablespoons sesame oil

For pickling the cucumber
1 teaspoon salt
1½ teaspoons caster sugar
1 tablespoon Chinese rice vinegar (if using white wine vinegar, a little less)

For marinating the duck
⅓ teaspoon salt
2 teaspoons light soy sauce
1 teaspoon dark soy sauce
1½ teaspoons Shaoxing wine or medium dry sherry
1 pinch ground white pepper or to taste
1 teaspoon potato flour or 1½ teaspoons cornflour
2 tablespoons egg white
1 tablespoon peanut or corn oil

For the sauce
½ teaspoon potato flour
1 tablespoon water
¼ teaspoon salt
1 teaspoon thin or light soy sauce

Wash and pat dry the cucumber. Halve lengthways then scoop out and discard the seeds. Cut diagonally into slices about 5mm (¼in) thick and put them into a clean bowl. Sprinkle on the salt. Mix together with chopsticks or a fork and leave for 1 hour. During this time the saltiness will sink in while the excess water will be drawn out. Pour into a sieve to drain, then squeeze out excess water by hand, a handful at a time, and put into a clean bowl. Sprinkle on the sugar, add the vinegar, then mix well. Leave for 2–3 hours at room temperature for the slices to pickle. They can be made in advance and refrigerated overnight.

Remove and discard the duck skin from the fillets. Starting from the smaller end of each fillet, and holding the knife at an angle, cut crossways into thin slices about 3mm (⅛in) thick. Put into a bowl.

Add the marinade of salt, soy sauces, wine or sherry, ground white pepper, potato or cornflour to the duck and stir to mix well. Add the egg white and stir vigorously to coat until absorbed. Leave for 30–60 minutes. Blend in the oil: this will help to separate the slices.

Skin and trim the pineapple. Quarter it, and remove and discard the hard core from each quarter. Cut the pieces across into slices 5mm (¼in) thick.

Just before cooking, make the sauce. Put the potato flour into a small bowl, and stir in the water. Mix in the salt and soy sauce.

Drain the pickled cucumber well. Also drain the pineapple if juices have oozed out.

Heat a wok over high heat until smoke rises. Add 1 tablespoon of oil and swirl it around. Add the white parts of 2 spring onions and stir a few times. Add the cucumber and pineapple and, maintaining the high heat, stir, turn and toss for about 2 minutes until they are piping hot and any exuded juices have been reabsorbed. Scoop on to a warm dish and keep nearby. Wash and dry the wok.

Reheat the wok over a high heat until plenty of smoke rises. Add the remaining 4 tablespoons oil and swirl it around to cover a large area. Add the garlic and let it sizzle for a few seconds. Before it gets burned add the ginger and then the remaining white spring onion. Stir a few times, then add the duck. Sliding the wok scoop down the sides of the wok, turn and toss vigorously for up to 1 minute until the duck slices, now separating, are becoming partially cooked, turning opaque. Splash in the wine or sherry around the sides of the wok. When the sizzling subsides (in seconds), lower the heat to minimum and push the duck mixture to the sides of the wok, leaving a small well in the centre. Add the well-stirred sauce to the centre and stir until it thickens. Return the cucumber and pineapple to the wok, turn up the heat and stir and turn to mix the contents until piping hot again. Stir in the green spring onion, and add the coriander leaves on top. Scoop on to a serving dish. Sprinkle the sesame oil on top to enhance the fragrance. Serve immediately.

Crisp Lettuce with Spicy Fermented Bean Curd

Serves 4 with 2 other dishes
Cheesy and salty, ivory in colour, white fermented bean curd comes in 2.5cm (1in) cakes floating inside a glass jar, sometimes labelled 'preserved' bean curd. It is often used as a seasoning for plain vegetables, or as a side dish to enhance the taste of plain rice and *congee* ('rice porridge'). It comes in two kinds – plain or spicy, with chilli flakes.

1 large head crisp lettuce
4 tablespoons peanut oil
Pinch of salt
60ml (2fl oz) water
3–4 spring onions, cut into 2.5cm (1in) sections, white and green parts separated
4 cakes spicy white fermented bean curd with chilli flakes, mashed with 1 teaspoon juice from the jar

Trim and rinse the outer leaves of the lettuce. Unwrap the rest and break it all into large pieces.

Heat a wok over high heat until smoke rises. Add 2 tablespoons of the oil and swirl it around. Add the lettuce, pinch of salt and the water. Turn the leaves and cook until just limp, when the excess water content will have been drawn out. Pour into a colander and lightly press the leaves so they drain well.

Reheat the wok over a high heat until smoke rises. Add the remaining oil and swirl it around. Add the white spring onions and stir a few times. Add the mashed bean curd and stir in to incorporate with the oil. Before fierce splashing occurs, return the lettuce to the wok, flip and turn with the wok scoop until piping hot, coating the leaves with the purée. Add the green spring onions, stir a few

more times, then scoop on to a serving dish and serve. The lettuce leaves, even though cooked, will still have the crunchiness so attractive to the Chinese palate.

Stir-fried Prawns with Mange-tout

Serves 6 with 3 other dishes
Whenever I make this dish for family or friends, or a version of it (using asparagus rather than mange-tout, for example), it never goes begging.

450g (1lb) medium raw prawns in the shell but without heads (26–30 prawns)
170g (6oz) mange-tout (snow peas), topped and tailed then rinsed
4 tablespoons peanut or vegetable oil
Salt
Vegetable oil for deep-frying
½–1 teaspoon finely chopped garlic
15–30ml (1–2 tablespoons) spicy hot soy bean or broadbean paste (or chilli sauce, at a pinch) or to taste
For the prawn marinade
½ teaspoon salt
1 teaspoon cornflour
1 tablespoon egg white
For the sauce
5 tablespoons chicken stock
1 teaspoon potato flour or 1½ teaspoons cornflour dissolved in 2 teaspoons water
1–2 teaspoons thin or light soy sauce

If the prawns are frozen defrost thoroughly and rinse the shells. Shell each prawn, and with the point of a small knife make a shallow slit along the centre of the back to remove and discard the black vein, if any. Lay them 23 on kitchen paper to absorb excess moisture. When all are done, put them into a large bowl.

To marinate the prawns, add the salt to the bowl and stir vigorously in the same direction for up to 30 seconds until the prawns feel elastic. Sprinkle with the cornflour and add the egg white. Stir again vigorously until both are completely absorbed. For a crisp result, cover the bowl and refrigerate for 2 hours or longer, or even overnight.

Blanch the mange-tout. Bring a pot of salted water to the boil. Add the mange-tout, plus 1 tablespoon of oil and stir a couple of times. Before the water returns to the boil, pour into a colander and refresh with cold water. This will keep the mange-tout vividly green and crisp. Leave to drain.

To prepare the sauce, add the chicken stock to the dissolved potato or tapioca flour in a small bowl. Add the soy sauce and stir to mix.

Sit a wok on the wok-stand (or ring) and half fill with vegetable oil. Heat over a high heat until it reaches 180°C (350°F). Meanwhile loosen the prawns in the bowl, then carefully add them to the oil, separating them with wooden chopsticks or a wooden spoon. Deep-fry for about 20 seconds or until the prawns have curled up and turned pinkish. Scoop up with a large perforated disc and put on to a dish. Turn off the heat. (The oil can be re-used two or three more times after being strained.) This step can be done a couple of hours in advance. Rinse and dry the wok.

Heat the wok over a high heat until smoke rises. Add the remaining 3 tablespoons oil and swirl it around several times.

Add the garlic, which will sizzle. Before it burns, add the soy bean or broadbean paste and give it a quick stir. Return the prawns to the wok and turn and toss with the wok scoop until well mixed with the spicy sauce. Add the mange-tout and stir. Reduce the heat and pour the well-stirred sauce into the centre, stirring as the sauce thickens. Stir and mix the ingredients with the sauce until very hot. Scoop on to a serving dish and serve immediately.

Chinese Leaf with Minced Dried Shrimps

Serves 4–6 with 2–3 other dishes
Shrimps preserved in salt then dried in the sun are a very popular accompaniment to Chinese celery cabbage, known and sold in supermarkets as Chinese leaf. Usually the shrimps are cooked at the same time as the cabbage, but the end result is far from satisfactory: the shrimps become chewy and unappetising. I have therefore devised the following variation in which the shrimps have a real role to play and the cabbage becomes even more flavoursome.

45g (1½oz) dried shrimps, rinsed
4 tablespoons peanut or
*   vegetable oil*
1 tablespoon Shaoxing wine or
*   medium dry sherry*
1 large head Chinese leaf, 1.1kg
*   (2½lb) or 2 smaller ones*
4 slices peeled ginger
4 spring onions, trimmed and
*   cut into 5cm (2in) sections,*
*   white and green parts*
*   separated*
¼ teaspoon salt

Put the shrimps into a bowl and add 3–4 tablespoons of warm water to barely cover. Leave to

soak for 1 hour or longer. Pour into a sieve to drain, but retain the soaking liquid.

Heat a wok over high heat until smoke rises. Add 1 tablespoon of oil and swirl it around. Add the shrimps and stir them around for 10-20 seconds. Splash in the wine or sherry along the sides of the wok, stirring continuously as it sizzles and evaporates, and enhances the fragrance. Scoop the shrimps on to a dish and leave to cool for a few minutes. Rinse and dry the wok.

Put the shrimps into a liquidiser, add the soaking liquid and process until the shrimps are finely minced. Remove to a dish. Minced shrimps can be made in advance and stored in a jar in a cool place.

Rinse only the outer leaves of the Chinese leaf to rid them of impurity. Cut all the leaves crossways at about 3.75cm (1½in) intervals; separate the white stalky parts from the leafy parts.

Reheat the wok over high heat until smoke rises. Add 3 tablespoons oil and swirl it around several times. Add the ginger, let it sizzle for a few seconds, then add the white spring onions and let them sizzle for a few seconds more. Add the white stalky parts of the cabbage, and vigorously turn and toss with the wok scoop in case they get burned. Turn the heat down to medium, sprinkle on half of the salt, cover the wok with the lid and continue to cook for 2–4 minutes or until the cabbage starts to yield its moisture. Remove the lid, add the leafy parts and the remaining salt. Turn up the heat, stir and turn the whole wokful rapidly several times. Reduce the heat again, put on the lid and cook for 3–5 minutes or until much moisture has oozed from the cabbage. Pour everything into a sieve placed over a large bowl. Press the leaves gently with the wok scoop to drain well. (The natural juices are quite sweet and can be saved to use as vegetable stock.)

Return the cabbage to the wok over a low to medium heat, and add the green spring onion and the minced dried shrimps. Turn and stir to mix until piping hot again. Scoop on to a serving dish and serve.

Steamed Plaice Fillets

Serves 2–4 with 1–2 other dishes
The better and fresher the fish, the more likely the Chinese are to steam it whole for the table. Their favourite sea bass, grouper and Dover sole are too expensive for anything but special occasions. For an everyday family meal, most of us have to look for something more easily affordable. Plaice, which is often sold ready filleted, fits the bill very well indeed. Its innate flavour is subtle if slightly insipid; by sandwiching all the condiments between the fillets you can upgrade the flavour to gourmet standard.

*1 knob ginger, about 3.75cm
   (1½in) long
4 spring onions
2 plaice fillets, 450–500g
   (1lb–1b 2oz), patted dry
¼ teaspoon salt
Ground pepper to taste
3 tablespoons peanut or
   vegetable oil
2 tablespoons thin or light soy
   sauce*

Peel the ginger and cut about 10 slices as thinly as you possibly can. Then cut the slices into very

Stir-fried Prawns with Mange-tout

narrow strips. You'll need about 2 tablespoons of this shredded ginger.

Rinse and trim the spring onions, then cut crossways into 5cm (2in) sections. Keep the white and green parts separate. Cut each section lengthways into very thin strips.

Lay the plaice fillets skin side down and sprinkle with salt and pepper. Place one fillet, skin side down, on to a heatproof dish with sloping sides. Spread it evenly first with the shredded ginger, then the white spring onion. Put the second fillet on top, skin side up.

Put the dish with the fillets into a steamer and steam, covered, over a high heat for about 6 minutes until they are cooked (the flesh will turn

white). Turn off the heat but leave the dish in the steamer. If there is too much liquid in the dish, spoon some off or dab away with kitchen paper, leaving just a few tablespoonfuls behind.

With a table fork and a knife, or a pair of chopsticks, remove and discard the skin of the top fillet. You'll find that it peels off like a glove. Spread the shredded green spring onion on top.

Put the oil in a small saucepan and heat it until smoke rises. Remove from the heat and, a little at a time, sizzle it all over the green spring onions, partially cooking them. Add the soy sauce. Remove the dish from the steamer. Just before serving, spoon the sauce in the dish over the fish.

Spiced Soy Sauce Chicken

Serves 4 with 1 other dish

The success of this very popular Chinese family dish depends on two factors: the proportions of sugar, soy and spiced liquid, and the technique used to reduce the sauce and braise the chicken.

12 quails' eggs
1 free-range chicken, cleaned,
* 1.35–1.4kg (3–3¼lb) with*
* giblets*
1 tablespoon peanut or
* vegetable oil*
1 thick slice peeled ginger
2 spring onions, trimmed and
* halved crossways*
300ml (½ pint) dark soy sauce
* or Kikkoman soy sauce*
2½ tablespoons demerara sugar
For the spiced liquid
2 whole star anise or 16
* segments*
2.5cm (1in) cinnamon stick,
* broken up*
600ml (1 pint) water

Put the quails' eggs in a saucepan and add water to cover. Slowly bring to the boil then simmer gently, uncovered, for 30–40 seconds for a soft-boiled result. Pour into a colander and refresh the eggs with cold water before leaving them in a pot of cold water for 15 minutes or longer. Peel and keep in a cool place.

Half fill a wok with water, bring to the boil and then turn off the heat. Submerge the chicken two or three times in the water, then lift it and put in a colander to drain. The hot water bath should facilitate even colouring of the skin when the chicken is cooked.

Prepare the spiced liquid. Add the star anise and cinnamon to a saucepan and pour in the water. Bring to the boil, reduce the heat and fast simmer, covered, for 30 minutes or until the liquid has been reduced to 300ml (½ pint). Drain and discard the spices.

Heat a wok over a high heat until smoke rises. Add the oil and swirl it around. Add the ginger and spring onions and stir a few times. Reduce the heat, pour in the spiced liquid followed by the soy sauce. Add the sugar. Slowly bring to a simmer, stirring a few times to make sure the sugar dissolves.

Pat dry the chicken, both the skin and the cavity. Slip it into the sauce in the wok, and lay it on its side. Using a large, long-handled spoon, continuously pour the barely simmering sauce over the chicken, 2 spoons over the thigh and leg against 1 over the wing. Carry on for 15 minutes. Adjust the heat occasionally to ensure that the sauce is barely simmering yet hot enough to release some smoke when poured over the skin of the chicken, colouring it russet brown. Turn the chicken over, and repeat the sauce-pouring action on the other side for another 15 minutes. The sauce itself is gradually thickening.

Turn the chicken back to its original side. Add the heart, gizzard and liver. Put on the wok lid and maintain a slow simmer for 25 minutes. Remove the liver after about 10, the heart after 25, and reserve. Once more turn the chicken on to the other side and simmer slowly for another 20 minutes. The chicken should be done by now, yet still juicy, and the sauce thicker yet not burned. Remove the chicken from the wok, letting the sauce drain out, and put it on a chopping board. Remove the gizzard.

Carve the chicken, either in the Chinese way or however else you like. If you want to do it in the Chinese way, use a kitchen chopper to joint the wings, the thighs and drumsticks first. Cutting down the sides, halve the body to separate the breasts from the back. Chop the back crossways through skin and bones at 2–2.5cm (¾–1in) intervals and arrange them along the centre of an oval serving plate. Likewise chop the wings and second joints and arrange them on the sides. Slit along the breast bone through the skin. With your hands remove the two pieces of breast meat from the main bone and wishbone, and cut crossways into pieces of similar size. Arrange them on top of the back pieces. Cut also the liver, heart and gizzard into slices and put on the plate. As the dish is usually served at room temperature, this step can be done in advance. This way of carving reflects the Chinese liking for gnawing poultry bones to savour the more succulent dark meat around them.

Just before serving, add the shelled quails' eggs to the sauce and simmer, uncovered, for about 20 seconds, pouring the sauce over them, until hot. (If you prefer them to be hard-boiled, simmer them longer, covered.) Remove and serve with the chicken. Some sauce can be served on saucers for individual dipping, and the rest reserved for use later.

Note The remaining sauce can be used in different ways: to poach more cooked and peeled quails' eggs (they make marvellous hors d'oeuvres); to braise drumsticks and chicken wings; to stew beef or pork spare-ribs; or just to enhance the flavour of plain boiled rice.

Ham-Fried Rice

Serves 2–3

A very easy and nutritious one-dish lunch or dinner, or accompaniment to meat or fish dishes. The rice itself can be cooked in the morning or even the previous evening (fried rice is best made with rice that has been left to cool and become firm). Be sure to keep it refrigerated.

170g (6oz) frozen garden peas
    or 225g (8oz) frozen petits
    pois
Salt
4 tablespoons peanut or
    vegetable oil
4–6 spring onions, trimmed and
    cut into small rounds, white
    and green parts separated
1 large egg, lightly beaten with 1
    pinch or ⅛ teaspoon salt
3 bowls cooked rice, about 500g
    (1lb 2oz), well loosened
170g (6oz) lean cooked ham,
    diced
About 60ml (2fl oz) chicken
    stock or water
Soy sauce

Put the peas in a saucepan. Pour boiling water in to amply cover, add about ½ teaspoon salt and 1 tablespoon oil and return to the boil. Continue to boil for about 3 minutes for garden peas and 1 minute for petits pois. Pour into a colander and drain.

Heat a wok over a high heat until smoke rises. Add the remaining oil and swirl it around to cover a large area. Add the white spring onion and stir several times. Pour in the egg and stir with the spring onion. Before it is completely set, add the rice. Sliding the wok scoop down the curve of the wok, turn and toss the rice for about 1 minute, separating the grains. Add the ham and the peas, continuing to stir until piping hot again. Taste the mixture. If you think it is too dry, sprinkle over some or all of the stock or water. Add the green spring onion and stir. Remove the wok from the heat and scoop the fried rice into a serving dish. Serve immediately, with other dishes if liked.

You may add soy sauce (sparingly please!) to your own serving to taste.

Steamed Pork Fillet in Black Bean Sauce

Serves 2 with 1 other dish

The essential condiment for this recipe is the inexpensive Chinese fermented black soy beans which are sold everywhere in Chinese stores. The best and most easily available brand is packaged in a round paper box pasted over with yellow paper and carrying an English label 'Yang Jiang Preserved Beans with Ginger'. These fermented soy beans, tangy and slightly bitter if tasted on their own, work wonders on a whole range of dishes, both meat and seafood, when fried in oil with garlic to become the famous black bean sauce.

225g (8oz) trimmed pork fillet
225g (8oz) closed brown or
    white mushrooms, washed
    then cut into 5mm (¼in)
    slices
4 spring onions, trimmed and
    cut diagonally at 1cm (½in)
    intervals, white and green
    parts separated
For the sauce
3 tablespoons peanut oil
2 teaspoons very finely chopped
    garlic
2 tablespoons fermented black
    beans (see above), rinsed
    then mashed
For the marinade
⅛ teaspoon salt
⅛ teaspoon sugar
1½ teaspoons light soy sauce
1 teaspoon Shaoxing wine or
    medium dry sherry
Ground white pepper to taste
2 teaspoons tapioca or potato
    flour
1 tablespoon sesame oil

Prepare the sauce first. Heat a wok over high heat until smoke rises. Add the oil and swirl it around. Add the garlic, stir and let it sizzle. Before it burns, add the mashed black beans. Stir and mix for a few seconds until the fragrance rises. Turn off the heat and scoop the mixture into a small bowl, scraping off all the oil as well. Leave to cool.

Cut the pork fillet crossways into slices about 3mm (⅛in) thick. Put into a bowl. To marinate the pork, add the salt, sugar, soy sauce and wine or sherry to the bowl, and stir to mix. Sprinkle on the pepper and the tapioca or potato flour, and stir to coat. Leave for 20 minutes, then stir in the sesame oil.

Line a 23cm (9in) round, slope-sided heatproof dish with half of the mushroom slices. Add the black bean sauce to the pork and mix to coat the slices well. Put the pork on the mushrooms and then cover it with the remaining mushrooms. Scatter the white spring onion on top.

Place the dish in a steamer and steam, covered, over high heat for 10 minutes, until the pork is cooked and the mushrooms tender and juicy. Add the green spring onion and steam for another 30 seconds. Remove the dish from the steamer. The juices in the dish deliciously combine the intense savouriness of the black bean sauce and the sweetness of the mushrooms. Serve immediately. 27

CHAPTER 2
ROASTING

Roasting cooks by dry heat. Traditionally, meat was roasted on a spit which had to be turned in front of an open fire so that the heat was applied evenly. Now, most roasting is done in ovens, in dry heat that hits the joint from all sides at once. The advantage of spit-roasting is that as the fat on the outside of the meat begins to melt, so the meat bastes itself as it turns slowly round. Some modern cookers are fitted with an electrically driven spit. This will not usually be large, or strong enough, to spit-roast really big joints or birds, but for small roasts it is very good indeed.

Roasting meat in a conventional modern oven is superficially the most straightforward of cooking processes. Yet no method arouses greater controversy about procedure. Is meat best roasted at high heat, or low, or a combination of both? Supporters of high-heat roasting claim that the flavour of their meat is the best, and that searing it at high temperatures produces a delectably browned exterior. Fans of slow-roasting note the shrinkage which occurs at higher temperatures, and point to the certain tenderness of meat cooked at lower settings. Advocates of the combination method sear their roasts in a hot oven, then reduce the heat for the remainder of the cooking time. This, they claim, gives them the best of both techniques.

So who is right? For once, the answer is everybody, because all the methods are correct choices for appropriate cuts of meat, and none of the methods is the best way of cooking all of them.

As a general rule, prime cuts can take high heat, when the meat is to be served rare, or medium. Tougher secondary cuts, which require more thorough cooking to tenderise them, and pork and veal which, although tender, should always be well-cooked, will generally benefit from slower roasting. But a variety of other factors have to be taken into account. These include the size and shape of the joint or bird, whether it is on or off the bone, and whether it contains a stuffing.

THE SEARING TRUTH ABOUT SHRINKAGE

One of the most persistent myths in cookery is the idea that searing meat at high temperatures seals in the juices and prevents drying. This is simply not so. Shrinkage, and consequently a degree of drying, are inevitable consequences of cooking meat and poultry. How much shrinkage occurs depends on how thoroughly the meat is cooked. The more it is cooked the greater the loss will be.

If two identical joints are roasted under the same conditions, one to medium-rare and the other to well-done, the joint which has been cooked to medium rare will lose less moisture than the well-done one. The same is true of smaller pieces of meat, such as steaks and chops, which are grilled or fried.

To see why this is true involves looking in microscopic detail at what happens to meat when it is subjected to heat. Proteins inside the long individual muscle cells or fibres become denser as they coagulate, allowing the connective tissue which surrounds them to squeeze out juices. In the oven these evaporate.

None of which is to say that searing meat at high temperatures in the oven, or anywhere else, is a bad idea. Searing is useless as a method of preserving moisture in meat, but nothing makes it taste better. The browning reactions, which only occur at fairly high temperatures, alter the flavour of the outer surfaces of the joint – an effect which is emphasised when exuded juices evaporate, leaving behind the concentrated layer of richly flavoured meat which forms the delectable crusty exterior of a roast. The art of roasting is to achieve an optimum balance between flavour and succulence.

EQUIPMENT

Not only are there many different designs of gas, electric and solid fuel ovens, but even ovens of the same make and model do not necessarily perform identically. Thermostats and temperature controls are not made to standards of accuracy that can be relied upon blindly. Conventional ovens are hotter at the top than at the bottom, and the indicated temperature, the one set on the dial, normally applies to the centre of the oven. The purpose of the fan in fan-assisted ovens is to spread the indicated heat evenly from top to bottom and side to side.

There is no substitute for getting acquainted with an oven. Some will be hotter, some cooler than the temperatures they are set for. Checking the temperature with a separate oven thermometer will settle the matter for those who prefer certainty to guesswork, and will allow adjustments to be calculated.

Another kind of thermometer, one which measures the internal temperature of the meat, is an invaluable aid to accuracy where it matters most. It takes the guesswork out of judging when meat is cooked to the exact degree of done-ness required (see Chart on page 40). The type most widely available consists of a skewer-like probe with an attached dial. Before the meat is put into the oven, the probe is inserted into the joint, with the tip aimed at the centre but not resting on bone or fat. The dial reads the temperature at the tip of the probe, and is left in place throughout cooking. Some ovens offer a meat probe with a digital read-out and a time's-up bleep built into the specification.

Roasting tins should be shallow, to allow the dry heat to brown the meat, but deep enough to catch melted fat and juices with no danger of spillage when the tin is removed from the oven. Racks are used to raise the meat above the juices and let the dry oven heat reach all its surfaces.

Two more pieces of equipment are particularly useful. A bulb baster allows the cook to extract fat and juices safely from the roasting tin without tipping it, and to baste the joint. A separator jug, with a spout which pours from the base, simplifies the job of separating the roasting

---

TRIMMING A RACK OF LAMB

A guard of honour and a crown roast are prepared in the same way from chined racks of lamb. First cut across the layer of fat about 10 cm (4 in) from and

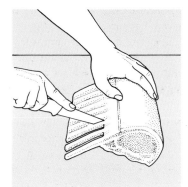

parallel to the rib tips, and cut and pull off, exposing the bones. With a knife, cut the meat and fat from *between* the bones. Scrape the bones clean.

29

juices from the melted fat. There is a fortune waiting to be made by someone who manufactures a robust, pint-sized jug of this type.

For tying meat and trussing poultry you will need string, a trussing needle, skewers and possibly a larding needle.

A razor-sharp knife is essential for carving. (Some sharpening steels are good, but your butcher may be able to advise you on how to get knives sharpened.) A traditional carving knife has rather an inflexible blade, and you may find that a knife with a long, supple blade gives better results with some cuts, such as saddles and legs of lamb or venison. A pair of heavy-duty poultry shears makes light work of dismembering birds.

WILL IT ROAST?

To make a good roast, meat must be young and tender. In the case of beef, veal, lamb and pork, the best roasting joints are the muscles which do the least work. Think how many times a day a grazing animal lifts its heavy head, and it's not difficult to understand why the neck is not one of the bits we roast. But the back, which does little more than follow the front, produces prime roasting cuts. Hind legs make good roasting pieces too, prime ones in the case of veal, lamb and pork, which are slaughtered at less than a year old, and very serviceable slow-roasting joints of beef, which are from more mature animals. For further guidance on the selection of meat, see Chapter 20.

BEEF

Prime cuts for roasting are fillet, forerib, wing rib (also known as prime rib), and sirloin. Fast-roast fillet and small rib joints. For joints weighing more than 1kg (2lb 3oz), the combined method gives better results.

Candidates for slow-roasting are back rib, and thick rib.

Although sold as roasting joints, and handsome looking in the butcher's window, silverside, top rump and topside are usually better suited to pot-roasting. Slow-roasting with frequent basting is the alternative.

VEAL

Most parts of the carcass can be roasted if cut into suitable pieces and prepared with a protective covering of added fat, or basted during roasting to prevent drying. Roasts weighing 1.5kg (3½lb) are more successful than smaller joints. For reasons of taste and digestibility, veal is cooked to an internal temperature of 75°C (165°F). A combination of high and lower oven heat achieves the best results.

LAMB

Leg, loin and saddle are prime candidates for roasting for those who enjoy their lamb pink. Use the combined high and low heat method for these and for crown and guard-of-honour roasts made from the best end of neck, and for those who prefer prime cuts cooked to medium or well-done. Shoulder, and stuffed, rolled breast of

CROWN ROAST OF LAMB

For a crown roast of lamb, curve two trimmed racks of lamb round into a circle, bones up and fat inside. Sew the ends together to form a circle, or tie

with string. For a guard of honour, interlace the bones of two trimmed racks, meat inside, and hold together with string tied round between the bones.

lamb are best suited to the combined method, or slow-roasting.

PORK

Loin is the tenderest cut of pork for roasting, but a whole roast leg, covered in crisp crackling, is the handsomest. The combined high and low heat method suits all roasting joints of pork which, because the animals are slaughtered young, can be cut from the forequarter as well as the loin and leg.

CHICKEN

Roasting chickens weighing 1kg (2lb 3oz) or more can be roasted using the combined high and low temperature method, or slow-roasted. Poussin and double poussin (see page 219) are fast-roasted at a high temperature.

DUCK

An initial blast of high heat is essential to draw off fat, so the combined high and low heat method is best suited to ducks and ducklings. Barbary ducks should be basted to prevent drying.

GOOSE

As with duck, an initial period of high heat draws off the fat, and the combined high and low heat method is the one to choose. Remove melted fat from the tin several times during roasting if you plan to save it for other purposes. (It is a delicious medium for frying or roasting potatoes, and is ideal for *confit*.)

GUINEA FOWL

Roast on high heat. Bard or baste. Remove the barding fat, dust lightly with seasoned flour, and return to the oven to brown a little in the last 5 minutes of cooking.

QUAIL

Roast as guinea fowl.

SQUAB

Bard and roast as guinea fowl.

TURKEY

Use the combined high and low heat method, or slow-roast. By far the best way of basting the bird, and ensuring that the skin does not burn, is to cover it with a double layer of butter muslin or cheesecloth soaked in melted butter, and spoon fat from the roasting tin over the bird occasionally during roasting.

GROUSE

Best eaten slightly pink. The bitter-tasting legs are not usually served. The breast meat, supported by its bones, can be separated in one piece from the legs, wings and back using poultry shears. This is most easily done before roasting. Bard the breasts with fat, then reassemble the birds by setting the breasts back on their bases to roast on high heat. Remove the barding fat, dust lightly with seasoned flour, and return to the oven to brown a little in the last 5 minutes of cooking.

CARVING A RIB OF BEEF

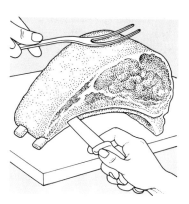

1. Remove the bones at the wide end of the rib before carving, then run the knife along between meat and contours of the ribs.
2. Steady the roast with the back of the carving fork, and slice vertically, with each slice falling free.

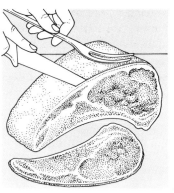

PARTRIDGE

Generally thought to taste best when cooked as thoroughly as chicken, neither pink nor well-done, but cooked through. Bard and fast-roast. Remove the barding fat, dust lightly with seasoned flour, and return to the oven to brown a little in the last 5 minutes of cooking.

PHEASANT

Because the legs benefit from longer cooking than the breast meat, roasting pheasant is a compromise. Bard and fast-roast. Remove the barding fat, dust lightly with seasoned flour, and return to the oven to brown a little in the last 5 minutes of cooking. The legs can then be removed and given an extra 4 or 5 minutes in the oven while the tender breast rests before carving.

PIGEON

Overcooking toughens dense pigeon meat, so it is best eaten slightly pink. Bard and fast-roast. Remove the barding fat, dust lightly with seasoned flour, and return to the oven to brown a little in the last 5 minutes of cooking.

SNIPE AND WOODCOCK

Both are usually eaten while the flesh is still a little pink. Bard and fast-roast. Remove the barding fat, dust lightly with seasoned flour, and return to the oven to brown a little in the last 5 minutes of cooking. The traditional way to serve them is to split the birds in halves and scoop out the cooked entrails on to a croûton of bread set under each bird while it roasts. The neck is discarded, but the head is served, split to expose the brain which is eaten as a delicacy. Following tradition is not obligatory.

WILD DUCK

Because the legs benefit from longer cooking than the breast meat, roasting wild duck, like pheasant, is a compromise. Bard and fast-roast. Remove the barding fat, dust lightly with seasoned flour, and return to the oven to brown a little in the last 5 minutes of cooking. The legs can then be removed and given an extra 7 or 8 minutes in the oven while the tender breast-meat rests before carving. An alternative strategy is to serve the pink breast meat as one course, then to finish the legs under the grill and serve them separately, perhaps with a green salad.

HARE

The dense, lean meat of young hares is best eaten pink, and benefits from an oil-based marinade (see page 46) to prevent it drying. Before marinating, remove as much as possible of the membrane which covers the flesh. If well-done meat is preferred, roasting is not the best treatment to choose because the meat will harden. Fast-roast, basting frequently.

RABBIT

Like hare, the dense, lean meat of young wild or hutch rabbits is best eaten pink. Marinate and treat as hare.

CARVING A 'LONG' SADDLE OF LAMB

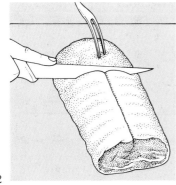

I. A long saddle of lamb comprises the loins plus the chumps. Cut lengthwise down one side of the backbone to the bone, then cut at right angles to remove one side of the saddle.
2. Remove the other side of the saddle in a similar way, then carve both pieces into slices. Carve the chump end of the roast on the bone.

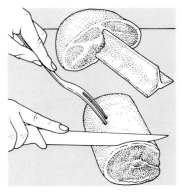

VENISON

Roast tender joints of young venison from the saddle or haunch. The meat is very lean and will need larding (see page 71) or marinating in an oil-based marinade (see page 69) and basting if the meat is not to become too dry. For the same reason it is best eaten pink. If well-done meat is preferred, braising is a more suitable cooking method. Roast using the combined high and low heat method.

WILD BOAR

The loin and hind leg of young wild boar provide the best roasting cuts. The meat is leaner than pork but, like pork, must be thoroughly cooked. Marinate in an oil-based marinade (see page 69), and slow-roast, basting frequently, to an internal temperature of not less than 70°C (160°F).

PREPARATION FOR ROASTING

Preparation for roasting may be no more elaborate than giving the joint or bird a smear of butter or oil and seasoning it.

SEASONING

Meat should be seasoned immediately before it goes into the oven. Salt draws out moisture, so seasoning in advance is not a good idea.

STUFFING

Stuffing can be used to add flavour, moisture and bulk to poultry and rolled roasts such as breast of lamb. Or it may be inserted into lean roasts such as a boned loin of pork. It is no longer thought advisable to stuff the main cavity of chickens, ducks or turkeys because of the risk of salmonella poisoning if the interior of the bird is not cooked sufficiently thoroughly. However, a stuffing can still be included if it is inserted under the skin of the breast (see *poule au pot* on page 12 and illustration on page 220), where it serves to give the bird an even more imposing appearance. An alternative is to cook a stuffing mixture separately.

BARDING

Barding meat with fat eliminates the need for constant basting. Prepared joints from the butcher, and oven-ready game birds, may already have a layer of fat tied on to them with string. If not, ask the butcher for a piece of pork back fat and do the preparation yourself. The fat can be flattened into thin sheets by putting it between two pieces of dampened plastic film and beating it flat with a rolling pin. Then tie it on neatly with string.

LARDING

Larding very lean cuts with thin strips of fat threaded through the meat is an alternative treatment, particularly suitable for large pieces which are roasted by the combined high and low heat method, or slow-roasted. If the meat is to be served pink, then the strips of fat are inserted just under the skin (see page 71). If the meat is to

CARVING A LEG OF LAMB

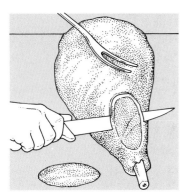

1. Holding the roast steady with the back of the fork, begin carving from the rounded side of the leg. Slice thinly away from yourself, gradually turning the knife to get large slices almost parallel to the bone.
2. Turn the leg over and, holding the bone in a cloth, carve long slices from the opposite side of the leg.

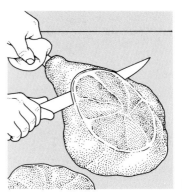

be well-cooked, they can be inserted right through the centre of the joint. They will melt during cooking to add succulence and counter dryness.

MARINATING

Oil is an important ingredient in marinades for lean roasts which benefit from lubrication. Herbs, spices and lemon juice, wine or vinegar add flavour. For an adaptable all-purpose recipe see page 46. If the meat is to be marinated for more than an hour before roasting, use an unsalted marinade because salt will draw moisture from the meat.

CALCULATING COOKING TIMES AND JUDGING DONENESS

Cooking times are calculated on the assumption that roasts are at room temperature before they go into the oven, because this is what gives the best results.

Stuffed roasts should be weighed *after* stuffing.

Use the cooking times shown in the Chart starting on page 38 for guidance, bearing in mind that ovens and ingredients vary. A long, thin roast will cook more quickly than one which has a more compact shape. If in doubt, start early and be prepared to increase the resting time rather than risk having everything else ready to eat except the meat.

Make sure that the oven has reached the required roasting temperature *before* putting the meat in.

Basting the meat during cooking is not necessary for barded roasts or those with their own layer of fat on the outside. Too frequent opening of the oven door allows the heat to drop in some ovens. For this reason it is better, whenever possible, to bard rather than baste.

To judge when a roast is cooked, rely on a meat thermometer and the Chart of internal temperatures (see page 40). Alternatively, test with a skewer inserted into the centre of the joint, or the thickest part of the thigh in the case of poultry, and examine the colour of the juices which emerge. For all poultry, veal, pork and well-done lamb, they will be clear, or tinged with gold. Pink-tinged juices indicate lamb, beef, and most game birds (except grouse) are cooked to medium. Deep pink juices indicate rare lamb, and medium-rare grouse, venison and beef. Rare beef and venison produce juices which are red.

RESTING ROASTS

Resting a roast after it is cooked is as important as every other stage of the cooking process, and the one most frequently skimped or overlooked. Resting allows the meat to settle down, and the temperature difference between the exterior and interior of the roast to decrease. Meat which has been adequately rested is easier to carve and loses far less of its juices.

CARVING A SHOULDER OF LAMB

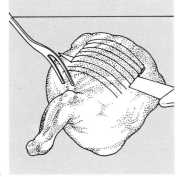

1. Place the joint, skin side uppermost, and make a series of parallel cuts in the middle of the joint. Run the knife horizontally along the length of the bone to release these short slices.
2. Turn the joint over, remove fat, and then carve in larger, horizontal slices.

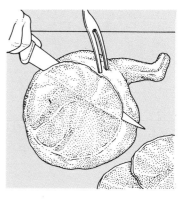

Instead of being grateful for having time to dish the vegetables and make gravy or finish a sauce without rushing, inexperienced cooks worry that the meat will be cold. Their concern is unnecessary. A large joint or bird will have a great deal of heat stored in it and would take hours, not minutes, to get cold. The length of the resting period will depend on the size of roast.

As soon as it is taken from the oven, set the roast in a warm spot, transferring it to a hot clean dish if the juices in the roasting tin are needed for a sauce or gravy. (Cover it loosely with aluminium foil if you like.) If space in the kitchen is tight, put it back in the oven (but switch it off first, and leave the door open).

Slow-roasted meat and poultry can be rested for a shorter time than roasts cooked with the combined or high-heat methods.

Roast Fillet of Beef

SERVES 4

Fillet of beef, roasted in a single piece, makes a quick, easily carved and very luxurious little roast for two to eight people, depending on the size of the piece.

Beef from the middle section of the fillet, where it has a cross section of approximately 7.5cm (3in) is ideal, and cuts into perfect slices. The narrow 'tail' end has to be doubled for roasting and falls apart when sliced, and the thicker end has an awkwardly shaped side-piece which also drops off.

There will be almost no juices left in the roasting tin to make a sauce, so serve it with a classic *béarnaise* (see page 82). This is a traditional accompaniment to a Châteaubriand, a French cut from the fillet; it is usually grilled, and served with Château potatoes as well.

680g (1½lb) fillet of beef
1 tablespoon melted butter or oil
Salt and freshly ground black pepper

Preheat the oven to very hot (240°C/475°F, gas mark 9).

Wipe the meat dry with kitchen paper and tie it with string in three or four places along its length. This will improve the shape of the piece by holding the sides in. Brush it with melted butter or oil and season it just before it goes into the oven.

Check the weight of the roast and set it on a rack in a roasting tin. Insert a meat thermometer, if you are using one, into the centre of the meat, which should be brought to room temperature before going into the oven.

For rare beef, roast for 12 minutes, or to an internal temperature of 60°C (140°F). For medium-cooked beef, roast for 15 minutes, or to an internal temperature of 70°C (155°F). The fillet is too special to cook to well-done. Rest the roast for 10 minutes before cutting into thick slices.

CARVING A CHICKEN

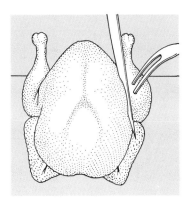

1. Place the bird breast side up, and remove the legs and wings on each side. If the chicken is large, separate drumsticks from thighs.
2. Carve thin slices diagonally from each side of the breast.

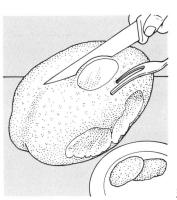

Roast Shoulder of Lamb

SERVES 4–6

A small shoulder of home-produced new season's spring lamb is meltingly tender and should not be very fatty. The larger shoulders from older animals sold in winter are fairly fatty but, as the meat is best cooked to well-done, a good amount of the fat will melt into the roasting tin during cooking, and the meat will still be succulent. A spring shoulder will feed four, a late-season shoulder feeds six.

1 shoulder of lamb
1 clove garlic
2 or 3 sprigs of fresh rosemary
Salt and freshly ground black pepper
1–2 teaspoons plain flour

Preheat the oven to hot (230°C/450°F, gas mark 8).

Wipe the shoulder dry with kitchen paper. Peel the garlic and cut it into thin slices. Use a sharp, pointed knife to make small, shallow incisions at approximately 4cm (1½in) intervals on both sides of the meat, and poke a sliver of garlic and 3 or 4 rosemary leaves into each hole. Season the meat on both sides.

Check the weight of the roast and set it on a rack in a roasting tin. Insert a meat thermometer, if you are using one, into the centre of the meat, making sure that it is not resting against the bone. The meat should be brought to room temperature before it goes into the oven.

Calculate the cooking time at 20 minutes to the 450g (1lb), including the initial searing time. Roast it for 10 minutes at the high heat, dust it with the flour, then reduce the oven temperature to moderate (180°C/350°F, gas mark 4) and continue roasting for the remainder of the calculated time. The meat will be well-done when it reaches an internal temperature of 80°C (175°F). Rest it for 10–15 minutes before carving.

ROASTING VEGETABLES

Starchy vegetables such as potatoes and parsnips can be roasted in the oven at the same time as the meat. They can be roasted from raw, but are more usually parboiled first, then cooked in the fat and meat juices surrounding the roast, or in a separate tin with oil or melted fat. When cooked round the roast they will absorb some of the juices and develop a toffee-like coat. For really crisp roast potatoes, cook them separately in oil, melted beef fat or lard. The oil or fat should be at least 1cm (½in) deep, and very well heated in the oven before the potatoes are added.

The temperature at which the meat is roasting will govern how long the vegetables will take, unless you have a double oven. Additional factors to consider when calculating how long to give them include the size and shape of the pieces, whether they are raw or parboiled, whether they are freshly parboiled and still hot, and whether the space available to cook them is at the top or bottom of the oven.

Ideally, potatoes should be roasted in a hot oven (230°C/450°F, gas mark 8) for the first 20 minutes, then turned over and cooked at a moderate heat (180°C/350°F, gas mark 4) until crisp and golden, usually about another 30 minutes.

Parboiled beetroot, carrot, celeriac, parsnip, plantain, sweet potato, whole onions and firm-fleshed varieties of squash are candidates for roasting in the drippings around the joint. Whole heads of unpeeled garlic can also be roasted, wrapped in foil, until the flesh is soft. The squeezed out purée can be spread on croûtons and served as an accompaniment to the meat.

Roast shoulder of lamb, served with roast potatoes, roast garlic, mint sauce and redcurrant jelly.

ROASTING TIMES AND TEMPERATURES

	Fast-Roasting	Combined High and Low Heat Roasting	Slow-Roasting
BEEF	240°C/475°F, Gas 9 for total roasting time	Sear at 240°C/475°F, Gas 9, for 15 mins then reduce the heat to 180°C/350°F, Gas 4	150°C/300°F, Gas 2 for total roasting time
FILLET	**Rare** 7 mins per 450g (1lb) **Medium** 10 mins per 450g (1lb)		
PRIME RIB WING RIB SIRLOIN RUMP FORE RIB	On the bone [Boneless]	**Rare** 8–10 mins per 450g (1lb) [10–12 mins] **Medium** 10–12 mins per 450g (1lb) [12–15 mins] **Well-done** 15–18 mins per 450g (1lb) [18–20 mins]	
AITCHBONE CUT BACK RIB THICK RIB TOPSIDE SILVERSIDE TOP RUMP	On the bone and boneless		**Medium** 20–25 mins per 450g (1lb) **Well-done** 30–35 mins per 450g (1lb)
VEAL		Sear at 190°C/375°F, Gas 6 for 15 mins then reduce the heat to 180°C/350°F, Gas 4	
All roasting cuts, on the bone or boneless		**Medium to well-done** 20–25 mins per 450g (1lb)	
GAME	230°C/450°F Gas 8 for total cooking time	Sear at 240°C/475°F, gas 9, for 10 mins then reduce heat to 180°C/350°F, gas 4	150°C/300°F, gas 2, for the total roasting time
VENISON *SADDLE* *HAUNCH*		**Rare** 8–9 mins per 450g (1lb) **Rare** 9–10 mins per 450g (1lb)	
RABBIT HARE GROUSE PARTRIDGE PHEASANT PIGEON SNIPE WOODCOCK WILD DUCK	30 mins 30–40 mins 20–30 mins 20–25 mins 30–45 mins 20–30 mins 10–15 mins 15–20 mins 20–30 mins		
WILD BOAR			35–40 mins per 450g (1lb)

	Fast-Roasting	Combined High and Low Heat Roasting	Slow-Roasting
POULTRY		Sear at 220°C/425°F, Gas 7 then reduce the heat to 170°C/325°F, gas 3	170°C/325°F, gas 3, for total roasting time
CHICKEN 1–1.5kg (2–3lb) 1.5–2.5kg (3–5lb) GOOSE 3.5–4.5kg (8–10lb) 4.5–5.5kg (10–12lb)		Sear 30 mins then 15–30 mins Sear 30 mins then 30–60 mins Sear 45 mins then 1¾–2 hours Sear 45 mins then 2–2½ hours	1¼–2 hours
		Sear at 220°C/425°F, gas 7 then reduce heat to 180°C/350°F, gas 4	
TURKEY 3.5–5.5kg (8–12lb) 5.5–7kg (12–15lb) 7–9kg (15–20 lb)		Sear 50 mins then 1½–2 hours Sear 50 mins then 2–2½ hours Sear 50 mins then 2½–3 hours	3½–4 hours 4–4½ hours 4½–5 hours
DUCK OR DUCKLING 1.5–3kg (3–6lb)		Sear 30 mins then 50 mins–1½ hours	
GUINEA FOWL 750g–1.5kg (1½–3lb) POUSSIN 500g–750g (1–1½lb) SQUAB 500g–750g (1–1½lb) QUAIL	220°C/425°F, gas 7 30 mins–1 hour 220°C/425°F, gas 7 20–30 mins 220°C/425°F, gas 7 20–30 mins 220°C/425°F, gas 7 15 mins		
LAMB		Sear at 230°C/450°F, gas 8 for 10 mins then reduce the heat to 180°C/350°F, gas 4	150°C/300°F, gas 2 for total roasting time
BEST END CROWN ROAST GUARD OF HONOUR LOIN SADDLE SHOULDER	On the bone	**Rare** 10 mins per 450g (1lb) **Medium** 12–15 mins per 450g (1lb) **Well-done** 20 mins per 450g (1lb)	
SHOULDER ROLLED BREAST	Boned or Boned & Stuffed		**Well-done** 35–40 mins per 450 g (1 lb)

	Fast-Roasting	Combined High and Low Heat Roasting	Slow-Roasting
PORK		Sear at 200°C/400°F, gas 6 for 10 mins then reduce the heat to 160°C/325°F, gas 3	
LOIN On the bone		**Medium** 25 mins per 450g (1lb)	
HAND } On the LEG } bone SHOULDER LOIN Off the bone		**Medium** 30 mins per 450g (1lb) **Well-done** 35 mins per 450g (1lb)	
LEG } Boned and } rolled SHOULDER } or stuffed		**Well-done** 35–40 mins per 450g (1lb)	

INTERNAL TEMPERATURES OF MEAT, POULTRY AND GAME

All domestic poultry, pork and wild board should be cooked to an internal temperature of not less than 70°C (155°F) to eliminate the risks of bacterial and parasite infection. Rolled joints of meat should also be cooked to at least the safe minimum of 70°C (155°F).

BEEF	Rare	60°C (140°F)	**DUCK**	Medium	70°C (155°F)
	Medium	70°C (155°F)		Well-done	80°C (175°F)
	Well-done	80°C (175°F)			
			GOOSE	Well-done	80°C (175°F)
VEAL	Medium	75°C (165°F)			
	Well-done	80°C (175°F)	**TURKEY**	Medium	70°C (155°F)
				Well-done	80°C (175°F)
LAMB	Rare	60°C (140°F)			
	Medium	65°C (147°F)	**RABBIT & HARE**	Rare	60°C (140°F)
	Well-done	80°C (175°F)		Medium	70°C (155°F)
PORK	Medium	70°C (155°F)	**VENISON**	Rare	60°C (140°F)
	Well-done	80°C (175°F)		Medium	70°C (155°F)
CHICKEN	Medium	70°C (155°F)	**WILD BOAR**	Medium	70°C (155°F)
	Well-done	80°C (175°F)		Well-done	80°C (175°F)

CHAPTER 3

GRILLING AND BARBECUING

Grilling appears to be one of the simplest of all cooking techniques but its simplicity is deceptive. Easy as it looks, and straightforward as the procedures are, it is one of the trickiest ways of cooking to get right every time. No other method involves quite so many variables or demands more judgement or watchfulness from the cook. How hot is the grill? Even the most sophisticated modern cookers offer no accurate measure of the grill's heat output. And of course barbecue cooking out of doors holds out even less hope of precision. How do you calculate the effects of wind-chill on Guy Fawkes night? How much more quickly will the steaks cook if they have been out of the fridge for a while, warming on a sunny patio?

Grilling uses intense, dry heat and cooks food fast. Characteristically, it produces a well-browned exterior and, when correctly judged, a succulent interior. The way in which browning by direct heat changes the flavour of meat, fish and vegetables seems to appeal to everyone. The special taste of grilled food always seems even better when it has been cooked over a fire or charcoal than when it has been cooked under a gas or electric grill. It is this 'taste of the fire', a combination of smoke flavours and juices from the food caramelising on the underside, that gives such a moreish savour to barbecued food.

Controlling the speed of grilling relies on the crude expedient of moving the food closer to or further from the heat. Small pieces of food, which cook fastest, are placed closest. So sardines, for example, need to be nearer than trout.

An even bigger fish, say a small salmon, would be grilled further away again, or it would be burned on the outside before the middle had cooked.

The distinction between roasting over an open fire and grilling is a matter of scale, obvious when the distinction is between a whole ox cooked for a day or more on a spit with a lamb chop grilled for 10 minutes in the kitchen. Whether a small shoulder of lamb cooked over charcoal is roasted or grilled is a matter of semantics. Here, grilling applies to small portions of quickly cooked foods.

Foods which can be grilled successfully are those which do not need long cooking to make them tender. Prime cuts of meat, most poultry and game, many types of fish and shellfish, and a suprisingly wide selection of vegetables need no more than a lick of olive oil or melted butter and seasoning to prepare them for the grill.

Marinades of oil, herbs and spices add exciting flavours to grills and barbecues, and prevent undue drying during cooking. Salt should nearly always be saved for last-minute seasoning because it draws out moisture from meat and fish. However, some vegetables benefit from salting in advance to draw off bitter juices.

SUITABLE INGREDIENTS FOR GRILLS AND BARBECUES

BEEF

Steaks – sirloin, rump, T-bone, fillet and porterhouse – and other lean, tender cuts of beef such as short ribs, cut singly. Skirt of beef is inexpensive and tender when well hung and cooked no more than medium rare. Hamburgers, home-made with lean beef finely chopped, as opposed to minced, are very good (opposite).

Beef cooked rare, or medium rare, will be more succulent than well-cooked meat or hamburgers.

VEAL

Chops taken from the ribs 'or loin, or boned medallions from the loin. The taste of under-done veal is unappealing, so it is usually cooked to medium or well done.

LAMB

Loin chops, or double loin chops called butterfly chops; chump chops; leg steaks or gigot chops; lamburgers.

Lightly cooked lamb is a less popular taste than rare beef, and most people enjoy it cooked to medium or well done.

PORK

Spare rib chops from the neck end of the pig; loin chops with or without the kidney; chump chops; leg steaks; spare ribs (see page 216); rissoles or *crépinettes* (see Glossary); cured pork; gammon steaks and bacon.

Pork is never eaten rare and should always be thoroughly cooked.

VENISON

Chops, medallions or steaks (see page 223), and burgers with some added fat.

Venison, like beef, can be cooked to any stage of doneness, from rare to well done.

SAUSAGES

All kinds of meat can be made into sausages. For grilling and barbecuing, recipes which include some fat and little or no rusk are best.

Sausages of any type should be thoroughly cooked.

OFFAL

Lamb and calves' kidneys will toughen if over-cooked. They taste best if a little pink in the middle.

POULTRY

Chicken pieces; split or butterflied poussin (see illustrations, page 46); kebabs; guinea-fowl, halved or in pieces; some breeds of duck (Barbary, for example), cut in pieces (see page 220); quail, whole or butterflied; turkey pieces.

All poultry should be cooked thoroughly. When pierced with a skewer the juices should run clear.

GAME BIRDS

Young pheasant, partridge, pigeon or wild duck, jointed, halved or butterflied (see page 46).

Pheasant tastes best when cooked through. Other game birds may be preferred medium rare.

FISH

Whole fish of almost any size from sprat to salmon. Relatively fatty fish such as sardines, pilchards, herring, mackerel, salmon trout and salmon are well suited to grilling whole. Trout and flat fish need special care if they are not to be dry. Any round fish large enough to make a single serving, or bigger, will cook more evenly if a few diagonal, slashing cuts are made in its sides. These are made in the thickest part of the fish and almost through to the bone. You can also grill steaks and cutlets of larger fish, and fish kebabs.

Fish of all types is cooked when it comes easily away from the bone and the flesh has turned from translucent to opaque.

CRUSTACEANS AND SHELLFISH

Halves of raw lobster; large shrimps and prawns; scallop cushions.

The flesh is cooked when it has turned from translucent to opaque.

VEGETABLES

Slices of uncooked potato can be grilled, but new and small whole potatoes are best par-boiled (see Glossary) before grilling. Red, green and yellow peppers, tomatoes, mushrooms, courgettes, aubergines, onions and chicory spears require only to be cut into suitable pieces. Corn cobs can be barbecued in their husks (after removing the silky threads inside). They can be parboiled or grilled from raw.

Potatoes and corn cobs are unappetising

unless cooked right through, but other vegetables can be cooked to any degree of doneness you like – from nearly raw to very well done.

KEBABS

All the foods listed here can be cooked in bite-sized pieces threaded on to skewers. When making up mixed kebabs, choose ingredients that will all cook in the same length of time. If in doubt, make up separate skewers of individual ingredients; those cooked first can be kept warm until the others are ready.

CHEESE

Toasted cheese; grilled goat's cheeses; cheese melted in vine-leaf packets.

If overcooked by direct heat, cheese toughens and develops unpleasant flavours. Grill toasted cheese (thin slices of hard cheese laid on buttered toast) under a high heat until it melts and begins to brown lightly. Slices of goat cheese are grilled under top heat until the surface melts and browns lightly, and the interior is just warm. Wrapping pieces of cheese in vine leaves is a good method on a barbecue. The cheese is cooked only until it melts.

OUTDOOR PUDDINGS

Caramelised fruit kebabs; barbecued bananas and pineapple; toasted marshmallows.

Bite-sized chunks of raw fruit (banana, pineapple, apple etc.) can be marinated in a mixture of juice, alcohol and sugar to taste, then threaded on skewers and cooked over a barbecue until lightly browned and warmed through. Toast marshmallows, one at a time, on the end of a skewer until the outside is coloured and the inside melting.

HAMBURGERS

Familiarity has bred contempt for the hamburger which, when well made, should be as good as steak. Making hamburgers at home is an opportunity to rescue a popular formula from commercial abuse. Buying high-quality lean beef, and chopping it by hand, are the basic essentials. Use chuck steak, rump or topside for flavour, and trim the meat of all connecting tissue. For hamburgers which are to be eaten rare, there is no need to include fat. If they are to be cooked to well-done, however, then a proportion of fat will help to stop them drying. You can use finely chopped beef fat or, more luxuriously, marrow fat scooped from the bones. If finely chopped onion or shallot is to be included in the mix, then the butter or oil it has been softened in can be included instead.

Why chop the meat by hand when mincing or processing it is quicker? Chopping the meat with a sharp knife or knives (chefs use matched pairs of heavy knives for this job) cuts the muscle fibres into short lengths with a minimum of squashing and squeezing so that meat retains more of its original character than if it is minced or processed. Mince made from lean, well trimmed meat is an acceptable substitute. Beef chopped in a processor will produce hamburgers with a softer, less steak-like texture.

Allow 110g (4oz) of trimmed, lean beef per burger. Chop the meat and shape the hamburgers as close to cooking time as is feasible for the freshest steak taste. Add up to a tablespoonful of finely chopped fat and up to the same amount of softened onion or shallot per burger. Both are optional. Season the meat very lightly and shape it into burgers using only enough pressure to make them hold their shape. Hamburgers which are to be cooked to well-done will cook without excessive drying if they are no more than 2.5cm (1in) thick. Those to be served rare can be up to twice that thickness. Grill hamburgers on high heat so that they brown fast on the outside and are still succulent in the middle. A 2.5cm (1in) thick burger takes about 3 minutes on each side to cook to rare, 5 minutes a side for medium.

RACKS AND SKEWERS

Simplicity is no small part of the appeal of grilling. Racks designed for grilling fish are the most useful piece of specialised equipment (see illustration overleaf), making it possible to turn fish without breaking it.

Large numbers of small fish such as sardines can be impaled on parallel skewers to make them easier to turn (see photograph on page 45).

Skewers for kebabs should always be flat so that the food can be turned as it cooks and does not simply swivel on the skewer instead. They are also useful for holding meat or poultry flat while they cook.

Small wooden skewers are useful for pinning the tails of chops. Twigs of rosemary, stripped of some of their leaves, make aromatic skewers.

COOKING UNDER A GRILL

Gas or electric grills should be turned on full for at least 10 minutes and thoroughly heated before cooking begins. Lay the food, which should be at room temperature, on the rack over the grill pan and position it under the heat.

Control the speed of cooking by adjusting the distance from the heat source, or, if adjustable, the temperature of the grill. Avoid allowing the outside to brown too much before the inside is sufficiently cooked. Blackening to the point of charring is always overcooking and tastes bitter.

Cook the food on one side, then turn it over and cook until done. Aim to grill each side for roughly the same number of minutes. With so many variables to control, not least the widely varying efficiency of different grills, it is impracticable to give more than the vaguest of timing suggestions. A 2.5cm (1in) thick sirloin steak may be cooked to rare in as little as 5 minutes and take 12 or more to reach well-done. A 7.5cm (3in) thick fillet steak would take a minimum of 12 minutes to reach medium. For other foods, see Assessing Doneness.

For pan-grilling, see Dry-Frying on page 64.

GRILLING ON A BARBECUE

The mistake most frequently made by inexperienced barbecue cooks is to rush, and to start cooking before the charcoal is ready. Once lit, the charcoal should be left to burn until it is covered with white ash. Then the glowing embers should be spread for cooking. The cooking temperature is controlled by adjusting the height of the food above the embers.

Avoid bad tastes by observing the following:

- Use an odourless firelighting liquid, gas starter or old-fashioned paper and sticks.
- Begin with clean grill racks and grids, and grease them lightly.
- Set the grill rack at a slight slope – if possible, with a tray to catch the drips. This will reduce flames from fat spatters, which can give the food an acrid taste.

ASSESSING DONENESS

Judging how thoroughly grilled meat is cooked can be done by pressing it with your fingers. The less resilient it is, the more cooked it is. But this method takes more practice than most of us get. Which leaves only one option – to prod the meat at its thickest part with a pointed knife and look at the colour of the juices which emerge. If the steak is rare the juices will be red. If it is medium

Brush skewered sardines during grilling or barbecuing with a marinade-moistened sprig of herbs.

BARBECUING FISH

Fish can fall apart or, if small, can be difficult to turn over on the barbecue. The answer is to use a double-sided grilling basket or rack; these can be

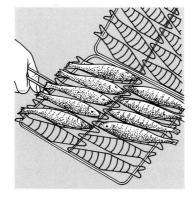

turned over, and they help the fish keep their shape. Some hold several small fish at the same time; some are shaped to hold one single, larger fish.

they will be pale pink and almost clear.

Pieces of meat cooked *over* heat may not need piercing. Beads of juice will appear on the upper surface after the meat has been turned.

With poultry the juices should run clear when pierced at the thickest point, close to the bone.

Fish is simpler to judge. Insert the point of a sharp knife into the thickest point, close to the bone. It is done when the flesh parts easily from the bone and has turned opaque.

Vegetables are easiest of all. They are done when they are as soft as you like them.

USING THE JUICES

Provided they have not been burned, any juices in the bottom of the grill pan can be used as the foundation of a simple sauce. Where a marinade has been used for basting, it may be necessary to do no more than taste for seasoning and pour it over the cooked food. Otherwise the juices can be strained into a small saucepan and reduced (see page 176), or thickened with *beurre manié* (see page 79) or butter. Small quantities of vinegar or lemon juice can be used to sharpen the taste, or cream or *crème fraîche* to soften it.

MARINADES

The purpose of marinades is twofold – to add flavour and prevent drying. The usual ingredients are oil for lubrication, wine, vinegar, citrus juice or yoghurt to enhance flavour, plus herbs and/or spices, or still more exotic condiments like the fermented fish sauce used in satay. Each marinade recipe is sufficient for 4–6 servings.

Herb Marinade

Oil and wine or lemon juice combine with herbs in an infinitely variable marinade for meat, poultry, fish or vegetables. Use well flavoured olive oil. The acid ingredient can be dry red or white wine, or lemon or lime juice, or wine or cider vinegar.

4 tablespoons olive oil
2–4 tablespoons wine, vinegar or lemon juice
1 clove garlic, finely chopped (optional)
1–2 tablespoons finely chopped fresh herbs
½ teaspoon freshly ground black pepper

Mix all the ingredients well together and turn the meat, fish or vegetables in the mixture. Leave them to soak for at least 2 hours before salting and grilling. The marinade can be used as a baste. Paint it on to the food during cooking.

Tandoori Marinade

This is an authentic-tasting tandoori marinade. Use it for skinned chicken joints, for cubes of lamb, chicken or firm-fleshed fish, or for raw jumbo prawns peeled except for the tail. Chicken and

BUTTERFLYING POULTRY

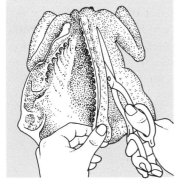

1. Place the bird on its breast and, using poultry shears, cut along the length of one side of the backbone. Cut along the other side of the backbone and cut off entirely.
2. Turn the bird over and open out as much as possible. Using the heel of your hand, strike the bird firmly on the breast – the object is to break the remaining bones so that the bird lies flat.

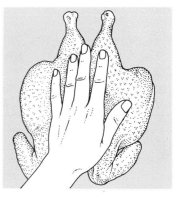

meat can be refrigerated for up to 24 hours in the marinade. Fish and shellfish need only 3 – 4 hours.

1 medium onion
4 large cloves garlic
30g (1oz) fresh green ginger
250ml (8fl oz) natural yogurt
4 tablespoons fresh lemon juice
4 tablespoons vegetable oil
1 tablespoon ground coriander
1 tablespoon ground turmeric
1 teaspoon ground cumin
½ teaspoon grated nutmeg
½ teaspoon ground cinnamon
½ teaspoon freshly ground black pepper
¼ teaspoon ground cloves
¼ teaspoon cayenne pepper or ground chilli
2 teaspoons salt

Peel and finely chop the onion, garlic and ginger. Reduce them to a smooth paste in a food processor, or with a pestle and mortar, then stir in all the remaining ingredients.

Use the marinade to baste the food as it grills. Serve the meat or fish with wedges of fresh lemon squeezed over it.

Yogurt Marinade

Yogurt is a useful tenderising agent in marinades. The herbs can be varied depending on which kind of meat or poultry is being used. Try tarragon, thyme or sage with chicken; rosemary with beef; tarragon, mint, thyme, rosemary or lavender leaves with lamb; sage or fresh bay with pork. Salt the marinated ingredients immediately before cooking.

4 tablespoons olive oil
150ml (¼ pint) natural yogurt
2 cloves garlic, crushed
1–2 tablespoons chopped fresh herbs
1 teaspoon freshly ground black pepper

Combine the ingredients and mix well. Soak joints of chicken or smaller pieces of meat or poultry in the marinade for at least 2 hours, or up to 12 hours in the refrigerator.

Soy Marinade

Soy sauce gives a slightly oriental flavour which works well with fish and poultry.

4 tablespoons vegetable oil
4 tablespoons dry sherry
1 tablespoon soy sauce
1 clove garlic, crushed
½ teaspoon freshly ground black pepper

Combine all the ingredients and mix well. Soak pieces of fish or chicken in the mixture for about 2 hours before grilling. Paint with the marinade during cooking.

Satay Marinade

The fermented fish sauce called *nam pla* (see page 288) which gives satay its distinctive flavour comes from Thailand. Tamarind pulp can be bought from oriental grocers (see Chapter 24).

¼ teaspoon tamarind pulp
1 tablespoon vegetable oil
2 cloves garlic, finely chopped
1 small onion, finely chopped
1 tablespoon each of brown sugar, fresh lime juice and nam pla

Dissolve the tamarind pulp in 2 tablespoons of boiling water, then put all the ingredients into a blender or food processor and process until smooth. Marinate thinly sliced ribbons of pork, beef, lamb or chicken in the mixture for about an hour. Thread them on wooden skewers and grill briefly on a high heat. Serve with a satay sauce.

The Cooking of Great Britain and Ireland

by ANTON MOSIMANN

When I first arrived in London in 1975, my knowledge of British cooking was not very extensive. I had heard many of the jokes current in kitchens around Europe – that the British had only one sauce, that they boiled everything to death, and that they ate nothing but oatmeal, roast beef and potatoes, preferably as chips.

Anton Mosimann, of Mosimann's dining club, London

But I was also aware that Britain was an agricultural land of plenty, and that the basic ingredients – beef, lamb, seafood, vegetables and fruit – were among the best in the world. It seemed a curious dichotomy, so I had to investigate to find out the truth for myself. Whenever I had time during those first few years at The Dorchester, with the help of a few stalwarts in the kitchen brigade, I set about researching the culinary history of the country in which I had chosen to work and live.

Rather like the English language itself, it appeared to me that much of the culinary tradition of Britain was polyglot, an amalgam of several differing national and imported foreign influences. Any cuisine borrows to a certain extent, and cannot stay permanently immune to infiltration from outside. The cooking of Britain was perhaps more open to this than others because of its geography – two main islands tucked into the lee of a great continental land mass – which made it subject from the earliest times to invasion and occupation.

The culinary basis on which these influences were to bear was one of seasonal food, plainly cooked. Meat, when available in Ireland, Scotland or Wales, would be boiled or stewed over furze or peat fires. Roasting was possible only over wood fires, and wood was particularly plentiful in England. These cooking techniques were inevitably dependent on the limited resources and fuel available to the cook: a slow fire and a single pot for the stews; a brisk fire and a spit for the roasts. The majority of people ate pottages or vegetable soups – the one-pot idea again – root vegetables, dried legumes, cheese and cereal-based bread or oatcakes. These last would be cooked on hot hearthstones or the forerunner of the girdle or griddle, said to be one of the oldest cooking utensils in the world. Any combinations of food were simple as well. Bread, cheese and onions, a marriage still offered today as a 'ploughman's lunch', would have been the most common of meals, and it required no basic cooking at all.

EARLY DAYS

The Romans were probably the first influence, credited with introducing to northern Europe the herbs which reminded them of their sunnier homelands, birds such as pheasants and guinea fowl, and various fruit trees, including cherries and apples. During their 400 or so years' occupation of Britain, the use of these introduced herbs in cooking would undoubtedly have become familiar to the natives. Thus, one can suppose, the much-loved British combination of lamb or mutton with a mint sauce would not have been possible but for the Romans!

The invading Celts, Saxons and Scandinavians had an effect too. The Saxons introduced good farming practice; the Danes brought Scandinavian methods of preservation such as smoking

Kipper Pâté

and drying, of fish in particular. Most of the famous Scottish smoked fish – Finnan haddock and Arbroath smokies among them – come from that east-facing coast, and Aberdeen Angus cattle are thought to have developed from Scandinavian stock. The Vikings, great voyagers who are said to have landed in America before Columbus, were also avid traders, a characteristic which may have laid the foundations of the great trading nation

Britain was later to become. (This in itself was to lead to many culinary adoptions and influences.)

At the Conquest in 1066, the Normans brought with them the cooking of France, which in turn had been influenced by that of Italy. The Anglo-Saxon inclination was still towards the simple and plain, but the Frenchmen from the north introduced more complicated and elaborate composite dishes which used combi- 49 nations of ingredients. The French in fact were horrified by the fact that the British farmed animals for eating at table – the French cooked only beasts which had given their best years to the land as working animals, and thought farming them very wasteful of resources. French joints had to be boned, rolled and braised or stewed with other ingredients to make them taste good. This was the fundamental difference in ways of cooking, and explains why the British could so excel at 'plain roasts'.

It was at this time, too, that new words for meat were adopted into the English language: ox became beef, calf veal, pig pork, and sheep mutton (from, respectively, the French *boeuf*, *veau*, *porc* and *mouton*). This particular trend was to be strongest in the far north of Britain. The 'auld alliance' between Scotland and France had its roots as early as the 9th century, and many French queens long before the tragic Mary Queen of Scots had influenced both kitchen and language. Even today in Scotland the French word *gigot* is used for a leg of lamb or mutton, and a large serving platter is called an asbet (from the French *assiette*).

These Gallic refinements, however, were confined to the court and the homes of wealthier Britons, and it was at this time that two disparate strands of British cooking began to appear. The rich and those who lived in the south – or near ports through which came foreign influences and ingredients – were open to new ideas. The poor, those who lived from the land, and those far from the trading centres (in Scotland, Wales, Ireland and the north of England) remained to a large extent unaffected. Theirs remained a simpler tradition, plain and uncluttered by foreign flavours, which was to form the bases of regional British cooking.

For the peasantry, as in any European country during the Middle Ages, had to make do with what they could seasonally grow, rear, catch, pick or poach. A pig and a few hens would be valuable staples in the farm or cottager's yard, and eggs and

By the end of the 18th century the potato was the most important vegetable crop in Britain, and it was probably then too that the British reliance on potatoes as an integral part of the meal – the cliché of 'meat and two veg' – originated.

salted pork of some kind ensured at least something to eat when harvests failed or spring was late. Now considered so characteristically British, the combining of a few slices of cured bacon with eggs is thought to have originated in those very early days.

SUGAR AND SPICE

Although the British have always been accused of being conservative in taste, many of the ingredients which have become basics of their cooking are exotic in origin. In the medieval era, major imports were spices, and

English 'high' cooking in particular was significantly affected. The foods of the wealthy would be heavily flavoured by cloves, mace, nutmeg, galingale, cubeb and grains of paradise. Pepper became an essential kitchen element of even the humblest household, and was considered so valuable that it was used as money or tribute (hence 'peppercorn rent').

It has been said that many festival English dishes of the Middle Ages could quite happily transplant to the Middle East of today: the recorded use of spicing, dried fruit, rose water and sweet nuts such as almonds are central to much Arab cooking. The medieval love of almonds is still seen in the cake covering, marzipan. Traditional gingerbreads, cakes and biscuits date from this time as well. This passion for spicing is said to have arisen because of the need to mask the flavour of tainted or over-salted foods, but this does not explain why many recipes of the period specify some five or so spices with fruit, for instance.

Much medieval food was also highly coloured, the tops of feast-day pastry pies being painted bright reds, yellows and greens. Those pies – pastry 'coffyns' or cases enclosing a mixture of ingredients – seem to be a British speciality, and probably evolved because they were easy to transport and eat before the fork came into general use. The tradition continues today, whether savoury (steak and kidney pie and the humbler Cornish pasty) or sweet (made with fruits such as apple, still spiced with its medieval clove).

Many of these pies, even the savoury ones, were very sweet by modern tastes, cane sugar having been introduced from the Orient during the early 16th century. Recipes of the period call for mixtures of boiled and shredded meats, suet, spices, dried fruits, orange peel and lots of sugar, all encased in pastry. This was the forerunner of the modern 'mince' pie, now made without meat.

Savoury puddings date from the medieval period as well, their concept echoing that of the pastry pie – a mixture of ingredients contained and cooked in a casing. In the 'high' tradition, meats, vegetables and spices would form the filling; in poorer households, cereal such as oats with some flavouring (blood, offal or onion) would be used. Some of these puddings were enclosed in the stomach bag of an animal. The Scottish haggis, black and white puddings, even sausages, are relics of this, as are the later sweet puddings made with a rich suet pastry and steamed in a cloth.

During the Tudor period, after Henry VIII had cut England off from the Pope and the rest of Catholic Europe, the infiltrating influences tended to reduce, and the people of Britain became more individual and insular. This was to have an effect on their eating habits, leading them back towards the plain and simple. Later the Puritans were to frown on anything involving sensual pleasure, whether social or culinary – theatrical performances and the feast of Christmas were abandoned, for instance. With the Restoration, the theatre may have leapt back to life with frothy and suggestive comedies, but the style of food had shown no forward development at all.

In France, the culinary arts were actively encouraged by the monarchy. In Britain, despite early royal enthusiasm for the French style, the population still relied basically on their plain boiled and roast meats, their pies, simple combinations and home-grown foods.

THE POTATO AND OTHER EXOTICS

There had, however, been several major importations of ingredients during the 16th and 17th centuries. One of the most significant was the potato, introduced in

It was an Italian who asserted that there existed in Britain 'sixty different religious sects, but only one sauce', and Somerset Maugham who swore that to eat well in Britain you had to eat breakfast three times a day.

around 1590 from the Americas. By 1650 it had become the staple food of Ireland, which was to lead to the tragic devastation caused by the potato blight in 1845: in that one-crop country, it is estimated that up to a million died of starvation.

The potato was cultivated in Scotland, Wales and the north of England too, but to a lesser extent than in Ireland, and it only gradually filtered into the diet of the more sophisticated south. Many of the best-known regional British dishes make use of potato – Irish stew, colcannon and champ, Lancashire hotpot, Welsh punch-nep and the Scottish stovies. By the end of the 18th century the potato was the most important vegetable crop in Britain, and it was probably then too that the British reliance on potatoes as an integral part of a meal – the cliche of 'meat and two veg' – originated.

The discovery of the New World had also led to the introduction of many other foodstuffs hitherto unknown in Europe, among them maize, tomatoes and the turkey. The latter was so-called because anything unfamiliar was deemed to have originated in the heathen east, thus the 'turkey cock'. (Indeed, maize was known at first as 'turkey corn'.) In Scotland in the early 18th century, a cargo of Seville oranges, bought cheaply from a Spanish vessel blown into Dundee, was made into a preserve by the buyer's wife, Janet Keillor. She usually used quinces (*marmelo* in Portuguese), but her new preserve was to become a unique part of the British breakfast and to acquire worldwide fame.

International trade led to the introduction of yet more 'foods' – coffee, chocolate and tea. Although the popularity of coffee led to the formation of coffee houses in the 17th century – forerunners of the British gentlemen's clubs – it was tea that was to become indissolubly linked with the British. Green tea from China had been the prerogative of the upper classes for some time – kept under lock and key in elaborate tea caddies – but, when the plants began to be cultivated in India and Ceylon by the British, the leaf became cheaper to buy at home. The drink cut across all classes, becoming a national passion by the 18th century, and virtually ousting coffee and chocolate (as well as the ubiquitous cheap gin and ale).

51

THE INDUSTRIAL REVOLUTION AND AFTER

Meanwhile the age of the machine had arrived, and this was to have a major effect on the whole social structure of Britain. Good food and its appreciation stem from an intimate association with the land. When rural workers turned or were forced from the land to find employment in the expanding cities, a simple culinary tradition was changed for the worse. In the towns and cities of an increasingly industrial Britain, fresh produce was less available, there were no smallholdings or gardens in which to keep even a hen or pig, lives were more rushed, and there was no time to spend on producing interesting meals. Ready-made foods appeared, and the food industry was born.

As many of the new city dwellers lacked cooking equipment, money for fuel, and an individual source of water, the cooked or hot foods offered by itinerant street vendors or stalls became essential. In London alone, fare such as hot eels, pea soup and hot green peas, fried fish, pies, trotters and baked potatoes were on offer. Interestingly, one of the most famous of British dishes – fish and chips – is thought to have derived from street foods introduced later by nationals of two other European countries: the fish from fried fish sold by Italians who had fled Italy after the Risorgimento, and the chips from the *frites* already famous in Brussels and recreated in Scotland by an expatriate Belgian. A reliance on such 'fast' foods is still obvious in Britain today, with its many take-aways.

The high cooking of Britain was not immune to change either. At one point it had been

Belfry Fish Cakes

considered to be on a par with that of the French, but the long rivalry was to result in a culinary victory for the French. As the rich and the new middle classes travelled and were impressed by the cooking of Europe, so the ideas they brought back with them began further to erode any individual British excellence. In the years following the French Revolution many French chefs came to England – among them Carême, Escoffier and Soyer – and it was their style of cooking that was to be the most influential through the 19th century. In cookery books of the period there are some detractors of the new 'Frenchification', but in Mrs Beeton's *Home Management*, widely presumed to be the ultimate overview of *British* food, there is an amalgam of national and regional dishes, British and French methods, and French and other foreign dishes. Later, two world wars, rationing and austerity were to sound the death knell of a continuance of old tradition.

THE GASTRONOMICALLY DISPOSSESSED?

Despite that magnificent early culinary history, the British had an unenviable reputation for dull cooking. There had been early detractors: in the middle of the 18th century, a Swedish traveller wrote that 'Englishmen understand almost better than any other people the art of properly roasting a large cut of meat', but then immediately qualified it by adding, 'because the art of cooking as practised by most Englishmen does not extend much beyond roast beef and plum pudding'. It was an Italian who asserted that there existed in Britain 'sixty different religious sects, but only one sauce', and Somerset Maugham who swore

that to eat well in Britain you had to eat breakfast three times a day.

That some British cooking has been poor is undeniable, but what went wrong? That very polyglot nature itself may hold the clues: without a basic *faith* in the traditional British ways of cooking, they would be undervalued and therefore less considerately followed. For however 'plain' a food and its cooking method may be, it needs as much loving attention and care as the most complicated or sophisticated of dishes. If something plain is cooked badly, it can be far worse than an indifferent composite dish, and many restaurants in Britain used to be guilty of this. It's significant, I think, that until quite recently British dinner-party hosts would choose to serve foreign dishes – a *boeuf bourguignonne* or *goulash* – presumably believing that their own native dishes were not 'special' enough.

One school of thought avers that the British have never had as much passion about food (or anything else) as have the French or Italians, and therefore cannot cook so creatively. National character has much to do with it, but so does a colder climate. The further north, the more comforting and stolid the basic food tends to be, and the quantity served will be greater (the British have always been thought of as large eaters). When food is viewed as fuel, there is little room for passion. Quentin Crewe put the problem rather succinctly in *Vogue* (1978): 'It is hardly surprising that there are so few real chefs in a country which has so little regard for food as an art, but thinks of it only as a necessity of life, like underpants.'

The British may eat out more often than they once did – the 53 restaurant tradition in fact came to Britain much later than to the rest of Europe – but they still do so less regularly and less generally than the French. There may be an element of subliminal 'guilt' involved at such extravagance, a lingering nuance of Puritanism. Inherent memories of wartime economies may also be involved, for even in home cooking there is occasional horror expressed at a recipe which uses too much butter or cream. Good cooking need not be monetarily extravagant, but a meanness of spirit, however fleeting, can result in a less than sensual result.

Much of the lack of real interest in food in Britain may be attributable to the plenty the islands have always enjoyed. In less agriculturally rich countries on the Continent, necessity would be the mother of invention, and of great cooking, whereas in Britain an amplitude of supply meant that *less* creativity was needed. Despite some fine hams, there is no *charcuterie* tradition as in France, Italy or Germany; despite a wealth of natural ingredients, there is but a limited use made of them. Much of the best seafood in Britain is still exported, for instance, and the wild mushrooms that flourish in English woods are ignored, whereas in Italy they are a national passion. (This of course may be put down to a curious British suspicion of things unfamiliar, first introduced to me 15 years ago by one of my English *sous-chefs*: whenever he went abroad, he always provisioned himself with packets of home-made sandwiches.)

A major force in the apparent British indifference to good food and good cooking was undoubtedly the Industrial Revolution and the continuing industrial nature of the country as a whole. Britain is a small country in comparison to France, and therefore the industrialisation was more far-reaching. In France there was more room, literally, for the survival of a strong agricultural tradition, and thus most of the French can have a closer relationship with their basic foodstuffs. A Frenchwoman will handle what she wishes to buy, sniffing a melon, squeezing a peach, snapping a bean to test for ripeness or freshness. Until very recently a British shopper would not conceive of such an approach, and a British greengrocer certainly did not encourage it.

A NEW SPIRIT ABROAD

It was not until the 1950s that the gastronomic depression was to lift. When the late Elizabeth David's *A Book of Mediterranean Food* was published, it opened the eyes of a whole generation of British professional and domestic cooks to a new awareness of food, its sensuality and its possibilities. Again it was a *French* influence, but from this was to grow a fresh enthusiasm. Robert Carrier and the late Jane Grigson, food writers rather than chefs, were also primary movers in this renaissance. Inspired by them, a whole new generation of cooks and restaurateurs, many of whom had not been professionally trained or exposed to French *haute cuisine*, began to produce food that once more was eclectic, borrowing from here and there, from other traditions and other countries, but which contained elements that were, nevertheless, essentially British in concept and feel.

And from that was to develop a confidence, in both professional and domestic cooks, which was slowly to lead to an exploration of British traditions and recipes, and a reconsideration of basic ingredients. It was at this turning point that I arrived in London and began my researches. They culminated in a revamped Grill Room restaurant at the hotel, with a menu devoted to British specialities and composed entirely of home-grown British foods.

A SPLENDID HERITAGE

The first thing that had struck me was how superlative British ingredients were. Aberdeen Angus beef is second to none, and Welsh and Scottish lamb are full of flavour. There are sheep in Shetland which feed on seaweed so that their flesh is virtually green; this is a delight which surpasses the *pré-salé* lamb of Brittany.

The seafood is wonderful: scallops, lobsters, crabs, mussels and fish from coastal waters, as well as deep-sea fish such as cod. Native oysters from Essex, Kent and Cornwall are as delicious as any Belons or *fines de claires*. Atlantic salmon caught in the great Scottish rivers, fresh or smoked over oak, are unique British delicacies.

Some of the best game in the world is found in Britain – venison, hare, partridge and pheasant – and one bird which is found only in Britain, the grouse, has become a personal passion. I can't wait for the Twelfth of August each year!

The vegetables, too, are good, even if at first I found the variety a little less than I might have hoped. English asparagus is the best I have tasted, and the tiny Jersey new potatoes which appear briefly in the spring taste sweet and of the volcanic soil in which they grow. I even encountered some new delights, which had always been part of the regional tradition. One of these was laverbread, the seaweed found on many British shorelines, but which has become a Welsh speciality and accompanies lamb so well. Carrageen, a seaweed used in Ireland as a natural gelatine, and rock samphire were other unfamiliar ingredients.

The fruits available in Britain astounded me – the many varieties of apples, pears, members of the plum family such as greengages and damsons, and the multitude of soft fruits and berries. The cheeses were a surprise to me as well, with regional specialities almost as varied as anywhere else in Europe.

With such basic excellence, there had to be traditional recipes to go with them, and there were, despite all the apparent evidence against. From countless books and manuscripts (my own personal collection, a majority of which are British in origin, now numbers more than 4,000), I discovered delicacies and subtleties that I would not have thought possible.

From Scotland there were mussel stew-soups directly comparable to the more renowned *moules à la marinière*; clear vegetable broths, smoked fish soups, and an elegant combination of leeks, chicken and prunes in cock-a-leekie; simple river trout coated in oatmeal and fried in bacon fat, or simply grilled; and fresh herrings, their oily flesh partnered by the tang of a mustard sauce. From Cornwall came fresh crabs, and mackerel with a sharp gooseberry sauce – an amalgam as sophisticated and intelligent as any of French *haute cuisine*. There was deep-fried whitebait – once a treat for Londoners on day trips to Greenwich – Dover sole and eels. (I must admit that I have not been won over by jellied eels, but eels with a traditional British sauce, green with herbs, is a favourite.)

It is in the poultry, meat and game recipes that the essential 'plainness' of British cooking is more evident, and most sensible. With such fine-quality produce, elaboration would be a mistake.

There are sheep in Shetland which feed on seaweed so that their flesh is virtually green; this is a delight which surpasses the pré-salé *lamb of Brittany.*

To the British, a good meat tends to be considered not as an ingredient for a dish but as something to be appreciated for itself and to be cooked to its own peak of perfection. Most meats or birds were simply roasted or grilled. The renowned roast beef of England was originally cooked on a spit over or beside the fire, the fat dripping into a tray below, in which the equally famous Yorkshire pudding would be cooked. (This was a regional speciality, often served with gravy before the meat so that appetites could be partially satisfied, and the meat itself would go further.) Roasting today is more akin to baking – in an enclosed oven – so I often grill or pan-grill small wing ribs for beef that is actually nearer to the original conception.

What surprised me most, in a country that was reputed to have only one sauce, was the disconcertingly wide range of sharp, sweet or subtle meat or bird accompaniments, traditionally called tracklements. These originated from the belief that if the animal or bird fed on or near a type of berry, for instance, it would make a perfect partner for the cooked flesh. These included creamy horseradish with beef, capers with boiled mutton, mint sauce with sweet lamb from the south, redcurrant or rowan jelly with venison or mountain lamb, and apples, gooseberry or rhubarb with pork. There were also bread sauce with poultry and game birds, and mustard or devilled sauces with kidneys. (There were even more fish accompaniments, sauces made from cider, anchovies, fennel, parsley or Stilton.) Such culinary thinking evokes a much more sophisticated approach than the British tradition is generally given credit for.

In the few casserole or stew dishes, the emphasis once again was on a basic simplicity, but the integrity of flavours was always retained. Irish stew, Lancashire hotpot, boiled beef and carrots are wonderful when cooked well. A beef stew moistened with Ireland's Guinness can stand alongside any French or Belgian equivalent, and I must admit to a weakness for boiled silverside, often more delicious than a *bollito misto*, and slowly braised oxtail.

It was the desserts that most intrigued me. Many hot puddings were rather heavy, such as the steamed suet sponges, but tasted wonderful, especially when accompanied by a well-made custard, the sweet sauce so disparaged by many Continental 55 commentators. This sauce in itself is the basis of many characteristic British puddings, among them custard tarts and pies (the name was originally 'crustade', referring to the crust of a pie rather than to the filling), trifle, bread-and-butter pudding and the famous burnt cream. Fruit pies as opposed to tarts seem to be uniquely British, and they and many other fruit desserts such as crumbles or fools, simple as they are in conception, show a respect for and appreciation of their ingredients equal to anything in the French or Italian canon. The use of leftover bread features in many cuisines, but several British examples are in a realm of their own: bread-and-butter pudding and the cold summer pudding, for instance. A fine syllabub is virtually the same as a cold French *sabayon* or an Italian *zabaglione*. One of my most prized possessions is a manuscript dating from 1733, a hand-written record of domestic hints and recipes in some wealthy English household. In it there is a recipe for chocolate sorbet which is as sophisticated as anything in *nouvelle cuisine*.

And as for baking, there is such a strong regional tradition of cakes, teacakes, scones, pancakes and breads that an entire new meal, that of afternoon tea, had to be invented in Britain to do justice to them. In every part of the British Isles there is some wonderful baked speciality.

This Great British tradition was thus one which I embraced with enormous enthusiasm. The so-called plainness was something dear to my own heart anyway: I have always believed that a wonderful piece of fish should actually look like and taste of itself, and be cooked and served simply.

The basic techniques of British cooking needed no adaptation – roasting, grilling, deep-frying and boiling are the same in any cuisine – but I knew I could contribute some of my own thoughts to traditional British recipes. The first change I made might seem rather mundane, but is essential to flavour – seasoning. I don't think the British ever season their food enough, despite their history of adventurous spicing. Many British dishes have probably been thought boring simply because there was not enough salt or pepper added in the cooking. This has led to a habit of putting salt on foods at table, before anything is tasted, which in turn has precipitated the ire of many a Continental chef.

Another aspect I thought I could gently alter was the heaviness of many of the recipes. I now make apple pies and mince pies in the traditional British style, for instance, but I use a mincemeat without suet, and filo instead of a sturdier pastry. The concept is the same, but the end product is lighter, and therefore a lot healthier. I've even made a Christmas pudding which is suitable for vegetarians and has fewer calories. Bread-and-butter pudding was one dish which really attracted me, but I felt that it too could be lifted: I did so by using less bread, slicing it much thinner, and by enriching the custard. By poaching it in a *bain-marie* – which offers a much less direct heat than baking – it becomes lighter and smoother, more akin to a soufflé.

Bread-and-butter pudding has now become one of my signature dishes, and whenever I cook and serve it, wherever I am in the world, I like to think of its humble origins – a use for leftover

bread – and how I am flying the flag for a great old British recipe, albeit with a touch of the new. Refinements such as these are being explored by many young British exponents of the culinary art, which is adding yet another element to a great tradition.

It gives me much pleasure to see such a resurgence of interest amongst British chefs, food writers and home cooks in their own culinary heritage. It is a heritage to take pride in, and I am very proud to have played a small part in its rebirth.

MENU I: LUNCH OR DINNER
SERVES 10
Kipper pâté
Lancashire hotpot
Summer pudding
Welsh rarebit

Kipper Pâté

The simple potted dishes of British cooking – whether of fish, meat or game – are the literal equivalent of French pâté, and many are very delicious. I have taken the idea a little further here, using the wonderful British cold-smoked herring.

340g (12oz) kipper fillets, skinned
255g (9oz) white fish fillets (eg lemon sole), skinned and chilled
20g (¾oz) unsalted butter, softened
2 tablespoons dry vermouth, cold
300ml (½ pint) double cream, very cold
Salt and freshly ground white pepper
4 large spinach leaves, blanched, refreshed and dried

Preheat the oven to 150°C/ 300°F, gas mark 2. Grease a 1.5 litre (2½ pint) terrine dish with the butter.

Bone the kipper fillets using tweezers. Reserve two of them. Purée the remainder in a pre-chilled food processor bowl with the white fish fillets. Add the vermouth and a quarter of the cream, and continue to purée. Turn the mix out into a chilled bowl, and beat in the remaining cream gradually. Season well.

Wrap the reserved kipper fillets in the blanched spinach leaves. Half fill the terrine dish with the creamy fish mixture. Take the wrapped fillets, trimmed to fit, and place lengthwise on the mixture, in the centre of the terrine. Fill the terrine with the remaining fish mixture and cover with a lid.

Place in a roasting tray half-filled with hot water and poach in the preheated oven for 1¼ hours. Remove from the oven and cool. Unmould and chill.

To serve, cut into slices and arrange on individual cold plates. It can be served with mayonnaise flavoured with mustard, or with horseradish.

Lancashire Hotpot

Traditionally a tall pot is used, so that the mutton chops can stand upright. The pot itself, taking the place of pastry, would at one time be put into the oven at the end of a baking day, when the fire had cooled, to cook slowly overnight. Later, hotpots would be left to cook all day so that factory workers could return at night to a hot meal. The oysters that were once so abundant were slipped into the stew beneath the potato crust.

Summer Pudding

10 lamb loin chops
10 middle neck chops
2 lamb's kidneys
60ml (2fl oz) olive oil
680g (1½lb) onions, sliced
Salt and freshly ground black pepper
680g (1½lb) carrots, cut into pieces
500g (1lb 2oz) button mushrooms, trimmed
1.5kg (3¼lb) medium potatoes, peeled and sliced into rounds
750ml (1¼pints) brown lamb stock, slightly thickened
A few sprigs each of fresh thyme and parsley
2 bay leaves

Preheat the oven to 160–180°C/ 325–350°F, gas mark 3–4. Trim the meats of any fat, and halve, clean and core the kidneys.

Heat the oil in a large pan and sweat and lightly colour the onions. Remove and reserve.

Season the meats with salt and pepper. Add a little more oil if necessary to the pan. Brown the chops briefly. Stand the loin chops, 'tails' up, on the bottom of a suitably large, tall pot. Scatter some of the onion and the carrot on top of the chops, filling any holes and spaces, seasoning again as you go.

Add the mushrooms and the kidneys, and some more carrot

57

and onion. Press slightly so that the surface is flat. Season. Arrange the middle neck chops on top and cover with the remaining carrot and onion.

Arrange the potato slices, neatly and slightly overlapping, over the top of the ingredients. Brush with a little more oil and season. Pour in the stock until it almost covers the potato slices, adding water if necessary. Add the herbs. Cover with a tight-fitting lid and bake slowly in the preheated oven for 1½–2 hours. Remove the lid for the last 30 minutes to allow the potatoes to become golden brown.

Summer Pudding

British dessert recipes abound in ideas for using up stale bread, but this cold pudding, which perhaps also catered for a glut of soft fruit and berries, is a wonderful invention. Some puddings can be too stolid, so I always use very thin slices of a good bread – wholemeal, which is healthier – and many more berries.

Large thin slices of wholemeal bread, crusts removed (you'll need at least 8)
4 gelatine leaves, soaked in cold water and squeezed dry
Juice of 1 lemon
200g (7oz) each of ripe strawberries, raspberries and blackberries (or blueberries)
Raspberry sauce
400g (14oz) raspberries
4 tablespoons icing sugar
Juice of 1 small lemon

Brush a 900ml (1½ pint) pudding basin with a little oil.

Cut the bread into tapered rectangles, and line the basin with some of it. Dissolve the gelatine in 120ml (4fl oz) water over a gentle heat, then stir in the lemon juice. Strain and divide this liquid between three small stainless-steel pans. Add the berries separately to these pans, and stew gently until just tender – just until their juices start to run, but they are still holding their shape and are a rich colour.

Place alternate layers of the individual fruits and bread in the basin, finishing with a layer of any fruit that is left, mixed, along with some juice if necessary. Top with the remaining slices of bread, cover with a saucer and weight down with something heavy (a large can of fruit, for instance). Allow to set in the refrigerator for at least 12 hours so that the juice can soak through the bread.

For the sauce, press the raspberries through a sieve, and mix with the sugar and lemon juice.

Unmould the pudding on to the centre of a serving plate and carefully pour the sauce over the top to cover it completely. Decorate with mint leaves and extra fruit if you like, and serve with whipped or clotted cream or – a healthier alternative – natural yogurt.

Welsh Rarebit
SERVES 4

The savoury (like afternoon tea) seems to be uniquely British. It is in essence a sharp little dish designed to clean the mouth after dessert, in preparation for the serving of the port. It was primarily a male tradition, but Queen Victoria is said to have been very partial to bone marrow on toast. Although the concept of savouries was new to me, Welsh rarebit – or rabbit – seemed familiar, rather like the Swiss *croûte au fromage*.

The recipe serves four only: generously double it if all your guests want a taste!

15g (½oz) butter
85g (3oz) each of Caerphilly and Cheddar cheeses, grated
1 tablespoon beer
A generous dash of made English mustard
Salt and freshly ground black pepper
4 slices of hot buttered toast (granary is good)

Melt the butter in a saucepan over a low heat. Add the cheeses, beer, mustard and salt and pepper to taste. Stir until the cheeses have melted and the mixture is smooth. Take care not to overheat, or the mix will become oily. Draw off the heat and allow to cool slightly.

Have the toast hot and ready, spoon the mixture on to each slice, and spread evenly. Place under a hot grill to lightly brown, and serve sizzling hot.

MENU 2: BREAKFAST
SERVES 4
Fruit or cereal
Kedgeree or
Belfry fish cakes
Tea or coffee

The hearty cooked breakfast for which Britain is famed did not become commonplace until Victorian times. Mrs Beeton listed a number of dishes she considered appropriate: '...veal and ham pies, broiled fish, mutton chops and rump steaks, kidney, sausages, bacon and poached eggs, muffins, toast, marmalade and butter'. Few households would today have the money, time or gustatory energy to contemplate such a spread, but some cooked dishes still prevail, such as the two following.

Start the meal with a fruit dish – some fresh grapefruit segments, strawberries with yogurt, a dried fruit compote – or home-made muesli or, like the Scots, porridge. Follow the hot dish with toast if you like.

Kedgeree

Trade with the East and the expansion of the Empire added numerous threads to the already polyglot patchwork of British cooking. The medieval passion for spices was rekindled by the foods encountered in India dur-ing the years of the Raj – mulli-gatawny soup, chutneys and ketchups among them. Kedgeree in fact is truly representative of what became known as Anglo-Indian cooking, for it exists properly in neither British nor Indian cuisine.

200g (7oz) prawns, cooked in their shells
200g (7oz) smoked Finnan haddock with skin
200g (7oz) fresh salmon, with skin, scaled
Salt and freshly ground pepper
4 teaspoons olive oil
1 large onion, finely chopped
150g (5½oz) basmati or other long-grain rice
1 teaspoon curry paste or powder
20g (¾oz) butter
Lemon juice to taste
2 hard-boiled eggs, sliced
20g (¾oz) parsley, finely chopped

Shell the prawns, saving four unshelled for decoration. Put the shells into a large saucepan and place the haddock on top.

Add 600ml (1 pint) boiling water, cover and leave for 10 minutes on a low heat.

Remove the haddock and poach the salmon in the liquid for a minute or so, or until just cooked, then remove and set aside with the haddock. Continue to simmer the stock with the prawn shells.

Skin the haddock and salmon, and remove all bones. Drop the skin and trimmings

From Scotland there were mussel stew-soups directly comparable to the more renowned moules à la marinière; *smoked fish soups; simple river trout coated in bacon fat, or simply grilled; and fresh herrings, their oily flesh partnered by the tang of a mustard sauce.*

into the stock pot. Mix the fish with the shelled prawns and season carefully with salt and pepper. Keep to one side.

In a large pan, heat the oil and sauté the onion until golden. Stir in the rice and, when it is transparent, add the curry paste or powder. Strain in the fish stock, cover and simmer over a very low heat for 20 minutes until the rice is tender and the stock has been absorbed.

Mix in the prepared fish and prawns, and enough butter to make the kedgeree moist. Adjust the seasoning, adding lemon

juice if liked, and heat through. Arrange in a warm dish or on individual plates. Place the sliced egg on top and sprinkle with parsley. Decorate with the warmed prawns and serve.

Belfry Fish Cakes

Fish cakes were probably first thought of as a vehicle for left-overs, but they can be much more exciting than that. Tradi-tional recipes use mashed pota-toes, but always too much in relation to fish. My version, with grated potato enclosing the fish – rather like a Swiss *rösti* – is much lighter, crisper and tastier. Serve with a parsley sauce if you like, or simply with lemon quarters.

450g (1lb) fish fillets (white fish, salmon, smoked haddock or a mixture)
2 tablespoons finely chopped parsley
1 tablespoon finely cut chives
Salt and freshly ground pepper
1 egg
255g (9oz) potatoes, peeled
1 tablespoon olive oil
15g (½oz) butter

Cut the fish into 1cm (½in) pieces, and place in a bowl with the herbs. Season to taste, then add the egg. Mix well to bind. Divide into eight portions, and roll into balls.

Roughly grate the potatoes and squeeze lightly to rid them of excess moisture. Place on a plate and season well. Roll the fish balls in this to coat them, then shape into little cakes.

Heat the oil and butter together in a frying pan and shallow-fry the cakes gently on both sides until crisp and golden brown, about 6–7 minutes. Drain well on kitchen paper.

59

CHAPTER 4
FRYING

Frying is not a sin. It is a technique with an image problem. The problem, of course, is fat, which is dietary enemy number one in current thinking on healthy eating. So frying is a method to be employed with discretion. The thoughtful cook reserves it for those dishes where it is simply the best technique to use, and then does it so skilfully that while the food is cooked in fat the result cannot be described as fatty.

Frying is an exceptionally appetising way of cooking the humblest of ingredients. Think of fried onions and of apple fritters. Frying is also an art, as the queues outside the best fish and chip shops testify.

In deep-frying, the food is completely immersed in oil or fat and all its surfaces are cooked at once. Shallow-fried foods are cooked on one side at a time, in a layer of oil or fat. It is because oils and fats can be heated to temperatures as high as double the boiling point of water that fried foods cook rapidly, forming a crisp, golden exterior.

A starchy coating of batter, crumbs, pastry or flour is used to protect foods from drying in the intense heat of deep-frying. Exceptions to the coating rule are potatoes, which are starchy themselves, and confections such as doughnuts and those *beignets* (see Glossary) which have starch, in this case flour, as the main ingredient. The same types of coating treatment are given to many shallow-fried foods.

Dry-frying is a further choice. Hard-wearing non-stick pans have made dry-frying in no more than a film of oil, or none at all, an increasingly popular method of cooking. A variation of this technique is dry-frying (or pan-grilling) using a heavy, ridged, cast-iron pan. In dry-frying, the ingredients – pieces of meat, fish or vegetables – are in direct contact with the cooking surface and are not coated with crumbs or batter. Stir-frying in a Chinese wok is another technique which uses little fat.

DEEP-FRYING

The narrow band of very high temperatures used in deep-frying, 180°C–200°C (350°F–400°F), sets the agenda of foods that can be cooked. Within this temperature range, the coating on the food is quickly sealed on contact with the fat. The food now enclosed has to cook before the coating becomes overdone. If food is fried too slowly, then the coating does not form a good seal and absorbs unpalatably large amounts of fat. If the fat is too hot, the outside will scorch before the inside is done.

The smallest pieces of food – whitebait and matchstick potatoes, for example – are cooked at the highest temperatures. Conversely the largest – thick pieces of battered cod or chicken Kiev, for example – are fried at the lower temperatures within the range. Anything much larger is too big for deep-frying and would be overdone on the outside before the centre had cooked.

Always cut food to be fried in batches – fritters, for example – to the same size as this makes for even cooking.

EQUIPMENT FOR DEEP-FRYING

A large deep pan is essential. Depth is required for safety because hot fat froths up when cold damp foods are put into it, and fat is, of course, dangerously flammable. Small pieces of food, such as chips, are cooked in a mesh basket which also serves to lift them in and out of the oil. A mesh skimmer is a better tool for handling batter-coated foods and larger pieces such as fish fillets and chicken Kiev.

Although it is possible to gauge the temperature of hot oil or fat by a variety of empirical methods (see Box), including the army cook's time-honoured test of spitting into it, using a thermometer eliminates guesswork. Thermometers for deep-frying clip on to the side of the pan.

A thermostatically controlled deep-fat fryer is a specialised electrical appliance which, in addition to controlling the temperature, will usually have the further advantage of a lid designed to absorb some of the smells. An ordinary pan can only be used without a lid. If it were covered, steam condensing on the lid would drip into the hot fat causing hazardous frothing and spattering.

OILS AND FATS FOR DEEP-FRYING

Oils and fats suitable for deep-frying are those which behave best at high temperature. Oils and fats have widely varying boiling points in the 260°C–399°C (500°F–750°F) range. But this knowledge is little help to the cook, because well before boiling point is reached, chemicals called triglycerides begin to break down, releasing

---

DEEP-FRYING TIMES AND TEMPERATURES

Remember that the speed of deep-frying is offset by the need to cook fairly small batches at a time, so that the temperature of the fat is not suddenly lowered too far when cold ingredients are put into it. It is usually necessary to raise the heat again immediately after adding a new batch of food, and in the case of larger pieces, such as chicken pieces or drumsticks, to regulate the heat throughout cooking so that the food cooks evenly through without excessively browning on the outside.

CHEESE BEIGNETS	UNCOOKED CHOUX PASTRY	6–8 MINS AT 190°C (375°F)
CHICKEN KIEV	BREADCRUMBED	10–15 MINS AT 180°C (350°F)
CHICKEN DRUMSTICKS	BATTERED OR BREADCRUMBED	15–20 MINS AT 180°C (350°F)
CHIPS	1CM (½IN) THICKNESS ONCE-COOKED: TWICE-COOKED: *THEN:*	10 MINS AT 190°C (375°F) 10 MINS AT 185°C (360°F) 1–2 MINS AT 195°C (390°F)
CROQUETTES	BREADCRUMBED	1–2 MINS AT 190°C (375°F)
DOUGHNUTS	RING – UNCOOKED YEAST DOUGH BALL – UNCOOKED YEAST DOUGH	2–3 MINS AT 190°C (375°F) 3–4 MINS AT 190°C (375°F)
FISH FILLETS	BATTERED OR BREADCRUMBED	7–12 MINS AT 180°C (350°F)
FRITTERS	BATTERED	1–2 MINS AT 190°C (375°F)
MATCHSTICK POTATOES		1–2 MINS AT 190°C (375°F)
ONION RINGS	FLOURED OR BATTERED	2–3 MINS AT 190°C (375°F)
POTATO CRISPS		1–2 MINS AT 190°C (375°F)
SAMOSAS	UNCOOKED PASTRY DOUGH	8–12 MINS AT 180°C (350°F)
VEAL ESCALOPES	BREADCRUMBED	3–5 MINS AT 200°C (400°F)
WHITEBAIT	FLOURED	1–2 MINS AT 190°C (375°F)

JUDGING TEMPERATURE BY SIGHT

Gauging temperature by the haze which rises from very hot oil or fat is not uncommon in professional kitchens but cannot be recommended at home. The dividing line between haze and smoke is not a suitable subject for domestic experiment, and in any case not all oils and fats give the same signals.

To gauge the temperature of oil or fat without a thermometer, use a 2.5cm (1in) cube of day-old white bread. The time it takes to fry to a crisp golden brown will vary according to temperature thus:

180°C (350°F) ....90 seconds
190°C (375°F) ....60 seconds
200°C (400°F) ....45 seconds

Another test is how the oil or fat bubbles when a piece of raw potato is lowered into it. At 180°(350°F) the action is a simmering one. At 190°C (375°F) the bubbles rise briskly.

unpleasant fumes. The smoke point of hot oil or fat is the temperature at which these vapours become visible, and as a rule is lower for animal fats than it is for vegetable oils. Smoke point is also a danger signal. In their vaporised forms, oils and fats are even more highly flammable.

Some chemical breakdown occurs even at deep-frying temperatures, with the cumulative result that the smoke point of any batch of oil or fat is lowered every time it is used. Contact with the air, and with the small particles of food inevitably left behind after frying, causes further decomposition which alters both taste and smell.

Accurate temperature control and filtering after each use will extend the life of oils and fats. Expect to use any one batch of oil or fat at least three times for deep-frying, but probably no more than six times. Oil or fat used to cook fish is best kept for fish alone. Filter deep-frying oil when it is cold, through a fine sieve or muslin, into a suitable container. Leave the 'dregs' behind.

Lard has always been a popular choice for sweet recipes. Beef fat is particularly tolerant of

high temperatures. As a result it lasts well and is an economical choice. Groundnut oil, sometimes labelled peanut or *arachide* oil, is virtually flavourless and one of the finest for deep-frying. Where its flavour is welcome, olive oil is also excellent. It is slow to develop off-flavours, which makes it a more economical choice than might at first appear. However, some olive oils produce a smoky haze at deep-frying temperatures which for other oils would be a danger signal of over-heating.

Other suitable vegetable oils include maize or corn oil, which has a flavour that not everyone likes, grapeseed, rapeseed, safflower, soya and sunflower oils. Blended vegetable oils are likely to be the least expensive choice. Check with the label that the oil is suitable for deep-frying. Do not use oil labelled as salad oil for deep-frying.

Fritto Misto di Mare

SERVES 4

Mixed mouthfuls of fish, each with its individual flavour sealed into a golden coat of crunchy deep-fried batter, are an Italian speciality that makes the most of what is in the market. Try to mix at least three types of fish, including squid and prawns. Bite-sized chunks of any firm-fleshed fish can be included, as can scallops, large mussels and sprats. Allow 110g–170g (4oz–6oz) of prepared raw fish per serving, depending on whether the dish is to be served as a first course or as the main dish. Wedges of lemon to squeeze over the fish are the only accompaniment this dish requires.

450g–680g (1lb–1½lb) prepared raw fish
300ml (½ pint) coating batter (see page 94)
Oil for deep-frying

Clean the squid (see page 234), discarding the ink sac. Cut the bodies into rings, and cut off the tentacles, keeping them whole. To prepare the prawns, remove the heads and peel off the shells, leaving only the fan-shaped tail. Remove the dark thread of gut. Cut the remaining fish into bite-sized pieces.

In a deep pan, heat the oil to 190°C (375°F). Dip the pieces of fish into the batter, then drop them carefully into the hot oil, a few at a time, and fry until golden on all sides, 3–5 minutes depending on size. Lift them out and drain on kitchen paper.

Keep warm in the oven while the remaining fish is fried. Serve as soon as possible before the batter loses its crispness.

Jane Grigson's Parsnip and Walnut Fritters

SERVES 4

'One would not think,' said Jane Grigson, 'that parsnips and walnuts would go well together. But they do. So do parsnips and almonds, or parsnips and hazelnuts. My preference, though, is for walnuts. Try these fritters, and see if you agree that they make a very special dish.'

900g (2lb) parsnips
110g (4oz) shelled walnuts
2 large eggs
85g (3oz) butter, melted
2 heaped teaspoons flour
Generous 150ml (¼ pint) milk.
Salt and freshly ground black pepper
Oil for deep-frying

Trim, clean and boil the parsnips in the usual way. When they are tender, put them through

TIPS FOR CHIPS
- Choose waxy potatoes.
- For a very crisp finish, wash and dry the raw chips carefully.
- For chips with a softer texture, dry the freshly cut chips but do not wash them.
- Preheat the empty deep-frying basket in the fat to stop the chips sticking to it.
- Cook the chips in small batches so that the temperature of the fat does not fall too sharply.
- Decide whether to cook the chips only once, or twice for an even crisper result (see Chart on page 61).

the *mouli-légumes* (see page 303), discarding tough bits of core. Mix to a smooth paste with the eggs, butter, flour and milk. Season with salt and pepper, and stir in the walnuts.

Heat a deep pan of oil to between 180°C–190°C (350°F–375°F). Slip in spoonfuls of the mixture, including a piece of walnut in each spoonful. Remove with a draining spoon when they are deep golden brown and drain well on kitchen paper. Serve as a course on their own, or with white fish baked in butter and a little white wine.

SHALLOW-FRYING

Shallow-frying is a more elastic and less narrowly defined technique than deep-frying. Where it is used for foods coated in batter, crumbs or flour, the temperatures used are in the same range as those for deep-frying, and the same points about fats and oils apply. Either method can be used for many foods such as crumb-coated fish fillets, battered fruit fritters and other flat pieces of food which only have to be turned once to fry both sides.

Shallow-frying at lower temperatures, and in a wider range of fats (including clarified butter and dripping), is used for cooking uncoated foods such as escalopes of chicken, fried eggs and omelettes. In some cases so little fat is used that its principal purpose is as a lubricant, ensuring maximum contact and minimum adhesion between pan and food.

A good conventional frying pan has a heavy base and shallow, sloping sides. Most are round, but there are also long, oval pans for frying fish.

Sole à la Meunière

SERVES 1

The French term *à la meunière* means 'in the manner of a miller's wife' and has been adopted for a technique that is all but universal. Dipping fish in flour and frying it in clarified butter or oil is simple cooking at its best.

Use the same method with scampi, and with other types of flat fish such as sole, flounder and plaice.

63

1 prime Dover sole
Salt and freshly ground black pepper
2 tablespoons flour
Clarified butter (see page 239), or oil to fry
1 teaspoon finely chopped parsley
30g (1oz) unsalted butter
1 lemon wedge

Remove the head, and skin the sole on the dark side (see page 227). If it is dry, dip it in milk or water. Season the flour with salt and pepper and spread it on a plate. Dip the fish in the flour to coat it all over, then lay it on a rack to dry for 5–10 minutes. This drying step has the effect of setting the flour coating, making the fish easier to turn and the final result crisper. Put about 5mm (¼ in) clarified butter or oil in a frying pan and heat it until very hot. Test the heat by dipping a corner of the fish into the pan. When it sizzles, put in the fish.

Fry until the first side is golden brown, 3–5 minutes depending on the size of the sole. Turn the fish carefully and fry the other side. It is done when the flesh comes away easily from the bone. Drain the fish well, transfer to a hot serving plate and sprinkle with parsley.

Pour out the fat in the frying pan and add the fresh butter. Swirl it over a high heat until it froths and starts to colour. Pour it over the fish and serve at once with a wedge of lemon.

DRY-FRYING

As a technique, dry-frying is unkind to pans and shortens their useful life while perhaps extending yours. But non-stick frying pans have a place even in the most exalted professional kitchens where they are used for dry-frying delicate foods like fish and chicken. The process is fast, direct and simplicity itself. In the case of fish, a thin fillet is seasoned and laid in a well-heated pan. In less than a minute, one side is lightly coloured. It is turned, and after a few moments more served, still moist, but with the added flavour of its own juices seared by the pan.

Dry-frying on a ridged cast-iron pan or plate (also called pan-grilling) is much liked as a method of cooking steaks, but can also be used for other meats, pieces of firm-textured fish, and for vegetables such as aubergines, courgettes or peppers cut in slices. The pan is heated until it is very hot indeed, and the seasoned food is cooked directly on the ridged surface which imprints it with characteristic dark stripes. This type of dry-frying can be done with no fat, or with foods which have been marinated (see page 46) or lightly painted with fat. The method's popularity is based on the extra flavour produced by the stripes of seared juices where the food has come in contact with the intense heat of the pan.

Chicken Escalopes with Parma Ham and Sage

SERVES 4

This easy recipe turns the most ordinary chicken breasts into a dish that bursts with flavour. The ham must be in the Italian Parma style, uncooked, unsmoked and wafer thin. The substitute for fresh sage in this recipe would not be dried sage but a light pass with a cut clove of garlic. Serve the escalopes with ribbon pasta or a green salad.

4 small chicken breasts, boned and skinned
8 leaves fresh sage, or 1 cut clove garlic
Freshly ground black pepper to taste
4 large or 8 small slices Parma ham
1 teaspoon clarified butter (see page 239)
4 lemon wedges

To flatten the chicken breasts into escalopes, lay them between two sheets of plastic wrap and beat them out until they are quite thin, say 5mm (¼ in) thick. Rougher underside up, unpeel the plastic from each escalope. Sprinkle with snipped sage and freshly ground black pepper, then lay the ham on top to cover the seasoned side completely.

Heat half the clarified butter or oil in a heavy frying pan, and when it is very hot lift two of the chicken breasts off the plastic and place in the pan, ham side down. Fry for about 1 minute, until the ham is lightly coloured, then turn and

Chicken escalope with Parma ham and sage, cooked on a ridged cast-iron pan.

fry until the chicken is lightly cooked, when the flesh becomes opaque. Remove to a warm plate while the other two escalopes are cooked in the same way. Serve at once with a squeeze of fresh lemon.

STIR-FRYING

Stir-frying in a wok is another technique which uses a minimum amount of fat, although Chinese cooks use their woks for deep frying too. It is the shape of the wok with its sloping sides which helps the cook to keep the food being stir-fried on the move over a high heat so that none of its surfaces remains for long in contact with the hottest area at the base of the pan.

It is a particularly good method to use for retaining the crisp texture and fresh flavours of tender young vegetables and seafoods such as raw prawns. (See also *The Cooking of China*, on page 16.)

Stir-Fried Spring Onions

SERVES 2

170g (6oz) spring onions
1 tablespoon groundnut oil
1 tablespoon dark soy sauce
Freshly ground black pepper to taste

Trim both ends of the spring onions and discard damaged leaves. Cut the onions in halves, and if the white ends are the thickness of a pencil, or fatter, slit them lengthwise. Wash and very thoroughly dry them. Heat the wok until it is very hot and add the oil, which should look shimmery at once. Add the spring onions and fry them for about 2 minutes, lifting and turning them constantly. Add the soy sauce and pepper and continue lifting and turning until the onions are cooked as you like them, and most of the liquid has evaporated. Serve immediately.

CHAPTER 5
BRAISING AND STEWING

Braises and stews are the quintessence of good home cooking. They are the hot pots, daubes, casseroles, pot roasts, civets, ragouts, fricassées and jugged game of our grandmothers' kitchens – substantial, comforting dishes with complex flavours. Some of the best are made with the cheapest cuts, cooked slowly and carefully to create memorable meals which are also economical.

Braising and stewing are variations on a single theme of cooking meat, fish, vegetables or fruit with liquid in a closed pot. Both can be done on top of the stove or in the oven. Whole joints or larger pieces of meat cooked in only sufficient liquid to create a moist cooking environment are usually described as braised. Pot roasting is another term for braising. Small pieces of meat cooked in rather more liquid are said to be stewed. Casseroling is virtually synonymous with stewing, although we usually think of it being done in the oven.

Many of the classic braises and stews of western cookery have taken their names from the pots and pans they are cooked in, and vice versa. French country cooking has contributed a disproportionate number of these. *Braisières* and *daubières* are still made with lids which include a depression to hold hot embers so that the food inside can be cooked from above as well as below. Casseroles have become international, while *marmites* and *toupins* have stayed at home. The round, brown glazed earthenware pot of English cooking is called, rather prosaically, a stewpot, although most cooks these days would no doubt call it a casserole too.

There are two good reasons for braising and stewing. The first is to tenderise meats which would otherwise be tough, and this involves long, relatively slow cooking. The second is to produce the pleasingly complex tastes which can be created by combining the flavours of several ingredients. Of course many recipes do both, but some need only relatively brief cooking times. When prime cuts such as lamb chops are braised, they are cooked only until the meat is done, otherwise they would be both tougher and drier than if cooked by another method. If you have ever thought to 'improve' a slow-cooked dish by making it with a 'better' cut than the recipe called for and were disappointed that the result was dry, crumbling meat and inferior flavour, this could be the explanation.

Long, slow braising is the best way to tenderise tough cuts taken from the hard-working neck, shoulder and leg muscles of grazing animals – pieces that score the highest marks for flavour, but contain connective tissue which needs prolonged exposure to heat to break it down. When it does finally soften and melt, the gelatine produced gives these dishes a luxurious unctuousness that can be produced no other way. There is no better method of cooking oxtail or *osso buco*. The pigs' trotters, cow heels and pieces of pigskin called for in many old recipes are there to contribute additional gelatine and flavour. Cooking times of 2 and 3 hours are common in dishes of this kind.

Fat, which is naturally present in larger

amounts in the muscles of mature animals than in the meat of young ones, also has an important job to do in improving the texture and taste of these slow-cooked recipes. Large pieces of very lean meat may need to be larded, threaded with slivers of fat which melt to baste the meat from within and vastly improve its texture. Whether naturally present, or added by larding, the fat is skimmed off at the end of cooking.

Most but by no means all braises and stews call for the meat to be browned before the liquid is added. Brief roasting or frying on a high heat with a minimum of fat adds flavour and colour to the finished dish. Experiments have shown that searing does not, as is widely supposed, seal in the meat's juices. But it really does bring out the the flavour which we value as 'meaty', so it still pays to do it.

SUITABLE INGREDIENTS FOR BRAISES AND STEWS

BEEF
Joints for braising include topside, silverside, aitchbone cut and top rump. Other pieces good for braising or stewing include neck, clod, chuck, blade, thick rib, thin rib, flank, skirt, shin, and leg.

VEAL
Joints for braising include rolled shoulder, and silverside, thick flank or cushion, which are cuts from the leg. Knuckle and shin are usually sold as *osso buco*. Neck, middle neck, breast and ribs can also be braised or stewed.

LAMB
The pieces of lamb usually braised are boned shoulders, boned and rolled breast, and neck. Scrag end and middle neck are stewed.

Legs and other cuts from older animals can be braised too.

PORK
Blade and shoulder, including the spare rib, hand and spring and chops from the leg can be braised or stewed.

Pieces of ham and bacon can be braised as well.

OFFAL
Tripe, heart, tongue and oxtail are the offal most often braised or stewed.

GAME
Shoulder of young deer is the piece most usually braised. The leg and saddle of an older animal may also be braised. Venison is very lean and large pieces will need larding (see page 71). Rabbit and hare – whole, jointed or in small pieces – plus older game birds, including wild duck, pheasant, partridge, grouse and pigeon, can also be stewed or braised.

POULTRY
Mature fowl braise well. Turkey legs, joints of goose and duck. Capons, boiling and roasting chickens and guinea fowl, whole or in pieces.

FISH
Any firm-fleshed fish can be braised (see Chart on page 229). Good for tuna, swordfish and steaks of large fish. Cooking times for fish braises and stews are shorter than those for most meats.

VEGETABLES
Ratatouille is a classic combination of stewed peppers, tomatoes and aubergine with onion. Single vegetables such as Florence fennel, onions, carrots, cabbage, celery and pulses can be braised, or several vegetables combined and cooked together.

FRUIT
Sour or hard fruits such as cooking apples, rhubarb, redcurrants, blackcurrants and gooseberries are stewed with sugar, water and sometimes spices. Cinnamon or cloves with apple, and elderflowers with gooseberries are usual combinations. Try a piece of vanilla pod or coriander seeds (toasted, crushed and tied in a scrap of muslin) with apple or rhubarb.

LIQUID INGREDIENTS
The liquid element of stews and braises can be water, or something stronger. Water is generally preferable to stock made with cubes, but the fresh or frozen stock now sold in supermarkets is excellent. Home-made veal stock (see page 76)

can be used with any meat or fish, and chicken stock (see page 76) or vegetable stock (page 76) are almost as adaptable. Keep lamb stock for lamb, game stock for game, and fish stock for fish.

Dry wines, light or dark beer or lager, and dry cider all add distinctive flavours, as does the slug of brandy so often called for in French country recipes. Fresh or tinned tomatoes are invaluable as a moistening ingredient. Milk is used in a classic Italian recipe for braised pork.

MARINADES FOR TASTE, NOT TEXTURE

Tenderising meat by chemical means, with acid marinades or protein-digesting enzymes such as those found in papaya or pineapple, is a waste of time and texture. It is not that they don't work, because, up to a point, they do. But their damaging effect on the structure of the meat leads only to unnecessary drying and crumbliness. What marinades lack in tenderising efficacy they may make up for in flavouring power. The use of wine marinades with game is a taste which continues to please, and is not the extravagance it may appear because the marinade can become the braising liquid.

Cooked Marinade

MAKES 1 LITRE (1¾ PINTS)

> *120ml (4fl oz) olive oil*
> *2 carrots, coarsely chopped*
> *2 stalks celery, coarsely chopped*
> *2 medium onions, coarsely chopped*
> *1 large leek, coarsely chopped*
> *2 cloves garlic, quartered*
> *1 handful parsley*
> *1 sprig fresh rosemary, or ½ teaspoon dried rosemary*
> *1.5 litres (2½ pints) dry wine, red or white*
> *250ml (8fl oz) red wine vinegar*
> *2 bay leaves*
> *2 cloves*
> *6 juniper berries*
> *6 black peppercorns, crushed*

Heat the olive oil in a large pan and add the chopped vegetables, garlic, parsley and fresh (not dried) rosemary. Cook for 10–15 minutes, stirring occasionally, until the vegetables are lightly coloured. Add the wine and vinegar. If using the dried rosemary, tie it with the bay leaves, cloves, juniper berries and crushed peppercorns in a piece of muslin and add to the pan. Bring to the boil, lower the heat, cover and simmer for about half an hour.

Allow it to cool completely before adding the meat. Turn the meat, say a shoulder of venison or a joint of beef or pork, in the marinade for up to 24 hours. Dry and brown it before braising in some of the strained marinade.

THICKENING AGENTS

Many recipes include finely chopped root vegetables or tomatoes which cook down to thicken the sauce or gravy. Flour may be used as a thickening in various ways. Sometimes pieces of meat are coated with seasoned flour before browning. Alternatively, flour is added later in the form of a *roux*, as in the following recipe for blanquette of veal. When thickening is required at the end of the cooking time, the method of choice depends on the character of the dish. Blanquettes use a liaison of cream and egg yolks but cannot thereafter be heated to boiling without curdling. When the quantity of sauce is too much as well as too thin, it can be reduced by boiling in a wide pan. But if the quantity is right and it is only too thin, it can be thickened by stirring *beurre manié* (equal quantities of plain flour and softened butter) a little at a time into the simmering sauce. Better still is potato flour, which will thicken the sauce without giving it a 'floury' taste. This is mixed with a little water and added to the simmering sauce as needed.

Blanquette of Veal

SERVES 4

A blanquette is a white stew made with meat which is not browned. It takes time and trouble to transform the coarser, cheaper cuts of veal into this creamy and surprisingly robustly 69 flavoured dish. Lamb, chicken or sweetbreads, which need less lengthy cooking, can also be made into blanquettes.

This is Richard Olney's recipe from the *The French Menu Cookbook*. He serves it with rice, but fluffy mashed potato would be just as good. Home-made veal stock can be used in place of the water.

> *1kg (2lb 3oz) breast or rib tips of veal, cut into 2cm (¾ in) slices*
> *170g (6oz) small, firm, button mushrooms*
> *1–2 tablespoons fresh lemon juice*
> *4 tablespoons water*
> *75g (2½ oz) butter*
> *Salt and freshly ground white pepper*
> *3 medium carrots, scraped and cut in 2.5cm (1in) lengths*
> *2 medium onions, peeled, 1 stuck with 4 cloves*
> *Thyme or mixed herbs*
> *Bouquet garni (see page 261) of parsley, celery, and bay leaf*
> *20 small onions, peeled*
> *1 tablespoon plain flour*
> *5 tablespoons double cream*
> *3 egg yolks*
> *Freshly grated nutmeg*
> *Chopped parsley to garnish*

Combine the mushrooms with most of the lemon juice, the water, 15g (½oz) of the butter, some salt and pepper, and boil them in a covered pan for 1 minute.

Arrange the pieces of meat in a heavy saucepan so that, without packing them in, they take up a minimum of space. Put the mushrooms aside; add their cooking liquid to the meat, and enough cold water to cover the meat by about 1cm (½in). Add salt, bring to the boil, and skim two or three times, adding small amounts of cold water each time the liquid returns to the boil. Add the carrots and medium onions, a large pinch of thyme or mixed herbs and the aromatic *bouquet garni*, making sure that all are submerged, and regulate the heat to maintain a bare simmer, with the saucepan covered, for 1½ hours.

Meanwhile put the small onions, with 30g (1oz) of the butter, into a saucepan just large enough to hold them in a single layer. Season the onions with salt and pepper, and stew them gently for about 15 minutes, tossing them from time to time. They should be soft and slightly yellowed but not browned.

Strain the contents of the saucepan containing the meat through a large sieve into a bowl. Pick out the two onions and the *bouquet*, and discard them. Put the bowl of liquid aside.

Return the meat and carrots to the saucepan, add the mushrooms and the little onions, and put the pan aside, covered. Skim any fat from the surface of the liquid. In another saucepan make the *roux*: melt the remaining butter over a low heat, add the flour and cook for about 1 minute, stirring regularly without allowing the flour to brown. Pour in the cooking liquid from the meat all at once, whisking until it returns to the boil. Lower the heat to maintain a simmer with the saucepan uncovered. Over a period of about 20 minutes, skim off the light, fatty skin that forms repeatedly on the surface and pour the resulting lightly thickened sauce over the meat and its vegetable garnish. Leave to simmer, covered, for about 20 minutes.

Mix together in a bowl the cream and egg yolks. Add a little pepper and a very little nutmeg. Slowly stir in a ladleful of the sauce. Then, away from the heat, stir this mixture into the stew. Return the saucepan to a medium-low heat, stirring constantly until the sauce is only thick enough to coat a spoon lightly; it must not approach the boil or it will curdle. Add a few drops of lemon juice; taste and add more if necessary. Sprinkle with chopped parsley and serve with rice.

Carbonade of Beef

SERVES 6

This richly flavoured dish of carefully browned beef and onions cooked slowly in beer is popular in the Low Countries. It is particularly famed in Belgium, which has a long tradition of brewing and a very wide variety of beers. Some recipes call for stout, which makes a beautifully dark gravy, but any beer, flat or fizzy, from Guinness to lager, is fine.

1.35kg (3lb) braising steak, trimmed of any
  fat
Salt and freshly ground black pepper
2 tablespoons olive oil
30g (1 oz) butter
680g (1½lb) onions, thinly sliced
1 tablespoon plain flour
600ml (1 pint) brown ale

Cut the beef into large cubes, 3.5cm (1½in), and season lightly with salt only. Heat the oil in a heavy, flameproof pan or casserole and brown the meat quickly on all sides in small batches. Set the beef aside and add the butter to the pan. Reduce the heat and add the onions, all at once, and brown them evenly, stirring to prevent them sticking and burning. When they are well coloured, stir in the flour and mix well. Return the meat to the pan and add the beer. Bring to the boil, reduce the heat and simmer, covered, for 2–3 hours, or until the beef is very tender. This can be done on top of the stove or in a pre-heated slow oven (150°C/300°F, gas mark 2).

If there is too much liquid when the meat is done, pour most of it off into another pan, skim any fat which rises to the surface, and reduce the sauce by fast boiling before reuniting it with the beef. Taste for salt and add freshly ground black pepper. Serve with mashed potatoes or wide ribbons of freshly cooked pasta.

Carbonade tastes even better if it is cooled and reheated, and cooling makes it easier to remove surplus fat from the sauce.

Braised Haunch of Venison

SERVES 6–8

The back leg of a deer, called the haunch, can be cut long or short in the same way as lamb. Size will depend on the type of deer and its age. Braising is a more reliable treatment than roasting for meat from any animal of uncertain age.

This recipe does need good home-made stock – veal, beef, or chicken – made with plenty of bones so that the liquid sets to a light jelly.

Approx. 2.5kg (5½ lb) haunch of venison
1 litre (1¾ pints) cooked marinade (see page
  69)
225g (8oz) pork back fat
2 carrots, finely chopped
2 large onions, finely chopped
1 stalk celery, finely chopped
Bouquet garni (see page 261) of parsley,
  thyme, bay leaf, and 6 juniper berries
600ml (1 pint) gelatinous stock (see above)
150 ml (¼ pint) crème fraîche
Salt and freshly ground black pepper

Marinate the haunch in the cooked marinade in the refrigerator for at least 12 hours and up to 2 days. Remove and dry the meat. Strain and reserve the liquid. Cut half the pork back fat into narrow ribbons about 5mm (¼ in) wide, and use them to lard the joint (see below). Put the remaining piece of fat between two sheets of plastic wrap and beat it out thinly. Lay the fat on

LARDING A HAUNCH OF VENISON

Cut back fat into 5mm (¼ in) wide strips and insert into a larding needle. With the haunch rounded side up, draw the needle through the flesh, leaving

ribbons of fat which you trim so that a short length of fat shows at each side of the 'stitch'. Do this at regular intervals across the whole haunch.

top of the joint and tie it on carefully.

Choose a casserole or roasting tin big enough to hold the haunch without too much space around it. Cover the base with the chopped vegetables and *bouquet garni*. Place the meat on top and add the strained marinade and stock. Cover the casserole or tin (with foil if there is no lid) and cook in a preheated moderate oven (160°C/325°F, gas mark 3) for about 3 hours, or until the meat is tender. Remove the cover and barding fat for the last half-hour to allow the meat to brown. Baste it once or twice.

Remove the haunch from the oven to a serving dish and keep it warm. Strain the cooking liquid into a pan, pushing through the cooked vegetables to thicken it. Skim off fat and boil it down to about 250ml (8fl oz). Stir in the cream and season to taste with salt and pepper.

Provençal Tuna Braise

SERVES 4

One thick tuna steak weighing about 680g (1½lb) or a little more is the basis for a robustly flavoured braise which will feed a family. Variations of this Mediterranean dish can be made with steaks of swordfish, bonito and shark. Alternatives to the lettuce include blanched spinach or chard. Use whichever is abundant in the market or garden.

> 680g (1½ lb) tuna steak
> 1 small tin anchovy fillets
> 4 tablespoons olive oil
> 2 cloves garlic, quartered
> 2 bay leaves
> 2 floppy cabbage lettuces
> 4 medium onions, finely sliced
> 500g (1lb 2oz) ripe tomatoes, skinned, seeded and quartered
> Large handful of sorrel leaves, if available
> Salt and freshly ground black pepper
> 250ml (8fl oz) dry white wine

Drain the anchovy fillets and halve them lengthwise. Use them to lard the fish steak, pushing evenly between the 'rings' of the flesh. Choose a heavy ovenproof pot or casserole into which the fish will fit quite snugly. Put half the olive oil, half the garlic and one of the bay leaves in the bottom. Lay the leaves from one of the lettuces over this base, and top with half the sliced onions and tomatoes. Season with salt and pepper and lay the tuna steak on the vegetables. Top with the remaining onions and tomatoes, the sorrel (if using), the remaining garlic, bay leaf, and seasoning. Remember that the anchovies are already salty. Top with the leaves from the second lettuce and pour over the remaining oil and the wine.

Cover the dish and bake it in a preheated moderate oven (160°C/325°F, gas mark 3) for about 1 hour. Serve hot or warm, directly from the casserole, with crusty bread or potatoes.

Braised Fennel

SERVES 4

This recipe demonstrates how browning before finishing the cooking in a little liquid can add interest and flavour to vegetables.

> 4 medium bulbs of Florence fennel
> 1–2 tablespoons olive oil
> 150ml (¼ pint) dry white wine or light stock
> Salt and freshly ground black pepper

Trim the fennel bulbs and cut them in halves from top to tail at their widest point to allow the pieces maximum contact with the pan. Choose a wide, shallow pan which will hold the fennel halves snugly in a single layer. Heat the oil in the pan and brown the fennel on both sides without allowing it to burn. This can be done fast or slowly, but needs watching because (like onions) the fennel will catch and burn quite suddenly.

When the fennel is coloured on both sides add the wine, stock or water, and salt and pepper. Cook, covered, on top of the stove or in a preheated moderate oven (160°C/325°F, gas mark 3) for about 20 minutes or until the fennel is as tender as you like it. Reduce any excess liquid by fast boiling until there is just enough to glaze the fennel. Good with plainly grilled meat, poultry or fish.

Tuna steak braised with lettuce leaves, onions and tomatoes in Provençal tuna braise.

CHAPTER 6

STOCKS AND SAUCES

Mastering the craft of sauce-making is straightforward. It is simply a matter of practice. Mastering the art – well, that is another thing. In sauce-making there is scope for imagination, inspiration, talent and taste and, when the first pair get the better of the last, for foodie hyperbole. But just as the virtuoso violinist must start with musical exercises, so the cook who can rely on his or her basic techniques is the one most likely to create a sauce worth an encore. So let's start, at the beginning, with stock.

STOCKS

Good stocks are not made by throwing an assortment of kitchen scraps and trimmings into a pot and boiling them up. They take time, trouble and some expense. The cook's care is repaid with broths whose bright appearance is matched with flavours which are true and clear.

How much the taste of the stock will need to be concentrated by reduction depends on its eventual role. Generally it will need to be stronger for sauces than for soups. A whole pot may be reduced to a cupful or two of intensely flavoured glaze which, when cooled, will be quite solid. To the keen cook this is treasure in store, a miracle-working ingredient that can be turned in an instant into a brilliant sauce, or used to transform an ordinary sauce into a great one.

The principles of making good stocks are invariable.

● Use generous quantities of good, fresh ingredients.

● All meat, poultry and game stocks can be made with browned or unbrowned ingredients. When browning, do it carefully so that none of the bones is burned. Even a small piece that is badly scorched will give a bitter taint to the whole pot.

● Consider the balance of meat and vegetable flavours. When the stock is destined to be reduced to a strong glaze it will taste disappointingly gluey unless an adequate quantity of vegetables has been included. The usual proportions are 90 per cent meat and bones, 10 per cent vegetables. *But*, for a broth which is to be used as a poaching liquid, or for soup, it may sometimes be preferable to omit the vegetables.

● Add an appropriate *bouquet* of herbs (see page 261) and other flavouring ingredients such as cloves, juniper berries or citrus peel.

● Do not add salt to the stock pot. Reducing the stock concentrates all the elements of its taste, including salt.

● Use sweet-tasting water. In areas where tap-water is heavily chlorinated or has other noticeable tastes, consider using bottled spring water with no overt flavour for making stock which is to be well reduced.

● The traditional stock pot is taller than it is wide, to reduce evaporation, but any large pan with a heavy base which discourages sticking will do.

● Bring to the boil slowly and skim repeatedly. As the temperature rises, so does scum – caused by the coagulation of albuminous proteins in the meat or fish. These would cloud the stock and need to be skimmed off, several times. To encourage scum to form, and so clear the stock, add a cup of cold water to the simmering pot to lower the temperature, then skim off the froth which will appear as it approaches boiling point again.

• Simmer, don't boil, the stock or it will be cloudy. Cook it, partially covered, at a gentle simmer, with small bubbles rising lazily to the surface.

• Don't stir the pot.

• Cook the stock for an appropriate length of time, from 20 minutes or so for a light fish stock to 5 hours for a hearty beef stock. Cooking for longer than necessary risks giving it a stewed bone taste.

• Skim off as much fat as possible from the cooked stock before lifting out the bones with tongs. Then ladle the stock into a bowl through a sieve lined with a double layer of dampened cheesecloth or muslin.

• Degrease the stock again, either by mopping its surface repeatedly with paper towels or by leaving it to cool and then scraping off the congealed fat.

Veal is the basis of the most important stock used in the best professional kitchens. The large quantities of gelatine released by the young veal bones gives stocks made with them an unctuous richness of texture. At home, beef and chicken stocks are more often made. A veal knuckle bone is a good addition to beef stock.

Brown Beef Stock

MAKES ABOUT 2.75 LITRES (5 PINTS)

1.5kg (3½lb) beef bones, sawn in short
  lengths
1.5kg (3½lb) shin of beef, cut in small cubes
1 medium onion with skin, halved
55g (2oz) carrot, coarsely chopped
55g (2oz) celery, coarsely chopped
55g (2oz) tomato flesh, coarsely chopped
55g (2oz) turnip, coarsely chopped
Bouquet garni (see page 261) of thyme,
  parsley, bay leaf, 1 clove garlic and 2
  cloves tied in a leek leaf

Spread the bones and beef on an oven tray and roast them in a hot oven (230°C/450°F, gas mark 8) until they are well browned on all sides, about 30 minutes. Pour off and reserve the fat. Transfer the meat and bones to the stock pot. Deglaze the roasting tin with water or wine (see page 176), and reduce the liquid to a spoonful by fast boiling. Add it to the pot.

Put the onion halves, cut side down, in a small dry frying pan or directly on to a solid electric or Aga hob. Brown without fat until the surface is well blackened but not bitter, and add to the pot.

In a non-stick pan without fat, or in the roasting tray with a little of the beef fat, brown the vegetables on top of the stove, or in the oven, then add them to the pot. Add the *bouquet garni* and water, covering the ingredients by 5cm (2in).

Bring slowly to the boil, skim, and simmer gently for 4–5 hours, skimming several times. Remove and discard the meat, bones, vegetables and *bouquet*. Strain and degrease the stock, which is now ready to be reduced and concentrated as required.

REDUCING STOCK

Choose a pan which the stock will almost fill, ideally one that is wider than it is tall, to assist evaporation. Heat to nearly boiling. Hold it at a gentle simmer, skimming off any skin that forms.

When it has reduced half-way down the pan, transfer it to a smaller pan which again it nearly fills. Continue reducing until it is the strength you require.

Glace de Viande or Meat Glaze

Reduce the beef stock to approximately a tenth of its original volume, using the method described above. It will be richly flavoured and coloured, and should be clear and syrupy.

To store the finished glaze, divide it between a number of small sterilised jars. When it is cool, seal the top with a 5mm (¼in) thick layer of melted lard, and label it. Sealed like this it will keep for several months in the refrigerator. Any meat, poultry or game stock can be reduced to a glaze if the original bones used contained enough gelatine.

75

White Veal Stock

MAKES ABOUT 2.75 LITRES (5 PINTS)

1 or more veal knuckle bones, sawn in short
lengths
1.5kg (3lb) stewing veal, shank, neck or rib
tips
240g (12oz) carrots, coarsely chopped
2 large onions, peeled and quartered
1 whole head garlic, unpeeled
1 stalk celery, coarsely chopped
1 leek, cut in short lengths
A generous bouquet garni (see page 261) of
thyme, parsley, bay leaf and 2 cloves tied
in a leek leaf

For a white veal stock, none of the ingredients is browned. The meat and bones are covered with water, brought to the simmer and thoroughly skimmed before the vegetables and *bouquet garni* are added. Simmer for about 4 hours.

Chicken Stock

MAKES ABOUT 2.75 LITRES (5 PINTS)

1 boiling hen, about 2.5kg (5lb) or chicken
carcasses and trimmings, raw or cooked
110g (4oz) carrot, finely chopped
110g (4oz) celery, finely chopped
110g (4oz) onion or white part of leek, finely
chopped
2 cloves garlic, peeled
Bouquet garni (see page 261) of parsley, bay
leaf, and a piece of lemon zest tied in a
leek leaf

The ingredients for chicken stock can be browned, or not, according to taste. A boiling hen gives excellent flavour without browning. Cut it into four or six pieces and proceed as for veal stock. If the stock includes leftovers from roast chicken, wash out any particles of stuffing which would cloud the stock, and brown the pieces lightly in a hot oven, being very careful that they do not burn. Chicken bones can scorch and taste acrid when they are golden brown, and

long before they are burned black.

Assemble and cook as beef stock if the chicken is browned, and as veal stock if not. Simmer for about 2 hours.

Lamb Stock

A sauce made with lamb stock, reduced to a glaze and enriched with butter (see page 83), beats traditional gravy as a sauce to serve with lean roast lamb. Use the bits and bones from one lamb roast to make a small amount of stock to form the basis of a sauce for the next; or proceed as for brown beef stock with stewing lamb and bones from the butcher and cook for 2–3 hours. Omit the cloves and add tarragon to the *bouquet*.

Game Stock

If instead of water the liquid element is made up of equal quantities of decent red wine and veal stock, the resulting game stock will be rich in colour, taste and texture. Brown the meat and bones well and add a few dozen juniper berries and a piece of orange zest to the *bouquet garni*. A sprig of rosemary is another possibility. Alternatively, game stock can be made, as brown beef stock, with water, but cooked for only 2 hours.

Vegetable Stock

Almost any fresh vegetables and herbs can be used to make vegetable stocks, although potatoes should be avoided if the stock is to be clear. Useful vegetables for stock include celeriac, fennel, peppers, mushrooms and tomatoes as well as the usual stockpot ingredients: onions, carrots and celery. Whether or not to peel is a matter of choice. Pea-pods and woody asparagus stems can be the basis of stocks for soups made with the peas or asparagus tips. A little lemon juice, wine or wine or cider vinegar will liven the taste of stocks made without tomatoes. Any of the fresh herbs are valuable ingredients, and a few slices of fresh ginger will add heat.

Chop the vegetables quite finely so that they

need a minimum of cooking to yield their flavour. Browning the vegetables lightly in a little oil or butter before adding the water gives a different, 'meatier' taste to the stock. Vegetable stocks are quickly made and cook for only about 30 minutes. Strain, cool and use within 48 hours to enjoy the fresh flavours.

Court Bouillon

MAKES ABOUT 1.2 LITRES (2 PINTS)
Court bouillon, or *nage*, is a light vegetable stock used for poaching fish and shellfish.

30g (1oz) butter
4 shallots, finely chopped
4 small white mushrooms, finely chopped
2 medium carrots, finely chopped
1 leek, white part only, finely chopped
1 celery stalk, finely chopped
1 slice or 'leaf' Florence fennel, finely chopped
2 tablespoons white wine vinegar
300ml (½ pint) dry white wine
1 litre (1¾ pints) water
1 clove garlic
Bouquet garni (see page 261) of parsley, bay leaf and a sliver of lemon zest tied in a piece of leek leaf
1 teaspoon peppercorns
Salt

Melt the butter in a deep pan and sweat the vegetables for about 10 minutes without allowing them to colour. Add the wine vinegar, wine, water, garlic and *bouquet garni*. Bring to the boil and simmer for 15 minutes. Crush the pepper coarsely and tie it in muslin. Add it to the liquid and simmer for 5 minutes more. Strain the *court bouillon* and add salt to taste.

Fish Stock

MAKES ABOUT 1.2 LITRES (2 PINTS)
Remember when making fish stock that fish bones are also used to make fish glue. This is a reminder to cook fish stock briefly (20–25 min-

utes) for a sweet taste, and not to over-do the reduction when cooking it down to make a stronger fish *fumet*. Freshness, as in all things fishy, is essential. The bones of flat fish, especially sole, are good for stock, as are cod, haddock and other white fish skeletons. Use heads and tails too, but make sure that all the blood has been washed off. Salmon and trout trimmings can be used for stock, but not herrings or mackerel which are too oily.

About 1kg (2¼ lb) fish trimmings
300 ml (½ pint) dry white wine
1 carrot, finely chopped
1 onion, finely chopped
Bouquet garni (see page 261) of parsley, bay leaf and fennel
2 tablespoons lemon juice or wine vinegar
1 teaspoon peppercorns, coarsely crushed

Put all the ingredients, except the pepper, in a pan and bring to the boil. Reduce the heat, skim and simmer for 15 minutes. Add the pepper and simmer for 5 minutes more. Strain the stock through a sieve lined with a double thickness of damp muslin or cheesecloth. Use immediately, or chill and use within 48 hours.

COMMERCIALLY MADE STOCK
Some of the fresh and frozen stocks now sold in supermarkets are of good quality and very useful for making flour-based sauces. They can also be reduced by simmering and combined with butter or cream.

The problem with stock cubes in general is their saltiness, which makes them unsuitable for reduction. However, they are a standby for flour-based sauces. They all taste different, so shop around for brands you like.

SAUCES THICKENED WITH FLOUR
Butter and flour cooked together to make a *roux* is the thickening agent used in béchamel, the most basic white sauce made with milk; in *velouté*, which is made with stock; and in *espagnole*, or brown sauce, which is made with stock and a *roux* which has been browned. These are 77

the 'mother' sauces of the classic repertoire, themes on which seemingly endless variations can be found in innumerable cookery books. They faded from fashion with the rise of *nouvelle cuisine* but are well on their way back into favour thanks to their good temper and keeping qualities.

Lumps are potentially a snag with flour-based sauces, but understanding how they get there is one step to preventing their formation in the first place. When dry starch is added to hot liquid it forms knots or clumps. Look at a lump in cross section and it is a ball of uncooked starch grains completely enclosed in a coat of cooked grains which have gelatinised on contact with the hot liquid and formed a barrier to the interior. The purpose of a *roux* is twofold. It wraps the separate flour grains in a coat of butter, so that they all have an equal chance of mixing with the hot liquid. It is also a preliminary stage in cooking out the cereal taste of raw flour.

For brown sauces the *roux* itself is cooked until it turns a rich biscuit colour. This adds flavour but reduces the thickening power of the flour in the same way that caramelising sugar reduces its capacity to sweeten. The proportions of *roux* to liquid depend on how thick the finished sauce is to be, and so they vary from recipe to recipe. Two factors to bear in mind are that long cooking, which is required to make a brown sauce clear and shiny, has a thinning effect, and that cooling, a usual result of serving any sauce, thickens those made with flour.

In professional kitchens, three-quarters of an hour is the minimum cooking time for any sauce made with wheat starch. This ensures that it will not taste of raw flour, and also makes a noticeable improvement to the texture.

Béchamel Sauce

MAKES ABOUT 300ML (½ PINT)

> *600ml (1 pint) milk*
> *1 bay leaf*
> *30g (1oz) butter*
> *30g (1oz) flour*
> *Salt and freshly ground black pepper*
> *Freshly grated nutmeg (optional)*

Hot liquid can be worked faster and more smoothly into a *roux*, so heat the milk, with the bay leaf, to boiling point and set it aside. Melt the butter in a small, heavy-bottomed saucepan. Add the flour all at once, and quickly stir it in. Stir the mixture over a low heat for about 2 minutes without allowing it to colour. Now start adding the hot liquid, a small ladleful at a time, stirring vigorously. It will immediately thicken the *roux*, which will gather round the wooden spoon or whisk and come away from the sides of the pan. Work quickly, and as soon as the mixture is an homogeneous mass, stir or whisk in another ladleful. Continue adding the liquid, a ladleful at a time, incorporating each addition thoroughly before adding the next.

At the point where half or more of the liquid has been added, the mixture will slacken a little, and the last additions will be easier to incorporate. Simmer the sauce very gently, stirring frequently to stop it sticking, for about 45 minutes. This can be done in the top of a double boiler. The long, slow heating produces a silky smooth sauce which has no taste of raw flour.

Season with salt, pepper and, optionally, nutmeg. Add up to 300ml (½ pint) of double cream to make this basic béchamel into a cream sauce. Add about 30g (1oz) each of freshly grated Parmesan and Gruyère cheeses to 600ml (1 pint) béchamel to make a *Mornay* sauce for fish or cooked vegetables. For a *sauce Soubise*, combine equal amounts of onion purée (made by sieving onions baked in their skins) and cream with béchamel. Serve with roasted or grilled lamb.

Velouté Sauce

Velouté is made with the same proportions of *roux* to liquid and the same technique as béchamel. The liquid can be veal, chicken or game stock, or fish *fumet*. The sauce is cooked for a minimum of 45 minutes, and benefits from being simmered for several hours.

While the sauce is reducing, periodically skim off the mixture of fat and gelatine which rises to the surface. Slow reduction develops a sumptuously velvety texture and concentrated taste. Expect a reduction of as much as two-thirds when calculating quantities.

Variations on *velouté* sauce are finished with double cream, or thickened a little more with a mixture of egg yolks and double cream stirred in at the last moment. The sauce cannot be returned to the boil after egg yolks have been added or it will curdle. Add cream and tomato purée for a *sauce Aurore*.

Brown Sauce

Brown sauce is made with the same proportions of *roux* to liquid, but the *roux* itself is browned on a moderate heat before the liquid, in this case good brown stock, is added. The addition of tomato purée turns it into a *sauce Espagnole*. Brown sauce should be simmered and skimmed for a minimum of 3 hours, and benefits from 5 or more hours' cooking. During this time the gluten proteins in the flour are gradually skimmed off and the sauce becomes glossy and clear.

Chasseur, Bordelaise, Lyonnaise, Madeira, Poivrade and *Zingara* are a few of the classic sauces based on brown sauce. Several include mushrooms, reduced wine and bone marrow.

GRAVY

There is a persuasive school of culinary thought which holds that there is no such thing as good gravy, and there is an element of truth in this. The residues in the roasting pan provide inadequate flavour to support the quantity of liquid that gravy-eaters demand. Hence the ubiquity of gravy mixes.

The problem with gravy made by adding flour to the roasting tin, to make a *roux* of the dripping, and then adding liquid, is that the starch does not cook for long enough, and the taste is weak. The flour itself masks flavour.

But there are other ways of meeting the problem. One is to make a good brown sauce in advance and freeze it in small quantities. It can then be used as a gravy base to which the deglazed pan drippings are added.

Another is to settle for unthickened pan juices. A third is to deglaze the pan with stock, home-made or one of the fresh or frozen stocks now sold in supermarkets, and thicken it with a *beurre manié* (see below), or a little corn starch or potato flour mixed with cold water.

LAST-MINUTE THICKENING OF SAUCES

Cornstarch or cornflour, potato starch (*fécule* or farina) and arrowroot are all useful for last-minute thickening because they need only brief cooking. Of the three, cornflour is the easiest to buy but the last to choose as it will taste floury.

In a small bowl, mix a spoonful or two of the starch with enough cold water to make a thin paste. Then stir the dilute starch into the simmering soup or sauce a little at a time. Thickening occurs almost immediately.

An alternative is *beurre manié*. This is a mixture of soft butter and plain flour mixed together in equal measures – an uncooked *roux* in fact. It is added to the simmering liquid in small pieces and stirred in thoroughly. It is added a little at a time, and has the inevitable disadvantage of a floury taste.

EGG EMULSION SAUCES

Getting the hang of making egg-based emulsion sauces is like learning to ride a bicycle or swim. Once you have succeeded, the feel and the skill are never forgotten. So it is worth cracking a few eggs to master it.

The similarities between the classic egg-based emulsion sauces are greater than the differences. *Hollandaise, béarnaise* and their variations are made with butter and served warm. *Mayonnaise* is made with oil, and served cold. Using the freshest possible egg yolks and putting plenty of energy into the work of whisking are essential to both.

The current advice on making emulsion sauces is based on a fuller understanding of science than was available to writers and chefs in the past. If a different, tried and tested method works for you, then there is no need to change your technique. But if the results are hit and miss, follow these recipes. The instructions may appear unorthodox, but be assured that the results are the classic sauces.

A note on pans. Avoid aluminium and non-stick pans for making warm emulsion sauces. 79

Aluminium causes discoloration and non-stick surfaces hinder the emulsification process.

Mayonnaise

MAKES ABOUT 350ML (12FL OZ)

> *2 very fresh egg yolks*
> *Salt and freshly ground pepper*
> *300ml (½ pint) oil (see below)*
> *1–2 tablespoons lemon juice, wine vinegar or*
> *water*

Very fresh egg yolks which have as little as possible of the white clinging to them are the most effective emulsifiers. Extra virgin olive oil contains elements which can gradually destabilise a successfully made mayonnaise. It is better to use refined olive oil, or another almost tasteless refined oil mixed with enough extra virgin olive oil for an appealing flavour. Have all the ingredients at room temperature.

Put the yolks in a bowl with a pinch of salt and one measured teaspoon of the oil and start whisking. The mixture should quickly start to thicken. Continue whisking and adding the oil a teaspoonful at a time until the emulsion is thick and glossy and a total of 6 teaspoons of the oil have been incorporated.

Now whisk in a teaspoon of lemon juice, wine vinegar or water. This will thin the mixture a little and the oil can now be added in the traditional thin, steady stream, while the sauce is whisked continuously and energetically. When all the oil has been incorporated, adjust the flavour and thickness of the sauce. Add lemon juice, wine vinegar or water, salt and pepper until flavour and consistency are as you like them.

RESCUING A MAYONNAISE WHICH SEPARATES

The capacity of each egg yolk to emulsify oil is vastly greater than the amount of oil called for in recipes, but using 2 yolks and no liquid to start with makes it much easier for the cook to initiate the process of emulsification and thickening. If this stage causes difficulty, then it is likely that the yolks were not sufficiently fresh, or that they had too much egg white adhering to them.

However, if the emulsion breaks after it has been formed successfully, the remedy is simple. Whisk in a little water to thin it slightly, then continue adding the oil as before.

MAYONNAISE VARIATIONS

Sauce tartare Stir in a mixture of finely chopped capers, sour gherkins, chives, chervil and parsley to taste. Serve with fish.
Green mayonnaise Stir in finely chopped spinach, watercress or sorrel which has been blanched and very well drained, plus any mixture of herbs to taste. Tarragon, chives, chervil, mint or parsley are all good. Serve with cold fish or poultry.
Garlic mayonnaise or aïoli Some versions of *aïoli* are based on mashed potato and oil strongly flavoured with garlic. Alternatively, it can be made by crushing two or more whole cloves of garlic with salt and adding this to the egg yolks. Then make mayonnaise as described. Use as a dip or with crudités.
Coating mayonnaise To cover pieces of cold poached fish or chicken. Dissolve half a sachet of gelatine in 4 tablespoons fish or chicken stock, as appropriate, or water. Cool to room temperature, then whisk the gelatine into 300ml (½ pint) mayonnaise. Use immediately.

Hollandaise Sauce

MAKES ABOUT 300ML (½ PINT)

The tricky part of making *hollandaise*, a light buttery emulsion sauce served warm as a classic accompaniment to steamed asparagus and poached fish, is warming the egg yolk sufficiently to maximise its thickening power without scrambling it. The American food writer Harold McGee has invented a non-traditional method for mak-

Even the simplest barbecued steak, piece of chicken or fish can be enlivened by a tangy salsa Mexicana *(see page 84)*

ing it by heating and whisking all the ingredients together at once. The point of his technique is that by dispersing the egg at the outset there is less danger of overheating it and curdling the sauce. The lemon juice, which is acid, also plays a role in helping to prevent the yolk from coagulating into lumps. Use very fresh egg yolks with as little of the white clinging to them as possible.

Choose a heavy pan with a wide curve between the base and sides so that all the sauce can be reached by the whisk.

3 very fresh egg yolks
1 tablespoon water
1 tablespoon lemon juice
Salt and freshly ground white pepper
225g (8oz) unsalted butter, cut into 16 pieces

Put the egg yolks, water and lemon juice into a cold saucepan with ½ teaspoon salt and some pepper, and beat them together thoroughly. Add the chunks of butter, place the pan over moderate heat, and begin whisking gently. Control the heat so that the butter melts gradually and evenly

EGG SAFETY

For as long as there remains any danger that some eggs may contain salmonella bacteria, sauces containing uncooked egg yolks pose a degree of risk. Commercial mayonnaise made with pasteurised egg yolk is safer for babies and the elderly. The warm emulsion sauces, such as *hollandaise*, cannot be heated sufficiently to kill the bacteria. Harold McGee in his book *The Curious Cook* (Harper Collins), describes experiments with what he calls 'near boiling' egg yolks in a microwave oven. The procedure is fiddly and has to be adapted to individual appliances, but other curious cooks may be interested in following this up.

HOLLANDAISE VARIATIONS

Béarnaise sauce Combine 150ml (¼ pint) dry white wine, 4 tablespoons wine vinegar, 2 finely chopped shallots and a tablespoon each of chopped chervil and tarragon into a pan and boil until only 2 tablespoons of liquid remain. Strain the reduction, discarding the shallots and herbs. Follow the recipe for *hollandaise* sauce using the reduced liquid in place of the water and lemon juice. If you have fresh herbs, stir a small quantity of finely chopped tarragon into the finished sauce. Serve with steak, chicken, fish or vegetables.
Sauce paloise Follow the recipe for *béarnaise* sauce, replacing the tarragon with mint. This sauce is especially good with salmon.
Maltaise sauce Follow the recipe for *hollandaise* sauce, omitting the water and whisking the juice of a blood orange into the finished sauce. Serve with fish.

into the yolk base. Once all the butter has melted, continue heating and whisking until the sauce just thickens, when it will be between 71° and 77°C (160–170°F). Turn the heat down and hold the sauce around 49°C (120°F) until serving.

An alternative strategy, using the same ingredients, is to make the sauce in the top of a double boiler or *bain-marie* (see Glossary). First ensure that the bottom of the inner pan or bowl is not touching the water simmering beneath it.

Put the egg yolks and lemon juice into the inner pan or bowl together with a little salt and pepper. Whisk over the heat until the mixture is smooth, then begin adding the melted butter, a little at a time, until the sauce is thick and smooth. Finally, whisk in the water and adjust the seasoning.

RESCUING A WARM EGG EMULSION SAUCE WHICH SEPARATES

There are two strategies for rescuing a sauce which separates, but neither is infallible, or even worth trying if the egg has scrambled. The first is quickly to whisk in an ice cube: this may cool the sauce before too much heat damage has been done. The second is to start again with fresh egg yolks and whisk the damaged sauce into them a little at a time.

USING A PROCESSOR

Food processors take the work out of making egg emulsion sauces, and some would say the aesthetic pleasure too. The main difficulty to overcome is how to work a very small starting volume of egg and liquid when the blade of the machine does not reach right down to the bottom of the bowl. Run the machine very briefly, stop it and use a spatula to push the embryo sauce into the path of the blade. Do this several times until there is enough sauce for the processor to work on. Or make a double quantity of the recipe.

To make the warm emulsion sauces, put the egg yolks and cold liquid in the machine and process it for half a minute. Then, with the machine running, pour in hot, bubbling melted butter in a steady stream. Adjust the seasoning.

EGGLESS EMULSION SAUCES

Emulsion sauces can also be made without the help of egg yolk. The classic vinaigrette dressing for salad is a cold emulsion sauce made without egg. Finely ground mustard seed, usually in the form of a commercially made up mustard, helps to form and stabilise the emulsion.

Vinaigrette

Shaking the ingredients vigorously in a screw-top jar or bottle is the least laborious method of making any vinaigrette.

The proportions of oil and vinegar can be varied greatly and will depend on the strength and flavour of the oils and vinegars used, and the flavour of the foods to be dressed. Wine vinegar, olive oil, salt, pepper and mustard are the basics. For every tablespoon of vinegar, use at least 3 tablespoons of oil and ½ teaspoon of a mild made mustard, with salt and pepper to taste.

Beurre Blanc

It is perfectly possible to form a warm liaison of water and melted butter without the help of egg yolk as *beurre blanc* proves. This sauce, very good with fish, is less thick than a *hollandaise*.

4 tablespoons dry white wine
4 tablespoons white wine vinegar
2 tablespoons very finely chopped shallots
Salt and freshly ground white pepper
110g (4oz) chilled unsalted butter, cubed

Put the wine, vinegar and shallots into a small pan and simmer until only a scant tablespoon of the liquid remains. Take the pan off the heat, season the mixture with a little salt and pepper and let it cool a little. Return the pan to a very low heat, using an insulating mat if necessary to regulate it, and whisk in the cold butter, a few pieces at a time, adding the next batch just before the first has entirely disappeared. When all the butter has been added, the sauce should have the consistency of thin cream. Serve at once.

Beurre Brun

This is one of the quickest, best and most useful sauces in the cook's repertoire. The marvellous flavours of well browned meat and poultry juices can be captured in a *beurre brun* made from the deposits left in the tin or pan after roasting, frying or grilling. Skim or pour off as much fat as possible and deglaze the pan by adding a splash of wine or stock. Stir and scrape up the deposits over a high heat. Strain the liquid through a fine sieve into a small pan and reduce the liquid to a scant tablespoon. Let it cool a little before whisking in an ounce or two of cold butter cut in cubes as for *beurre blanc*. Adjust the seasoning and serve at once. Don't even think about trying to keep *beurre brun* warm.

RESCUING A BUTTER EMULSION SAUCE

A safe maximum temperature is 54°C (130°F). When heated a few degrees more, oily puddles of clear melted butter start to appear. If you catch it quickly enough you can save the sauce by taking the pan off the heat and whisking it for a minute.

If the temperature drops so sharply that the sauce starts to solidify, it cannot be resurrected by reheating. It will no longer be a sauce, though you could serve it as a flavoured butter.

83

PUREED VEGETABLE SAUCES

Several reasons explain the growing popularity in recent years of another group of healthy sauces, cooked and uncooked, which are thickened with vegetables. One, of course, is the ever-increasing variety and year-round availability of raw materials and fresh herbs to complement them. The spread of food processors is another.

All this is without taking into account more adventurous tastes and the influences of travel, the food media, and ethnic restaurants. Add the beguiling lack of difficulty which *salsas* and purées present even to the least able of cooks, and the absence of an inhibiting classic tradition, and it is easy to see why everyone feels free to invent and experiment. Technique is subservient to taste, and recipes are almost superfluous.

To make puréed vegetable sauces choose top-quality ingredients with plenty of flavour. Skinned and deseeded red or yellow peppers, carrots, parsnips, celeriac, leeks and watercress are prime candidates. Cook the vegetables plainly and process them until smooth. Add stock, olive oil or cream until the mixture has a sauce-like consistency.

Salsa Mexicana

MAKES ABOUT 300ML (½ PINT)
This fiery concoction of tomato and chilli appears on every Mexican table and it does not take long to develop an insatiable taste for it. Serve it with grilled meat or fish, or avocado.

> *225g (8oz) ripe tomatoes*
> *1 or 2 hot green chillies*
> *1 small onion*
> *1 clove garlic*
> *10 sprigs coriander*
> *½ teaspoon salt*
> *1 teaspoon fresh lime juice*

All the ingredients must be very, very finely chopped. The sauce looks best if this is done by hand. A processor produces irregular pieces, or mush. Skin the tomatoes (see page 194), deseed and chop them. Using gloves (see page 185), deseed the chillies, and chop the flesh. Peel and chop the onion and garlic. Chop the coriander. Put them all in a bowl and stir in the salt and lime juice. Set aside for half an hour.

Shallot and Coriander Salsa

SERVES 4–6
Lynn Hall of La Petite Cuisine cookery school teaches a shallot and coriander *salsa* for marinating pieces of very lightly cooked chicken or fish. The acid in the *salsa* completes the 'cooking'. Allow portions of 111–170g (4–6oz) each.

> *150ml (¼ pint) peanut (groundnut) oil*
> *4 tablespoons wine vinegar*
> *Salt and freshly ground black pepper*
> *6 tablespoons tomato ketchup*
> *1 teaspoon Worcestershire sauce*
> *5 drops Tabasco sauce*
> *110g (4oz) shallots, very finely chopped*
> *1 tablespoon each of finely cut chervil, chives and tarragon*
> *4 tablespoons finely cut coriander*

In a large bowl whisk together the oil, vinegar, a pinch of salt and 3 turns of the pepper mill. Mix in the tomato ketchup, Worcestershire sauce, Tabasco and shallots. Leave for about an hour.

Place the hot fish or chicken, which should be three-quarters cooked, taken off the bone and cut into attractive bite-sized pieces, in a shallow serving dish. Pour over the shallot vinaigrette which will continue to 'cook' the fish or chicken. Add half of the herbs to the dish. Leave to stand in a cool place for 3–4 hours. Finally add the remaining herbs.

FRESH FRUIT SAUCES

All the soft fruits make glorious *coulis*, or sauces.

Raspberries and strawberries, peaches and nectarines need only be puréed and sweetened – icing sugar is best – to taste. This is easiest in a processor or blender, of course, but can be done by pushing the fruit through a sieve. (Raspberry *coulis* will need sieving anyway to remove the pips.) Blackcurrants and redcurrants will need to be lightly cooked before puréeing and sieving.

CHAPTER 7
YEAST COOKERY

Yeast is the most magical of ingredients, half feared because it really does have a life of its own. It is yeast that leavens, or lightens, doughs made with flour, water and salt, and turns them into bread. There is no better smell than the wholesome aroma of wheat and yeast transformed in the oven to a warm loaf with a golden crust and tender, honeycomb interior.

From plain bread for everyday sustenance have evolved innumerable enriched bread doughs which are made into rolls, buns and cakes. It is interesting how many of the cakes made in this country and elsewhere in Europe to celebrate Christmas and other festivals are in fact enriched breads. Italy's sweet and light *panet-tones*, Scotland's black bun and Germany's fruit and marzipan laden *Stollen*, all made with many variations, are examples. At one time Simnel cakes were raised with yeast, as many other traditional regional recipes still are. *Bara brith*, the Welsh fruit bread, Cornish saffron cake, lardy cakes and Sally Lunns are all leavened with yeast. A number of old-fashioned teatime specialities such as crumpets, pikelets and muffins (the English not the American type), are made with yeast, as are doughnuts, and *blinis* (see page 93), the lightest of savoury pancakes to accompany caviar.

Not all enriched breads are sweet, of course. Nuts, herbs, spices, olives, even sun-dried tomatoes, are used to flavour small fancy loaves and rolls, and what is pizza but bread with a savoury topping?

None of these good things could be made without the astonishingly powerful engine set to work when we combine yeast with flour and water.

YEAST

Of the many species of yeast, only one, a strain of *Saccharomyces cerevisiae*, which translates as 'brewer's sugar fungus', is used in baking. The particular strain used to raise dough produces large quantities of carbon dioxide as it ferments, unlike other strains of the same species which specialise in producing alcohol and are used in brewing. The cook can buy it in three different forms.

FRESH YEAST

Also called compressed yeast, fresh yeast is sold by bakeries and health-food shops. Fresh yeast should feel cool, and like putty. It is beige in colour. It is very perishable and can be stored, closely wrapped, in the fridge for only a few days. But it freezes successfully, for three months or longer. Thaw before using.

Shrinking, dryness and the appearance of white spots are indications that the yeast is stale.

GRANULAR DRIED YEAST

The granular form sold in tubs and packets by supermarkets is every bit as effective as fresh yeast. It needs reconstituting with liquid before being mixed with the flour. Always store granular dried yeast in a cool place and be careful to note the use-by date.

EASY-BLEND DRIED YEAST

The latest addition to the range, this is mixed directly with the flour, making it the simplest form to use. Store in a cool place.

WHICH YEAST?

Choosing which type of yeast to use is more a matter of aesthetics than efficacy. When home-made bread has a 'beery' flavour it is probably because the proportion of yeast is too high. This is likeliest to occur when using dried yeast. Weight for weight, granular dried yeast is twice as potent as fresh compressed yeast.

Manufacturers' advice on dried yeast is calculated to produce gratifyingly fast fermentation. But excellent though the results may be, many cooks believe better loaves are made using less yeast and a slower rise.

TEMPERATURE CONTROL

All three forms of yeast are 'live', but yeast is usefully active only within a clearly defined temperature range. The most critical temperature to note is 54°C (130°F), the heat at which yeast finally dies in the heat of the oven.

Fresh or granular dried yeasts are activated in lukewarm liquid before being added to the flour. Lukewarm means a temperature of blood heat, or a little hotter, 37–43°C (98–108°F).

For fermentation, or rising, to take place at an *optimum* rate, it needs warm, moist conditions – a covered bowl and a room temperature of 21–24°C (70–75°F). Fermentation is sometimes deliberately slowed down by leaving the dough to rise in a much cooler spot, even in the fridge. Slow fermentation offers four potential advantages. It:

- Improves the flavour of plain breads.
- Improves texture, distributing small air bubbles evenly through the dough.
- Allows the cook to postpone baking until a convenient time. Doughs could be fermented overnight for a breakfast baking, for example.
- Uses less yeast, minimising 'beery' flavour, and cost.

ACTIVATING YEAST

Activating the yeast is the first instruction in most recipes. If you are using fresh yeast, crumble the measured amount into a small bowl or cup, and add a few tablespoons of lukewarm water, or whatever liquid the recipe requires. Stir. As soon as the yeast has dissolved, it is ready to use.

To activate granular dried yeast, add a pinch of sugar to the warm water before sprinkling the yeast on it in a cup or small bowl. Stir and set aside in a warm place for 10–15 minutes until all the granules have dissolved and the liquid has a head of creamy froth, very like a pint of porter.

Easy-blend dried yeast does not need preliminary activation.

FLOUR AND OTHER YEAST-DOUGH INGREDIENTS

FLOUR

Strong flour milled from hard wheat makes the finest bread. The important difference between wheat and other grains is the greater amount of gluten it contains, and hard wheat has more of this useful protein than the soft wheat flours used in cakes and pastries.

Strong white bread flour, bleached or unbleached, has more gluten than wholemeal flour does; more also than flours and meals milled from other grains such as rye, which make denser, heavier loaves. It is for this reason that most of the bread recipes which use oats, maize, barley or other ingredients to give different flavours and textures also include a proportion of strong wheat flour for its texture-improving gluten.

SALT

Bread made without salt would be unpalatably insipid, and so its principal function as an ingredient is taste. It also improves bread's keeping qualities. The thing to remember is that salt inhibits yeast fermentation. Cooks who like their bread to taste quite salty therefore may find it takes a little longer to rise. Too much salt will tend to produce a loaf with a hard crust.

LIQUID

Water is the only liquid required for making plain bread. The *average* proportion is about 300ml (½ pint) water to 450g (1lb) or a little more flour. The capacities of different brands and types of flour to absorb water is very variable, however, and recipes are only a guide where liquid is concerned. Some brown flours are exceptionally thirsty.

A half-and-half mixture of milk and water produces rolls with a softer crust than a dough made with water alone. Milk is also said to improve the crumb of wholemeal bread and its keeping qualities.

OILS AND FATS

Small amounts of oil or fat make the dough a particular pleasure to knead and improve the keeping quality of the baked bread. Fat also inhibits the action of yeast, which is why lavishly enriched breads such as brioche take longest to rise.

ADDITIONAL ENRICHMENTS AND FLAVOURINGS

Eggs, sugar, dried fruit, nuts and spices are ingredients which occur in endless permutations in recipes made with yeast-raised doughs. Seeds and cracked grain, too, can be incorporated into the dough, or used to give the crusts of bread or rolls additional interest. Savoury enrichments include cheese, olives, sun-dried tomatoes, fried onions and herbs.

MIXING

Recipes adapted from commercial techniques, and old domestic recipes from the days when baking for big families involved larger quantities of dough than anyone would make at home now, sometimes call for the yeast and liquid to be combined with a small amount of flour to form a batter known as a sponge. This is quite unnecessary, and today all the ingredients are simply mixed together to form a dough.

KNEADING

When flour and water are combined, the gluten proteins interact with the liquid to give dough its characteristic texture: its plasticity, which allows it to be pushed out of shape; and its elasticity, or inclination to spring back to its original form.

Kneading the dough is said to 'develop' the gluten, which is a good description of what the process feels like as an inert lump of new dough comes to life in your hands. During kneading it becomes firmer and more resilient as the molecules of gluten are reorganised to form an ever denser web of protein strands. It is these which trap the gas bubbles which form when the yeast goes about its fermentation business and the dough begins to rise. The more elastic the dough, the greater will be its capacity to trap bubbles of gas, and so produce a loaf of good size and even texture.

The action of kneading is a pleasant one. Place the ball of dough on a floured surface. Fold it towards you, then use the heel of one hand to push the dough down and away from you. Fold the stretched dough back towards your body again, give it a quarter turn, and repeat the action of pushing, stretching, folding and turning for 5–10 minutes.

Kneading by hand, there is no danger of overworking the dough – stretching the gluten molecules to the point where they lose their strength and the mixture starts to soften again. This is a real risk with an electric mixer or processor, however, so be sure to refer to the manufacturer's instructions for guidance on timings.

RISING

The freshly made and kneaded dough is put into a clean bowl, covered to prevent moisture loss, and set aside at warm room temperature for an hour or so until it has doubled its original volume. It must be covered to prevent a skin forming: use a damp cloth, or lightly oiled cling film. Maximum fermentation has taken place when the dough no longer springs back when lightly pressed, but retains the impression of the finger that poked it. Then the dough is punched down, the cook quite literally knocking the air out of it. At this stage it is either formed into loaves, or – in the case of white bread made with strong flour – left to rise again in a covered bowl, and punched down a second time. The second rising will usually take about half as long as the first.

The dough is then shaped into loaves, which are allowed to prove, to double in size, before 87 being baked. Set the loaves or rolls well apart. Again the rising dough should be covered to prevent moisture loss.

BAKING

The final stage of rising is called 'oven spring', the yeast's last burst of activity before it dies in the heat of the oven combined with a rapid expansion of the gases trapped in the dough. Elizabeth David in her encyclopaedic *English Bread and Yeast Cookery* wrote at length about the history and attributes of ovens old and new. To create the ideally steamy baking conditions which maximise a loaf's volume and at the same time allow it to form a crust which is thin and crisp, she experimented with baking her bread under a cloche or bonnet. The technique of covering the loaf with a large heatproof bowl or metal pot for the first 30 minutes or so of baking is most suitable for loaves baked without a tin, or in a shallow pan. The cover is then removed and the baking is continued until the loaf is fully cooked.

Another way of improving the crust is to place a flat pan of boiling water in the bottom of the oven just before the bread is put in, and leaving it there throughout the baking. The steam from the water forms a coating of moisture on the top of the dough which gives it time to expand and develop a crust. You could also brush the loaf tops with lightly beaten egg whites or cold water 10 minutes before the end of the baking time.

The oven temperatures suitable for baking plain breads are generally in the 204–218°C (400–425°F) range. When baked, a loaf should be well risen and brown, and sound hollow when rapped on the base.

COOLING AND STORING

Cooling freshly baked bread too quickly can spoil a good loaf. Set it on a wire rack, or stand it across the tin it was baked in, and allow to cool slowly in the warmth of the kitchen. The air will then circulate around the bread and prevent any moisture from spoiling the crispness of the crust. Do not wrap or store until completely cold. The bread-bin should not be airtight.

Crusty White Coburg Loaf

MAKES 1 LOAF

This round, free-standing loaf needs no special equipment and the small quantity of dough, which has two rises but only one kneading, is easy to handle.

400g (14oz) strong, unbleached white flour
2 teaspoons salt
8g (¼oz) fresh yeast, or ¼ teaspoon granular dried yeast and a pinch of sugar
Approx. 250ml (8fl oz) warm water

Mix together the flour and salt and sift them into a large bowl. Warm the flour in a low oven (140°C/275°F, gas mark 1) for a few minutes while preparing the yeast. If you are using fresh yeast, mix it with a little of the warm water to make a smooth, runny cream. If you are using granular dried yeast, sprinkle the granules and sugar on a little of the warm water. Mix well and leave until the mixture begins to froth and the granules have dissolved completely. Make a well in the warm flour and pour in the yeast mixture and most of the water. Mix to a soft dough, adding as much of the remaining water as required. Do not knead the dough at this stage; cover and leave it in a warm place to rise.

When the dough has doubled its bulk, in 1–2 hours, knock it down and knead it until it is smooth and supple. Form it into a ball and set it on a floured baking sheet. To prevent the loaf from spreading too flat in the oven, tuck the edges of the ball of dough underneath it as if they were a loose bedcover. Cover the dough and leave it to rise again until it has doubled its bulk once more. Cut a cross in the centre of the loaf with a very sharp knife or razor blade. As soon as the cuts open, which should happen very quickly, cover the loaf with a large bowl or casserole and bake it in the preheated oven (230°C/450°F, gas mark 8) for 20 minutes. Remove the cover, reduce the temperature to moderately hot (200°C/400°F, gas mark 6), and

Crusty white Coburg loaves, basic wholemeal bread and brioches, with a further bowl of yeast dough proving in the background.

continue baking the loaf for about 20 minutes, or until it sounds hollow when tapped on the base.

Basic Wholemeal Bread

MAKES 1 LOAF

Making good 100 per cent wholemeal bread is not quite as simple as the recipe suggests. Variations in the thirstiness of different batches of flour or meal are disconcertingly large, so the liquid measures given in recipes are not much more than suggestions. Too wet a dough will produce a heavy loaf. Too stiff a dough will result in a dry crumb.

> *570g (1¼lb) stoneground wholemeal flour*
> *15g (½oz) fresh yeast, or 1 teaspoon granular dried yeast and a pinch of sugar*
> *300–350ml (10–12fl oz) water*
> *4 tablespoons whole milk or light cream*
> *15g (½oz) salt*

Sift the flour into a large bowl and warm it in a low oven (140°C/275°F, gas mark 1) while the yeast is being activated. Heat the water to warm blood heat and add the milk or cream. Mix the yeast with a little of the warm liquid (and sugar, if using granular dried), and add the salt to the remainder in a measuring jug. Grease a loaf tin of about 2 litres (3½ pints) capacity. Make a well in the middle of the warm flour and pour in the yeast mixture plus 300ml (½ pint) of the measured liquid. Mix thoroughly, adding more flour if the dough is too wet to handle, or more liquid if it seems too stiff. Aim for a dough which is soft, but which holds together well enough to shape and lift into the tin.

Transfer the dough to the tin. Push it into the corners and flatten the top. Cover and leave in a warm place to rise for about 45 minutes to one hour. Wholemeal dough does not rise in the spectacular manner of white bread. When it reaches the top of the tin it is ready to go into the oven.

Bake in a preheated hot oven (230°C/450°F, gas mark 8) for about 20 minutes, then lower the heat to moderately hot (190°C/375°F, gas mark 5) and bake for another 20 minutes. Turn the loaf

TROUBLESHOOTER'S GUIDE
- Beery flavour – using too much dried yeast.
- Heavy bread with too little aeration – inadequate fermentation time; excessive fermentation time resulting in over-stretched gluten; stale yeast, poor flour, or too wet a dough.
- Crumbly, cake-like crumb – too much fat in the dough, or too stiff a dough.
- Sour flavour – over-fermented dough with too little salt.
- Insipid flavour – too little salt, immature dough, poor flour.
- Hard crust – too much salt in the dough, or overbaking.

out of its tin, and if it sounds hollow when rapped on the base it is done. Probably it will need another 5 or 10 minutes' baking. Return it to the oven without its tin for as long as it needs.

Brioches

MAKES 12 OR MORE

Home-baked brioches fresh from the oven, feather-light and meltingly tender, are a treat for high days and holidays. Brioche dough can be frozen, closely wrapped, immediately after the knocking back stage. Let it thaw slowly in the refrigerator then shape, prove and bake it. Brioche tins have sloping fluted sides which flare out from a narrow base. Muffin tins can substitute for individual moulds and a loaf tin will do for a single large brioche.

> *15g (½oz) fresh yeast, or 1 scant teaspoon granular dried yeast*
> *2 tablespoons warm water*
> *2 teaspoons sugar*
> *450g (1lb) strong white bread flour*
> *1½ teaspoons salt*
> *6 large eggs, lightly beaten*
> *225g (8oz) unsalted butter, softened*
> *1 egg yolk beaten with 2 tablespoons water, to glaze*

Activate the yeast in the water, adding a pinch of the sugar if using granular dried yeast. Sift the flour, salt and remaining sugar into a warm bowl. Make a well in the centre and add the beaten eggs and the yeast mixture. Working by hand, or using the dough hook of an electric mixer, mix then knead the dough for at least 10 minutes.

Now add the butter, a tablespoon or two at a time, making sure that each piece is amalgamated completely before the next is added. Continue kneading the dough for another 5 minutes or so. It will be very soft and tacky, so you may need to work with a scraper in one hand. Cover the bowl and leave the dough to rise in a warm place until doubled in volume, about 2 hours.

Knock the air out of the dough and transfer it to a clean bowl. Cover it again and chill it overnight. It will rise again very slowly in the refrigerator, and it is this slow rising which gives the bread its distinctive fine texture.

Brush the brioche mould or moulds generously with melted butter and set on a baking sheet. Turn the dough on to a lightly floured surface and form it into a ball.

To make one brioche loaf Cut off a third of the dough to make the traditional top knot which gives *brioche à tête* its name. Roll the larger piece into a ball and place it in the mould. Roll the smaller piece into an elongated egg shape. Using your fingertips, press a hole into the centre of the dough in the mould, and insert the narrow end of the dough egg.

To make individual brioches Take a piece of dough which will half fill one of the moulds, and pinch off a quarter to make the top knot. Roll the larger piece into a ball and put it in a mould. Roll the smaller piece into another ball. Use scissors to snip a cross in the top of the larger ball, and press the smaller one into the cross. Shape the remaining dough in the same way. Cover the brioches and leave them to rise again until they have doubled their bulk.

Brush the tops with the egg yolk and water glaze and bake them immediately in a preheated moderately hot oven (200°C/400°F, gas mark 6). Individual brioches will take between 10 and 20 minutes, depending on their size; a single large one 40–45 minutes.

Turn brioches out of their tins as soon as they are out of the oven, and cool them on a wire rack. Serve warm.

Pizza Dough

SERVES 6

This recipe makes two rectangular pizzas the size of a standard 30 x 23cm (12 x 9in) baking sheet.

> *250ml (8fl oz) milk*
> *15g (½oz) fresh yeast, or 1 teaspoon granular dried yeast, or 1 teaspoon easy-blend dried yeast*
> *Scant ¼ teaspoon sugar (if required)*
> *450g (1lb) strong plain white flour*
> *1 teaspoon salt*
> *1 large egg*
> *6 tablespoons olive oil*

Heat the milk to boiling point, then set it aside until lukewarm.

Using fresh or granular dried yeast Use about 4 tablespoons of the milk to activate the fresh yeast or granular dried yeast. Add the sugar to the latter. Sift the flour and salt into a bowl. Mix the remaining warm milk with the egg and oil, and stir lightly together. Make a well in the centre of the flour and pour in the yeast and egg mixtures all at once. Mix to a dough.

Using easy-blend dried yeast In a bowl, sift together the flour, yeast and salt. Mix the egg with the oil and milk and stir lightly together. Add the egg mixture to the flour all at once and mix to a dough.

Turn out the dough, which will be very sticky at this stage, on to a well-floured surface and knead it for about 5 minutes or until it is springy and elastic. Form the dough into a ball, put it in a bowl, cover and leave to rise until it has doubled in volume. This will take 1–2 hours at room temperature – longer in a cool place.

Punch down the dough and knead it briefly before rolling it out fairly thinly – 5mm (¼in) is thick enough. Pizza toppings of tomato sauce and other ingredients can be added immediately, and the pizzas baked in a preheated very hot oven, 240°C/475°F, gas mark 9 for 20–25 minutes until sizzling and slightly risen.

CHAPTER 8
BATTERS

Batters are the basis of any number of irresistibly good things, all quickly made from common ingredients – flour, eggs and milk or beer. They are the fast food of yesterday, recipes which have survived virtually unchanged from the days before everyone had a freezer and shops stayed open round the clock. What could be quicker to make, or more appetising to eat, than Scotch pancakes warm from the griddle, spread with fresh butter and home-made jam? Or tender crêpes sprinkled with sugar and a squeeze of lemon juice. It is a brave cook who would risk the howls of protest that would greet roast beef without Yorkshire pudding, or Shrove Tuesday without pancakes.

These are instant foods made for instant eating. With the exception of thin pancakes used as wrappers or re-heated in sauce, as in *crêpes Suzette*, batter-based foods are best eaten straight from the pan or griddle. This applies equally to batter-coated dishes like apple fritters or deep-fried fish.

The first, indeed almost the only, rule of batter-making is to begin with a mixture which is too thick rather than too thin. It is easy to add more liquid to thin it down, but almost impossible to add more flour without forming lumps. How thick to make a batter is a matter of experience, but experience is easily acquired. Err on the side of thickness when making any type of pancake, and cook a trial pancake or two, gradually adding more liquid until you get the required result, or the texture you like.

The best way to keep pancakes warm is to transfer them immediately from the griddle or pan to a plate over a pan of simmering water and cover them with a clean napkin or teacloth.

Batters call for ordinary plain flour. The strong flours used in bread are a positive disadvantage in batters. The elasticity produced by their high gluten content would toughen pancakes and hinder a coating batter's capacity to adhere. This is why batters should be mixed as briefly as possible, so that the gluten is not encouraged to develop. Some recipes call for the batter to be rested after it is mixed and before it is cooked. This allows the starch granules in the flour to swell a little, and is useful for crêpes and other thin batters which are used to make tender, fragile pancakes.

American Buttermilk Breakfast Pancakes

SERVES 2–4

A 'short stack' of three or four thick, light pancakes served with maple syrup and bacon cooked to a frazzle is the epitome of American breakfasts. Traditional recipes use lavish amounts of raising agents, and the taste of these, which comes through in the cooked pancakes, has become part of the expected flavour. Buttermilk pancakes, which were enormously popular before packet pancake mixes took over in American kitchens, rise with less chemical assistance and taste the better for it. Use cultured buttermilk or plain yogurt (not the set type), thinning it with milk or water if need be.

175ml (6fl oz) buttermilk or plain yogurt
2 tablespoons melted butter
1 large egg, separated
140g (5oz) plain flour
½ teaspoon baking soda (bicarbonate of soda)
2 tablespoons caster sugar
½ teaspoon salt
Oil or melted butter for frying

Beat the buttermilk, melted butter and egg yolk together in a large bowl. Sift all the dry ingredients together and stir them quickly and lightly into the buttermilk mixture. In a separate bowl whisk the egg white until stiff, then fold it quickly into the batter. Heat a griddle or heavy frying pan very well, and grease it lightly with oil or melted butter. About 2 tablespoons of batter will make a small pancake. Double or treble the amount for larger ones. Drop the measured batter on the griddle and cook until the underside is golden brown and bubbles are bursting through the top. Turn and cook briefly on the other side.

Grease the griddle lightly between cooking each batch.

Blini

SERVES 4–6

Blini, the yeast-raised pancakes that are such an improvement on the hot toast usually served with caviar, can be made with ordinary wheat flour, or with a mixture of wheat and buckwheat. The buckwheat gives them a curious beige colour and a marvellous nutty taste. Serve the blini hot or warm, with soured cream, chives and caviar. This can be from the Beluga sturgeon or, less exotically, from salmon or trout. The batter can be made up to 24 hours in advance.

15g (½ oz) fresh yeast
450ml (¾ pint) lukewarm milk
110g (4oz) plain flour
110g (4oz) buckwheat flour
1 large egg, separated
1 tablespoon lightly flavoured vegetable oil
½ teaspoon salt
Oil for frying

Activate the yeast in 4 tablespoons of the warm milk (see page 86). Sift the plain flour into a large mixing bowl and the buckwheat flour into a smaller one. Make a well in the plain flour, pour the dissolved yeast into it and mix with a wooden spoon, gradually drawing in the flour from the edges to the centre. Beat the mixture well, adding enough of the warm milk to make a thick, smooth batter. Cover the bowl and leave the batter to rise in a warm place for about 2 hours, or until it is light and bubbly and has doubled its volume.

Now beat in the buckwheat flour and enough of the remaining milk to produce a smooth batter with the thickness of pouring cream. Beat in the egg yolk, oil and salt. In another bowl, whisk the egg white until it will hold a peak, and then fold it into the batter. Now cover the batter and let it rise again for another hour or so at room temperature, or more slowly (even overnight) in the refrigerator. Let it come back to room temperature before cooking the blini.

Blini are cooked on a flat cast-iron griddle, or in a heavy shallow frying pan. They can be made large or small as you wish. To make them all the same size, choose a spoon or small ladle which will hold the right amount for a single pancake. Heat the griddle or pan well, and grease it very lightly with oil. Drop spoonfuls of the batter on to the cooking surface, spacing them well apart. Cook until the underside of the blini are golden and bubbles begin to burst through the top. Turn them and cook on the other side. Grease the griddle sparingly between each batch with more oil.

Scotch Pancakes

MAKES ABOUT 18

225g (8oz) plain flour
½ teaspoon salt
2 teaspoons cream of tartar
1 teaspoon bicarbonate of soda
30g (1oz) caster sugar
1 tablespoon runny honey
1 large egg
Approx. 300ml (½ pint) milk
Lard or oil for frying

Sift all the dry ingredients together into a bowl and make a well in the centre. Add the honey and egg and gradually beat in the milk to make a thick, smooth batter. A heavy cast-iron griddle is traditional for cooking pancakes, but a good thick frying pan will do very well. Heat it slowly and thoroughly before beginning to cook the pancakes. When the pan is hot, grease it lightly with lard or oil. Drop tablespoonfuls of the batter on to the griddle, spacing them well apart. When bubbles begin to break on the surface, and the underside is a pale biscuit brown, turn the pancakes over and cook them briefly on the other side. When fully cooked they should be no darker than a pale, golden brown.

Crêpes

MAKES ABOUT 18

Crêpes are time-consuming to make but can be stored, interleaved with greaseproof paper, for two or three days in the refrigerator, or two or three months in the freezer. They are equally good served with sweet or savoury fillings.

> *110g (4oz) plain flour*
> *¼ teaspoon salt*
> *3 large eggs*
> *250ml (8fl oz) milk*
> *2 tablespoons melted butter.*
> *Clarified butter (see page 239) or oil for frying*

Sift the flour and salt into a bowl and make a well in the centre. Beat the eggs with a little of the milk and add them to the flour. Mix lightly, drawing in the flour to make a smooth thick batter, then stir in the melted butter and half the remaining milk. Set the batter aside for at least an hour, or up to 24 hours in the refrigerator. The finished batter should have the thickness of single cream, so just before using it, stir in some or all of the remaining milk.

Heat a well-tempered crêpe or omelette pan and grease it very lightly with clarified butter or oil. It should be hot enough to sizzle a drop of batter immediately. Pour in just enough batter to cover the base of the pan and swirl it out to the edge. Cook until the underside is golden brown, then toss or turn it with a spatula, and cook it briefly on the second side until golden and nicely coloured.

Expect to cook two or three less-than-perfect test crêpes to work out the best combination of heat and batter thickness. Adjust the heat so that the crêpes cook quickly, but not so fast that the batter sets before it can reach the edges of the pan. Too high a heat produces thick crêpes; too heavy a hand greasing the pan results in heavy ones.

Galettes de Sarrasin

MAKES ABOUT 12

Watching a skilled galette-maker at work, spreading batter impossibly thin over a wide circular griddle with a practised flick of the wrist and a little paddle made for the purpose, is enough to put anyone off trying to make them at home. We cannot make galettes the size of dinner napkins as the professionals do, but smaller ones cooked in a crêpe or omelette pan are perfectly feasible. These, made with buckwheat flour, are best eaten at once sprinkled with melted butter and a savoury filling of ham and grated cheese, or sweet with a spoonful of jam.

> *110g (4oz) buckwheat flour*
> *¼ teaspoon salt*
> *300ml (½ pint) milk*
> *3 large eggs*
> *2 tablespoons melted butter or oil*

Make the batter and cook the galettes in exactly the same way as the crêpes above.

Coating Batter

MAKES 300ML (½ PINT)

This is a basic batter for coating food to be deep- or shallow-fried. A thicker or thinner coating can be made by increasing or decreasing the proportions of liquid and flour. A thin batter cooks to a crisper and lighter coating than a thick one. A thick batter clings to the food better, but can be stodgy.

110g (4oz) plain flour
½–1 teaspoon salt
1 tablespoon olive oil
200ml (⅓ pint) beer or water
2 egg whites

Sift together the flour and salt in a bowl and make a well in the centre. Add the oil and gradually mix in the beer or water, working from the centre outwards. Rest the batter at room temperature for about an hour.

Just before using the batter, whisk the egg whites until they are stiff and fold them into it.

Yorkshire Pudding

MAKES 1 LARGE OR 8 SMALL PUDDINGS
Traditionally Yorkshire pudding is cooked in beef dripping under the roast, where it soaks up a ration of meat juices as it cooks. The result is full of flavour but heavier than individual puddings baked in oil. These rise very dramatically in the oven and are easily overcooked. Timing depends on the heat of the oven. If there is only one oven, the meat roasting setting, which may be hot or moderate depending on the cut of meat, will govern the temperature at which the batter cooks. A hot oven (230°C/450°F, gas mark 8) is ideal for Yorkshire pudding, but it can be cooked at any temperature from moderate (160°C/325°F, gas mark 3) upwards. Allow extra time for cooking at lower settings.

110g (4oz) plain flour
¼ teaspoon salt
2 large eggs
150ml (¼ pint) milk
Oil, or fat from roasting tin

Sift the flour and salt into a mixing bowl and make a well in the centre. Mix the eggs with a little of the milk and add to the flour. Stir until a smooth paste is formed, then gradually add the remainder of the milk. The batter can be mixed up to an hour before it is needed.

About 15 minutes before the beef is due to come out of the oven (30 minutes before it is carved after a 15-minute rest), put 2 tablespoons of fat from the roast into a baking tin about 25cm (10in) square, or its equivalent. Put the tin in the oven and, when the fat is very hot, pour in the batter and set the pudding as high up in the oven as possible. Bake for about 30 minutes, or until well risen and golden. Cut in squares to serve.

Individual puddings will take a few minutes less to cook. About 5 minutes before the meat is due to come out of the oven, put 2 teaspoons of oil or dripping in each hollow of a Yorkshire pudding tray, or muffin tin. Heat the oil to sizzling in the oven before filling each hollow almost to the top and returning the tin to the oven.

Vary the flavour of the pudding by adding some chopped herbs. Par-cook some good sausages and bake in the batter for a toad in the hole.

MAKING CREPES

Lightly grease a crêpe or omelette pan with clarified butter or oil and pour in just enough batter to cover the base of the pan. When bubbles form

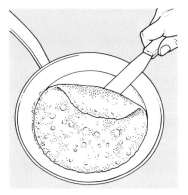

on the surface of the crêpe, or the underside is golden, lift the edge using a spatula, to check. Turn with the spatula, or toss, and cook the second side.

CHAPTER 9
PASTRY

Pastry in all its splendid variety demonstrates the cook's ingenious manipulation of a handful of everyday ingredients – flour, fat and water, with sugar and salt for flavouring, and eggs for richness. The competent pastry-maker's repertoire includes shortcrust, rough puff, full puff, *pâte sablée*, choux paste, hot water crust, and that old English standby suet crust. Each has its own technique and uses, its particular reasons and rules.

Puff and shortcrust dough can be bought, fresh or frozen. One reason for making them at home is the superior flavour that using good fresh butter gives to the finished pastry. Filo is also sold fresh or frozen, and the commercial product, sometimes labelled strudel pastry, is so good that few cooks will attempt to make it except for fun, or to produce a very big sheet of dough to make a single party-size strudel. All the other kinds of pastry have to be made at home, or else bought ready-cooked as shells or finished tarts, pies and puddings.

Pastry-making calls for exactness. Even among the specialist professionals, there are few chefs who do not measure their ingredients accurately even when they are making the same recipes every day of their working lives. Taking pains with pastry pays mouthwatering dividends.

lated too much and the gluten proteins in the flour are allowed to develop. While the adult cook's pastry is crisp and tender, the child's off-cuts from the same batch are hard and tough. This is why plain flour is the best choice for most pastry making.

Only in filo or strudel pastry is the elasticity of the gluten in strong flour an asset, allowing the dough to be stretched transparently thin. Two factors restrict gluten development in most pastry doughs. These are the small amount of water used, and the relatively large amount of fat.

Fat is the ingredient which gives pastry its texture: friable in the case of shortcrust, flaky in puff, and tender in choux. Different ways of incorporating it into the dough are what gives pastry its varied textures. In puff, separate thin layers of butter and dough are interleaved ready to spring apart in the heat of the oven. In shortcrust the butter is as finely dispersed as it can be in its solid form. In hot-water crust the fat is even more closely allied to the flour by being melted – as it is also for choux, where the starch in the flour is partly gelatinised in the preliminary cooking of the dough.

Margarine made from vegetable oil, lard, or white vegetable fats can be substituted for butter, but butter gives the finest flavour.

INGREDIENTS

The child's inedible pastry playthings rolled repeatedly at the edge of the kitchen table illustrate just what happens when dough is manipu-

EQUIPMENT

Pastry-making demands a minimum of equipment. A cold marble slab on which to make dough by hand and roll it out is a great pleasure to use, and helps to keep the dough cool while it is worked. But any clean, flat surface will do. Apart from a rolling pin, scales, a sieve, measuring spoons and jugs, the most useful accessory for pastry-making is one of the cheapest – a flexible plastic scraper for gathering together partially blended dough, and for clearing the work surface afterwards.

A food processor is an invaluable assistant, speeding the work of rubbing fat into flour for all the short pastry variants. A selection of specialised tins and cutters helps to give the work a professional-looking finish. One or more heavy-duty flat steel baking sheets, the largest that will fit the oven, is essential. Much can be accomplished free-hand.

For pastry-*baking* equipment, see page 302.

CHILLING, STORING AND FREEZING

Where recipes call for pastry dough to be chilled during its making or before rolling out, it should be closely covered with cling film or foil to prevent moisture loss. Wrapped like this, puff, shortcrust, sweet pastry and filo doughs can be stored for several days in the refrigerator, or deep frozen for two or three months. Thaw pastry dough thoroughly in the refrigerator before attempting to roll it out.

ROLLING AND SHAPING

● To prevent pastry dough from sticking when it is rolled out, dust the work surface lightly with flour before starting. If the half-rolled dough threatens to stick, lift it, one edge at a time, and dust underneath with flour.

● Roll pastry dough from the centre towards the edges using a light, firm action. The idea is to re-form the shape of the dough, not to stretch it. Stretching causes pastry to shrink in the oven.

● Allow chilled dough to soften a little at room temperature before rolling. When puff pastry is rolled too cold, the layers of fat break rather than spread, wasting the effort that has gone into it already. Over-cold short pastry dough will split and crack at the edges.

● There is less danger of tearing rolled-out pastry dough if it is lifted on the rolling pin. Hold the pin in one hand just above the mid-line of the dough and use the other hand to lift up one edge of the pastry and drape it over the pin. Then, holding both ends of the pin, transfer the dough to its tin or baking sheet, stretching it as little as possible.

● Use very sharp knives to cut puff pastry dough. A blunt knife will squash the layers together and discourage them from separating in the oven.

BAKING BLIND

● Where recipes call for short, sweet or savoury pastry cases to be blind baked – that is, cooked without a filling – the pastry will shrink less if it is well rested between shaping and baking. If possible, line the tin with pastry dough the day before and chill it overnight.

● To prevent blind-baked pastry from bubbling up in the oven, put a greaseproof paper lining over the dough and weight it down, not too heavily, with dried beans. When the pastry is set and partly cooked, lift out the beans and paper and continue baking until it is done.

GLAZES AND FINISHES

An egg yolk mixed with a little water produces a shiny golden glaze. Brush the mixture lightly on to the uncooked pastry, before making any decorative cuts and, in the case of puff pastry, avoiding the edges so that they are free to rise. Egg glaze is also useful for sticking on pastry leaves and other decorative flourishes.

Icing sugar sprinkled on puff pastry for the last few minutes of cooking time produces a deep chestnut-coloured gloss.

Caster sugar sticks best to hot pastry straight from the oven for a dusted sugar finish. Icing sugar dustings are applied just before serving.

Shortcrust

MAKES ABOUT 340G (12OZ) DOUGH
Shortcrust is the most useful all-purpose pastry and the most quickly made, for filled pies of meat or fruit, for flans, quiches, and sweet or savoury 97

tarts. This quantity is sufficient to make a 25cm (10in) pastry case for a family-sized flan or tart giving six to eight portions. When using a small food processor, it is better to make two small batches of dough than one large one when doubling or trebling recipe quantities.

To rub in means to lift small handfuls of fat and flour and to rub lightly between thumbs and fingertips as it drops back into the mixing bowl.

> 225g (8oz) plain flour
> 1 teaspoon salt
> 110g (4oz) butter
> 2–3 tablespoons iced water

By hand Sift the flour and salt into a large bowl. Cut the butter, which should be cool, but not chilled hard, into small dice and toss them lightly in the flour. Rub in the fat with fingertips or a pastry blender until the mixture looks like fine breadcrumbs. Sprinkle 2 tablespoons of water over the mixture and blend, using a fork, until it can be formed into a ball. Add the remaining water if needed.

Turn the dough out on to a floured surface and press it gently into a stiff dough. Rest it, covered, in a cool place for at least 10 minutes before rolling out.

In a food processor Put the flour and salt into the bowl and process briefly to aerate. Cut the butter, which can be very cold, into dice and add them to the bowl. Process until the mixture has the texture of fine breadcrumbs. With the machine turned off, sprinkle 2 tablespoons of water over the mixture. Process briefly, stopping the machine as soon as a ball of dough begins to form around the blade.

Turn out the dough on to the floured surface and press it gently into a ball. Cover and rest in a cool place for at least 10 minutes before rolling.

Wholemeal Shortcrust

Good stoneground wholemeal flour does not, sadly, make good pastry. Use wholemeal pastry flour, or a half-and-half mixture of stoneground wholemeal and plain white flour, and the quantities and method described above for shortcrust.

Pâte Brisée

MAKES ABOUT 450G (1LB) DOUGH

This is a richer shortcrust made with egg. It is a light, crumbly pastry well suited to wrapping fish or meat *en croûte*, or for pasties or small savoury tartlets.

> 255g (9oz) plain flour
> 160g (5½oz) butter
> 1 large egg
> ¾ teaspoon salt
> ¼ teaspoon sugar
> 1 tablespoon milk (if needed)

By hand Sift the flour into a large mixing bowl, or on to a clean work surface, and make a well in the centre. Cut the butter, which should be quite soft, into small dice, and put them in the well together with the egg, salt and sugar. Rub the fat mixture into the flour using the fingertips of one hand, gradually drawing in the flour with the other hand. When the mixture is almost blended, add the milk and knead it very lightly into a homogeneous dough. Cover and chill for at least an hour before rolling out.

In a food processor Put the flour, salt and sugar into the bowl and process briefly. Add the butter, cut in dice, and process until the mixture resembles fine breadcrumbs. Mix the egg with the milk in a cup and, with the machine turned off, add the egg to the bowl. Process until the mixture begins to form a dough around the blade. Stop the machine and turn out the dough on to a lightly floured surface. Press it very lightly into a homogeneous mass. Cover and chill it for at least an hour before rolling out.

Pâte Sablée

MAKES ABOUT 310G (11OZ) DOUGH

This is a very sweet, short, melting pastry. Bake it blind to make fragile cases for soft fruit tarts, or bake in discs, large or small, which can be used to sandwich layers of fruit or as a base for uncooked cheesecakes and other dessert assemblies set with gelatine. This is a tricky dough to roll out in large pieces, but cracks and joins will soon knit together as the pastry bakes.

140g (5oz) plain flour
55g (2oz) icing sugar
¼ teaspoon salt
110g (4oz) unsalted butter
Yolk of 1 large egg
A few drops of vanilla essence

By hand Sift the flour, icing sugar and salt into a large mixing bowl, or on to a clean work surface, and make a well in the centre. Cut the butter, which should be quite soft, into small dice, and mix the egg yolk with the vanilla essence. Put the butter and egg mixture into the well and rub in, using the fingers of one hand, gradually drawing in the flour with the other hand. When the mixture is well blended knead it very lightly into a homogeneous dough. Cover and chill for at least an hour before rolling out.

In a food processor Put the flour, salt and icing sugar into the bowl and process briefly. Add the butter, cut in dice, and process until the mixture resembles fine breadcrumbs. Mix the egg yolk with the vanilla essence in a cup and, with the machine turned off, add the egg to the bowl. Process until the mixture begins to form a dough around the blade. Stop the machine and turn out the dough on to a lightly floured surface. Press it very lightly into a homogeneous mass. Cover and chill it for at least an hour before rolling out.

Rough Puff

MAKES ABOUT 450G (1LB)
Rough puff is a multi-purpose dough used for pies and tarts of all kinds from steak and kidney pie to cream horns and fruit turnovers.

225g (8oz) plain flour
½ teaspoon salt
170g (6oz) butter
150 ml (¼ pint) cold water
1 teaspoon lemon juice

Sieve the flour and salt into a large mixing bowl. Cut the butter, which should be malleable but

---

OVEN TEMPERATURES FOR PASTRY

The oven temperatures used for cooking pastry range from moderately hot, through hot to very hot. The highest temperatures are used for puff. Those recipes which combine pastry with a filling which also needs cooking are usually baked at a high temperature to set the pastry, then cooking is completed at a lower setting.

The chart shows the range of oven settings typically advised.

Shortcrust	hot	220°C/425°F,	gas mark 7
	moderately hot	190°C/375°F,	gas mark 5
Sweet shortcrust	moderately hot	200°C/400°F,	gas mark 6
	moderate	180°C/350°F,	gas mark 4
Puff	very hot	240°C/475°F,	gas mark 9
	moderately hot	190°C/375°F,	gas mark 5
Choux	hot	220°C/425°F,	gas mark 7
	moderately hot	190°C/375°F,	gas mark 5
Hot-water crust	moderately hot	200°C/400°F,	gas mark 6
	moderate	160°C/325°F,	gas mark 3
Filo and strudel	hot	230°C/450°F,	gas mark 8
	moderate	180°C/350°F,	gas mark 4

not soft, into 12 fairly uniform cubes and add it to the flour, followed by the water and lemon juice. Use a knife to mix the ingredients into a rough dough that begins to cling together. Turn the mixture on to a lightly floured surface and press it lightly into a rectangle. Roll it out into a strip that is approximately three times as long as it is wide. Mark the strip into thirds. Fold in three as in the illustration below. Give the pastry a quarter turn, press the open edges lightly to seal them, and repeat the rolling, folding and turning routine four times more, resting the dough, wrapped in the refrigerator, for about 15 minutes after the second and fourth rollings. Rest the finished dough for an hour before rolling out.

Puff Pastry

MAKES ABOUT 1.25 KG (2¾ LB)
Puff pastry makes the airiest vol-au-vents, mille-feuilles, and pie tops. It is also used, dramatically, to top individual bowls of consommé, perfumed with mushrooms, truffles or a distinctive herb such as lemongrass or tarragon.

There is no advantage in making a smaller quantity of puff pastry because any that is not used immediately can be frozen with no detectable loss of flavour or performance. There is a school of thought that favours using strong flour for puff. The high gluten content is to some extent counteracted by the large amount of fat, but the result is less tender and melting.

500g (1lb 2oz) plain flour
2 teaspoons salt
1 tablespoon lemon juice
250–275ml (8–9fl oz) iced water
500g (1lb 2oz) unsalted butter

Sift the flour and salt on a clean surface and make a well in the centre. Mix together the lemon juice and iced water, and pour about one-third of this liquid into the well. Using one hand to beat the mixture and the other to support the walls of flour, draw in the flour until the centre has the consistency of a cream sauce. Add more water and continue mixing until you have a dough which can be formed into a ball. Wrap the dough and chill it for about 30 minutes.

Prepare the butter by working it with a knife or spatula into a block measuring about 15cm (6in) square. Then chill it.

Rolling the dough and butter together will be easier if they have roughly the same consistency. As this makes the following stages less fraught, it

---

MAKING PUFF PASTRY

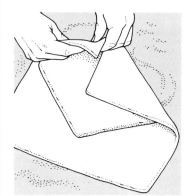

1. Place the block of butter on the square of pastry dough and fold over the edges of dough to make an envelope.

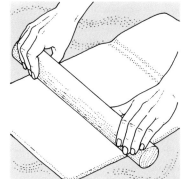

2. Starting in the middle of the envelope, roll the dough, working towards and away from you only, to a rectangle of about 20 x 40 cm (8 x 16 in).

3. Mentally divide the rectangle into thirds. Bring one-third over the middle third, then the remaining third over both. Chill. Repeat six times (see method).

is worth a little patience at this stage to try to achieve it.

Lightly flour the work surface and roll out the dough to a square large enough to wrap the butter block with just a little overlap. Place the butter in the middle of the dough with the sides of the butter opposite the corners of the pastry. Fold the corners to the centre envelope style (see illustration) and press the joins lightly with the rolling pin.

Starting with the rolling pin in the middle of the envelope, roll out the dough, working towards and away from your body only, to a rectangle measuring about 20×40cm (8×16in). The short side should face you. Use a rule or long knife to nudge the edges straight and square up the corners.

Mentally divide the rectangle into thirds. Take the third nearest to you and fold it over the middle third, then bring the top third down over the other two. Square up the package and lightly tap the edges with the rolling pin. Press a shallow dent in the top with a finger as a reminder that the dough has been turned and folded once. Wrap the dough in cling film and chill it for at least 30 minutes.

Unwrap the pastry. Two sides have folds in them (think of the pages of a book). Place the 'book' on a lightly floured surface with the spine on the left and the turn-marking dent uppermost. Roll it out again to the same size as before. Fold it in three again, keeping the edges and corners square, and make two turn-marks. Wrap and chill it for another 30 minutes.

By repositioning the dough with the spine of the book on the left, you are turning it each time through 90°. The turn-marks keep track of the number of times the dough has been rolled. Puff pastry is turned six times in all, making 730 leaves in the finished dough. The third and fourth turns should be possible without chilling the dough between them, likewise the fifth and sixth. But if the dough becomes too warm and soft, stiffen it up in the refrigerator. If the worst happens and butter starts to leak through the dough, dust the afflicted area with a little flour and chill well before carrying on. After the sixth and last turn, mark and wrap the pastry as before and chill again before using it.

Hot-Water Crust

MAKES ABOUT 900G (2LB) DOUGH

This is the pastry to use for grand and elaborate game pies and home-made pork pies. The warm dough is pleasingly malleable and easily worked into the elaborate flutings of a traditional game pie mould. Walls of dough can also be raised freehand around a large jar or wooden pie mould in the manner of the pastry coffyns of olde English pyes.

> *450g (1lb) plain flour*
> *1 teaspoon salt*
> *1 egg yolk*
> *225g (8oz) lard, or half-and-half lard and butter*
> *175ml (6fl oz) water*

Sift the flour and salt into a warmed mixing bowl. Make a well in the centre, drop the egg yolk into it and cover it with flour. Heat the lard, or lard and butter, with the water in a small pan until the fat has melted, then bring to the boil. Pour immediately over the flour and stir vigorously with a wooden spoon until the dough is cool enough to handle. Turn the dough on to a lightly floured surface and knead it until it is smooth and pliable. Cover and rest it in a warm place for about 20 minutes before shaping.

Choux

MAKES ABOUT 10 ECLAIRS

Use it for eclairs, choux puffs or profiteroles. To make savoury, cheese-flavoured *gougères* or deep-fried *beignets*, stir 45g (1½oz) finely grated Parmesan or Gruyère into the paste with the eggs.

Choux paste is too soft and sticky to be rolled out, and is spooned or piped on to dampened baking trays. In the oven the paste expands to three or more times its original volume, leaving a hollow interior.

Making a small slit in the base of eclairs and profiteroles as soon as they are out of the oven will help any excess moisture to evaporate, and the pastry to stay crisp.

120ml (4fl oz) water
55g (2oz) unsalted butter
75g (2½oz) plain flour
½ teaspoon salt
2 large eggs

Put the water and butter into a heavy saucepan and heat until the butter melts. Sift the flour and salt on to a sheet of paper. Bring the water to the boil. Off the heat, slide all the flour off the paper into the liquid and stir vigorously until well combined. Return the pan to a medium heat and cook the mixture, stirring, until it forms a solid mass and comes away cleanly from the sides of the pan. Take the pan off the heat and allow the mixture to cool a little before beating in the eggs, one at a time. The paste is now ready.

Filo

Paper-thin sheets of filo pastry dough should not be allowed to dry out. Once the packet has been opened and the leaves of pastry unrolled, they will need to be kept covered with plastic wrap or a damp cloth. The dough is virtually fatless, and when cooked without additional oil or melted butter it is dry and brittle. It can be moulded without fat into fanciful shapes such as token pastry cups to hold soft fruit for dieters. But it is at its best brushed with fat or oil and baked in stacks of six or more sheets. Layered with finely chopped nuts and sugar, filo is the structural element in the Greek sweet *baklava*. It can also be layered with olive oil, salt and dried herbs and topped with finely cut raw vegetables – say tomatoes, courgettes and aubergines – then cut into fingers after baking.

Suet Crust

MAKES ABOUT 450G (1LB) DOUGH

Suet pastry is steamed, not baked. Its characteristic softness and unique taste are a cornerstone of traditional British cooking, for dishes such as steak and kidney pudding, and Sussex pond pudding, which is filled with a whole lemon and lots of butter and sugar. Suet crust is also used to make suet dumplings.

This quantity is enough to make a filled meat or game pudding for six people using a 1.75 litre (3 pint) pudding basin. Up to one-third of the flour can be replaced with fresh white breadcrumbs for a lighter crust. Vegetable suet is an alternative to beef suet.

285g (12oz) self-raising flour
170g (6oz) shredded beef suet
1 teaspoon salt
About 175ml (6fl oz) water

Sift the flour into a mixing bowl, add the suet and salt and mix lightly together. Sprinkle the mixture with water, mix lightly with a fork, and continue adding water and mixing until the dough will just hold together. Turn it out on to a generously floured surface and gather it into a ball. Suet crust pastry should be used as soon as it has been made.

CHAPTER 10

PASTA

There is more to Italian pasta than starch – quite a lot more. Hard durum wheat ground into semolina, from which dried pasta is made, contains not less than 12 per cent protein. Fresh pasta made with eggs has substantially more. Our increasing consumption of pasta, fuelled by new nutritional thinking as well as changing tastes, has led to a vastly expanded choice. It has also spawned one widespread misunderstanding. The notion that fresh pasta is better than dried pasta is a myth. It is true that well-made fresh egg pasta is a delight which can hold its own in the best gastronomic company. But some factory-made fresh pasta is quite simply unpleasant. Its taste is floury and its texture sticky, and there is nothing the cook can do to improve it. So if one brand name proves disappointing, try another. There are plenty of good makes to choose from.

Of course dried pasta may be second rate too. Look for brands made with durum wheat, and Italian makes with *pasta di semola di grano duro* on the packet. Yellowness alone is not an indication that dried pasta includes eggs. Italian brands which do will be labelled *pasta all'uovo*.

Dark specks are an indication that the germ of the wheat has been included in the milled grain. Wholewheat pasta, including bran as well as wheatgerm, is also widely available, but even wholefood enthusiasts can be forgiven for preferring pasta made from refined flour.

There are quite literally hundreds of pasta shapes, styles and fillings, and many of them have several names. Italian regional diversity means that, confusingly, one name may be used to describe several different pastas. Take *tortelloni*, for example. It can mean large *tortellini* – stuffed circles of pasta folded to look like little ears – as well as small squares of stuffed pasta. Between small round meat-stuffed *agnolotti* and the big tube pasta called *zitoni* there is a fanciful alphabet of descriptive imagery – little priest's hats, *capeletti di preti*; little ears, *orecchiette*; cock's combs, *cresti mezzane*; elephant's teeth, *dente d'elefante*; snails, *lumache*; quills, *penne*, and worms, *vermicelli*. The definitive list has yet to be compiled.

MAKING PASTA

To make pasta at home with semolina is a task balked by even the most intrepid cooks. The long, laborious kneading demanded by semolina dough is a task best left to machinery. But egg pasta made with strong bread flour is a pleasure to work, and the pasta it produces has a pleasingly lively texture and a fresh flavour.

Kneading the dough is the step which gives pasta its liveliness. When the proteins in the flour come into contact with the moisture in the eggs, the long gluten molecules begin to unravel and form an elastic network. Kneading stretches and reorganises them. You can feel tension building in the dough as the elasticity develops.

A wide selection of pasta shapes can be made by hand with no more equipment than a sharp knife and a pastry wheel to cut pinked, zig-zag edges. Sheets of lasagne and ribbons of pasta can be cut to any width. To make bows, cut short wide ribbons with pinked edges and pinch them in the middle. Offcuts can be trimmed into squares and triangles for soup.

Filled pasta offers another range of shapes and endless scope for stuffings.

Egg Pasta

SERVES 4–6

Pasta dough can be made in a food processor or by hand. Rolling it out and cutting it into thin ribbons is simplified by using a pasta-rolling machine which works on the principle of the old-fashioned clothes mangle. It presses the dough between two rotating rollers which are moved progressively closer to squeeze the pasta thinner and thinner. Using a machine ensures pasta of a uniform thickness, though of course it can also be rolled by hand. An Italian pasta rolling pin is longer and thinner than the standard British model and has no handles.

3 large eggs
310g (11oz) unbleached strong white flour

To make pasta dough by hand Beat the eggs lightly. Sift the flour into a mound on a clean work surface. Make a well in the centre and add the eggs. Using one hand to beat the mixture and the other to support the walls of flour until the eggs have been incorporated, work the flour gradually into the eggs to form a stiff dough.

Knead the dough for about 5 minutes until it is smooth and elastic. Wrap it to prevent drying and rest it for about 30 minutes before rolling.

To make pasta dough in a food processor Fix the metal blade in the bowl. Drop in the eggs and process them briefly. With the machine running, add the flour through the feed tube. Continue processing until the dough forms a ball, and then for another minute to knead it. Turn out the dough and wrap it to prevent drying. Rest it for about 30 minutes before rolling.

To roll pasta dough by hand Divide the rested dough into two or three pieces. Cover the dough waiting to be rolled to prevent it drying. Dust the work surface lightly with flour or fine semolina.

Roll and stretch the dough into thin sheets, working quickly and firmly. About 3mm (⅛in) is right for *fettucine* (narrow noodles), but you need it thinner still for *tagliatelle*, which are about 5mm (¼in) wide, or to make sheets of pasta for stuffing.

To roll pasta dough in a pasta machine Take an egg-sized piece of pasta dough (covering the remainder to prevent drying), dust it with flour and work it through the rollers, dusting again with flour as often as necessary. Start with the rollers wide apart and put each piece of dough twice through this setting, folding it double before rolling it the second time. Then work down through progressively finer settings until the pasta is as thin as you need it. The second finest of the six or more settings will roll the dough as thin as is usually required.

To cut pasta ribbons by hand Hand-cut pasta ribbons can be any width you care to make them. Having rolled out a sheet of pasta by hand, dust the top surface with fine semolina to prevent it sticking. Working from one side towards the centre, fold the dough over on itself in a flat, loose roll (see opposite). Now roll in the opposite edge until the two rolls meet in the middle (see opposite). Use a sharp knife to slice through the double roll. To unroll the ribbons, slide a knife under the pasta where the two rolls meet and lift the knife, keeping its blunt edge uppermost (see opposite). The rolled pasta ribbons will unravel on each side of the blade. Allow them to dry for at least 5 minutes before cooking.

To cut pasta ribbons in a machine Set the machine to cut fine or wide as appropriate, and pass the rolled dough through the cutting rollers. Allow the pasta to dry for at least 5 minutes before cooking.

FLAVOURED AND COLOURED PASTA DOUGHS

Home-made pasta can be coloured, and to a lesser extent flavoured, by the addition of strongly pigmented ingredients. Squid ink turns pasta a sinister dark grey, even black. Cooked spinach, squeezed as dry as possible and chopped finely, makes green pasta, and cooked, puréed beetroot will turn it any shade from pale pink to crimson. For orange pasta add tomato purée, and for a rich yellow include saffron. Very finely chopped fresh herbs will give it a speckled, tweedy appearance.

With the exception of saffron, which is mixed with the flour either in powdered or filament form, all the other flavourings are added at the same time as the eggs. If required, a little extra flour can be incorporated at the kneading stage, and when rolling out. Fine ribbons of black pasta are especially good with shrimps, clams and other seafood combinations.

STUFFED FRESH PASTA

Ravioli, tortellini and many more stuffed pastas are easy to make, and the results are such an improvement on anything available outside a good Italian restaurant or a traditional Italian home that once you've tried it you are sure to do it again and again. Highly flavoured game meats and wild mushrooms make excellent fillings for pasta, but traditional recipes use all manner of ingredients from pumpkin to *prosciutto*, sea bass to Swiss chard.

Stuffings should be well-seasoned to offset the blandness of the pasta dough. And because the traditional shapes hold only a small amount, usually a teaspoonful or less, stuffings need to be fine-grained and well mixed. The mild, almost sweet fresh Italian Ricotta cheese is mixed with fresh herbs and a little Parmesan to make a light, summery filling.

Ravioli Stuffed with Ricotta and Herbs

SERVES 4–6

> *1 quantity fresh pasta (see opposite)*
> *110g (4oz) fresh Ricotta cheese*
> *55g (2oz) best Parmesan cheese, freshly grated*
> *2 tablespoons finely chopped fresh basil, sage or parsley*
> *1 egg yolk*
> *Salt and freshly ground black pepper*
> *Freshly grated nutmeg*

Make the pasta but do not roll it out until you are ready to assemble the ravioli. Keep the dough covered.

Mix the Ricotta with the grated Parmesan, chopped herbs and egg yolk. Season the mixture with salt, pepper and a little nutmeg. Roll out the dough finely. Place ½ teaspoonfuls at regular 3.5cm (1¼in) intervals on one sheet of dough (see page 108). Lay the second sheet of dough

CUTTING PASTA RIBBONS BY HAND

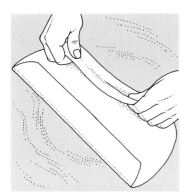

1. Dust the rolled sheet of pasta with fine semolina, then, fold in (or roll) both long sides towards the middle.

2. Cut through both folds or rolls into thin strips as shown.

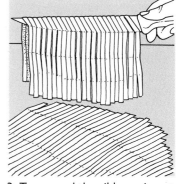

3. To unravel the ribbons, insert a knife where the two edges or rolls meet then lift, blunt edge uppermost.

over the first. Using floured fingers, or a small lump of dough, press the two sheets of pasta together between the blobs of filling.

Use a knife or serrated pastry wheel to cut the pasta into neat squares – each a pillow of dough enclosing a morsel of filling (see overleaf). Place the filled ravioli on a clean cloth dusted with flour or fine semolina and allow them to dry a little before cooking. If they are to be left for more than a few minutes, turn them over from time to time so that the moistness of the filling does not make the underside too soft.

Boil the ravioli for about 5 minutes in plenty of boiling salted water. Drain and serve at once with a little melted butter and a sprinkling of freshly grated Parmesan. The melted butter can be infused with a few leaves of whatever fresh herb you've used in the filling.

To shape tortellini Roll out the dough and use a biscuit cutter to stamp out circles about 7.5cm (3in) in diameter. Put a teaspoon of stuffing in the middle of a circle and moisten the edges with water. Fold over the circle to make a half moon enclosing the stuffing, and pinch the edges closed. Holding the straight edge against your index finger, fold the two ends round it. The seam will turn up like a hat brim. Pinch the two ends together firmly. Dry and cook as for ravioli. (See illustrations below.)

COOKING PASTA

All types of pasta demand extravagant quantities of boiling salted water. The standard allowance for half a kilo of dried spaghetti is 5 litres; that is over a gallon of water for a pound of pasta.

To cook long spaghetti without breaking it, let it 'melt' into the boiling water. The brittle strands soften almost immediately and can be pushed into the pan quite quickly. As soon as all the pasta is immersed, and the water is boiling energetically again, give the pot a stir to make sure none is sticking to the bottom. Other types of pasta are simply dropped into rapidly boiling salted water and cooked until done.

Fresh pasta can take 30 seconds or less to cook once the water has returned to the boil, while dried pasta can take up to 20 minutes. Timing depends on the shape and thickness of the pasta, whether it is fresh or dried, and the ingredients used to make it. Guidance on cooking times for dried pasta is given on the packets. Start testing well before the expected cooking time is up. Fish out a sample (without letting the pot go off the boil) and bite into it. It is ready

Ravioli stuffed with Ricotta and herbs, served with a little melted butter and some freshly grated Parmesan (see page 105).

MAKING TORTELLINI

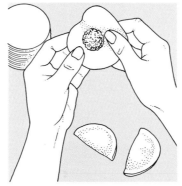

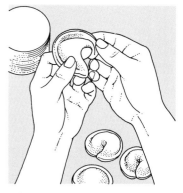

1. Place a teaspoon of filling in the middle of each circle of rolled-out dough. Moisten the edges of the circle with water.

2. Fold over the circle to make a half moon enclosing the stuffing, and pinch the edges closed.

3. Holding the straight edge against your index finger, fold the two edges around it. Pinch the ends together.

when it is soft enough to eat with pleasure but still offers some resistance to the teeth – *al dente* in fact.

Immediately it is ready, drain the pasta – not too thoroughly or it will stick together – and mix it with a sauce.

- Always boil pasta uncovered.
- Do not add oil to the cooking water.
- Do not over-drain cooked pasta.
- Do not rinse cooked pasta.
- Always sauce and serve boiled pasta as quickly as possible.

An alternative method of cooking dried pasta is particularly useful for anyone who has to feed a gas meter or cook on a single ring. Start in the usual way with a large pan of boiling salted water. Add the pasta, let the water return to the boil, then boil for 2 minutes more. Take the pot off the heat, clamp on a tight-fitting lid and leave it to stand for the whole of the cooking time advised on the packet. Drain and serve in the usual way.

HOW MUCH PASTA TO COOK

Deciding how much to cook will depend on whether the pasta dish is to begin the meal, as it usually does in Italy, or whether it is to be the main event. It will also depend, of course, on the appetites of the diners. As a general rule, fresh pasta will absorb twice its weight of water; dried pasta three times.

About 100g (3½oz) of dried pasta is a generous first course serving, or a modest main-course one. An equivalent quantity of freshly made pasta is about 150g, or just over 5oz. For a substantial main course serving, allow about 140g (5oz) dried pasta, or 200g (7oz) fresh.

SAUCING PASTA

Pasta demands no elaborate sauce-making skills. A spoonful or two of extra virgin olive oil or good butter to lubricate it, and a little something for flavour, are all it needs. New season's garlic, finely chopped, freshly grated Parmesan cheese, chopped fresh herbs, or in early winter a few shavings of fresh white Italian truffle, are as good or better than more laborious confections. Olive oil scented with truffles, or with *porcini* – the mushrooms called *Boletus edulis* in field guides – can now be found in some supermarkets as well as in Italian grocers.

Sauces made with fresh or tinned tomatoes, basil-scented *pesto*, and *ragù bolognaise* made with minced beef, chicken livers and tomato are perennially popular choices. Italian cookery books have recipes for pasta with seasonal vegetables, including courgettes, cauliflower, peas, and many more.

Taste is the most important consideration in saucing pasta. Matching texture to the pasta shape's sauce-holding capacity repays some thought too. As a rule, spiral, ruffled and twiddly

MAKING RAVIOLI

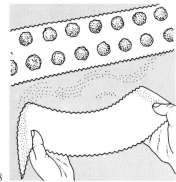

1. Place teaspoonfuls of filling at regular intervals on one sheet of dough, then lay the second sheet over the first.
2. Press the two sheets together with your fingers between the blobs of filling, then cut with a knife – or use a pastry wheel as here – into neat squares.

shapes are best able to hold tomato and thin sauces. Shells and pasta shapes such as *rigatoni* and big macaroni are good for catching meat and seafood sauces with larger pieces of meat or fish in them. When mixing vegetables with pasta, think about cutting the vegetables in pieces which will match the size of the cooked pasta as in, say, *penne* with slivers of cooked red peppers.

Baked pasta dishes such as *cannelloni* and *lasagne* are usually made with fillings of meat and tomato, or spinach and Ricotta layered with béchamel sauce, topped with cheese and baked until golden.

Pesto

SERVES 6–8

85g (3oz) fresh basil leaves
2 cloves garlic, peeled and crushed
30g (1oz) pine kernels
1 teaspoon salt
55g (2oz) Parmesan cheese, freshly grated
30g (1oz) Pecorino cheese, freshly grated
8 tablespoons olive oil
30g (1oz) butter, softened

To make pesto traditionally in a mortar, put the basil leaves, garlic, pine kernels and salt in the mortar and grind them to a smooth paste. Add the cheeses and incorporate them into the basil mixture, then transfer the paste to a larger bowl and beat in the oil and butter.

To make pesto in a blender or food processor, put all the ingredients except the cheeses into the machine and process them until smooth. Add the cheeses and process again briefly, or beat in the cheeses by hand for a coarser texture.

Spaghetti alla Carbonara

SERVES 4–6
Spaghetti alla carbonara is one of the ways bacon and eggs are eaten in Italy and this recipe does not include cream as it sometimes does in Anglo-Italian restaurants.

225g (8oz) pancetta or streaky bacon, in 1
thick slice
4 cloves garlic, peeled
2 tablespoons olive oil
30g (1oz) butter
4 tablespoons dry white wine
salt and freshly ground black pepper
450g (1lb) spaghetti
3 large eggs
85g (3oz) Parmesan cheese, freshly grated
3 tablespoons finely chopped parsley

Chop the *pancetta* or bacon into sticks or dice, and bruise the garlic with the flat of a knife. Heat the oil and butter together in a small saucepan and add the *pancetta* or bacon and garlic. Cook them together until both are golden, then add the wine. Boil until the wine is well reduced, then discard the garlic. Keep warm.

Cook the spaghetti, uncovered, in plenty of boiling salted water and drain it as soon as it is tender but still has a little bite.

Meanwhile, break the eggs into a warmed serving bowl. Add the cheese and parsley and a generous sprinkling of freshly ground black pepper. Beat lightly together. Add the hot spaghetti and toss it in the egg mixture until it is well coated. The eggs form an instantly creamy sauce and need no further cooking. Add the *pancetta* or bacon with its fat and toss the spaghetti again to mix the ingredients. Serve immediately.

The Cooking of Italy

by VALENTINA HARRIS

Italian food? In a sense there is no such thing. Italy is far too staunchly separatist and proud of its regional differences for there to be anything you could describe – yet – as a national cuisine.

Valentina Harris, food writer and broadcaster

Flavours, ingredients, colours and textures vary almost from village to village, from one end of the country to the other.

Wherever he or she comes from, the skill of the Italian cook is based on family tradition and local availability of ingredients rather than the teachings of gastronomic luminaries. Italy has developed at a tremendous pace over the last fifty years or so, yet few have forgotten the hardship which parts of the country were suffering right up until the 1950s. Hunger, disease and an almost complete lack of communication are still fresh in the memory, which is what makes Italy's vast culinary heritage so precious and so interesting.

Inevitably, things are changing. The developing motorway network, rail, sea and air links mean that food can be moved around with a speed and efficiency previously unthinkable. As the ingredients are transported from region to region, so the recipes, the styles, the specialities and the traditions are swapped and personalised. Eventually there *will* be something like 'Italian food' in a much broader sense: already the regional boundaries are beginning to blur.

Yet I still believe it is important to recognise that the food of Lombardy is light years away from the food of Campania, and that the desserts of Rome have almost nothing in common with the cakes of the Veneto.

On the other hand it is just as important to remember that this vast cornucopia of specialities has common threads that bind it all together. However different a finished dish may be, it is more than likely to contain ingredients common to thousands of others. Pasta, for example, is eaten all over Italy. But it is very different in Piemonte, say, where they eat very fine, sophisticated *tajarin* (ribbons), from what it is in Basilicata, where they prefer stodgy, thick *cavatielli* (hand-made shells). Olive oil is produced as far north as Lake Como and as far south as Sicily, yet the north has traditionally preferred to cook with butter. Only since olive oil has been proved healthier are the cholesterol-conscious northern industrialists and bankers turning to the golden elixir of the south.

In very broad terms, the cuisine of the south is what one would think of as typically Mediterranean. The emphasis is on pasta dishes with vegetables; vegetables in their own right, cooked in a myriad ways or preserved in olive oil or sun-dried; olive oil used in everything from salad to cakes; fresh fish and/or *baccala* and *stoccafisso* (dried salt cod and stockfish); fresh fruit, pulses, bread and a limited number of dairy products. In the north, by contrast, meat reigns supreme – along with a vast array of dairy products, polenta, risotto, creamy sauces and cakes.

The most important factor in all this is climate. In the north the weather is colder, wetter and damper, providing ample pasture for large herds of cattle. The south has scorching heat and is so arid that only a small range of crops will grow.

Central Italian cooking tends to combine the best of what the north and south have to offer. The climate, being generally more temperate, yields an enormous range of specialities that are not as rich as northern cuisine, nor yet as spartan as the food of the south. The islands of Sicily and Sardinia are quite different again.

For all the differences, however, cooking throughout Italy depends on some very simple rules: take the very best, freshest ingredients available and cook them as simply as possible, but with plenty of imagination, flair and love. It is a very *emotional* cuisine, but no less serious for that. Probably the most obvious example is pasta itself. What other nation in the world has

Risotto con Gambaretti (risotto with prawns)

ever put flour and water together so lovingly to make something which is so pretty to look at, so delicious and so versatile?

When I last researched the subject of pasta manufacturing, there were no fewer than 652 different shapes available on the market. The idea of Italian *mammas* spending hours and hours rolling out huge sheets of handmade pasta is becoming more of a myth as each new generation of Italian *mammas* comes along. If the truth be known, Italians eat far more factory-made, dried durum wheat pasta than fresh pasta. Fresh pasta is either bought at a specialist shop or

made at home in honour of a special occasion.

The other famous Italian first course is risotto – a dish whose traditions are strictly embedded in the north. The reason for this is simple enough: only in the north is there enough rain for rice to be grown in paddy fields. Contrary to what many people seem to think, making risotto does not mean simply throwing a few leftover vegetables and bits of cooked chicken into some boiled rice. Risotto is an art form, and should be respected as such.

In Britain now it is a pleasure to see how the new style of Italian cuisine is gradually replacing 111 what has been fondly called 'Britalian' cookery. When the first Italian restaurants opened here, they simply cooked to fulfil the demands of their somewhat unadventurous patrons. A decade or so ago, for a restaurant to qualify as Italian it simply had to serve lasagne, cannelloni, a spurious version of *spaghetti* Bolognese, a strange concoction called *pollo sorpresa* and a few other bland and uninteresting dishes which bore little resemblance to the native originals.

The new generation of chefs worldwide has taken up the cause of Italian food with a passion. It is tremendously exciting to see how Italian cuisine has taken off all over the globe, proving again and again just how innovative and imaginative it can be when lovingly prepared. The new Italian cuisine observes all the same rules as the old, yet the new recipes have a particular style about them, making use of techniques that are not necessarily part of the Italian tradition, and introducing a whole new range of flavourings and ingredients that are not indigenous to the home country. This makes them no less Italian than the classics, and paves the way for yet more expansion and development in the future. As long as the finished dish is palatable, looks attractive and is essentially worth repeating, there is no reason to shun it for not being altogether 'authentic'. For example, chargrilled squid dressed with pesto sauce may not be traditional, but it is delicious.

Alongside this innovative thrust, Italian chefs and home cooks are also rediscovering their ancient recipes and are bringing them up to date – cooking them with renewed enthusiasm in case they should be swamped in the tide of frozen pizza. There is a protective spirit in Italian cooking which is enormously inspiring, and which keeps alive one of the most vital strands of the national culture.

There are too many 'typical' Italian ingredients to consider them all in detail, but here are some of the most important.

SAUSAGES AND PRESERVED MEATS

These include sausages, *salame*, *prosciutto*, and various other specialities such as Mortadella, *coppa*, *bresaola*, *guanciale* and *pancetta*.

Italian sausages tend to have a very coarse texture which becomes quite crumbly when cooked, and a very strong peppery flavour. They are made all over the country in various guises. One of the best-known varieties is the *Lucanica*, *Luganeghe* or *Luganega* sausage, which is made in a continuous coil, and can be boiled or grilled.

Other sausages made from pork include *zampone di Modena*, a boned pig's trotter stuffed with pork, normally cooked to celebrate New Year's Eve and served hot with lentils. *Cotechino* is a very rich, thick pork sausage for boiling, also served on New Year's Eve with lentils. (The lentils represent the gold coins you'll earn in the coming year – the more you eat, the richer you'll become.)

The largest of all the cured meats is Mortadella. Made entirely from pork it tends to be quite fatty. It is pale pink, with large white spots of fat and a fairly bland flavour. Some of the more interesting varieties have slivers of pistachio nuts and/or whole peppercorns added.

Prosciutto is simply the Italian name for ham, and it covers cooked as well as cured (raw) ham – frequently miscalled Parma ham. The reason for this common mistake is that the valley of Langhirano, near Parma, is the best place in Italy for making perfect cured ham, known simply as *prosciutto crudo*. The climatic conditions here are unique, with gentle air currents running through the valley from one end to the other and keeping the raw hams in peak condition as they are cured.

Although the very best comes from the Langhirano valley, *prosciutto crudo* is also made very successfully in other parts of the country. The only other cured hams which merit a special prefix are *prosciutto San Daniele*, from the village of the same name in Friuli-Venezia-Giulia, and *prosciutto di Carpegna* from further south, in the Marche.

Coppa is rather like poor man's *prosciutto crudo* in that it contains various offcuts such as shoulder, collar, skin etc., which are compressed into a knobbly shape and sliced thinly in the same way as cured ham. The meat tends to be quite dark in colour and streaked with fat. It has a much stronger flavour than *prosciutto crudo*.

Guanciale and *pancetta* are two versions of Italian bacon. They are fattier and much more highly flavoured than English bacon and are used principally as ingredients in recipes. *Guanciale* is made from pig's cheek; *pancetta* from the belly.

Salami is the name given to various cured sausages that are thinly sliced and served cold, normally as part of an antipasto. There are many different varieties, the most popular being *salame Milano*, which is fairly bland and relatively lean. *Salame Napoletano* contains a little chilli and is therefore reddish in colour and more spicy in flavour. *Salame cacciatorino* is small and stubby but quite similar to *Milano* in flavour. *Salame felino* is the most narrow of them all, with a lovely spicy, meaty flavour, and *finocchiona* is a *salame* made with fennel seeds.

Good *salame* needs to be gently squeezed and smelled in order to decide if it is a good buy or not. It should give slightly under the fingers, must never be hard, but not soft like a sausage either. It must smell sweet and meaty, never musty or sour.

The one preserved meat not made out of pork is *bresaola*, which comes from Lombardy. This delicious and very special meat is air-dried fillet of beef. It is served very thinly sliced with a sheen of extra virgin olive oil, a squeeze of lemon and a dusting of freshly milled black pepper.

CHEESE

A great many cheeses are made throughout Italy – far too many to do more here than introduce a few of the most important. I hope that sampling and enjoying these will encourage you to explore the subject further.

Parmigiano Reggiano and *Grana Padano* are both hard grating cheeses that are essential to many pasta recipes, risottos and other dishes. *Parmigiano Reggiano*, as the name suggests, comes from the Parma area of Reggio-Emilia. *Grana Padano*, from the Po valley, is generally not considered to be as good as *Parmigiano*, but is very similar. Both cheeses are excellent when eaten on their own or with fruit, vegetables or nuts, especially when they are young and moist. As the cheeses age they become drier and harder, with a much stronger flavour.

Mozzarella came originally from Campania, though it is now produced in several other parts of the country. It is a pure white, springy cheese which becomes delightfully stringy in cooking. The best variety is made from the milk of the water buffalo and is called *Mozzarella di Bufala*. Until recently the buffalo variety

Cooking throughout Italy depends on some very simple rules: take the very best, freshest ingredients available and cook them as simply as possible, but with plenty of imagination, flair and love. It is a very emotional cuisine, but no less serious for that.

was almost impossible to find, but renewed interest from all over the world has meant a great resurgence in production. *Mozzarella di Bufala* is more difficult to make because the buffaloes have a much lower milk yield than cows, and tend to be more awkward to keep. This makes it more expensive than the cow's milk version, although certainly worthwhile. Buffalo *Mozzarella* tastes less bland than cow's milk *Mozzarella*; both varieties can be smoked, but *Bufala* is really too good to smoke.

Ricotta is a soft, crumbly, creamy cheese made from whey, which is used a great deal in cooking, not only for savoury dishes but also in cakes and pas-

tries. The name means 're-cooked' – a reference to the manufacturing process.

Pecorino is the name given to various ewe's milk cheeses which vary in texture from relatively soft varieties to hard grating cheeses.

Provolone comes in large 45cm (18in) sausage, pear and cone shapes and can be bought in two forms: *dolce* and *piccante*. *Dolce* is made with calf's rennet. It is not actually sweet, as its name suggests, but blander and smoother in flavour. *Piccante*, made with kid's rennet, is spicier, sharper, and has a much stronger smell and flavour.

Gorgonzola is an Italian cheese that almost everybody knows – a salty, very full flavoured blue cheese with a deliciously gooey texture which is usually eaten with bread rather than used in cooking. *Dolcelatte* is similar, though it is considerably milder in flavour.

Mascarpone is more like clotted cream than cheese. Thick, white and stiff enough to hold its peaks, this is the vital ingredient of that most moreish of all Italian puddings, Tiramisú. It also makes delicious pasta sauces, and is the most wonderful partner for ripe, juicy pears.

TOMATOES

Although it is untrue, as I've heard it said, that 'all Italian food is smothered in tomato sauce', tomatoes are certainly used a great deal in Italian cookery. As succulently fresh, sun-ripened Italian tomatoes are not available in Britain – and I can't think of a way they ever could be – one has to rely on the canned or bottled varieties.

The most basic is the canned plum tomato, which can be bought whole or chopped. 113

Tomato purée is available in cans, tubes (like toothpaste) or jars. This is a product to be used very sparingly: it is highly concentrated. *Passata* is a marvellously useful product available in wide-necked bottles or cartons. It consists of canned tomatoes which have been sieved to make a smooth pulp. You can buy it completely seedless or in a slightly coarser version with some seeds and lumps left in.

OLIVE OIL

Olive oil has been a major cooking ingredient all around the Mediterranean for literally thousands of years. It can now safely be said that the whole of Italy has embraced olive oil with a fervent passion. Olives which produce a dense and fruity oil grow profusely all over the south. In the north the groves are sparser and fewer, and the oil has a lighter texture and milder flavour. Tuscan and Ligurian oil are both justly famous for their excellence.

On the question of extra virgin and virgin olive oil there is not very much to say except that the one with the least acidity is the most highly prized. Extra virgin will have less acidity than virgin and will be oil from the first pressing. The second pressing – the virgin oil – has a slightly higher acidity level. The third (and sometimes fourth) pressing is called simply olive oil without any kind of virginal prefix.

Olive oils differ quite widely, depending upon the quality and variety of the olives used, and which part of Italy the oil comes from. I think the wisest thing to do is to have two or three different bottles on the go at the same

Scaloppine con Limone e Capperi (veal escalopes with lemon and capers)

Budino di Ricotta (Ricotta pudding)

time. In this way you can have a really fruity, rich oil for salads, a milder oil for adding to sauces, and a very fine olive oil for certain cooking techniques such as shallow-frying. Save the strongest flavoured oil as a partner for things that are very bland – lettuce, bread, boiled rice, plain boiled pasta.

BREAD

Bread is a tremendously important part of the Italian way of eating. Nobody would dream of sitting down to a meal without a basket of bread with which to dip, mop up or otherwise nibble. The type of bread varies widely from region to region.

Bread is also important not just in its own right, but as an ingredient in other dishes. For example, in southern Italy breadcrumbs are lightly fried in oil and sprinkled over pasta in lieu of grated cheese. All over the country, bread is often the basic ingredient for many different kinds of soup. Originally, as the soup would represent the only meal which an Italian peasant was likely to eat all day, the bread made the soup more satisfying and nourishing.

Many different kinds of Italian bread are available in the UK now, the most popular of which must be the lovely light *ciabatta*. The name translates as 'slipper', which is what it looks like. It has lots of holes, which makes it so light, but has a nice chewy crust in contrast. Made with olive oil and seasoned with salt, it has plenty of flavour as well as tex- 115 ture. Other varieties of bread widely available here include *focaccia*, flat pizza dough baked with no topping except for a generous smearing of olive oil and plenty of rock salt; olive bread, a soft thick bread baked with olives kneaded into the dough; and, by complete contrast, *grissini*, long, thin and very crisp bread sticks.

Bruschetta and *crostini* are two snacks or antipasti which have their origins in Italy but which have become popular in the UK. They are nothing more than slices of bread such as ciabatta covered with a topping and served as open sandwiches. The topping can be as simple as a sliced fresh tomato coated in olive oil and fresh basil, or as complicated as finely chopped cooked chicken livers, mashed into a hot paste with olive oil, herbs, capers and seasonings.

PASTA

What more can I say? Only to reiterate, perhaps, that there is a tremendous difference between fresh pasta and dried durum wheat pasta. The former is richer, more filling and nourishing. It cooks very quickly and tends to be saved for special occasions. The latter is more for everyday use and generally speaking takes longer to cook.

The relationship between the shape of pasta and the sauce that goes with it is very important. Generally speaking, more delicate pasta sauces are better suited to delicate shapes, whereas sturdy, chunky sauces – with or without meat – are better with thick, chubby shapes. Largely it is a matter of practice. You will soon discover what works well and what does not, but do remember that the shape of the pasta is designed to hold more or less sauce, and to suit the texture of the sauce in the best possible way. Some marriages of shape/sauce are instantly destined for divorce!

RICE AND RISOTTO

You can't get away from it: risotto will take you 20–30 minutes to make, and you will need the right sort of rice to do it properly – a plump Italian variety such as Arborio, Nano Fino or Carnaroli. No other rice can absorb so much liquid without becoming too soft: the 'bite' at the heart of each grain of rice is what produces the distinctive risotto texture. The other vital ingredient for risotto is stock. No matter whether it's chicken, meat, vegetable or fish, to be good enough for risotto it has to be good enough to eat on its own. The relationship between the stock and the kind of risotto you are planning must be carefully considered as well. For example, a risotto containing a very strong tasting vegetable such as artichoke can be made very well with vegetable stock, while a more delicate risotto – asparagus, say – is best made with chicken stock.

Add to all this a very finely chopped onion (or in some cases garlic), a little butter and, sometimes, freshly grated Parmesan cheese.

PESTO

This magically green sauce is currently very fashionable in Britain. In Liguria where it comes from, pesto is much more than a sauce, it is a religion. In its simplest form it is fresh basil pounded in a mortar with grated Parmesan, olive oil, pine kernels, garlic, salt and pepper. In Liguria, however, purists will insist that pesto can be made only when the plant is flowering, and that cubed potatoes must be boiled with the pasta and served as part of the dish. In this way, any excess oil from the pesto will be absorbed by the hot potatoes and the pasta will get the full benefit of the pesto itself. Many Ligurian cooks like to add curd cheese to the pesto. Some prefer to make it with walnuts rather than pine kernels, and many like to add slivers of *pancetta* to the finished dish.

POLENTA

Polenta is finely or coarsely ground maize, a type of cornmeal.

Classic polenta takes between 40 and 50 minutes to cook from start to finish, but the quick-cook variety takes only 5 minutes. In Italy it is normally eaten as a basic carbohydrate alongside a casserole or stew of some sort. Polenta can also be allowed to cool and set, then sliced and grilled or fried, or layered in an ovenproof dish with Mozzarella and tomatoes rather like lasagne.

GNOCCHI

Gnocchi is the name given to pasta shapes, but actually the word means 'lumps', which is a far better description of what they are – dumplings.

Gnocchi need to be made with great care so that they do not end up being heavy. Spinach *gnocchi* are made by lightly blending finely chopped spinach with Ricotta, Parmesan and egg. Pumpkin *gnocchi* are made by blending puréed pumpkin with breadcrumbs, Parmesan, egg and a little flour. Potato *gnocchi* are much smaller and are made by mixing together mashed floury potatoes, salt and a little flour.

The dough is rolled into a long cylinder and cut into small

116

sections about the size of a walnut (or cherry for potato *gnocchi*). Each section is rolled across the back of a fork or cheese grater to give it indentations: this allows as much sauce as possible to cling to it. The *gnocchi* are cooked in salted boiling water: when they bob up to the surface they are ready to scoop out into hot bowls.

MENU I
SERVES 4
Polenta con Gorgonzola
Risotto con Gambaretti
Scaloppina con Limone e
    Capperi, con Peperoni in
    Padella
Budino di Ricotta

Polenta con Gorgonzola (Polenta with Gorgonzola)

255g (9oz) easy-cook polenta
    (you can use the classical
    type if you prefer)
1 litre (1¾ pints) cold water
Salt and freshly ground black
    pepper
200g (7oz) Gorgonzola cheese,
    thinly sliced

Bring the water to the boil and rain the polenta flour into the water, stirring constantly. Add a pinch of salt and keep stirring. With easy-cook polenta you will need to stir for only about 5 minutes. The classic type takes up to 45 minutes to cook properly. Stir until the polenta is solid and comes away easily from the sides of the pan, then turn it out on to a board, smooth out and leave to cool. When it is cold, slice it thinly and place under a medium-hot grill. When the slices are lightly browned, turn them over and cover with Gorgonzola. Return

to the grill and allow to heat through until the cheese is just running. Transfer to a platter, sprinkle with freshly ground black pepper and serve at once.

Risotto con Gambaretti (Risotto with prawns)

450g (1lb) risotto rice
90g (3¼oz) unsalted butter
1 onion, finely chopped
175ml (6fl oz) dry white wine
Approx. 1.5 litres (2½ pints) fish
    or vegetable stock, hot
450g (1lb) fresh raw prawns,
    peeled (raw are preferable,
    but cooked will do at a
    pinch)
Salt and freshly ground black
    pepper
3 tablespoons chopped fresh
    parsley

Melt the butter in a large pan and fry the onion lightly until just soft and blond but not browned. Tip in all the rice and stir it around until coated in butter and onion and lightly toasted. The rice must be incredibly hot when you move to the next step – adding the wine. When you pour this in, it must sizzle audibly and make a lovely steamy hiss. Stir until all the wine has been completely absorbed.

Begin to add the hot stock – *only one ladleful at a time*. Stir after each addition of liquid, and keep stirring. After about 10 minutes add the prawns. Keep stirring and adding liquid until the grains are soft and plump but still with a little bite in the centre (*al dente*). You can make the risotto as dry or as wet as you like. Take off the heat and stir in salt and pepper to taste. Then stir in the parsley and cover. Leave to stand for 3

minutes, then transfer to a platter and serve.

Scaloppina con Limone e Capperi (Veal escalope with lemon and capers)

4 veal escalopes, about 750g
    (1¾lb) total weight, trimmed
    and beaten flat
2 tablespoons plain white flour
30g (1oz) unsalted butter
Juice of 1 lemon
Salt and ground black pepper
90ml (3fl oz) dry white wine
55g (2oz) capers, rinsed, dried
    and coarsely chopped
½ lemon, sliced

Dust the meat lightly on both sides with the flour. Melt the butter in a heavy frying pan and fry the meat quickly for 2 minutes on each side. Add the lemon juice and turn the escalopes over in the butter and juice to flavour them thoroughly. Add the wine and allow to evaporate for about 1 minute. Season the meat and take it out; put it aside on a platter to keep warm. Add the capers to the pan and stir everything together very thoroughly. Pour the hot capers over the meat and serve at once, garnished with slices of lemon.

Peperoni in Padella (Pan-fried peppers)

4 medium peppers (preferably
    yellow and red)
1 onion, chopped
2 cloves garlic, chopped
4 tablespoons olive oil
1 tablespoon tomato purée,
    diluted in 4 tablespoons
    warm water
Salt and ground black pepper
5 leaves fresh basil, torn

117

Bring a large pot of salted water to the boil. Drop the peppers in and allow them to soak for about 1 minute. Take them out of the water and quickly peel off the outer skin while they are still hot. Make it easier by holding them in a cloth and using a sharp, small knife. Cut the peeled peppers in half, remove all the seeds and membranes and cut them into thick strips.

Put the onion, garlic and olive oil into a deep frying pan. Fry until the onion is soft, about 7 minutes, then add the pepper strips and stir together thoroughly. Pour on the diluted tomato purée and cover. Leave to simmer, stirring occasionally, for about 20–30 minutes, or until the peppers are tender. Season with salt and pepper to taste, and stir in the fresh basil. Serve at once or leave to cool and serve lightly chilled.

Budino di Ricotta (Ricotta pudding)

500g (1lb 2oz) fresh Ricotta
½ tablespoon plain white flour
5 eggs, separated
140g (5oz) caster sugar
60g (2¼oz) mixed candied peel, chopped
1 large pinch ground cinnamon
Grated zest of 1 lemon
2 tablespoons brandy
Butter for greasing
Flour for dusting

Push the Ricotta through a sieve into a bowl, then add the flour, 5 egg yolks and 2 egg whites, 75g (3oz) of the sugar, the candied peel, the cinnamon and lemon zest. Mix all this together very thoroughly and add the brandy. When you have a well-amalgamated mass, preheat the oven to 180°C/350°F, gas mark

4. Whisk the remaining egg whites until stiff and then fold them into the mixture. Butter and dust with flour a 750g (1¾lb) mould and pour in the mixture. Bake in the oven for 30 minutes, then remove and allow to rest for 5 minutes before turning out on to a platter (or serve from the bowl). Dust with the remaining sugar and serve.

MENU 2
SERVES 4
Caponatina
Penne con le Noci e il Mascarpone
Pesce al Forno, con Carciofi alla Romana
Tiramisú

Caponatina (Warm aubergine and olive salad)

1kg (2lb 3oz) aubergine, cubed
100ml (3½fl oz) olive oil
40g (1½oz) onion, chopped
255g (9oz) assorted pickles such as gherkins, peppers, carrots etc.
30g (1oz) capers, rinsed and dried
6 celery leaves, rinsed and dried
55g (2oz) stoned green olives
30g (1oz) stoned black olives
1 tablespoon granulated sugar
150ml (¼ pint) red wine vinegar or half-and-half wine vinegar and red wine
2 tablespoons pine kernels

Cover the cubed aubergines with salt, put them in a colander in the sink and leave them to drain out their bitter juices for 1 hour – longer if possible. Then wash and dry them thoroughly.

Divide the oil between two deep frying pans and fry the aubergine cubes in one pan. In

the other pan fry the onion, pickles, capers, celery leaves and olives for about 15 minutes. When the aubergines are soft and well coloured, remove them from the oil and let them drain on kitchen paper. Add the sugar and vinegar to the onion mixture, cook until the fumes of the vinegar disappear – a few seconds only – and then stir in the aubergine and pine kernels. Serve warm or cold on slices of toasted *ciabatta* bread rubbed lightly with a peeled clove of garlic and coated generously in olive oil.

Penne con Noci e il Mascarpone (Penne with walnuts and Mascarpone)

40g (1½oz) butter
110g (4oz) Mascarpone cheese
400g (14oz) penne
Salt and freshly ground black pepper
15 walnuts, shelled, peeled and coarsely chopped
85g (3oz) Parmesan cheese, freshly grated

Put a large pot of salted water on to boil. Melt the butter in a small saucepan. Mash the Mascarpone to make it smooth. Toss the pasta into the boiling water, stir and return to the boil. Cook until tender. Drain carefully and return to the pot. Pour over the melted butter and toss together thoroughly, then add the Mascarpone and the walnuts and toss again. Season with a little salt and pepper, and add half the Parmesan cheese. Toss together again, and transfer to a warmed serving dish. Sprinkle with the remaining Parmesan cheese – use a little extra if you like – and serve at once.

Pesce al Forno (Baked fish)

*Approx. 1.35kg (3lb) whole
white-fleshed firm fish – eg
grey mullet or bass*
*6 anchovy fillets, washed, dried
and finely chopped*
90ml (3fl oz) olive oil
2 cloves garlic, chopped
*2 tablespoons chopped fresh
parsley*
*½ tablespoon chopped fresh
rosemary*
*Salt and freshly ground black
pepper*
*150–300ml (¼–½ pint) dry white
wine*

Gut and wash the fish carefully
and, if necessary, remove the
coarser scales. Mix the anchovy
with half the olive oil and the
garlic, parsley and rosemary,
until the anchovies begin to
dissolve into a creamy dressing.
Season this with salt and pepper
and thoroughly smear the fish
with it inside and out. Oil an
ovenproof dish large enough to
take the fish with the remaining
oil. Preheat the oven to
160°C/325°F, gas mark 3. Lay the
fish in the ovenproof dish and
sprinkle liberally with about half
the white wine. Bake the fish for
about 1 hour, sprinkling
frequently with white wine to
prevent it from drying out. Serve
as soon as the fish is tender and
cooked through.

Carciofi alla Romana (Artichokes with mint and garlic)

*12 globe artichokes, prepared
for cooking*
5 cloves garlic
6 sprigs fresh mint
*2 heaped tablespoons fresh
breadcrumbs*
175ml (6fl oz) olive oil
Salt and ground black pepper

Wear rubber gloves to prevent
the skin on your hands going
black as you prepare the
artichokes. Be completely
ruthless about stripping off as
many of the hard exterior leaves
as you can, right down to the
tender, pale green interior. Cut
the top off so that you have a flat
surface and no sharp points
anywhere. Pull open the
remaining leaves to expose the
hairy choke inside. Scoop this
out with a teaspoon, a sharp
knife or with your fingers. Peel
the stalk carefully and cut off any
section that seems woody and
hard. The artichoke should now
look like a chunky flower. Drop
into cold water with lemon juice
to keep them fresh and
unblackened until you need to
cook.

Chop together the garlic and
mint, and mix these with the
breadcrumbs, a little of the oil,
and salt and pepper. Insert a
little of this mixture inside each
of the artichokes, in the space
from which the choke has been
removed. Arrange the artichokes
upright in an oiled, ovenproof
dish. Pour a little water into the
dish to keep them moist and
sprinkle with the remaining oil.
Any leftover filling can also be
scattered around the artichokes.
Cover very loosely with foil and
bake for 1 hour in a moderate
oven – 190°C/375°F, gas mark 5
– basting frequently. Serve hot
or cold.

Tiramisú

*255g (9oz) Mascarpone or very
rich cream cheese*
4 eggs, separated
4 tablespoons caster sugar
*100ml (3½fl oz) strong espresso
coffee*
*110g (4oz) best bitter chocolate,
broken into small pieces*
8 tablespoons weak coffee
*5 tablespoons rum, brandy or
Tia Maria, or other liqueur of
your choice (Amaretto is
delicious)*
*About 20 boudoir biscuits or
Savoiardi (large light spongy
biscuits from Piedmont)*
*2 tablespoons each of cocoa
powder and instant coffee*
4 amaretti biscuits, crumbled

Whisk the cheese until soft and
manageable. Beat the egg yolks
until pale, then whisk them into
the cheese. Add the sugar
gradually to the cheese and egg
yolk mixture, stirring and
whisking constantly. Pour in the
strong espresso coffee and mix
thoroughly. Beat the egg whites
until very stiff, then fold them
into the egg mixture. Mix the
broken chocolate gently into the
mixture. Mix the weak coffee
and the alcohol together. Dip
the biscuits in the liquid one at a
time and line the bottom of a
dish with them. (This should be
about 15cm/6in deep, and 20cm/
8in across; or make individual
tiramisús.) Pour in half the cheese
mixture. Dip more biscuits in the
liquid and cover the cream layer
with soaked biscuits. Pour over
the remaining cream. Bang the
dish down lightly to settle the
layers. Using a sieve, dust with
the cocoa powder mixed with
the instant coffee, then sprinkle
with the crumbled amaretti and
chill until required, at least 3
hours. Best if made a day ahead. 119

CHAPTER 11

CAKES AND BISCUITS

Cakes are certainly not one of life's essentials. Their reputation is frivolous, but their reasons exactly calculated. Sweet nothings are the product of attention to detail, right down to the correct size of baking tin. Reliable recipes are the cornerstones of successful cake-making.

There are four traditional methods, each applicable to a different style of cake. Whisked mixtures based on eggs are used to make the lightest of fatless sponges. Creamed mixtures of fat and sugar are the basis of a range of cakes from buttery Victoria sponges to fruit-laden Christmas cakes. Less rich everyday fruit cakes are made by rubbing the fat into the flour. And sticky cakes like gingerbread are made by melting together sugar and syrup and adding them to flour mixed with chemical raising agents. Newer methods utilise the speed of machines, and ingredients like soft margarines to achieve results which are comparable with, but slightly different from, traditional recipes.

INGREDIENTS

FLOUR

Plain household flour is the best for cakes and biscuits. It contains less protein than strong bread flour, and when mixed with water produces less gluten. Cake making usually calls for the flour to be folded into a more liquid mixture, and this gentle treatment is designed to minimise gluten development and so produce a tender texture. Strong flour would produce chewier, heavier results.

Recipes dependent on chemical raising agents will specify self-raising flour. Or, if more or less than the standard proportion of raising agent is needed, plain flour and a measure of baking powder is specified.

Wholemeal flour is not ideal for making light cakes, but it can be used successfully, even in sponge recipes formulated to overcome its drawbacks. Use recipes intended to be made with wholemeal flour.

SUGAR

The fine grains of caster sugar make it the best choice for most cakes. More air can be incorporated into whisked and creamed mixtures made with caster sugar than with coarser granulated sugar. Where brown sugar is called for, use the soft varieties, whether light or dark.

EGGS

Adding cold eggs to creamed mixtures invites curdling and some loss of lightness. So make sure eggs are at room temperature before incorporating them. For mixtures which require egg whites to be whisked separately from the yolks, eggs which are fresh but not new-laid are best.

FATS

Butter is the preferred fat for flavour, though margarine (but not whipped spreads, which contain too much water) produces lighter cakes because more air can be beaten into it. Soft margarines can be used for sponge cakes made with the all-in-one processor method. Fats should be at room temperature for cake making.

SALT

Yes, salt is required to balance taste. A little brings out the flavour of the other ingredients, although there may be sufficient in the butter or margarine.

FRUIT, NUTS AND FLAVOURINGS

Beware of ingredients from the back of the store-cupboard. The oil in nuts which have been badly stored or kept overlong may have turned rancid, so taste any batch that may be doubtful. Glacé cherries and candied peel may need to be washed and dried if they have heavy deposits of syrup or crystallised sugar on them. Check spices, especially ground spices which lose their flavour faster. Use real essences in preference to cruder artificial flavourings whenever possible. The weasel word to watch for on labels is 'flavouring'. Note use-by dates on baking powders.

MASTERING THE CRAFT

CAKE TINS

Shiny cake tins look handsome, but tins with dull or black walls are more efficient heat-conductors and are preferable. Various sorts of failure can be caused simply by using a tin which is not matched to the quantity and character of the mixture. Cakes which rise and overflow too small a tin are likely to collapse and fall again. Sandwich tins for sponge cakes should be about 2.5cm (1in) deep. If the tin is too high the sides will cook much faster than the centre, which is shielded from the heat, but the slower-cooking centre will rise for longer, forming a dome which will have to be cut off if the cake is to be decorated.

LINING TINS

Lining cake tins with buttered greaseproof paper or baking parchment is well worthwhile, even when using non-stick tins. Freshly baked cakes are fragile, and one stuck corner or edge is easily broken off. See below and overleaf.

OVENS

Ovens are individuals, and no two seem to behave exactly alike. If you suspect that the indicated temperatures are inaccurate, check them with an oven thermometer hung between the centre and top of the oven, about half-way back. Cakes are usually baked near the centre of a moderate (180°C/350°F, gas mark 4) to moderately hot oven (190°C/375°F, gas mark 5). Large, rich fruit cakes which are baked at lower temperatures are an exception.

Always bake a cake as soon as it is mixed in an oven which has already been heated to the correct temperature. During the early stages of baking, when the cake is still liquid, all the tiny air bubbles beaten into the mixture expand, and, if

LINING A ROUND CAKE TIN

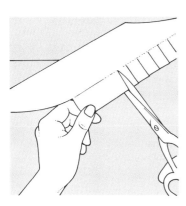

1. Measure height and circumference of tin. Cut a strip of greaseproof longer than the circumference and wider than the depth. Fold over a good 1 cm (½ in) paper lengthwise, then snip to the fold line.

2. Sit tin on doubled greaseproof, and pencil round the bottom. Cut two circles. Place one in greased tin, then the strip, slashed edges folding inwards. Add other circle.

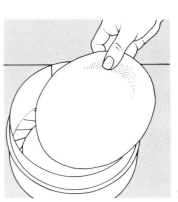

raising agents have been used, new bubbles of gas are formed. As the temperature of the mixture itself increases, so the risen cake begins to set. Proteins in the flour and eggs coagulate and the starch gelatinises. The last stage of baking completes the process and the cake browns and solidifies further.

Ovens with glass doors are a boon to the curious or nervous cook who wants to see what is going on in there. Whether the cake is visible or not, resist the temptation to open the oven door until at least three-quarters of the expected baking time has passed.

TESTING CAKES

Sponges are tested for doneness while still in the oven. They are baked when the tops feel springy to the touch of a fingertip, and the touch leaves no dent. Other types of cake are tested with a warmed skewer. Towards the end of cooking time slip a skewer into the centre of the cake. Draw it out, and if no uncooked cake mixture is sticking to it, the cake is done.

COOLING CAKES

It is at this stage that the trouble you took to line the tin with paper pays off. Sponges should be rested in their tins for a minute or two after they come out of the oven, then turned out of their tins on to a wire drying rack and the base papers peeled off immediately. Leave them to cool completely.

Leave rich fruit cakes to settle in their tins for

an hour or so before turning them out on to a wire rack and leaving them to cool for several hours.

STORING CAKES

Fatless sponges should be eaten the day they are made, or frozen and eaten on the day they are thawed. Victoria sponges are best eaten fresh, but can be stored briefly in a tin, or frozen.

Rich fruit cakes improve with keeping, and mature best wrapped in greaseproof paper and stored in a tin. Two or three months' storage is not too long. Freezing them arrests the maturing process.

WHISKED CAKES

Fatless Sponge

MAKES ONE CAKE

Whisked sponges are the lightest cakes in the cook's repertoire. A filling of soft fruit and whipped cream turns a fresh sponge into a delectable summer pudding or teatime indulgence. Sugar that has had vanilla pods buried in it will scent the cake beautifully.

85g (3oz) plain flour
½ teaspoon baking powder
3 large eggs, separated
85g (3oz) caster sugar

LINING A SQUARE (OR RECTANGULAR) TIN

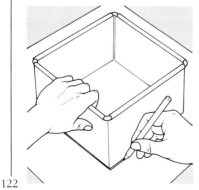

1. Grease the tin, then stand on a large piece of greaseproof paper, at least the size of the tin plus the depth all round. Pencil round the base of the tin. Cut in diagonally from the corners of the paper to the pencilled corners of the tin.
2. Fit paper into the tin, pencilled lines precisely along the base, and overlap at paper corners. Trim if necessary.

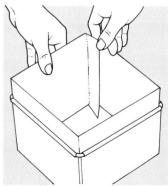

Preheat the oven to moderate (180°C/350°F, gas mark 4) and prepare two 18cm (7in) sandwich tins by greasing them generously and lining the bases.

Sift together the flour and baking powder. Do it to mix and aerate the mixture thoroughly. Combine the egg yolks and sugar in a bowl and whisk until the mixture leaves a trail when dropped from the whisk. It will fall in ribbons which lie on the surface of the mixture for a moment before settling into it. This will take about 10 minutes by hand – less using an electric beater. Using a clean, dry whisk, whip the egg whites until they are stiff, but not dry.

Now use a large metal spoon to combine the ingredients lightly, folding alternate spoonfuls of egg white and flour into the egg yolk mixture.

Divide the mixture equally between the two prepared tins and bake for 20–25 minutes. The sponges are cooked when they feel firm and springy in the centre and have begun to shrink a little from the sides of their tins.

CREAMED CAKES

The alchemy of cake-making is gloriously demonstrated by the judging table of the Victoria sponge section of any summer show or fête. What can happen when one recipe is attempted by a variety of different hands is there for all to see. There will be sponges high and low, pale and golden, moist and dry, all made with the same classic four-ounce mixture.

Victoria Sponge

MAKES ONE CAKE

110g (4oz) butter
110g (4oz) caster sugar
2 large eggs
A few drops vanilla essence
110g (4oz) self-raising flour
½ teaspoon baking powder
2 tablespoons milk or water (if necessary)

Preheat the oven to moderate (180°C/350°F, gas mark 4) and prepare two 18cm (7in) sandwich

WHAT CAN GO WRONG?

- Curdled mixture   Fat and sugar not creamed thoroughly
Eggs too cold
- Collapsed cake   Oven door opened too soon during baking
Tin size inappropriate
- Cake too domed   Oven temperature too low
Tin size inappropriate
- Burned edges   Oven temperature too high
Cake not protected from scorching
- Sinking fruit   Cake mixture too liquid
Pieces of fruit too large
Fruit not dry nor dusted with flour. Flouring helps to keep fruit suspended through fairly plain fruit cakes. Rich fruit cakes are so closely packed with fruit that sinking raisins should not be a problem, provided the mixture is not too wet.

tins by greasing them generously and lining the bases. Begin with all the ingredients at room temperature.

Put the butter in a mixing bowl and beat it until it is pale and light, using a wooden spoon or an electric beater. Add the sugar and continue beating until the mixture is so light and fluffy it drops from the spoon. Break the eggs into a separate bowl and beat them lightly. Add the eggs, a spoonful at a time, to the butter mixture, beating in each addition thoroughly before adding the next. If the mixture shows any inclination to curdle, add a spoonful of the flour and continue

123

beating. Beat in the vanilla essence.

Sift the flour and baking powder together to blend and aerate the mixture well. Then use a large metal spoon to fold the flour, a little at a time, into the creamed mixture. If the mixture is now soft enough to drop easily off a spoon tapped on the side of the bowl, it is ready to bake. If it is a little too dry, add the milk or water.

Divide the mixture equally between the two prepared tins and bake for 25–30 minutes. The sponges are cooked when they feel firm and springy in the centre.

Rich Fruit Cake

Rich fruit cakes have long been symbols of celebration. What would Christmas, birthdays, wed-

FOR THE CAKE	15cm (6in) round or 13cm (5in) square	23cm (9in) round or 20 cm (8in) square	29cm (11in) round or 25cm (10in) square
Currants	170g (6oz)	450g (1lb)	680g (1½lb)
Raisins	110g (4oz)	285g (10oz)	450g (1lb)
Sultanas	110g (4oz)	285g (10 oz)	450g (1lb)
Glacé cherries	55g (2oz)	100g (3½oz)	170g (6oz)
Candied peel	30g (1oz)	40g (1½oz)	55g (2oz)
Brandy	3 tablespoons	4 tablespoons	6 tablespoons
Plain flour	110g (4oz)	285g (10oz)	450g (1lb)
Salt	¼ teaspoon	½ teaspoon	1 teaspoon
Freshly grated nutmeg	¼ teaspoon	½ teaspoon	scant teaspoon
Ground cinnamon	¼ teaspoon	½ teaspoon	scant teaspoon
Unsalted butter	110g (4oz)	285g (10oz)	450g (1lb)
Soft brown sugar	110g (4oz)	285g (10oz)	450g (1lb)
Eggs	2 large	5 large	8 large
Chopped almonds or pecans	40g (1½oz)	75g (2½oz)	110g (4oz)
Molasses or black treacle	1 teaspoon	1 tablespoon	1½ tablespoons
Finely grated lemon zest	½ lemon	1 lemon	2 lemons
Finely grated orange zest	½ orange	1 orange	2 oranges
Baking time	**3½ hours**	**4¾ hours**	**5½ hours**
FOR THE MARZIPAN			
Ground almonds	225g (8oz)	450g (1lb)	680g (1½lb)
Caster sugar	225g (8oz)	450g (1lb)	680g (1½lb)
Brandy	1 tablespoon	2 tablespoons	3 tablespoons
Lemon juice	1 teaspoon	2 teaspoons	1 tablespoon
Almond essence	¼ teaspoon	½ teaspoon	1 teaspoon
Egg yolks	3	5	8
Sieved apricot jam	6 tablespoons	120ml (4fl oz)	175ml (6fl oz)
FOR THE ROYAL ICING			
Icing sugar	450g (1lb)	680g (1½lb)	900g (2lb)
Egg whites	3	4	6

dings and christenings be without them? Make the size to suit the occasion – a single cake for Christmas, two or three tiers for a wedding. If an immaculate icing job is more than you can face, bear in mind that home-made cakes can be professionally decorated for a big occasion.

Use the best quality of dried and candied fruit available. Lusciously flavoured muscatel raisins, stoned of course, are worth searching for. So is the high-grade candied peel sold in big pieces. It is tough stuff to chop, but worth the chore.

To make the cake If you have time, plump up the dried fruit in the brandy overnight. Put the currants, raisins and sultanas in a bowl. Chop the cherries and candied peel and add them to the bowl with the brandy. Cover and leave.

Next day, preheat the oven to cool (140°C/275°F, gas mark 1). Prepare the baking tin by greasing it well and lining the sides and base.

Begin with all the ingredients at room temperature. Sift the flour, salt, nutmeg and cinnamon into a large mixing bowl. In another bowl cream the butter and sugar together until the mixture is pale and fluffy. Beat for at least 10 minutes by hand, or 5 minutes with an electric beater.

Break the eggs into a third bowl and beat them lightly. Beat the eggs into the creamed mixture, a spoonful at a time, beating in each addition thoroughly before adding the next. If the mixture shows any inclination to curdle, add a spoonful of the flour and continue beating. When all the egg has been incorporated, fold in the flour and spices using a large metal spoon. Fold in the soaked fruit and peel, the nuts, molasses, and lemon and orange zest.

Spoon the mixture into the prepared tin and spread the top flat. Bake it below the centre of the oven for the time indicated in the chart. Don't open the oven door until at least three-quarters of the expected baking time is up, and then only to lay a double sheet of greaseproof paper over the top if it appears to be in danger of scorching. Test the cake with a warmed skewer towards the end of the expected baking time.

Cool the cake in its baking tin for at least an hour before turning it on to a wire cooling rack and stripping off the papers. When it is cold, wrap it greaseproof paper and store it in a tin.

Note Feeding rich fruit cakes with a little additional brandy at intervals over several months of storage certainly makes them taste delicious. Be cautious with a wedding cake, however, because an over-indulged cake may stain the icing.

To make the marzipan Mix the almonds and sugar in a bowl before stirring in the brandy, lemon juice, almond essence and egg yolks. Turn out the stiff paste on to a board dusted with icing sugar and knead it into a ball.

Roll out half the marzipan to cover the top of the cake, using the cake tin as a template to cut it out. Roll and cut out two strips for the sides.

Paint the cake with warmed apricot jam and apply the marzipan, pressing it on firmly and smoothing over the joins. The marzipan will need to dry for several days before the cake is iced. Cover it with a clean cloth or paper, and leave it in a cool, dry place.

To ice the cake Make sure that the egg whites are free of yolk and that the bowl, spoon and whisk are free of grease. Put the egg whites in the bowl and stir in the icing sugar a little at a time. When it has all been incorporated, whisk the icing vigorously, for about 15 minutes by hand, or 7 minutes with an electric beater. When it is ready the icing can be pulled up into extravagant but stable peaks. Use it immediately, or cover to keep it from drying and use within half an hour.

Smooth coats of icing as a basis for piped decorations are applied with a palette knife dipped into hot water and shaken almost dry.

Cake boards and supports are required for multi-tiered wedding cakes and these are available, together with advice and tuition, from specialist suppliers.

For Christmas cakes the simplest decoration – icing pulled up into rough peaks with the tip of a knife – is still one of the most effective.

ALL-IN-ONE-SPONGES

Electric whisks and food processors revolutionised cake making and made this all-in-one-method for light cakes a practical proposition. Omitting the usual creaming of the fat and sugar is compensated for by additional raising agent. 125

110g (4oz) self-raising flour
1 teaspoon baking powder
110g (4oz) soft margarine or butter
110g (4oz) caster sugar
2 large eggs
Vanilla essence

Preheat the oven to moderate (160°C/325°F, gas mark 3) and grease two 18cm (7in) sandwich tins and line the bases. Begin with all the ingredients at room temperature. Sift the flour and baking powder into a large bowl or a food processor. Add all the remaining ingredients and whisk or process them together, adding, if needed, a spoonful of water for a dropping consistency.

Divide the cake mixture equally between the prepared tins and bake for about 30 minutes or until the tops feel springy to the touch. Turn on to a cooling rack and strip off the papers.

THE RUBBING-IN METHOD
Substantial cut-and-come-again cakes are quick to make with a rubbed-in mixture of fat and flour. This is the method to use for family fruit cakes which keep for a week or more if they are stored in an airtight tin.

Jasper's Fruit Cake

MAKES ONE LARGE CAKE

When Seville oranges for marmalade-making are in season in January use the zest to flavour this substantial family fruit cake.

450g (1lb) plain flour
½ teaspoon salt
450g (1lb) mixed dried fruits
225g (8oz) butter
400g (14oz) caster sugar
Freshly grated zest of 1 orange
2 large eggs
250ml (8fl oz) milk

Preheat the oven to moderate (180°C/350°F, gas mark 4). Grease and line a deep 23cm (9in) round cake tin. Sift the flour and salt into a large bowl. In another bowl mix the dried fruits with a little of the flour to coat them lightly and keep each piece separate. Cut the butter in dice and add it to the flour mixture. Rub it in until the mixture looks like coarse breadcrumbs. Mix in all but a tablespoon of the sugar, the dried fruits and freshly grated orange zest. Beat together the eggs and milk and add it, all at once, to the dry mixture. Stir to incorporate all the ingredients evenly.

Turn the mixture into the prepared tin, spreading the top with a shallow depression in the centre. Sprinkle with the reserved sugar and bake for 1 hour, then reduce the temperature to cool (150°C/300°F, gas mark 2) and bake for another 1–1½ hours. Leave the cake in its tin for 20 minutes before cooling on a wire rack.

THE MELTING METHOD
When a cake's sweetness is provided by molasses, black treacle or honey, melting the fat and syrup together is the method of choice. A reaction between acids in the molasses or honey and the bicarbonate of soda aerates the mixture with bubbles of carbon dioxide. Eggs provide an additional lift. These moist, slightly sticky cakes, are at their best a few days after they are baked.

Edinburgh Gingerbread

MAKES ONE LARGE CAKE

450 g (1 lb) plain flour
¼ teaspoon salt
1½ teaspoons ground ginger
1½ teaspoons ground cinnamon
1½ teaspoons mixed spice
½ teaspoon ground cloves
225 g (8 oz) stoned dates
110 g (4 oz) shelled walnuts or pecans
225 g (8 oz) butter
340 g (12 oz) molasses or black treacle
200 g (7 oz) dark brown sugar
4 large eggs, beaten
1 teaspoon baking soda (bicarbonate of soda)
A little warm milk

Jasper's fruit cake, a sandwiched ground nut cake, and tuiles (see overleaf).

Preheat the oven to moderate (180°C/350°F, gas mark 4). Grease and line a deep 20 cm (8 in) square baking tin. Sift the flour, salt and spices into a large bowl. Coarsely chop the dates and nuts and add them to the flour.

In a small saucepan melt together on a low heat the butter, molasses or treacle, and sugar. Stir this mixture into the flour, followed by the eggs and the baking soda mixed with a tablespoon of warm milk. Stir just enough to blend the ingredients thoroughly, adding a little more milk if it is needed to make a mixture which will just drop from the spoon. Turn the mixture into the prepared tin and spread the top evenly. Bake for about 20 minutes, then reduce the temperature to cool (150°C/300°F, gas mark 2) and continue baking for another 2 hours, or until a skewer inserted comes out clean.

Cool the gingerbread on a wire rack, then strip off the papers. Store in an airtight tin.

CAKES FOR SPECIAL DIETS

For people who are not allowed to eat some of the usual cake ingredients a home-baked cake that fits in with their dietary restrictions is especially welcome. The recipe for a nut cake is suitable for people on gluten-free diets. Flour is replaced by ground nuts, which make it moist and full of flavour. The second cake, made without sugar, includes one of the newer artificial sweeteners which have no bitter after-taste and should be suitable for most diabetics.

Ground Nut Cake

MAKES ONE CAKE

110 g (4 oz) unsalted butter
140 g (5 oz) caster sugar
Finely grated zest of 1 orange
½ teaspoon salt
3 large eggs, beaten
100g (3½oz) finely ground almonds or
*   hazelnuts*

Preheat the oven to moderate (180°C/350°F, gas mark 4) and prepare a 20 cm (8 in) round sponge tin by greasing it well and lining it.

Begin with all the ingredients at room temperature. Put the butter in a mixing bowl and beat it until it is pale and light using a wooden spoon or an electric beater. Add the sugar and continue beating until the mixture is so light and fluffy it drops from the spoon. Beat in the salt and orange zest followed by alternate spoonfuls of egg and ground nuts.

Spoon the mixture into the prepared tin and level the top. Bake it for about 45 minutes, or until a skewer inserted comes out clean.

Cool the cake in its tin for about 15 minutes before turning it on to a wire rack and peeling off the papers. Cakes made without flour will sink as they cool, but this is at no cost to their flavour. They taste even better a day or two after.

Sprinkle the top with icing sugar and serve plain. Or make two cakes and sandwich them together with whipped cream flavoured with an orange liqueur.

Chocolate and Coffee Roulade

MAKES ONE CAKE

2 large eggs
2 tablespoons Canderel Spoonful
40g (1½ oz) plain flour
1 teaspoon cocoa powder
1 tablespoon instant coffee powder or
*   granules*
1 tablespoon warm water
For the filling
1 teaspoon powdered gelatine
1½ tablespoons hot water
140g (5oz) natural fromage frais
1 teaspoon Canderel Spoonful

Preheat the oven to moderately hot (200°C/400°F, gas mark 6), and prepare a Swiss roll tin about 18 × 28cm (7 × 11in) by lining it with baking parchment.

To make the cake, combine the eggs and Canderel in a bowl and whisk until the mixture leaves a trail when it falls from the beaters. Sift the flour and cocoa together and dissolve the instant coffee in the water. Fold the flour and coffee mixtures into the eggs and spread the mixture over the prepared tin. Bake for about 10–12 minutes.

Turn the cake out on to a sheet of baking parchment. Trim about 5mm (¼in) off all sides of the cake, roll it up loosely together with the baking parchment, and set it aside until cold.

To make the filling, dissolve the gelatine in the hot water and stir it into the *fromage frais* together with the sweetener. Refrigerate until partially set.

Unroll the cake and spread the filling over it. Roll it up again without the paper. Serve, cut into slices. Fresh raspberries made a very good addition to this cake.

BISCUITS

Home-made biscuits are quite literally child's play, quick to make, and irresistibly moreish.

Because they are small, sweet, and baked at quite high temperatures to make them crisp, the danger of burning them is the biggest hazard. But, unlike cakes, they will not spoil if the oven door is opened to check how they are doing.

Tuiles

MAKES ABOUT 50 SMALL BISCUITS
Thin, crisp tuiles have never been bettered as an accompaniment to ices, syllabubs or creamy fruit fools. While they are still hot from the oven they remain pliable and can be moulded. Drape them over a rolling pin to make the classic tuile shape. Make them larger to mould over upturned cups. They will harden into little bowls of biscuit to hold ice cream or berries.

110 g (4 oz) unsalted butter
110 g (4 oz) caster sugar
5 large egg whites
Vanilla essence
¼ teaspoon salt
110g (4 oz) plain flour

Preheat the oven to moderately hot (200°C/400°F, gas mark 6), and prepare one or more baking sheets by greasing them well.

Begin with all the ingredients at room temperature. Cream the butter in a mixing bowl, add the sugar and beat until the mixture is pale and fluffy. Beat in the egg whites, a little at a time, and a few drops of vanilla essence and the salt. Fold in the flour. Pipe or spoon small mounds of the mixture (about a teaspoonful is enough) on to the prepared baking sheet, spacing them wide apart because they will spread in the oven. Bake them for about 10 minutes, until they are pale gold in the centre and a little darker at the edges. Cool the tuiles on a wire rack and store in an airtight tin as soon as they are cold.

Shortbread Thins

MAKES ABOUT 50 SMALL BISCUITS
These are melting shortbread biscuits made from a dough which is rolled out and so can be cut into plain or fancy shapes. Once made, the wrapped dough will keep in the refrigerator for several days, or it can be shaped and refrigerated, then baked shortly before needed.

85g (3oz) unsalted butter
140g (5oz) caster sugar
1 egg yolk
Vanilla or lemon essence
½ teaspoon salt
170g (6oz) plain flour

Preheat the oven to moderate (180°C/350°F, gas mark 4) and prepare baking sheets by greasing and flouring them well. Begin with all the ingredients at room temperature. In a mixing bowl cream the butter and sugar until the mixture is pale and fluffy. Beat in the egg yolk, a few drops of essence and salt, then stir in the flour to make a stiff dough. Gather the dough into a ball, wrap and refrigerate for 30 minutes.

On a lightly floured surface, roll out the dough to a thickness of about 5mm (¼in) and use plain or fancy cutters to stamp out the biscuits. Arrange them on the prepared sheet and bake them for about 10 minutes until pale gold.

Cool the shortbread thins on a wire rack where they will crisp as they cool. When they are quite cold, store them in an airtight tin.

CHAPTER 12

CREAMS, CUSTARDS, MOUSSES AND ICES

Cool and sweet, smooth and light, creams, custards, mousses and ices are happy endings to family and festive meals. Make them at home with fresh eggs and cream, fruit and nuts, and you know what good things have gone into them. Try a crisp vanilla ice made the old-fashioned way with real vanilla, egg yolks and sugar. Use the very best chocolate and a splash of liqueur for a chocolate mousse so rich and light that it is best served in individual pots. Make a honey junket set in a shallow glass bowl, or an intensely flavoured sorbet with ripe raspberries and red wine. Puddings bought in plastic pots pale in comparison.

The melting textures of cold desserts are achieved in various ways. Sweet nothings such as fools, possets and syllabubs are little more than whipped cream flavoured with something. Mousses are sometimes, but not invariably, set with gelatine; junkets with rennet; ice creams and sorbets by freezing.

Then there are all the recipes which utilise the extraordinary chemistry of eggs. Crème caramel, a baked egg custard made with whole eggs, sets to a tender gel. Egg yolks alone thicken real custard, made with milk for pouring, or to freeze in ice cream; with added starch for pastry cream; or with cream to set in a crème brûlée. Whisked egg whites give mousses their light, airy texture, and small quantities of uncooked meringue can be used to give sorbets a creamy smoothness and extra volume.

Cold desserts are fertile territory for culinary imagination and inspired improvisation. Experi-

menting with flavourings has few pitfalls. But if cutting calories is your aim, remember that it is the high fat content of double cream that allows it to be whipped until light and firm. Single cream will not whip, and whipping cream, although it does whip, is unsuitable for recipes which call for double cream to be whipped with additional liquid.

Reducing the amount of sugar specified will only make a syllabub or junket less sweet, though in some recipes its role is in part structural. In custards, egg yolks and sugar are beaten together before the milk or cream are added. The beating process coats individual yolk molecules with sugar. This has two purposes, both of which reduce the tendency of the mixture to curdle. It separates the yolk molecules from each other, discouraging them from clumping together, and increases the temperature at which they will coagulate with other proteins in the milk or cream to thicken the custard. Which is not to say that the amount of sugar specified in recipes cannot be reduced, and artificial sweetener substituted for some of the sugar.

In ices, the function of sugar is quite different. Here it reduces the size of the ice crystals and has a crucial role in determining the finished texture of the ice. Granitas, ices which are intentionally coarse-grained, contain half or even less of the sugar used in smooth ices; these are the ones which remain scoopable at deep-freeze temperatures.

The perfect combination – crème brûlée *garnished with soft summer fruits.*

SIMPLE CREAM-BASED DESSERTS

Syllabub

SERVES 6–8

A traditional English creamy dessert.

1 lemon
120ml (4fl oz) dry white wine
110g (4oz) caster sugar
300ml (½ pint) double cream

Pare the zest thinly from the lemon and add it to the wine in a bowl. Cover and leave to steep for an hour or two in the refrigerator.

Remove the zest from the bowl and add the juice of the lemon, strained, plus the sugar and cream. Whisk the mixture until it is thick and light.

Divide the syllabub between six or eight glasses or small bowls, and chill well before serving with crisp, sweet biscuits.

Rhubarb Fool

SERVES 4–6

A wonderful way to use new or older rhubarb.

450g (1lb) rhubarb
170g (6oz) dark brown sugar
175ml (6fl oz) double cream

Cut the rhubarb in short lengths and put it in a pan with the sugar. Cook, covered, on a very low heat until the rhubarb is tender, about 10 minutes for spring rhubarb, longer for more mature stalks. It will produce more than enough liquid of its own. Strain the fruit well; the juice can be used on breakfast cereal or for another dish. Pass the rhubarb through a *mouli-légumes* (see page 303), or sieve or process it.

When the purée is completely cold – or, better still, chilled – whip the cream until it is thick and light, and fold the two lightly together. Turn the fool into individual glasses or bowls, and chill well before serving with crisp biscuits.

CUSTARDS AND JUNKET

Baked Egg Custard

SERVES 4

A baked custard will set at a temperature of between 82–88°C (180–190°F). If it is overcooked it will separate. By absorbing some of the oven's heat, the water bath or *bain-marie*, in which the custard cooks, allows the custard to reach setting point slowly, maximising the cook's chances of getting it out of the oven when it has set but is not overcooked.

600ml (1 pint) milk
4 large eggs
30g (1oz) caster sugar
Freshly grated nutmeg

Preheat the oven to moderate (160°C/325°F, gas mark 3), and butter a 900ml (1½ pint) baking dish.

Put the milk in a pan and heat it almost to boiling. Break the eggs into a bowl and add the sugar. Beat lightly together, then gradually stir in the hot milk.

Set the prepared baking dish in a roasting pan or baking tin, and pour the custard through a sieve into the dish. Sprinkle the top with freshly grated nutmeg.

Pour cold water into the tin to a depth of about 2.5cm (1 in). Bake the assembly in the centre of the oven for 40–45 minutes, or until the custard has set. Shake the dish gently. When the centre is no longer liquid but trembles like a jelly, it is ready. Remove the dish carefully from the water bath.

Serve hot, warm or cold, with a sprinkling of caster sugar and a spoonful of cream, or with poached fruit.

Crème Brûlée

SERVES 6

Crème brûlée, or burnt cream, can be set in the oven, in one large dish or in individual servings, using the same method and temperature as a baked egg custard. Or it can be made as follows.

4 large egg yolks
100g (3½oz) caster sugar
600ml (1 pint) double cream, or equal
*   quantities of double and single cream*

Make sure that the egg yolks are completely free of white, including the stringy bits that anchor them inside the eggs. Put the yolks in a bowl with 1 tablespoon of the sugar and beat them well.

Put the cream in a pan with a heavy base and bring it to the boil. Let it boil for about 30 seconds.

Now whisk the cream gradually into the yolk mixture. Rinse the pan and return the mixture to it. Cook, stirring, on a very low heat until the custard thickens and will coat the back of a spoon.

Pour the custard into one large dish or divide it between six ramekins or custard pots. Leave it until cold, then chill well.

About 2 hours before the meal, heat the grill to maximum. Sprinkle the remaining sugar on to the custard in an even layer and place it under the grill until the sugar melts and caramelises. Watch it carefully, turning the dish or pots so that the sugar cooks evenly.

Cool and chill before serving.

Crème Anglaise

MAKES 600ML (1 PINT)
A pouring custard is made with egg yolks, real vanilla and milk, a formula that commercial custard powders set out to ape. It can be served hot or cold. A sweeter version is frozen to make a traditional vanilla ice cream.

1 vanilla pod or real vanilla essence
600ml (1 pint) milk
6 large egg yolks
110g (4oz) caster sugar
A pinch of salt

If using a vanilla pod, halve it lengthways and add it to the milk in a heavy-based pan. Heat to boiling point, then set it aside for about 30 minutes to infuse. Remove the vanilla pod, which can

be washed and dried and used once more. If using vanilla essence, there is no need to heat the milk. Add vanilla essence after the custard has cooled (see below).

Make sure that the egg yolks are completely free of white and put them in a bowl with the sugar and salt. Whisk until the mixture is very pale and falls back in ribbons when the beaters are lifted. Whisk in the milk then return the mixture to the pan and cook over a very low heat, or in the top of a double boiler, stirring constantly until the custard is thick enough to coat the back of a spoon. At the point at which it starts to thicken, the froth which has covered its surface will disappear, a sign that the critical heating point has been reached.

Immediately take the pan off the heat and stand the base in cold or iced water to stop the cooking process. Stir in vanilla essence to taste.

If the custard is to be served cold, or made into ice cream, stir it from time to time as it cools.

Pastry Cream

MAKES ABOUT 500ML (18FL OZ)
Pastry cream, or *crème pâtissière*, is the unctuous custard layer that you will find in vanilla slices, or between the crisp pastry and sharp fruit in raspberry and strawberry tarts. The small amount of flour in the standard recipe does away with the danger of curdling the custard, which firms as it cools. For a light cake filling, mix it with whipped double cream. A spoonful of Benedictine will make it taste extraordinarily French. Vanilla essence can be substituted for the vanilla sugar, or you may use the infusing method described in the recipe for *crème Anglaise*.

6 large egg yolks
110g (4oz) vanilla sugar
30g (1oz) cornflour
450ml (¾ pint) milk

Make sure the egg yolks are completely free of white. Beat them with the sugar until the mixture falls in ribbons from the whisk. Beat in the cornflour, making sure there are no lumps. Heat the milk to boiling, then whisk it into the yolk mix- 133 ture. Rinse the pan and pour the mixture into it. Bring slowly to the boil, stirring. Before it reaches the boil there is an alarming stage where the yolks begin to coagulate and it looks like scrambled egg. Stir steadily and it will smooth out again. Simmer gently for 2 minutes to get rid of the floury taste, then remove from the heat. Press a piece of greaseproof paper over the surface to prevent a skin from forming, and leave to cool.

Junket

SERVES 4

Junkets are almost puritanically plain. Miss Muffet's curds and whey need not be nursery fare if flavoured elusively with brandy or a strongly perfumed honey. Use unflavoured rennet from chemists or health-food shops. The alternative is rennet with synthetic-tasting fruit flavours.

600ml (1 pint) full cream milk
1 tablespoon caster sugar
2 tablespoons brandy
1 teaspoon rennet

Junket sets best at room temperature. It must not be jogged or disturbed while it is setting or it will break into curds and whey. So decide first where you are going to stand it.

Heat the milk to blood heat, 37°C (98°F), and stir in the sugar and brandy. When the sugar has dissolved, add the rennet and immediately pour the mixture into its serving bowl. Leave it undisturbed until it has set – up to 2 hours on a warm day. Chill. Serve with lightly whipped cream.

MOUSSES

Mousses, which are firm enough to turn out of a mould, or to hold their shape as in this cold lemon soufflé, are set with gelatine. The light texture of mousses is best set off by well-defined flavours. Seville oranges, or purées of dried apricots or fresh raspberries work well.

Hurrying to combine the ingredients before the gelatine mixture is cool enough will cause the mousse to set with a denser layer at the base.

Cold Lemon Soufflé

SERVES 4–6

15g (½ oz) powdered gelatine
4 tablespoons cold water
4 large eggs, separated
170g (6oz) caster sugar
Juice and finely grated zest of 4 juicy lemons
300ml (½ pint) double cream

Fit a 15cm (6in) diameter soufflé dish with a collar of greaseproof or waxed paper standing 7.5cm (3in) above the rim.

Sprinkle the gelatine on to the cold water in a cup or very small pan and set it aside to swell and soften.

Put the egg yolks and sugar into the top of a double boiler, or a bowl set over (but not touching), a pan of hot water, and whisk over the heat until the mixture is pale and light and falls in ribbons from the beaters. Whisk in the lemon juice, and continue beating over the heat until the mixture thickens a little again. Take the bowl off the heat and set it to one side, whisking it occasionally as it cools.

Heat the gelatine gently, stirring until it has dissolved, then allow it to cool a little, but do not let it set. Whisk the gelatine and lemon zest into the egg yolk mixture.

Lightly whip the cream and fold it into the lemon mixture. Lastly, using a clean dry whisk, whip the egg whites until they are stiff but not dry, and fold them lightly into the lemon cream.

Pour or spoon the mixture into the prepared dish and chill it until firmly set, about 2-3 hours. Just before serving the soufflé, carefully peel off its collar.

Chocolate Pots

SERVES 6–8

Use the best quality dark chocolate you can find for this chocolate mousse. It is made without gelatine and is too light to mould, or even to serve attractively from a large dish. Make individual servings by spooning it into custard cups, glasses or ramekins and leaving it to set.

110g (4oz) dark dessert chocolate
120ml (4fl oz) double cream
3 large eggs, separated
*2 tablespoons brandy, whisky or orange
    liqueur*

Break the chocolate into a bowl, or the top of a double boiler, and add the cream. Melt the chocolate over hot but not boiling water.

In another bowl, chosen similarly to fit over the pan of hot water, beat the egg yolks, then gradually whisk in the melted chocolate. Whisk the mixture over the heat until it is thick, then add the spirit or liqueur and set it aside.

Using a clean, dry whisk, whip the egg whites until they are stiff but not dry. Fold the meringue thoroughly into the chocolate mixture. Divide it between six or eight pots and refrigerate until set, at least 4 hours.

ICES

Ice creams and sorbets freshly made with ripe fruit, fresh cream and real egg custards have true, natural flavours that even the best commercially made ices never quite match. One reason is freshness, but another is that making ices in small quantities at home we can afford to be generous with the fruit and liberal with the cream. There are no E numbers, artificial sweeteners or synthetic colourings in home-made ices.

FREEZING

A few very rich ices can be still-frozen without stirring and will turn out creamy. But most ice creams and sorbets need beating during the freezing process to break up the ice crystals and make the texture pleasantly smooth.

As a rule, the richer or sweeter the recipe, the less beating it will need. Large flakes or crystals of ice form most readily in the least sweet or cream-rich ices. These must be taken out of the freezer and beaten vigorously at least once, and better twice, to reduce the size of the ice crystals. The optimum moment to beat an ice is when the sides and bottom of the freezing mixture are almost firm and the centre is still fairly liquid. The ice should then be tipped into a chilled bowl and whisked hard, preferably with an electric

beater. It can be done in a food processor, but this does not have the same aerating effect as a well-timed beating which visibly increases the volume of the ice. The softened ice is then returned to the freezer to firm again.

If the ice has frozen too hard to be beaten, it is best softened slowly in the refrigerator.

Before still-freezing ices, always turn the freezer to its coldest setting for at least an hour beforehand. The colder the temperature, the smaller will be the crystals of ice formed in the mixture. For the same reason, it helps to still-freeze ices in shallow, preferably metal, containers which are better conductors of cold.

Freezing times are so variable that even the vaguest instructions can be more misleading than helpful. Obviously the ice-making compartment of a small refrigerator will take very much longer than a modern freezer switched to fast-freeze. The shape and volume of containers affect freezing times and so do ingredients. Sugar, fat and alcohol all inhibit freezing and favour the production of small ice crystals. Recipes with a high proportion of sugar and alcohol will take longest to freeze.

SORBETIERES AND
ICE-CREAM CHURNS

The smoothest, lightest ices are made in electric sorbetières, or in the old-fashioned hand-cranked churns which have to be packed with ice and salt. Sorbetières range in sophistication from costly and heavy machines, which freeze and churn quite large volumes of ice cream very efficiently, to inexpensive appliances which simply churn. These too are efficient, but limited. The bowl in which the ice is churned has to be cooled for 24 hours in the freezer before it can be used, and only small quantities can be made at once.

RIPENING ICES

After a day or two in the deep freeze, many home-made ices will be too hard to scoop and will need 'ripening' or softening. This should always be done slowly, in the refrigerator, and never hurried in a warm kitchen. Small quantities, individual servings and ices in shallow containers will ripen more quickly than ices in large containers, or bombes. The sweetest and most 135 alcoholic ices will ripen fastest. Allow 5–10 minutes for small ices, 30 minutes for bombes.

Old-Fashioned Vanilla Ice Cream

SERVES 4–6

> *1 vanilla pod, or vanilla essence*
> *750ml (1¼ pints) whole milk*
> *6 large egg yolks*
> *225g (8oz) caster sugar*
> *A pinch of salt*

Make the custard using the method described for *crème anglaise* on page 133 but increase the amount of vanilla flavouring to counter the effect of freezing the custard. This can be done by using vanilla sugar, or by scraping some of the minute black seeds out of the vanilla pod into the mixture, or by adding vanilla essence to the cool custard. Chill the custard in the refrigerator before freezing it in a sorbetière. Or still-freeze it, whisking the mixture vigorously at least once during the freezing process.

Lemon Ice Cream

SERVES 6

This rich, creamy ice can be still-frozen without stirring, so it can be frozen in serving dishes or glasses, or in the hollowed-out fruits. The same recipe can be made with 4 limes.

> *3 juicy lemons*
> *170g (6oz) icing sugar*
> *450ml (¾ pint) double cream*
> *3 tablespoons iced water*

Finely grate the zest from two of the lemons and squeeze the juice from all three. Combine the zest, juice and icing sugar.

Whip the cream with the water until it holds soft peaks, then whisk in the sweetened lemon juice. Turn the mixture into a freezer tray, or individual serving dishes. Cover and still-freeze, without stirring, until firm.

Strawberry Ice Cream

SERVES 6

Any soft fruit can be made into ice cream using this method and very similar proportions. How sweet or strongly flavoured to make the ice is a matter of taste.

> *340g (12oz) ripe strawberries, hulled*
> *Juice of 1 orange*
> *Juice of 1 lemon*
> *170g (6oz) caster sugar*
> *450ml (¾ pint) whipping cream*

Rub the berries through a sieve, or process them briefly and strain the purée. Combine the pulp with the citrus juices and sugar. Ideally the mixture should stand for an hour, to allow the flavours to develop. Stir from time to time.

Whip the cream until it holds soft peaks, add the sweetened purée and whisk lightly together.

Freeze in a sorbetière, or still-freeze, whisking the partially frozen ice at least once.

Red Wine Sorbet with Raspberries

SERVES 4–6

This recipe is from *A Table in Tuscany* by Leslie Forbes. In Italian it is *sorbetto al vino rosso con profumo de lampone*, which sounds even better. It is a posh slush with a marvellous flavour.

> *600ml (1 pint) fizzy young red wine*
> *200g (7oz) fresh raspberries, slightly crushed*
> *140g (5oz) sugar*
> *6 fresh mint leaves (and more for garnish)*

Boil the sugar, mint leaves and wine together for 2 minutes, or until the sugar has dissolved. Add to the raspberries and allow to sit for at least 1 hour, stirring occasionally. Remove the mint and put the mixture through a food processor. Freeze in an ice tray in the freezer (normal ice-making setting) for about 3 hours, stirring frequently until no more ice crystals form. Serve with more mint leaves dipped in sugar and water then frozen as a garnish.

CHAPTER 13

THE CONFECTIONER'S ARTS

Making sweets involves pushing sugar to extremes. There is not much more to it than that. Sugar syrup is heated to temperatures well above the boiling point of water, then cooled. It is by controlling how the syrup is heated and cooled that the cook creates a range of textures from creamy fondant to glassy brittle.

EQUIPMENT

No special equipment is needed for making sweets. Even a sugar thermometer is of limited use since it is so easy to judge the ascending stages of sugar boiling from soft ball to caramel in the time-honoured way shown in the table. Accurate measurement, and the ability to regulate quite low temperatures, is necessary only for working with chocolate.

For boiling sugar use a good pan with a heavy base and straight sides. Many syrups foam up when boiling, so it is important to choose a pan that is large enough. Unlined copper or brass, or stainless steel or aluminium are best because they cook syrups evenly, and withstand the high temperatures involved.

Marble is the ideal surface for working fondant on, and for making pulled sugar sweets, but any clean, steady, heat-resistant work surface can be used.

For making fondant, a heavy-duty metal scraper with a hefty wooden or rolled metal handle is a great help.

Non-stick tins for setting fudge and toffee in are a boon.

INGREDIENTS

Sugar is the main ingredient. White sugar is 99.8 per cent pure sucrose, and whether it comes from sugar cane or sugar beet is of no importance to the sweet-maker. Brown sugar made from cane contains some of the naturally occurring molasses (see Glossary). The word 'raw' may appear on the label to distinguish it from beet sugar to which cane molasses has been added for flavour.

Liquid glucose, from chemists, is sugar in another form which has longer molecules than sucrose. When added to sucrose syrups it inhibits crystallisation. Corn syrup, which is an ingredient in many American recipes, and cream of tartar, are also used to control crystallisation.

Chocolate, whether used for flavouring or coating, should be of good quality. A high percentage of cocoa solids is the indication. Look for 50 per cent or more on the label. The best has up to 70 per cent and is increasingly widely available despite its very high cost. Chefs use a top grade chocolate called *couverture* which has a high proportion of cocoa butter. The fats which make up cocoa butter are particularly unstable and *couverture* has to to be tempered by heating and cooling it to accurately controlled temperatures. *Couverture* can be bought from specialist suppliers, and instructions for tempering it are given on the packaging. Dipping chocolate, also from specialist suppliers, is less tricky to work with and melts to a good consistency for coating home-made centres. All types of chocolate come in dark, milk and white varieties.

Vanilla Caramels

MAKES ABOUT 680G (1½LB)
Wrap rich, chewy caramels in individual squares of cellophane, or dip them in melted chocolate.

> *500g (1lb 2oz) granulated sugar*
> *450ml (¾ pint) double cream*
> *85g (3oz) salted butter*
> *120ml (4fl oz) runny honey*
> *2 teaspoons vanilla essence*

Butter a 20cm (8in) square tin, lining the base with buttered greaseproof paper if it does not have a non-stick finish.

Put the sugar, cream, butter and honey into a large pan and heat slowly, stirring occasionally until the sugar has dissolved completely. Wash down any sugar crystals on the sides of the pan with a pastry brush dipped in water. Then boil the mixture to the hard ball stage (121°C/250°F), with a minimum amount of stirring just to stop it catching on the bottom of the pan. Stir in the essence and pour the syrup into the prepared tin.

When it is cool and firm, turn it on to a clean cutting surface and use an oiled knife to cut it into squares. Store in an airtight container.

Fudge

MAKES ABOUT 900G (2LB)
Fudge can be flavoured traditionally with vanilla, or with all sorts of other ingredients. Chopped walnuts or pecans and raisins are incorporated into the fudge about half-way through the graining process. Have them ready before beginning to beat the syrup. Interrupting the beating, even briefly, will allow large crystals to form, coarsening the finished fudge. Failure to ensure that the sugar is completely dissolved before boiling it, and beating it when it is too hot, will also produce hard, gritty fudge.

> *680g (1½ lb) soft brown sugar*
> *175ml (6fl oz) water*
> *400g (14oz) tin sweetened condensed milk*
> *110g (4oz) salted butter*

Butter or oil a tin measuring about 20cm (8in) square.

Put the sugar in a large pan with the water, condensed milk and butter. Heat slowly, stirring occasionally, until the sugar has dissolved completely. Wash down any sugar crystals from the sides of the pan using a pastry brush dipped in water.

Raise the heat and boil the syrup without stirring to the soft ball stage (113°C/235°F). Take the pan off the heat and dip the base in cold water to prevent the temperature rising any higher.

Allow the syrup to cool until the base of the pan feels no more than comfortably warm. Now grain the fudge by beating the mixture vigorously with a wooden spoon. When it begins to stiffen, pour it into the prepared tin, and while it is still warm mark it into squares. Cut it up only when it is quite cold. Store in an airtight container.

Fondant

MAKES ABOUT 400G (14OZ)
Peppermint creams, and the smoothest icing for little cakes and for dipping soft fruits to make *petits fours*, are all made with fondant. Transforming hot syrup into a malleable ball of smoothly recrystallised sugar will take 15–20 minutes of hard work. Once made, however, fondant keeps almost indefinitely.

> *450g (1lb) granulated sugar*
> *2 tablespoons liquid glucose*
> *150ml (¼ pint) water*

Put the sugar, glucose and water into a pan and heat slowly together, stirring occasionally until the sugar has dissolved completely. Wash down any sugar crystals from the sides of the pan with a pastry brush dipped in water.

Bring the syrup to the boil on a high heat and boil it to the soft ball stage (116°C/240°F). Take the pan off the heat immediately and stand the base in cold water to arrest cooking.

Sprinkle a clean, steady work surface with a little cold water and pour the syrup on to it. Allow it to cool for a minute or two before starting to work it with a metal scraper or wooden spatula (see illustrations). First fold the edges of the syrup puddle into the centre to help it to cool evenly. Then, as it thickens, work it in a figure-of-eight motion until it becomes white and crumbly.

Now, making sure that it is cool enough to touch, knead it with wet hands until the sugar, which is hard and stiff at first, becomes smooth and plastic. Form the fondant into a ball, wrap it tightly to prevent drying, and leave it to ripen for at least 12 hours before moulding or melting it.

With a few drops of concentrated essence and food colouring, plain fondant is quickly transformed into a great variety of sweets. Peppermint creams demonstrate the method used to shape the fondant by rolling and cutting it like pastry. Coffee creams demonstrate how fondant can be melted and poured into moulds to set. Sweets shaped in either way can be used as creamy centres for dipped chocolates.

flatten it roughly. Sprinkle a few drops of flavouring oil or essence on to it, and a very small quantity of colouring if you are using it. Knead the fondant well, adjusting the flavour and colour only when the first additions are thoroughly worked in.

Divide the fondant into quarters, and roll and cut one piece at a time. Keep the remainder covered to prevent drying.

Dust the work surface lightly with icing sugar before rolling out the fondant with a sugar-dusted pin to a thickness of about 1cm (½in). Use a small, plain cutter to stamp out the fondant, dipping it in icing sugar to prevent sticking.

Lay the cut sweets on trays lined with baking parchment or greaseproof paper and leave them to dry for about 12 hours, turning them two or three times. Rework and roll the offcuts.

Store in a separate airtight container so that the peppermint cannot taint other sweets.

Peppermint Creams

MAKES 400G (14OZ)
Rose, violet, lemon, vanilla and almond creams can be made in the same way.

400g (14oz) ripened fondant
Peppermint oil or essence to taste
Green food colouring (optional)
Icing sugar

Turn the fondant on to a clean work surface and

Coffee Creams

MAKES ABOUT 400G (14OZ)
Moulds for shaping fondant are made of hardened rubber and are sold in specialist kitchen shops.

400g (14oz) ripened fondant
2 tablespoons instant coffee powder or granules
2 tablespoons hot water

MAKING FONDANT

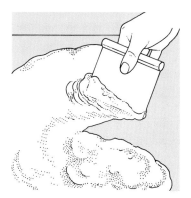

1. Pour the syrup on to a clean, lightly dampened work surface. Leave to cool for a minute or two, then start to fold the edges into the middle, using a dampened metal scraper.
2. Use a dampened wooden spatula to work the syrup in a figure of eight motion until it becomes first thick and opaque, then white and crumbly.

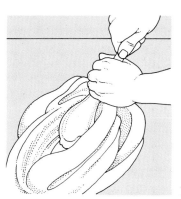

SUGAR BOILING

The texture of a sugar syrup once it has cooled depends on the temperature to which it was first boiled. The higher the temperature, the more moisture is driven off and the harder it will set. The temperature bands, their names, and how to test them, are as follows:

SOFT BALL
Fondant
Fudge

112–116°C (234–240°F)
Drop a small spoonful of syrup into iced water. When rolled with the fingers it will form a soft, sticky ball.

FIRM BALL
Soft caramels

118–121°C (244–250°F)
Drop a small spoonful of syrup into iced water. It will form a firm but still rather sticky ball which loses its shape quite quickly when out of the water.

HARD BALL
Marshmallow
Nougat

121–130°C (250–266°F)
Drop a small spoonful of syrup into iced water. It will quickly form a ball which, although sticky, does hold its shape out of water.

CARAMEL
Praline
Brittle

160–177°C (320–350°F)
Smell and colour are caramel's distinguishing marks. The colour can range from pale gold to rich chestnut, but should not be darker or the caramel will be more bitter than sweet.

HARD CRACK
Barley sugar
Hard toffee
Fruit drops

149–154°C (300–310°F)
Drop a small spoonful of syrup into iced water. Take it out and break it. It should snap easily and will not be sticky.

SOFT CRACK
Toffee
Butterscotch

132–143°C (270–290°F)
Drop a small spoonful of syrup into iced water. Take it out and pull it. It will draw into hard, pliable strands.

Put the fondant in the top of a double boiler and melt it slowly. The temperature of the fondant must not exceed 60°C (140°F). If you exceed this temperature, the fondant will be hard instead of creamy when it cools again. Dissolve the coffee in the hot water and stir it into the fondant carefully and evenly.

Use a spoon to fill the the moulds with melted fondant. You could also pour the fondant from a pan with a pouring spout, or from a jug. (Paper sweet cases can be used instead of rubber moulds.) Leave the coffee creams to set for about 2 hours before unmoulding them. Dry them on a wire rack in a dry airy spot before storing them in an airtight container or dipping them in chocolate.

Dipped Fruit Petits Fours

Strawberries, grapes, cherries and Cape gooseberries all make attractive *petits fours* when dipped in melted fondant. Soften as much fondant as you need in the top of a double boiler. Add 1 tablespoon of water for every 200g (7oz) of ripened fondant, and keep the temperature below 60°C (140°F). Fruit for dipping should be firm and dry. Hold the fruit by its stalk and lower it into the melted fondant, then set it on greaseproof paper or foil to harden. Allow the fondant to cover half the fruit's surface so that its colour contrasts with the white sugar. Except in very humid conditions, dipped fruits should keep well for a day or two.

Praline and Praline Powder

MAKES ABOUT 450G (1LB)

Praline, a mixture of toasted nuts and deep golden caramel set hard, then chopped or ground to a fine powder, is one of the classiest tastes in the cook's repertoire. Use it to flavour pastry cream, ices made with real egg custard, brioche dough, cakes and chocolate centres.

225g (8oz) blanched almonds
225g (8oz) caster sugar

Lightly oil or grease a non-stick baking sheet.

Put the almonds and sugar in a pan with a heavy base and heat slowly until the sugar has melted. Cook, stirring to distribute the heat, until the almonds are toasted and the sugar has turned to a rich, amber-coloured caramel. Immediately pour the mixture on to the prepared baking sheet and spread it in a thin layer. When it is quite cold, break it up and, if required, grind it to a fine powder using a pestle and mortar.

Stored in an airtight container, praline will keep for several weeks.

CHOCOLATES

Temperature control is the key to handling chocolate successfully. Overheating it can result in a grey bloom on the finished sweets. To prepare chocolate for dipping home-made centres, break a good quantity into a wide bowl. It is much easier to work with a generous pool of melted chocolate than with a shallow puddle, and a larger quantity is less likely to be accidentally overheated. Any left over can be cooled and reheated another time or used for flavouring.

Keeping moisture out of the chocolate is also critical. Even a few puffs of steam can cause it to seize, or stiffen irreparably. So set the wide bowl over a smaller pan of hot water, making sure that the base of the bowl is not in direct contact with the water.

Melt the chocolate slowly until it is liquid, making sure that the temperature never rises above 49°C (120°F). Stir the chocolate until it is completely smooth. The optimum temperature range for dipping is 32–43°C (90–110°F).

Hard centres, such as caramels, are easier to handle than soft ones. Forks designed for dipping chocolates have thin, straight tines, but a table fork does very well with a little practice.

Dip one centre at a time. Drop it into the molten chocolate and submerge it. Use the fork to lift it out, holding it above the bowl for a moment or two to allow the excess chocolate to drip back. Draw the fork over the rim of the bowl to wipe off any drips and set the covered centre down on a tray lined with greaseproof paper. The chocolate should harden almost immediately. If it does not, allow the molten chocolate to cool a little before coating the remaining centres, using the same procedure.

Traditionally chocolates are decorated with patterns made by touching the top of each sweet with a dipping fork, or another of the confectioner's tools, a dipping ring. This is done as the chocolate begins to stiffen. Setting small fragments of crystallised flower petals into the chocolate is the traditional decoration for rose and violet creams.

SAFETY PRECAUTIONS

Boiling sugar syrups can cause very serious burns. Work carefully and methodically. The best first-aid treatment for burns, however slight or severe, is to hold the burned area of skin under cold running water for a full 10 minutes to minimise the damage. Then keep the wound dry and clean, and seek medical attention if necessary.

CHAPTER 14
PRESERVING

Look around the supermarket shelves and see what a huge proportion of the food is in a state of suspended animation – frozen, canned, dried, salted, vacuum-packed or chilled. Many methods of food preservation were used originally to produce survival rations for winter, and continue in use today because we have grown accustomed to their tastes. It is no longer necessary to salt legs of pork and hang them in chimneys to dry and smoke. Fresh pork is available all year round, but we like the flavour of ham and bacon. There is no necessity to preserve milk, but life without cheese is unthinkable. Freezing gives us soft summer fruits in midwinter; but who would willingly forego the old methods of keeping them, as jams and jellies, in pickles or soaked in alcohol?

Preservation techniques all have the same purpose, to arrest the natural spoilage processes set in motion by enzymes in the foods themselves, or by external agencies such as moulds, yeasts and bacteria.

Freezing has long been known to slow the rate at which foods spoil, but until modern technology produced the means to exploit this knowledge, harnessing the potential of extreme cold was not a realistic possibility in the home. At temperatures below −18°C (0°F), micro-organisms in food do not grow or produce toxins. They hibernate. Enzyme activity, although greatly slowed down, is not stopped by freezing, and deterioration slowly continues. The rate at which different foodstuffs are gradually rendered less palatable by the activity of their own enzymes is reflected in the recommended freezer storage times. Frozen foods remain safe for far longer than they are pleasant to eat.

Extremes of heat also inactivate enzymes and bacteria. The precise temperature required to make food safe depends on the individual foodstuff and the length of time for which it is heated. But heating alone will not protect foods from the activities of airborne bacteria, or yeasts and moulds, and additional measures such as the creation of a partial vacuum, as in bottling, are required.

Salting, drying and potting all exploit the fact that micro-organisms need moisture to grow, and each method deprives them of moisture in a different way. Sugar, vinegar and alcohol also have preservative powers when used in high enough concentrations.

Nowadays we make preserves at home for fun and eat them for pleasure. Sometimes there are financial savings to be made too, but our priorities are more likely to be gastronomic than economic.

HYGIENE

For obvious reasons, preserving demands especially high standards of hygiene. Freezer cartons, jars, bottles and other re-usable containers and accessories such as rubber sealing rings should be carefully washed and dried. Glass jars and bottles can be sterilised in a preheated cool oven (140°C/275°F, gas mark 1). Give them a good 10 minutes.

142

Discs of waxed paper are sold in packets with jam-pot covers and should be applied to sweet preserves, wax side down, as soon as the jars are filled.

SALTING, POTTING AND DRYING

Salting requires pure sea or rock salt without additives. Iodised salt treated with iodine, and table salt with magnesium carbonate and calcium carbonate to keep it flowing freely in damp weather, are not suitable.

Salt Beef

SERVES 8–10

Brisket is a coarse, fat and unlovely cut of beef for every purpose except salting. Then, simmered with root vegetables and served with fluffy dumplings, it is transformed into a real delicacy. The meat is rosy, succulent and full of flavour.

The biggest hurdle the cook faces is getting hold of the necessary saltpetre (chemically, potassium nitrate). Its potential as an ingredient in explosives has made it difficult, but not impossible, to get hold of if you are persistent. Chemists require a signature. Failing that, a friendly butcher may be persuaded to provide it, already mixed with ordinary salt in a commercially produced salting mixture. Without saltpetre, the beef will not be a rosy pink colour when cooked.

In the following recipe, brining is for flavour rather than long preservation. To keep meat for several months without deterioration, old-fashioned brining proportions of 450g (1lb) salt to 2.75 litres (5 pints) of water would be needed.

170g (6oz) salt
1 teaspoon saltpetre
85g (3oz) demerara sugar
2.3–2.7kg (5–6lb) boned brisket, not rolled
1 clove garlic, quartered
1 teaspoon mixed pickling spice
1 teaspoon black peppercorns, crushed
4 bay leaves
1 large onion, quartered

Mix together the salt, saltpetre and sugar and rub the mixture into the beef on all sides. Sprinkle the garlic, pickling spice and pepper over the meat. Put the brisket in a large earthenware bowl or a plastic bucket with 2 bay leaves and cover it with cold water. Stand the container in a cool place, or in the refrigerator, and turn the meat daily for 7–10 days. By this time the liquid may be off-puttingly slimy, but as long as it is fresh smelling all is well.

Take the meat from the brine and wash it well in cold water. Roll and tie it neatly.

To cook the beef, put it in a large pot and cover it with cold water. Bring it very slowly to the boil and skim it carefully. Add the quartered onion and remaining bay leaves, cover and simmer the beef very gently for about 4 hours, or until tender.

Serve it hot with carrots, onions and parsnips added for the last 40 minutes of the cooking time, and suet dumplings (see page 102) popped into the pot for the last 20 minutes. Plain boiled or mashed potatoes, cooked separately, a jug of the stock and a little fiery English mustard complete this traditional meal.

Confit of Duck

MAKES 16 PIECES

Geese and ducks which have been fattened to produce *foie gras* are traditionally made into *confit* in south-western France. The flesh is salted to extract some of its moisture, seasoned with herbs and spices, then cooked in rendered goose or duck fat until it is so tender that it can be pierced with straw. The cooked pieces are packed into jars and covered with melted fat which sets to form a seal against air contamination. Stored in a cool place, *confit* will keep for many months. It is a key ingredient in *cassoulet*, the rich haricot bean stew so characteristic of the region.

The *confit* procedure alters and enriches the flavour of the main ingredient in a way that is comparable with baconing pork. Increasingly, modern chefs are making *confit* with ordinary, not fattened, ducks and geese, and with chickens and rabbits.

143

*2 ducks, preferably Barbary ducks, or 8 large
    duck legs*
110 g (4oz) salt
½ teaspoon saltpetre (optional)
4 bay leaves, crumbled
*1 teaspoon dried thyme, preferably from
    Provence*
Duck fat and lard (see below)

Divide the ducks into serving portions, taking the breast off the bone but leaving the skin intact and cutting each side in two. Divide the legs into thighs and drumsticks. Save any loose lumps of fat or skin to render down, and the carcasses for stock.

Mix together the sea salt (pounded if it is very coarse), saltpetre if using, bay leaves and thyme and rub this mixture into the pieces of duck. Pack them closely into a large bowl and sprinkle with the remaining salt mixture. Cover loosely and put the bowl in a cool place, or the refrigerator, for about 12 hours.

Render the reserved duck fat and skin by cooking it very slowly until all the fat has melted and only the golden crackling remains. Strain the fat.

Wipe the excess salt and moisture from the duck pieces with kitchen paper and pack them into a large casserole or heavy pot. Add the reserved duck fat, plus enough additional duck fat or melted lard to cover the duck pieces completely. Cook, uncovered, in a preheated cool oven (150°C/300°F, gas mark 2) for about 3 hours, or until the duck is very tender. When the meat is ready, most of the fat under the skin will have melted, and if the meat is pierced no juices will run out.

Sterilise (see page 142) one or more large preserving jars or crocks. Pour a ladleful of fat into the bottom of the jar, then pack in pieces of duck to within 5cm (2in) of the top. Pour in more fat to cover the pieces completely. Tap the jars firmly on a solid surface to release any air bubbles trapped with the meat, and leave them in a cool place until quite cold. Top up the jars with a good layer of hot fat or melted lard. Seal with lids if using preserving jars, or with foil pressed down on top of the fat, and store in a cool, dry place for at least a week to mellow the flavours.

When you want to retrieve one or more pieces of the *confit*, heat the jar gently in a pan of hot water or a very low oven, and fish out the quantity you need, making sure that the remaining pieces stay covered with fat. Cool and reseal the remainder for later use.

Regardless of how you serve the *confit* – on its own, in cassoulet or in another recipe, it should be very well heated for at least 5 minutes.

Potted Crab

SERVES 6

Sealing pots of well-seasoned fish or shellfish with clarified butter preserves their contents for a couple of weeks, which was no mean feat in the pre-freezer age. Potted char was a popular Lake District speciality, and potted shrimps are still made today. Potted crab, or better still potted lobster, delicately spiced with mace and cayenne pepper are – and there is no other word for it – delicious.

450g (1lb) very fresh cooked white crab meat
¼ teaspoon ground mace
¼ teaspoon cayenne pepper
Salt and freshly ground black pepper
110g (4oz) butter, softened
110g (4oz) clarified butter (see page 239)

Preheat the oven to moderate (180°C/350°F, gas mark 4).

Make sure that the crab meat is completely free of small chips of shell. Shred the meat roughly with a fork and season it with the mace, cayenne, salt and pepper. Pack the crab into one ovenproof dish, or divide it between six ramekins or cocotte dishes. Spread the softened butter over the crabmeat, cover the dish or dishes with foil and bake for 35 minutes for one large dish, 25 for the small ones. Remove from the oven and leave to cool until the butter has solidified.

Heat the clarified butter until it has just melted and pour it over the crab to make an airtight seal. Chill the potted crab for a day or two to allow the flavours to blend. Serve it at room temperature with freshly made toast.

AIR-DRYING

Air-drying is particularly well suited to flavouring ingredients such as herbs, citrus peel and mushrooms. The process could not be simpler. Moulds cannot grow without moisture, so thoroughly dried leaves, peel and fungi can be successfully stored from one season to the next.

DRIED HERBS

Some varieties keep their flavour better than others when dried. Good candidates for drying are bay, rosemary, sage, marjoram, oregano, thyme and savory. The flavour of basil, tarragon and mint changes and the dried herbs taste pleasant but different. Parsley, chervil and chives are better frozen than dried.

The time to pick and dry herbs is when they are in their prime and at their most pungent. With the exception of thyme, marjoram and oregano, which are best harvested as soon as their flowers open, herbs are at their best just before they flower. Tie the freshly gathered herbs in small bunches and hang them up, somewhere dry and airy, until the leaves are dry and crumbly. Spikes of rosemary can be laid side by side in layers in a basket to dry over a boiler or in the airing cupboard.

Dried herbs can be used just as they come. Alternatively, rub the leaves off the stalks and store them in airtight jars, or grind the leaves finely in a processor, and sieve the now almost powdered leaves before storing.

DRIED CITRUS PEEL

Use a small piece of dried orange peel in casseroles as you would a bay leaf, and note the subtle flavour it imparts to daubes and game. Use oranges and lemons which have not been treated with fungicides and wax. Bitter Seville oranges for marmalade-making are untreated, and organically grown lemons are widely available.

Use a small sharp knife to pare off the zest in ribbons, taking as little as possible of the underlying white pith. Thread the ribbons on to a piece of string, using a darning or trussing needle, and spacing them well apart. Hang them up to dry and when they are curled and brittle, after a few days, store them in an airtight jar. The flavour will last for a year or more.

DRIED FUNGI

Drying changes and intensifies the fragrance and flavour of mushrooms in a most interesting way. Reconstituted dried mushrooms smell meatier than fresh ones. For drying, use only perfect specimens, correctly identified and as fresh as possible. Good candidates for drying include field mushrooms and edible ceps, morels and blewits. On no account eat or dry any fungus that has not been positively identified.

Cut the mushrooms in slices about 5mm (¼in) thick, then either thread them on strings to dry, spacing the pieces well apart, or lay them on wire racks and dry in a very cool oven (110°C/225°F, gas mark ¼) until they are shrivelled and completely dry. Cool and store in an airtight container for a year or more.

PICKLING IN VINEGAR AND ALCOHOL

Both alcohol, in the form of distilled spirits, and vinegar are potent preservatives which, when used in sufficient concentration, inhibit the growth of micro-organisms. Wine vinegar or the harsher distilled malt vinegars can be used in pickles, but the quality of the preserve will always depend partly on that of the vinegar.

Green Tomato Chutney

MAKES ABOUT 2KG (4½LB)
It is pleasing to find a good use for unripened green tomatoes. If green tomatoes are not available, try unripe mangoes. Ripe fruit cooks down to a mushier texture.

900g (2lb) green tomatoes
900g (2lb) cooking apples
450g (1lb) onions
6 cloves garlic
30g (1oz) fresh green ginger
680g (1½lb) dark brown sugar
450g (1lb) stoned or seedless raisins
2 tablespoons salt
2 teaspoons ground allspice
2 teaspoons freshly ground black pepper
900ml (1½ pints) red wine vinegar

145

Roughly chop the tomatoes, cutting out the hard cores at the stalk end. Peel, core and roughly chop the apples. Peel and roughly chop the onions. Peel and chop more finely the garlic and ginger. Put all the prepared fruit and vegetables into a pan made of a material that will not react with the vinegar – a large brass preserving pan, or a wide pan made of stainless steel, or one with an enamelled interior. Add the remaining ingredients and mix well.

Bring the mixture to the boil, stirring until the sugar has dissolved. Then reduce the heat until the fruit simmers gently and cook the mixture down slowly for about 1 hour, or until the chutney has a pleasing consistency.

Put the chutney into prepared jars. When it is cold, cover tightly using coated lids which will not corrode in contact with the vinegar, or a double layer of greaseproof paper and an airtight layer to prevent evaporation. Chutney tastes best after it has matured for a few weeks, and keeps well for a year or more.

Mincemeat

MAKES 1.8KG (4LB)
The top quality candied orange and lemon peels sold in segments is preferable to chopped peel, which includes a proportion of peel from the less universally liked citron fruit.

> *340g (12oz) pippin type dessert apples*
> *225g (8oz) currants*
> *225g (8oz) stoned raisins*
> *225g (8oz) sultanas*
> *170g (6oz) candied orange peel*
> *170g (6oz) candied lemon peel*
> *170g (6oz) dark brown sugar*
> *110g (4oz) chopped almonds*
> *225g (8oz) shredded beef suet*
> *1 teaspoon mixed spice*
> *½ teaspoon freshly grated nutmeg*
> *½ teaspoon salt*
> *Finely grated zest and juice of 1 lemon*
> *6 tablespoons brandy or whisky*

Peel and core the apples. Pass them through the coarse blade of a mincer together with the currants, raisins, sultanas, and candied orange and lemon peels. Put the minced fruit in a large bowl and add all the remaining ingredients. Mix very thoroughly. Pack the mincemeat in clean jars, seal tightly to prevent evaporation, and store in a cool, dark place to mature for 4 weeks before using. Keeps for at least 6 months.

Rumtopf

As each of summer's fruits ripen, they can be preserved, layer by layer in alcohol and sugar to brighten winter meals. This recipe is from *Jane Grigson's Fruit Book*.

Before you start, a word of warning. The method is easy, foolproof. The tricky part is the quality of the fruit. It must be of the finest, and preferably from a garden that you know has not been much subjected to sprays: in the opinion of one expert, whom I consulted after a batch had developed mould for no reason that I could see, it is difficult these days to make a *rumtopf* that you can rely on, and he is convinced that the reason is the chemical treatment that commercially grown fruit undergoes.

This poses a real dilemma with soft fruit. You can scrub an orange or an apple without harming it: a strawberry that becomes acquainted with water loses its virtue.

Another point to watch is the alcohol. Cheap rum and brandy sometimes means weaker rum and brandy. If after these warnings you decide to try your luck, this is what you do.

You need a 5 litre or a gallon stoneware jar, or a special *rumtopf* from Austria or Germany which can sometimes be bought in this country.

Prepare 1kg (2lb 3oz) of strawberries, removing their hulls. Sprinkle them with 500g (1lb 2oz) sugar and leave overnight. Next day tip the whole thing, juice included, into a well washed and dried *rumtopf*. Pour on 1 litre (1¾ pints) of rum (as in Germany) or brandy (as in France).

Put a clean plate directly on to the fruit to make sure it stays below the surface. Cover the jar with plastic film and the lid. Keep in a cool, dark place.

Add more soft fruit and sugar – half quantities are fine – as the summer progresses. Add more alcohol, too, from time to time to keep the liquid level up. It should clear the fruit comfortably. Remove and replace the plate each time.

Suitable fruits include sweet and sour cherries (including stones), raspberries, loganberries, boysenberries, mulberries, peaches, apricots, greengages, mirabelles (include an occasional stone), melon, pineapple (cubed), one or two apples and pears. Although gooseberries, currants and blaeberries can go in, they do tend to go hard and uncomfortable.

When the pot is just about full, top it up with a final dose of alcohol. Cover with fresh cling film, then the lid, and leave until Christmas – or at least for a month.

Serve in wine glasses with cream floated on top. Serve as a sauce with ice creams – vanilla or honey, for instance. Mix with champagne, using mostly the liquid with not too much fruit, for a champagne cocktail.

JAMS, JELLIES AND SUGAR PRESERVES

Fruit can be preserved for a year or more in the form of jams and jellies, relying on strong concentrations of sugar to inhibit the development of micro-organisms. For preserves with good keeping qualities, the proportion of sugar to fruit is 340–450g (¾ –1lb) for every 450g (1lb) of fruit, or 600ml (1 pint) of juice.

Two more ingredients play a part in successful preserves. Pectin is a gum-like substance naturally present in fruit, which helps preserves to set by forming a gel in conjunction with sugar, and the third vital ingredient, acid.

Citrus fruits have plenty of pectin and acid as well as strong flavour, which is why marmalade usually sets well with little trouble. Gooseberries, blackcurrants, redcurrants, damsons, plums and apples are also adequately endowed with flavour, pectin and acid. Raspberries and loganberries score high marks for flavour but may need help to set well. Strawberries taste good but have little pectin or acid.

The chart overleaf shows typical acid and pectin values for a selection of fruits.

Fruits with poor acidity can be boosted with the addition of 2 tablespoons of fresh lemon juice per 450g (1lb) of fruit or 600ml (1 pint) of juice.

To compensate for low pectin levels, add commercially prepared pectin sold in bottles by chemists, or use sugar with added pectin which is sold everywhere for preserving. Note that the term 'preserving sugar', used without any reference to added pectin, means only that it is a quick dissolving type. Cooks persistently claim that cane sugar makes better preserves than beet sugar, but there is no conclusive evidence that this is so.

To test the setting potential of a particular batch of fruit, put a teaspoonful of the juice in a small bowl and add 2 tablespoons of methylated spirit. Mix well and leave for a moment or two for clots of gel to form. If the juice forms a single, large clotted mass, the pectin level is high. Small scattered clots indicate low pectin levels.

MAKING GOOD SUGAR PRESERVES

- Use top quality ripe fruit.
- Test for acidity by tasting it.
- Test for pectin if a medium or low score is expected (see Chart).
- Boost acid or pectin levels if required.
- Don't add more water than the recipe specifies.
- Add the sugar only after the fruit has softened sufficiently. Citrus peel, in particular, will not soften further after the sugar is added.
- Warm sugar dissolves more quickly when added to the fruit. Heat through in a cool oven.
- Make quite sure that the sugar has dissolved completely before boiling for a set, or it may re-crystallise later in the jars.
- Make small quantities at a time in a large pan. Preserving pans are wider at the top, assisting rapid evaporation. Once the sugar is added, preserves are boiled rapidly and rise up the pan. Lowering the heat to prevent the syrup boiling over prolongs cooking with a resultant loss of good colour and fresh flavour.
- Test for setting in one of two ways:
  1. Boil until a sugar or deep-frying thermometer registers 105°C (220°F).
  2. Put a small spoonful of the boiling liquid on to a chilled plate and leave it to cool. The preserve will set when a sample forms a

147

PECTIN AND ACID CHART FOR FRUIT

FRUIT	PECTIN	ACIDITY
Apples	***	**
Apricots	**	**
Blackberries	**	**
Blackcurrants	***	***
Blaeberries	**	**
Blueberries	**	**
Cherries	*	**
Cranberries	***	**
Damsons	***	***
Elderberries	*	*
Figs	*	*
Gooseberries	***	***
Grapefruit	***	***
Grapes	**	**
Greengages	**	***
Lemons	***	***
Limes	***	***
Loganberries	**	**
Mangoes	*	*
Medlars	**	*
Melons	*	*
Mulberries	**	**
Nectarines	*	*
Passion fruit	*	**
Peaches	*	*
Pears	*	*
Pineapples	*	**
Plums	***	***
Quinces	***	*
Raspberries	**	**
Redcurrants	***	***
Rhubarb	*	***
Seville oranges	***	***
Strawberries	*	*
Sweet oranges	***	**
Tangerines	**	**

Key: *** high: ** moderate: * low

skin that is firm enough to wrinkle when pushed with a fingertip.

- When setting point is reached, take the pan off the heat and skim any froth from the surface with a large spoon.
- To make sure that the pieces of fruit are distributed evenly through the set jam or marmalade, allow it to cool for about 10 minutes in the pan and stir it before potting.
- Store in a cool, dark place.

Dark, Thick-Cut Marmalade

MAKES ABOUT 3.2KG (7LB)

900g (2lb) Seville oranges
2 lemons
2.25 litres (4 pints) water
900g (2lb) granulated or preserving sugar
900g (2lb) demerara sugar
2 tablespoon molasses or black treacle

Line a sieve with a square of muslin and set it over a bowl. Cut the oranges and lemons in halves, squeeze the juice and strain it into the bowl. Use a spoon to scoop the pips and ragged pieces of pith from the peel halves into the lined sieve. Keep the orange peel halves aside. Tie up the muslin into a bag and put it in a preserving pan with the juice.

Cut the orange peel halves into short, thick strips and add them to the pan with the water. Bring to the boil, reduce the heat and simmer gently until the peel is very tender and the liquid is well reduced. This takes at least 2 hours.

Lift out the muslin bag and squeeze as much as possible of its pectin-rich juice back into the pan. Now add all the sugar and the molasses or treacle and stir the mixture on a low heat until the sugar has dissolved completely.

Increase the heat and boil the marmalade rapidly. After 10 minutes test it for setting, and repeat the test every 2 minutes until setting point is reached. Skim and leave the marmalade to stand for 10 minutes before stirring and potting.

An ideal way to use up green tomatoes – making a green tomato chutney (see page 145).

DEEP-FREEZING MEAT, POULTRY, GAME & FISH

	FREEZER LIFE IN MONTHS	THAW BEFORE USING	COOK FROM FROZEN	FREEZE WITH SUGAR OR SYRUP	FREEZE COOKED	FREEZE WRAPPED	FREEZE ON OPEN TRAYS	BLANCHING TIME IN MINUTES
BACON AND SALT CURED MEATS	1	✔				✔		
BEEF	12	✔				✔		
BONES FOR STOCK	2		✔			✔		
BRAINS	2	✔				✔		
CHICKEN	12	✔				✔		
COOKED DISHES OF MEAT, POULTRY AND GAME	2		✔			✔		
COOKED DISHES OF OFFAL	1		✔			✔		
CUBED MEAT	4	✔				✔	✔	
DUCK	6	✔				✔		
FURRED GAME	6	✔				✔		
GAME BIRDS, FAT, EG WILD DUCK	6	✔				✔		
GAME BIRDS, LEAN, EG GROUSE	9	✔				✔		
GIBLETS, POULTRY	2	✔				✔		
GUINEA FOWL	6	✔				✔		
HEARTS	2	✔				✔		
KIDNEYS	2	✔				✔		
LAMB	9	✔				✔		
LIVER	2	✔				✔		
MINCED MEAT	4	✔				✔		
OXTAIL	2	✔				✔		
PORK	6	✔				✔		
SAUSAGES AND SAUSAGEMEAT	2	✔				✔		
STOCK	1	✔	✔			✔		
SUET	2	✔				✔		
SWEETBREADS	1	✔				✔		
TONGUE	1	✔				✔		
TRIPE	2	✔				✔		
TURKEY	6	✔				✔		
VEAL	9	✔				✔		
FISH STOCK	1	✔	✔			✔		
FATTY FISH	4	✔	✔			✔		
SHELLFISH, COOKED	1	✔				✔		
SMOKED FISH	3	✔	✔			✔		
WHITE FISH	6	✔	✔			✔		

DEEP-FREEZING VEGETABLES

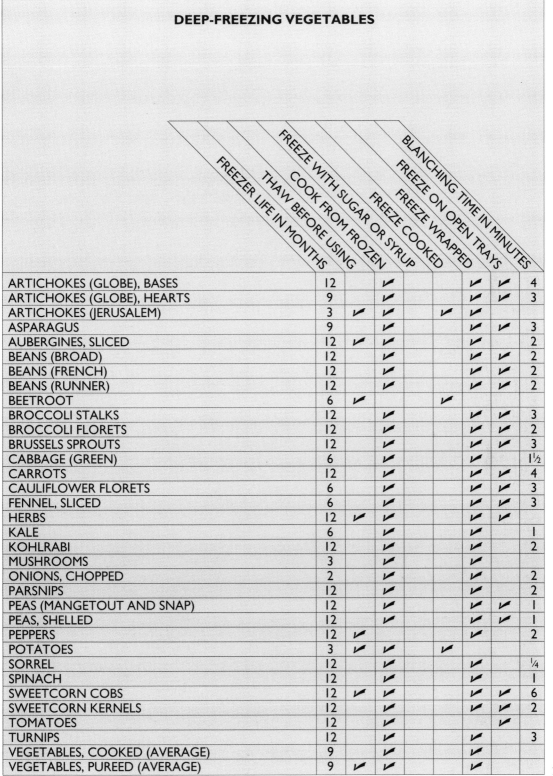

	FREEZER LIFE IN MONTHS	THAW BEFORE USING	COOK FROM FROZEN	FREEZE WITH SUGAR OR SYRUP	FREEZE COOKED	FREEZE WRAPPED	FREEZE ON OPEN TRAYS	BLANCHING TIME IN MINUTES
ARTICHOKES (GLOBE), BASES	12		✓			✓	✓	4
ARTICHOKES (GLOBE), HEARTS	9		✓			✓	✓	3
ARTICHOKES (JERUSALEM)	3	✓	✓		✓	✓		
ASPARAGUS	9		✓			✓	✓	3
AUBERGINES, SLICED	12	✓	✓			✓		2
BEANS (BROAD)	12		✓			✓	✓	2
BEANS (FRENCH)	12		✓			✓	✓	2
BEANS (RUNNER)	12		✓			✓	✓	2
BEETROOT	6	✓			✓			
BROCCOLI STALKS	12		✓			✓	✓	3
BROCCOLI FLORETS	12		✓			✓	✓	2
BRUSSELS SPROUTS	12		✓			✓	✓	3
CABBAGE (GREEN)	6		✓			✓		1½
CARROTS	12		✓			✓	✓	4
CAULIFLOWER FLORETS	6		✓			✓	✓	3
FENNEL, SLICED	6		✓			✓	✓	3
HERBS	12	✓	✓			✓	✓	
KALE	6		✓			✓		1
KOHLRABI	12		✓			✓		2
MUSHROOMS	3		✓			✓		
ONIONS, CHOPPED	2		✓			✓		2
PARSNIPS	12		✓			✓		2
PEAS (MANGETOUT AND SNAP)	12		✓			✓	✓	1
PEAS, SHELLED	12		✓			✓	✓	1
PEPPERS	12	✓				✓		2
POTATOES	3	✓	✓		✓			
SORREL	12		✓			✓		¼
SPINACH	12		✓			✓		1
SWEETCORN COBS	12	✓	✓			✓	✓	6
SWEETCORN KERNELS	12		✓			✓	✓	2
TOMATOES	12		✓				✓	
TURNIPS	12		✓			✓		3
VEGETABLES, COOKED (AVERAGE)	9		✓			✓		
VEGETABLES, PUREED (AVERAGE)	9	✓	✓			✓		

DEEP-FREEZING FRUIT

	FREEZER LIFE IN MONTHS	THAW BEFORE USING	COOK FROM FROZEN	FREEZE WITH SUGAR OR SYRUP	FREEZE COOKED	FREEZE WRAPPED	FREEZE ON OPEN TRAYS	BLANCHING TIME IN MINUTES
APPLES, SLICED	12		✔	✔		✔		
APRICOTS, STONED	12	✔	✔	✔		✔		
BLACKBERRIES	12	✔	✔	✔		✔	✔	
BLACKCURRANTS	12	✔	✔	✔		✔	✔	
BLUEBERRIES	12	✔		✔		✔	✔	
CHERRIES, STONED	12	✔	✔	✔		✔		
CRANBERRIES	12			✔		✔	✔	
DAMSONS	12	✔			✔	✔		
FIGS	12	✔	✔	✔		✔		
GOOSEBERRIES	12		✔	✔		✔	✔	
GRAPEFRUIT SEGMENTS	12	✔		✔		✔		
GRAPES, PIPPED	12	✔		✔		✔		
GREENGAGES, STONED	12	✔			✔	✔		
LEMONS AND LIMES, SLICES	12					✔		
LOGANBERRIES	12	✔	✔	✔		✔	✔	
MANGOES	12	✔		✔		✔		
MELONS	12	✔		✔		✔		
MULBERRIES	12	✔	✔	✔		✔	✔	
NECTARINES, STONED	9	✔		✔		✔		
ORANGE SEGMENTS	12	✔		✔		✔		
PEACHES, STONED	9	✔		✔		✔		
PEARS, SLICED	12	✔		✔	✔			
PINEAPPLE, SLICED	12	✔		✔		✔		
PLUMS, STONED	12	✔	✔	✔		✔		
QUINCES, SLICED	12	✔		✔	✔	✔		
RASPBERRIES	12	✔		✔		✔	✔	
REDCURRANTS	12	✔	✔	✔		✔	✔	
RHUBARB	12	✔		✔		✔		
STRAWBERRIES	12	✔		✔		✔	✔	
FRUIT PUREE, COOKED	9	✔			✔	✔		
FRUIT COULIS, RAW	4	✔				✔		
FRUIT JUICES	4	✔				✔		

DEEP-FREEZING DAIRY PRODUCE

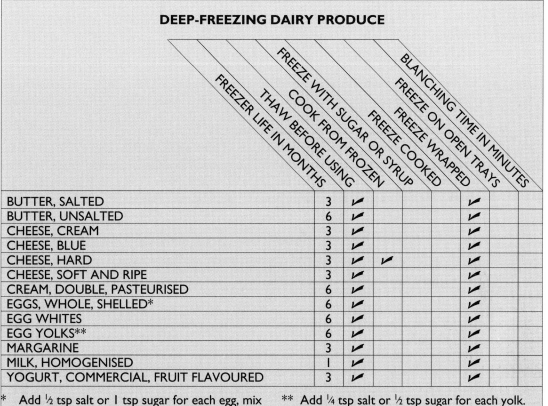

	FREEZER LIFE IN MONTHS	THAW BEFORE USING	COOK FROM FROZEN	FREEZE WITH SUGAR OR SYRUP	FREEZE COOKED	FREEZE WRAPPED	FREEZE ON OPEN TRAYS	BLANCHING TIME IN MINUTES
BUTTER, SALTED	3	✔				✔		
BUTTER, UNSALTED	6	✔				✔		
CHEESE, CREAM	3	✔				✔		
CHEESE, BLUE	3	✔				✔		
CHEESE, HARD	3	✔	✔			✔		
CHEESE, SOFT AND RIPE	3	✔				✔		
CREAM, DOUBLE, PASTEURISED	6	✔				✔		
EGGS, WHOLE, SHELLED*	6	✔				✔		
EGG WHITES	6	✔				✔		
EGG YOLKS**	6	✔				✔		
MARGARINE	3	✔				✔		
MILK, HOMOGENISED	1	✔				✔		
YOGURT, COMMERCIAL, FRUIT FLAVOURED	3	✔				✔		

* Add ½ tsp salt or 1 tsp sugar for each egg, mix and freeze.

** Add ¼ tsp salt or ½ tsp sugar for each yolk. Mix and freeze.

DEEP-FREEZING BAKED GOODS

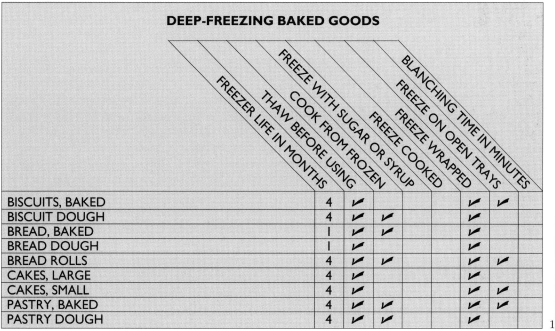

	FREEZER LIFE IN MONTHS	THAW BEFORE USING	COOK FROM FROZEN	FREEZE WITH SUGAR OR SYRUP	FREEZE COOKED	FREEZE WRAPPED	FREEZE ON OPEN TRAYS	BLANCHING TIME IN MINUTES
BISCUITS, BAKED	4	✔				✔	✔	
BISCUIT DOUGH	4	✔	✔			✔		
BREAD, BAKED	1	✔	✔			✔		
BREAD DOUGH	1	✔				✔		
BREAD ROLLS	4	✔	✔			✔	✔	
CAKES, LARGE	4	✔				✔		
CAKES, SMALL	4	✔				✔	✔	
PASTRY, BAKED	4	✔	✔			✔	✔	
PASTRY DOUGH	4	✔	✔			✔		

Raspberry Jelly

MAKES ABOUT 1KG (2LB 3OZ)

Home-made raspberry jelly has an intense, fresh flavour that no commercially produced jelly can match. Eat it with buttery croissants or brioche, or use a little, melted, to glaze fresh raspberry tarts. Without extra pectin, raspberry jelly will usually be lightly set, which is quite acceptable on the breakfast table and for glazing. For a stiffer set, use extra pectin.

1.8kg (4lb) fresh ripe raspberries
Granulated or preserving sugar (see below)

Put the raspberries in a pan and squash a few against the base. Heat gently to release the juices, squashing the fruit against the sides of the pan. Strain the juice through a jelly bag which you have scalded by pouring boiling water through it. To improvise a jelly bag, line a sieve with a clean teacloth and set it over a large bowl. Pour in the fruit pulp, tie up the corners of the cloth and hang it over the bowl for an hour or two until it stops dripping. For maximum clarity in the finished jelly, resist the temptation to squeeze the bag.

Measure the juice and put it in a preserving pan with 450g (1lb) sugar for every 600ml (1 pint) of juice.

Stir over a low heat until the sugar has dissolved completely, then boil for a set. Skim and pot while the jelly is very hot.

FREEZING

People used to talk of storing food in the deep freeze. Now we have dropped the deep and simply call it the freezer. Yet the old expression is a useful reminder that we are not talking about food which is merely *frozen*, but is frozen to −18°C (0°F) or lower. This temperature is the key to safe and successful freezing. In addition to immobilising the bacteria that spoil food, freezing food as fast as possible minimises the damage done to it. Water that freezes slowly forms large ice crystals. Water frozen fast forms much smaller ones. When the freezing liquid is inside meat and fish, much less damage is done to the structure of the flesh by the small ice crystals formed by fast freezing. As a result, there is a minimum loss of moisture from the flesh when it is thawed and cooked.

Use the fast-freeze control or switch the freezer to its coldest setting before freezing more than about 1kg (2lb 3oz) at a time.

WHAT WILL FREEZE?

Only a few foods cannot be frozen successfully. These include whole eggs in the shell, emulsion sauces such as mayonnaise, and recipes with sauces thickened with egg or starch such as pastry cream.

The Chart on page 150 shows how different foods should be prepared for freezing, and how long they can be stored.

PREPARING FOOD FOR FREEZING

Careful preparation and wrapping ensure that food keeps well for the maximum length of time. 'Freezer burn' is a form of dehydration at low temperatures which occurs when inadequate wrapping allows the dry air in the freezer to come in contact with the food. Use heavy duty wrappings designed for freezer storage. Eliminate as much air as possible, except when freezing liquids or semi liquids such as stews and purées which need head-space for expansion. Close all packages securely and label them clearly.

While all foods suitable for freezing can be frozen wrapped or in containers, some types of food can also be frozen laid out on trays, then, once frozen, wrapped and stored in the freezer. Berries, some vegetables, bread rolls and small cakes are candidates for 'open freezing'.

Fresh raw vegetables need to be blanched before freezing. Blanching destroys enzymes which, left untreated, would continue to work, gradually spoiling the colour, texture and flavour of the vegetables. However, freezing itself is destructive because ice crystals break down cell walls. Firm-textured vegetables stand up best to freezing. Leaves which will be eaten cooked, such as spinach, can also be frozen, but not lettuce and leaves to be eaten raw in salads.

Blanching must be accurately timed to destroy the enzymes without cooking the vegetables. Prepare the vegetables as if for cooking – topping and tailing beans, shelling peas, separating cauliflower into florets etc. Then blanch them (see Chart on page 150) in small batches in a large quantity of rapidly boiling salted water. This ensures that the heat does its job as quickly as possible. Transfer each batch immediately into iced water or cool it quickly under a cold tap. Drain and dry the vegetables before packing and freezing them. A robust wire basket with a handle is invaluable for transferring the vegetables into the boiling water and lifting them out again.

Cooked vegetable dishes such as gratins of root vegetables, purées, ratatouille and tomato sauces for pasta or pizza freeze well.

BOTTLING

Bottling is a dying folk art in this country. Domestic freezers have given us a quicker and more versatile method for fruit, and a faster, safer way of keeping vegetables and meat. Just 50 years ago every household had a store of the necessary jars with their special seals and lids, and replacements were widely available. Now they are more difficult to buy, though they can still be found on the shelves of serious kitchen suppliers.

The principle of bottling is a simple one. Food is packed in a container, usually a glass bottle or jar, covered and heated to kill the spoilage organisms. As the container cools, a partial vacuum forms between the food and the cover, preventing re-contamination.

Because most of the bacteria which cause food to spoil are killed at temperatures lower than that of boiling water, processing bottled foods by submerging the containers in boiling water is an effective form of sterilisation. (Timings vary, so follow a good recipe.) It works well for foods such as fruit which have high acidity. However, this domestic treatment is unsuitable for meat, poultry and most fresh vegetables, all of which have low acidity and can harbour heat-resistant bacterial spores. Botulism, a fatal form of food poisoning, is the risk. Leave foods with low acidity to commercial processors.

Firm fruits are bottled whole, or in large pieces. Soft fruits, such as berries, can be bottled whole, but their texture and appearance suffer during the heat treatment, so they are often preserved in purée or cordial form. Stored in a cool, dark place, bottled fruits should keep their colour and flavour for up to a year, but any that look or smell at all odd should on no account be tasted, and should be disposed of safely.

CHAPTER 15

COOKING WITH LEFTOVERS

Leftovers occur even in the best ordered households, and common sense demands that they should be used. The aim of recycling leftovers is to transform them into dishes which are worth making in their own right. Panache is the secret ingredient.

Now let us drop the dispiriting word leftovers, and think positively about some of the very good dishes which can be based on previously cooked ingredients, or on offcuts and trimmings from the raw materials. It is quite surprising how little need go to waste.

SAFETY

The fact that reheated food is one of the commonest causes of food poisoning is a poor excuse for wasting good ingredients. Two firm rules ensure safety. The first is to reheat food *thoroughly*. This applies regardless of the reheating method used, and particular care is required when microwaving in a low wattage oven.

The second rule is *never to reheat food more than once*. See also Chapter 27.

REHEATING MEAT

What could be more disappointing than reheating meat from a roasted joint that was tender and full of taste at the first eating, only to find it tough and poorly flavoured second time round? The problem of toughness, and how to rectify it, is more fully understood than what happens to the flavour.

When beef or lamb are roasted so that the meat is still pink, cooking is stopped when the internal temperature of the meat reaches about 60°C (140°F) and it remains tender and moist. When rare-roasted meat is reheated to 70°C (158°F), the muscle fibres shorten and the meat becomes tough. To tenderise it again, you need to cook it at a temperature higher than 80°C (176°F), until the tough connective tissue melts into gelatine. This applies whether the meat is sliced and reheated in gravy, or reheated in one large piece, or minced. Allow 20–30 minutes' cooking for finely chopped or minced meat, and up to 1½ hours for larger pieces.

Well-done roast meat, stews, casseroles, daubes, pot roasts and braises need only to be reheated.

Deterioration in the flavour of cooked meat is caused by oxidisation of its fats, a process which has been accelerated by the initial cooking. Oxidisation can be minimised by using pans and utensils made of materials other than iron and aluminium, and by closely covering the cooked meat for storage.

CHECKLIST OF IDEAS FOR LEFTOVERS

MEAT

Roast beef Cottage pie, rissoles, stuffed vegetables (peppers, courgettes, onions, mushrooms or cabbage leaves), samosa fillings, pasta stuffings, meatballs, toasted sandwiches.

Salt beef Corned beef hash.
Roast lamb Shepherd's pie, moussaka, rissoles, stuffed vegetables, meatballs.
Roast pork Rissoles, meatballs, stuffed vegetables, pasta stuffings.
Ham Omelettes, croquettes with rice or potato, stuffed vegetables, pasta stuffings, sauced in vol-au-vents or stuffed crêpes, potted ham paste.
Poultry Sauced in vol-au-vents or stuffed crêpes, in croquettes of rice or potato, in pilau with rice, soup, pasta stuffings, toasted sandwiches, with velouté sauce and pastry topping in pies.
Game Pasta stuffings, sauced in crêpes or vol-au-vents, potted with butter, with velouté sauce and pastry topping in pies.

FISH
Fish Fish cakes, fish balls, sauced with velouté or béchamel encased in *mousseline* (see Glossary).
Smoked fish Flaked smoked haddock in kedgeree, or sauced with béchamel on buttered toast, in vol-au-vents, or topped with grated cheese and grilled. Smoked salmon in scrambled egg or omelette.
Crustaceans Sauced with fish velouté or béchamel in vol-au-vents, pancakes, or encased in *mousseline* (see Glossary), or topped with grated cheese in ramekins and grilled.

VEGETABLES
Boiled potatoes Hashed, sautéed, Spanish omelettes, samosa fillings, curried.
Mashed potatoes Croquettes, in fish cakes, with egg in potato pancakes, thickening soups, topping.
Puréed vegetables Soups, gratins.

FRUIT
Soft fruits Sweetened purées frozen as *coulis* sauces, or ices; trifles.

RICE
Risotto Croquettes, *supplì* (see recipe).
Boiled rice Stuffed vegetables.

BREAD
White bread Bread puddings, *pain perdu*, French toast, cinnamon toast. Freeze fresh breadcrumbs for stuffings and mixing with herbs

or cheese for topping gratinéed dishes. Cheese pudding.
Brown bread Stuffings, and toppings with cheese or herbs.
Brioche Bread puddings, *pain perdu*.

PASTRY
Puff pastry dough trimmings Cheese straws, anchovy straws, cocktail pizzas.
Sweet pastry dough trimmings Biscuits for ices and creams.

Polpettini

SERVES 6
These Italian meatballs taste outstandingly good. In this recipe from *A Table in Tuscany* by Leslie Forbes they are coated in breadcrumbs or cornmeal and deep-fried to serve as an appetiser. They can also be rolled in flour, shallow-fried, and served with a bowl of buttered pasta, *tagliatelle, for instance.*

> 500g (1lb 2oz) cooked pork or beef, cut into cubes
> 2 potatoes, peeled and cooked
> 85g (3oz) Parmesan or Pecorino cheese, grated
> 110g (4oz) prosciutto (or ham)
> 2 eggs, beaten
> 1 handful of parsley, chopped
> 4 sage leaves, chopped
> Juice of 1 lemon
> Salt and freshly ground pepper
> ½ teaspoon grated nutmeg
> ¼ teaspoon ground cinnamon (optional)
> Cornmeal or breadcrumbs for coating
> Oil for deep-frying

Put the meat and potatoes through a fine grinder, mincer or food processor, then mix well with the other ingredients. Form tiny, round meatballs of a maximum 2.5cm (1in) diameter and roll in cornmeal or, better still, breadcrumbs.

Deep-fry (see page 60) a few at a time in hot oil until crunchy and golden brown. Drain well and serve hot with a selection of other *antipasti*. 157

Supplì

SERVES 4–6

When Elizabeth David's *Italian Food* was published in 1954 she had to advise her readers of a substitute for Mozzarella, the fresh white cheese which, thanks to the popularity of pizzas, is now widely available. This is her recipe.

Supplì are rice croquettes containing in the centre a slice of Mozzarella cheese and a piece of ham or Mortadella sausage. They can be made most successfully with leftover risotto, and are so good that it is worth cooking enough risotto to have about 2 cupfuls of rice left to make *supplì* the next day.

About 450g (1lb) cold risotto (see page 247)
2 eggs
100g (3½oz) thinly sliced ham, cut in squares
100g (3½oz) Mozzarella cheese, cut in squares
Fine breadcrumbs
Fat or oil for frying (deep or shallow)

Stir the beaten eggs into the cooked rice to bind it. Take about 1 tablespoon of the rice and put it flat on the palm of your hand; on the rice lay a little slice of ham and one of cheese. Place another tablespoon of rice on the top of the ham and cheese and form it into a ball about the size of a small orange so that the ham and cheese are completely enclosed. Roll each *supplì* very carefully in fine breadcrumbs, then fry them in hot fat or oil, turning them over and round so that the whole of the outside is nicely browned. Drain them on kitchen paper. The cheese inside should be just melted, stretching into threads (to which the dish owes its nickname of *supplì al telefono*, telephone wire croquettes) as one cuts into the rice. An attractive dish for a first course at lunch, and liked by everybody. But it needs a deft hand.

Fish Cakes

SERVES 2–4

Cooked smoked or fresh haddock or cod, salmon, tuna, or any other fish with plenty of flavour make good fish cakes to serve for break-fast, lunch or supper. The best sauce for fish cakes is a squeeze of fresh lemon juice.

225g (8oz) cooked flaked fish, free of skin and bones
225g (8oz) mashed potato
1–2 eggs, beaten
Salt and freshly ground pepper
2 tablespoons chopped fresh herbs (parsley, chives, chervil, dill, or a mixture)
Fine white breadcrumbs
Oil or fat for shallow-frying

Mix the fish and mashed potato with enough of the beaten egg to bind them together, and season the mixture well with salt, pepper and one or more of the herbs. Chill the mixture before forming it into balls, then flatten them a little to make thick cakes.

Turn the fish cakes in the remaining beaten egg, then in breadcrumbs to coat them well. Shallow-fry in hot oil or fat until golden brown on both sides.

Cottage Pie

SERVES 4

Making a shepherd's pie from cold roast lamb, or a cottage pie from roast beef, demands some thought to produce a good result. Quantities are variable, and the left-over meat will usually include well-roasted pieces from the outside of the joint and pink meat from the centre, or around the bone. Ideally, these meat pies, with a topping of creamed potato, are made with raw mince which is browned and then fully cooked with liquid and a little thickening before the topping is added and the finished dish baked to heat it through thoroughly and brown the potato.

When using cold roast meat, the browning stage is eliminated, but if the roast provides bone, it is well worth using it to make a stock to boost the flavour of the pie. The cold meat is minced, using the coarsest blade of the mincer, or very finely chopped. Alternatively, a food processor can be used to chop it, but this is the least satisfactory method because it is difficult to produce small, evenly sized pieces, and only too easy to overdo the chopping and to make a sticky mush.

Additional ingredients are all optional. Finely chopped onion, softened in oil or butter, and finely chopped root vegetables can be added for flavouring, or to stretch small amounts of meat a little further. The recipe gives proportions which can, of course, be varied.

2 tablespoons oil or butter
1 large onion, finely chopped
450g (1lb) cooked beef, minced
200ml (⅓ pint) stock or water
1 tablespoon cornflour
Salt and freshly ground black pepper
2 tablespoons finely chopped fresh parsley
680g (1½lb) potatoes, cooked and mashed

Heat the oil or butter in a saucepan and add the chopped onion. Fry until the onion is soft and lightly coloured. Add the minced meat and stock and simmer, covered, for about 15 minutes. Mix the cornflour with 2 tablespoons of cold water until smooth. Stir the cornflour into the minced meat mixture and stir well. Season the meat with salt and pepper to taste, and add the fresh parsley. Cook for 5 minutes more before turning the meat into a greased oven dish. Spoon the mashed potato over the meat and spread it evenly. This is more easily done if the meat is allowed to cool until solid. Dot the top of the pie with a little additional butter and bake it in a preheated moderate oven (180°C/350°F, gas mark 4) for about 40 minutes, or until the dish is bubbling and the top is well browned.

CHAPTER 16

COOKING WITHOUT A RECIPE

De gustibus non est disputandum. In matters of taste there is no dispute. The time-honoured dictum has never had to work harder than it does today when new ingredients, new influences, and new technologies make themselves felt in the kitchen. Coupled with the notion that novelty is a good thing for its own sake, an idea that gets more respect that it deserves in culinary matters, everyone feels free to kick the orthodoxies in the teeth. And why not? If the cucumber sauce on salami ice cream was not very nice, at least it was a talking point.

A more helpful adage for the guidance of creative cooks is the one about necessity being the mother of invention. You planned an apple pie for Sunday lunch, but the cupboard offers only strong bread flour or cornstarch, not plain flour. No problem. Dilute the gluten in the strong flour with a few spoonfuls of cornstarch and make pastry as usual. Or use the strong flour to make a crumble topping, which has no liquid in it to get the gluten working. If strong flour has run out and what is needed is fresh bread, then make a soda bread or use plain flour as you would strong. The yeast-raised loaf made with plain flour will not be as light as usual, but at least it is freshly baked bread.

So are there rules for breaking the rules, for escaping the tyranny of recipes? Indeed there are, as the flour examples illustrate. An understanding of the techniques described in the earlier chapters, and of the physical characteristics of basic ingredients, allows the cook to improvise substitutions and variations.

A mental checklist of points to consider will include texture and timing as well as taste. Think about how changed ingredients will behave.

TIMING

Will the new ingredient cook faster or more slowly? In the flour examples there is no reason to expect any difference in timing. But if the change is, say, fish for chicken in a curry, then you will need to bear in mind that most types of fish need less cooking than poultry does. This might lead you to adjust the sequence of the recipe, adding the fish at a later point in the procedure to avoid overcooking.

TEXTURE

In the example of yeast-raised bread made with plain flour, you would expect the loaf to be denser than usual because plain flour has less gluten to trap the aerating bubbles of gas. So would extra yeast improve the rise? No, because the limiting factor is the gluten, not the yeast.

Think about the textural implications of substituting fish for chicken in the curry. Firm-fleshed fish such as fresh tuna, big, juicy prawns or squid are going to be a better choice than soft-fleshed varieties like whiting or plaice.

TASTE

Here it is every man for himself. Recipes tell us to add salt to taste, to adjust the amount of sugar according to the tartness of fruit, to add a few drops of lemon juice to give life to a sauce. We are all practised tasters, so thinking about how changing or substituting ingredients will alter the taste of a recipe is only an extension of a skill we exercise every day.

Going back to the bread made with plain instead of strong flour, it is safe to predict that there will be no material alteration in the taste.

The curry is more complicated because fish and chicken taste different from each other, and tuna tastes different again from prawns or squid. Would a slightly different blend of spices – hotter, milder, or with a different emphasis – be an improvement? And what about herbs? Would fresh coriander leaves sprinkled over the cooked fish be a small change that makes a big difference?

STARTING POINTS

Apparently outlandish flavour combinations such as chocolate in a sauce for game, or vanilla in a sauce for fish, can be inspirations in subtle hands, vile if overdone. Explorers are not too proud to use maps to guide them to their starting points, and cooks who are adventurous by inclination or necessity can find tracks to follow in tried and tested combinations of tastes.

There are all sorts of good reasons for experimenting. The garden is full of bolting spinach and the family has had spinach twice already this week, so you want to do something different with it. Seasonal ingredients at glut prices and special offers in the supermarket are not to be missed. Making a meal from what is available when plans are changed and there is no opportunity to shop, is another chance to improvise. But who needs excuses? It is fun.

Here our starting point is the main ingredient which is to form the basis of a meal. Listed under each one (below) are herbs, spices and other flavouring ingredients with which they have a particular affinity. The list is not, of course, exhaustive. Anyone who has been cooking Japanese, Thai, Indonesian, Mexican, African or Middle Eastern dishes will find more condiments in the storecupboard to play with.

In the chapter on herbs and spices (see page 260), flavour combinations are approached from the opposite direction, putting the flavourings first and then listing their known affinities with various foods.

EGGS

Herbs: basil, chervil, chives, dill, fennel, lemon balm, parsley, sorrel, tarragon.
Spices: celery salt (with hard-boiled eggs), cayenne pepper, curry powders or pastes in mayonnaise or hot sauces.
Oils and fats: butter, olive oil.
Vinegars: wine, sherry or balsamic vinegar (to deglaze frying residues).
Vegetables: artichoke bottoms, asparagus, cauliflower, garlic, mushrooms, onions, potatoes (fried), spinach, spring onions, truffles, watercress.
Good companions: cheese, bacon, ham, salt and smoked fish, caviar.

CHEESE

Herbs: most fresh herbs go well with cream cheese or in dips. In other cheese dishes consider chervil, chives, dill, marjoram, oregano and parsley.
Spices: cayenne pepper, caraway, cumin, mustard.
Oils and fats: butter.
Vegetables: garlic, tomatoes, truffles. Cheese sauces, and cheesy toppings, go with virtually all vegetables.
Good companions: eggs, fish and shellfish, ham, pasta, sweet pickles, Worcestershire sauce, apples, pears (blue cheese), grapes.

FISH AND SHELLFISH

Herbs: basil, bay, burnet, chervil, chives, coriander, dill, fennel, lemongrass, marjoram, mint, oregano, parsley, savory, sorrel, tarragon, thyme.
Spices: allspice, anise, annatto, cardamom, celery seed, chilli, curry paste or powder, dill seed, fennel seed, galangal, ginger, green peppercorns, mustard, nutmeg and mace, paprika, red peppercorns, saffron, sassafras, star anise, vanilla.
Oils and fats: butter, olive oil, herb oils, bacon fat for frying.
Vinegars: all types.

161

Vegetables: edible seaweeds including fresh samphire, carrots, celery, celeriac, fennel, garlic, mushrooms, onions, peas, tomatoes.

Good companions: white wine, potatoes, rice and cream are particularly useful in fish cooking. Anchovy sauce, soy sauce.

CHICKEN

Herbs: basil, bay, bergamot, burnet, chervil, chives, coriander, fennel, lemon balm, lemongrass, marjoram, mint, oregano, parsley, rosemary, sage, savory, tarragon, thyme.

Spices: allspice, annatto, chilli, cumin, curry paste or powder, galangal, ginger, nutmeg, paprika, saffron, sassafras, tamarind, turmeric.

Oils and fats: butter, olive oil, herb-flavoured oils, sesame oil.

Vinegars: balsamic, cider, herb, sherry and wine vinegars.

Vegetables: most vegetables can be combined with chicken. Asparagus, garlic, mushrooms and truffles have a particular affinity with it.

Good companions: bacon and ham, lime and lemon, toasted pine kernels, white wine, cream, yogurt, and rice.

DUCK AND GOOSE

Herbs: bay, bergamot, hyssop, lemongrass, lovage, marjoram, oregano, parsley, sage, savory, thyme.

Spices: allspice, anise, caraway, chilli, cinnamon, cloves, fennel seed, fenugreek, galangal, ginger, juniper berries, sassafras, star anise, tamarind.

Oils and fats: added fats are seldom necessary.

Vinegars: balsamic, cider, herb, sherry and wine vinegars.

Vegetables: garlic, celery, celeriac, leeks, onions, spring onions, turnips.

Good companions: dried beans, lentils, apples, sour cherries, cranberries, lemons, lime and oranges (especially Seville oranges), redcurrant jelly, soy sauce.

GAME

Herbs: bay, lemon balm, lovage, marjoram, oregano, parsley, rosemary, savory, thyme.

Spices: allspice, cloves, coriander seed, juniper berries, paprika, sassafras.

Oils and fats: butter, olive oil, pork fat, including lard and bacon fat.

Vinegars: balsamic, fruit, sherry and wine vinegars.

Vegetables: all root vegetables, mushrooms (especially wild), Savoy cabbage, red cabbage.

Good companions: red wine, port, chestnuts, plums, prunes, Seville oranges, sour cherries, blaeberries, myrtle berries, cranberries, rowan jelly, redcurrant jelly, mushroom ketchup, dark chocolate in minute quantities, suet pastry for game puddings.

BEEF

Herbs: bay, chervil, lovage, marjoram, oregano, parsley, rosemary, savory, tarragon, thyme.

Spices: allspice, annatto, celery seed, chilli, cinnamon, cloves, coriander seed, cumin, curry paste or powder, dill seed, fenugreek, galangal, ginger, green peppercorns, juniper berries, mustard, paprika, sassafras, tamarind, turmeric.

Oils and fats: butter, olive oil, beef dripping, pork fat.

Vinegars: balsamic, sherry and wine vinegars.

Vegetables: most vegetables can be combined with beef. The entire onion and root tribes, okra, and tomatoes have a particular affinity with it.

Good companions: kidney, horseradish, soy sauce, mushroom ketchup, Worcestershire sauce, pickled walnuts, dumplings.

VEAL

Herbs: basil, bay, chervil, fennel, lemon balm, lovage, marjoram, oregano, parsley, rosemary, sage, savory, sorrel, tarragon, thyme.

Spices: mustard, nutmeg, paprika.

Oils and fats: butter, olive oil.

Vinegars: balsamic, herb and white wine vinegars.

Vegetables: artichoke bottoms and hearts, garlic, mushrooms, tomatoes.

Good companions: ham (especially *prosciutto*), cheese, tuna mayonnaise, anchovies, lemon, Marsala, white wine, cream.

LAMB

Herbs: bay, chervil, chives, coriander, dill, fennel, hyssop, lemon balm, lovage, marjoram, mint, oregano, parsley, rosemary, savory, sorrel, tarragon, thyme.

Spices: annatto, cardamom, celery seed, chilli, cinnamon, cloves, cumin, curry paste or powder, fenugreek, galangal, ginger, mustard, paprika, saffron, sassafras, tamarind, turmeric.

Oils and fats: butter, olive oil, lard.

Vinegars: balsamic, herb, sherry and wine.

Vegetables: garlic, fresh haricot beans, broad beans, peas, aubergines, cooked cucumbers, and tomatoes.

Good companions: dried beans and lentils, bulgar, capers, lemons, yogurt, redcurrant jelly, mint sauce.

PORK

Herbs: bergamot, fennel, lemon balm, lemongrass, lovage, marjoram, oregano, parsley, rosemary, sage, savory, thyme.

Spices: allspice, anise, annatto, caraway, chilli, cloves, fennel seeds, galangal, ginger, juniper berries, mustard, nutmeg, paprika, sassafras, star anise.

Oils and fats: butter, olive oil, lard.

Vinegars: wine vinegar.

Vegetables: cabbage, mushrooms, onions.

Good companions: prunes, apples, plums, dried apricots, fresh pineapple, dried peas and beans, *sauerkraut,* barbecue sauce, soy sauce.

VEGETABLES

Fresh young produce and unusual vegetables from the market garden, or your own, need no more adornment than salt, pepper and a little butter or oil. Indian cooking makes inspired use of herbs and spices, transforming the humblest of vegetables into dishes which can stand on their own. But last-minute additions, sprinkling a single herb, finely chopped, or a few seeds, crushed or whole, adds variety to the vegetables we eat most frequently.

Brussels sprouts: nutmeg.

Beetroot: chives, lemon thyme, parsley.

Cabbage: caraway, cumin, dill or fennel seeds, nutmeg, juniper berries.

Carrots: chervil, chives, coriander, dill, fennel, parsley, tarragon leaves, lemon juice, fresh ginger.

Green beans: garlic, slivered toasted hazelnuts or almonds, toasted sesame seeds, bacon croûtons, hazelnut oil.

Mushrooms: parsley, garlic, lemon juice.

Peas: chives, hyssop, mint.

Potatoes: chervil, chives, mint, parsley, garlic, spring onions, onion seeds.

Spinach: toasted coriander seeds, nutmeg.

White turnips: orange juice and zest.

FRUIT

Herbs and spices go well with some fruits. Raspberries, strawberries, mangoes and many others need no embellishment, but some fruits are lifted from ordinary to exquisite by additions which are sometimes surprising.

Apples: stewed with vanilla pod, cinnamon or cloves. Angelica leaves, sweet cicely, lemon balm or mint with cooked apple.

Bananas: fried with cinnamon and lemon juice.

Gooseberries: stewed with elderflower.

Melons: angelica leaves, lemon verbena, mint, lime and lemon juice.

Oranges: cinnamon, cloves or coriander in syrup.

Peaches and nectarines: cinnamon in poaching syrup, or sprinkled for grilling or baking.

Pears: bay, cardamom, cloves, cinnamon, fresh ginger, vanilla, and citrus zest in red wine for poaching.

Plums: stewed with angelica leaves, cloves or cinnamon.

Rhubarb: stewed with vanilla pod, or fresh ginger, or orange. Angelica leaves, sweet cicely or lemon balm on stewed rhubarb.

Compotes of dried fruits: bay, cardamom, cloves, cinnamon, fresh ginger, vanilla, citrus zest, wine and tea leaves.

Fresh fruit salads: lemon verbena, mint, sweet cicely.

The Cooking of America

by RICHARD CAWLEY

To an uninformed European, it might appear that American cooking has not much heritage of note and little in the way of important regional dishes – its only dubious claim to fame being perhaps the invention of fast-food delicacies such as Chicken McNuggets.

Richard Cawley, food writer and broadcaster

After all, how can a country whose national pedigree only dates from 1776 possibly have any culinary tradition?

A little investigation, however, reveals a fascinating and complicated history of cross-cultural recipe-swapping that began when the early English settlers were helped through their first winter by the native American Indians. This American tradition of embracing the cuisines of other cultures and synthesising them into 'American Food' continues today, creating a true gastronomic melting pot.

While America's political history stretches over a mere 200 years or so, as opposed to the millennia claimed by some European or Eastern cultures, it would take that many pages to explore the myriad cultural, historical and economic events that shaped American cooking into today's hearty amalgam.

This penchant began when the only 'Americans' were the native Indians. When the various groups of English settlers arrived in the early 1600s, they were relieved to have survived the treacherous Atlantic crossing but dismayed at having to face a formidable winter in unfamiliar terrain. Fortunately they were able to rely on 'recipe tips' from the Indians to get them through their first disastrous year.

The most important gift the American Indian gave to the first settlers was corn. This corn, which we know as maize or sweetcorn, was their staple food and was to become also the staple of the white man in a land which seemed unsuited to the cultivation of wheat. The unfamiliar maize kernels could be eaten raw, boiled, roasted or dried. Once ground, the resulting meal or flour could be mixed with water and made into porridges, puddings or loaves.

The early colonial housewife quickly learned from her Indian counterpart to bake these simple flat breads by either resting the dough on a wooden plank, which was then wedged in an almost upright position in front of an open fire, or by burying the discs of dough in hot ashes. These early loaves came to be known as johnny (or journey) cakes and ash cakes. Small loaves were also placed on metal farm implements and cooked over the flames – aptly named hoe cakes – and larger round loaves, called griddle cakes, were produced by the lucky housewife who had brought a flat metal griddle with her from England.

The transplanted English cooks also learned the Indian method of using a lye, made from soaking woodash in water, to remove the tough outer skin from the corn kernels. The Indians also used woodash as an ingredient in their breads, both to add flavour and to act as a leavening agent. The alkaline ash not only balanced the amino acids in the corn as a valuable food supplement, but also reacted with them to produce carbon dioxide, which lightened the breads.

This chemical reaction was refined in the mid 19th century by American chemists to produce the first version of baking powder, thus revolutionising the art of baking, which had formerly relied on eggs, slow-rising yeasts and natural fermentations.

As the colonial cook became more skilled, she refined her simple corn mixtures, adding eggs and wild fruits to make soufflé-like spoon breads and variations of traditional English sweet puddings.

The American taste for corn has far from diminished, and a list of modern uses for this most ancient of grains shows its astonishing versatility. The aisles of any American supermarket are

Boston Fish Chowder

stocked with cornflakes, corn oil, cornstarch (cornflour) and corn syrup, margarine, corn kernels either frozen or in tins; corn ground into cornmeal, processed into hominy to make grits or pickled in jars to make relish.

Corn is dwarfed, popped, made into fritters, bread, pancakes and muffins, brewed into beer, distilled to produce bourbon and fed to chickens to fatten them for the table. Then there are all the Mexican and southwest American Indian variations on the corn *tortilla*.

The Indians taught the settlers their ingenious and efficient methods of farming, and introduced the new arrivals to the wealth of wild foods – how to hunt for wild game, catch fish and gather the countless varieties of wild fruits and berries.

The English settlers soon became organised, planting their kitchen gardens with familiar fruit, vegetables and herbs, including English apples. These fared so well in the New England that they soon became a staple for Indians and settlers alike, with apple cider becoming as popular as beer. By the time of the revolution in 1776, English apples grew in every corner of 165 every colony in America.

Though fresh produce was abundant in season, every available method of preservation was used to store precious food for the winter. The settlers learned from the Indians how to dry and smoke fish, meat and game. They also cured foods in salt and pickled them in vinegar made from cider, making relishes from glut crops of cucumbers, peppers, onions and corn. They combined the sweet syrup extracted from the native maple tree with wild fruits to make preserves, jams and jellies. Apples were dried and made into sauce.

Up and down the Atlantic coast fish was extremely plentiful, with cod the backbone of the New England diet, eaten fresh in the summer months and salted for the rest of the year. It was 'grilled' in front of the fire, tied to an upright plank in the Indian way, and made into countless *chowders*. The name derives from the French word for cauldron, *chaudron*.

Early chowders were made from the same recipes used on board ship during the long journey from England. Fresh or salted fish was cooked in a pot with water, onion and a little salt pork, and thickened with crushed ship's biscuits.

The inland equivalent of chowder was a one-pot dinner based on meat and vegetables called New England boiled dinner – a meal which at its best, like the French *pot au feu*, can be delectable but whose early incarnations in a frugal colonial household were unlikely to be more than a bit of salt beef and a few vegetables boiled in plain water – virtuous food indeed.

That well-loved and universal dish of Boston baked beans also has its roots in this early period of American culinary history. The strict Puritan rules prohibited any cooking on the sabbath. It was a simple step to substitute traditional English peas with the Indians' beans, adding a little onion with a scrap of cured pork or bacon and a little maple syrup for sweetness. This could easily be prepared on Saturday to cook slowly overnight and be ready to eat for breakfast, dinner and supper on the sabbath.

The Dutch colonists, predom-

> *The Indians taught the settlers their ingenious and efficient methods of farming, and introduced the new arrivals to the wealth of wild foods – how to hunt for wild game, catch fish and gather the countles varieties of wild fruits and berries.*

inantly traders and merchants, who occupied much of New York (including the island of Manhattan, formerly called New Amsterdam), left a culinary legacy that includes more light-hearted fare than the stodgy New England classics. From those early days, Americans have delighted in pancakes and waffles, now inseparably paired with maple syrup, and that American favourite, the cookie.

Another group of religious refugees from Europe were to have a lasting influence on American food. The first settlers of what was to become Pennsylva-nia were known as Pennsylvanian Dutch, though they were actually Swiss-German (the confusion arising from the German word for German – *Deutsch*).

By the time the Pennsylvanians arrived in America, all the easily cleared land had been claimed by the English. The Germans, however, were used to woodland and moved inland, aware of the fact that where there were black walnut trees there would also be limestone – which meant good farming land.

They brought with them dumplings and noodles, the art of fine sausage-making, and they introduced vinegar as a flavouring rather than as a mere preserving agent in dishes such as *sauerbraten*. They also began to add sugar to their pickles, a habit which has passed down the centuries and accounts for the American fondness for combinations of sweet and sour.

A sausage stuffed in a piece of bread, christened a 'hot dog', was a much later invention by a German immigrant, and another German gave America, and the world, the hamburger.

We can also thank the Pennsylvanian Dutch for that other great American classic, the doughnut. Originally made without the hole, doughnuts were traditional for Shrove Tuesday, another custom happily integrated into mainstream American life.

To the cook in the simple kitchen of the early New England colonies, the preparation of food must have been a chore indeed – particularly as the cook was invariably also the woman of the house, servantless and convinced that any fancy food was the food of the devil.

Down south, however, for many women of the house, the

lifestyle was more lady of the manor than drudge. Looked after and cooked for by slaves, she presided over her spacious plantation home, organising tea parties, dinners and balls in the manner of *Gone with the Wind*. Her culinary skill lay in selecting menus, not cooking them.

These southern belles probably rarely saw their kitchens, which – because of the warmth of the climate and the abundance of fuel and labour – were housed in separate buildings some distance from the house. This differed from the northern kitchen, which by necessity was in the centre of the house. Whereas most northern food was typified by being cooked in an enclosed pot, these separate kitchens and the warmer climate encouraged outdoor cooking over an open fire. This has developed through history to become what is now modern American barbecue cookery.

Food supply in the south was also more plentiful and available, including an abundance of game. In North Carolina, for example, there were no fewer than 35 species of wild duck. There were wild grapes along the coast, plus all the wild berries. The first American turkeys were, of course, wild, and it must have been a natural step to sauce the rich gamey meat with a tart berry – resulting in the classic roast turkey with cranberry sauce.

The Carolinas were populated in part by French Huguenots. These were expert farmers, grape-growers, wine-makers and bakers. They quickly introduced their refined French cooking methods to the southern kitchen, adding wine and delicate sauces to the more rustic techniques of the English and German colonists.

The Huguenots also brought with them the recipes and skills for making frozen sherbets and ices, using the abundance of dairy produce and fruit. Thus began America's perpetual love affair with ice cream.

Rice arrived in the New World from Madagascar in 1685, and the freshwater swamps of the Carolinas proved the perfect place for it to grow. By the early 18th century, the success of the

American food was influenced not only by those who chose to migrate to America, but also by the vast population of Africans who were unwilling immigrants during slavery.

French Huguenot rice plantations worked by slaves was such that rice became known as 'Carolina gold' and soon became the staple of the south, replacing corn and wheat. Black cooks combined it with beans to produce dishes with such evocative names as Hoppin' John (cow peas), Limpin' Susan (red beans) and Moors and Christians (black beans).

Dairy food was plentiful in the south because the warm climate provided year-round grazing for cattle as well as a constant supply of fresh fruit and vegetables. Peanuts were introduced to fatten the hogs, which would eventually become fine hams, especially famous in Virginia. The Indians had long been in the habit of grinding seeds to a paste to thicken stews, and the grinding of peanuts to produce today's peanut butter was a natural progression. Further south in Georgia, farmers developed many new crops including watermelons, sweet potatoes and pimento peppers as specialities.

American food was influenced not only by those who chose to migrate to America, but also by the vast population of Africans who were unwilling immigrants during slavery. Black cooks in their turn added their own cultural touches to southern cooking to produce the fascinating hybrid dishes which constitute what is now considered southern cuisine. From Africa and the Caribbean they introduced *bene* (sesame) seeds, incorporated the local pecan nut, cooked meat with fruit, used coconuts and oranges, and soaked their cakes in rum. They also became expert at baking the hot breads and 'biscuits' which are now synonymous with southern cooking.

Further west in Louisiana, a pair of culinary styles developed – Cajun and Creole – that shared similar ingredients but which reflected the different cultural backgrounds of their practitioners. 'Cajun' derives from 'Arcadian' and refers to the white inhabitants of the region who migrated from France, making their way eventually to the muddy Mississippi delta via Nova Scotia. Cajun culture and cooking centres on the swamp lands of the delta region, where the abundant fish and shellfish highlight a gutsy and flavourful style of cooking. Crayfish, oysters, crab and shrimps (prawns) are the most popular ingredients, accented by hot chillies, sausages and quantities of rice.

Though the spicy heat of 167

Cajun cooking would make a French chef pale, French terminology peppers the Cajun repertoire, with terms such as *étouffée* and *gratinée* common.

The citified cousin to backcountry Cajun is Creole, a fancier kind of food with marginally less robust flavours, which flourished in the restaurants and wealthy homes of New Orleans, employing a new generation of professional black cooks. Creole cooking incorporated Spanish, French, African and Caribbean elements into the native Louisiana context, manifesting itself in such famous dishes as *jambalaya* – a dish very similar to Spanish paella based on rice, ham and shellfish. Its name speaks volumes about this jazzed-up, cross-cultural style of cooking. '*Jamba*' from the French *jambon* or Spanish *jamón*; '*ala*' from the French *à la*; and '*ya*' from the African word meaning both rice and an expletive.

The other most famous dish of this region, claimed by Cajun and Creole alike, is *gumbo*, a stew featuring any number of meats or shellfish, but invariably thickened with okra – gumbo being African Bantu for okra.

While the east coast of North America was being settled by predominantly English, French and German settlers, 3,000 miles to the west were Spaniards busily exploiting the riches of California, Arizona, Texas and New Mexico. These early settlers were also swapping recipes with the native residents, learning to appreciate the virtues of corn, beans and chillies. The cross-breeding of these staple Indian foods with cooking practices of the early Spanish conquerors led to the development of Tex-Mex or Mexamerican food which, enriched by the continued settlement of the region by Hispanic groups, remains foremost in America's 'ethnic' culinary consciousness.

In the 19th century a second wave of settlers began in America from all over the world – Scandinavia, Ireland, Scotland, China and Italy. Again, many of these were escaping religious or political persecution in Europe. With the fertile and easily accessible lands of the Atlantic coastal plain already spoken for, the new settlers began to move inland across America's broad heartland, and were eventually attracted by prospects of the Pacific coast and California. Each of these new 'foreigners' brought their own familiar dishes and cooking styles with them. Italian immigrants introduced one particular traditional dish which would eventually become an icon of American food – pizza.

Before the mid 20th century, most immigrants came from north-western Europe, but in recent decades many have arrived from south-eastern Europe, Latin America, the Middle East, Africa and Asia (Japan, Korea, Thailand and Vietnam). Restaurants serving the foods of these countries and markets selling ethnic ingredients are springing up in every major city. 'Going out for a pizza' is echoed by 'Going out for *sushi*/Lebanese/Ethiopian'.

While Americans have always been vaguely aware of the ethnic and cultural sources of the food they ate, it is only in the last few decades that the diversity and authenticity of American food has been more thoroughly examined and celebrated. In the post-World War II years, food in the States became homogenised, mainly as a result of the advances in food technology, such as deep-freezing and refrigerated railroad cars, and of the mass culture created by the media. Flavours were muted for the sake of pleasing the widest range of people; the further from the field an ingredient was, the better. 'Convenience foods', such as packet mixes and frozen 'TV dinners', were part of the American dream, and while they undoubtedly liberated the home-maker from some of the tedium of cooking, they also drew her and her family further from their culinary traditions.

In the late 1960s and early 1970s, some Americans began to look more closely at what they were eating, spurred perhaps in part by the 'counter-culture's' interest in ideas such as back-to-nature vegetarianism and organic foods. Hand-in-hand with this awareness of ingredients went a curiosity about the cuisine of other countries and the culinary roots of America's own food. Ethnic dishes grown dreary and diluted over the years – spaghetti and meatballs, chop suey – were replaced by more esoteric and adventurous dishes. Courageous hostesses began offering the likes of bouillabaisse, pesto and paella; Chinese restaurants distinguished between Szechuan, Cantonese and Hunan; and formerly humble fare such as barbecued ribs was blessed by liberal chic as 'soul food'.

In perhaps typically American fashion, this appreciation of ethnic ingredients and cuisines was at times taken to extremes, with juxtapositions of international styles that would try the skills of the most seasoned diplomat. Chef practitioners of what was

168

Chicken 'n' Dumplings

generously labelled 'fusion cuisine' were dishing up such combinations as Cassoulet of Lobster with Oriental Black Bean Salsa.

Trendy exaggeration notwithstanding, what has emerged from this period of culinary soul-searching is a pride in the multicultural traditions that are the foundation of today's American table.

MENU 1
SERVES 6
Caesar Salad
Chicken 'n' Dumplings
Shoo Fly Pie

Caesar Salad

This is one of those classic dishes where there are as many 'authentic' recipes as there are restaurants that serve it. This one was given to me by my friend Martha Holmberg, the American food writer and editor.

1 large head of Cos lettuce (no other kind will do)
For the dressing
1 egg yolk
3 tablespoons lemon juice
½ teaspoon Dijon mustard
1 clove garlic, crushed
6 anchovy fillets, drained and very finely chopped
Dash of Worcestershire sauce
Freshly ground black pepper
120ml (4fl oz) virgin olive oil
For the croûtons
3 tablespoons virgin olive oil
1 clove garlic, sliced
3 slices of white bread, cut into 1cm (½in) cubes
To serve
110g (4oz) Parmesan cheese, freshly grated

Discard any coarse or damaged outer leaves of the lettuce. Wash the rest and dry thoroughly, then tear into bite-sized pieces and put in a serving bowl.

To make the dressing put the first six ingredients in the bowl of a food processor or liquidiser, and season to taste with pepper. You should not need to add extra salt as the anchovies should provide enough. Process until smooth, then add the oil in a thin steady stream until well blended. Check seasoning.

To make the croûtons, heat the oil in a large frying pan. Fry the garlic over a medium heat until golden brown then remove and discard. This will have flavoured the oil. Fry the cubes of bread in the garlic oil, stirring constantly until crisp and golden. Drain and cool.

Pour the dressing over the lettuce and toss well, sprinkle over the croûtons and Parmesan, and serve at once.

Chicken 'n' Dumplings

This wonderfully comforting homey dish is in the tradition of the one-pot dinner of the early settlers, and is the sort of recipe which was and is adapted to the budget and taste of the cook.

6 chicken quarters (or chicken portions of your choice)
55g (2oz) butter
1 tablespoon corn oil
2 onions, chopped
4 stalks celery, chopped
4 carrots, sliced
1 tablespoon flour
300ml (½ pint) white wine
300ml (½ pint) chicken stock
4 tablespoons double cream
110g (4oz) button mushrooms, quartered
¼ teaspoon ground allspice
Salt and freshly ground black pepper

For the dumplings
225g (8oz) plain flour
1 teaspoon sugar
1 scant tablespoon baking powder
½ teaspoon salt
30g (1oz) chilled butter
150ml (¼ pint) milk

Heat the butter and oil in a large lidded frying pan, and fry the chicken portions over a low heat, in manageable batches, for about 15 minutes, or until browned all over. Remove and reserve.

Stir-fry the vegetables for 5–10 minutes in the same fat or until softened. Stir in the flour and continue to stir-fry for another minute.

Add the wine, stock and cream and bring to the boil stirring, then simmer for a few seconds until thickened. Stir in the mushrooms and allspice and season well.

Return the chicken pieces to the pan, pushing them well down so that they are surrounded by vegetables and sauce. Cover the pan tightly and cook over the lowest possible heat for 30 minutes.

To make the dumplings, sift the flour into a bowl and stir in the sugar, baking powder and salt. Cut in the butter as you would for making pastry or scones, then quickly mix in the milk with a fork to form a soft scone-like dough.

Either form into small equal balls, or roll or pat out to about 2cm (¾in) thick and cut out 12 x 3cm (1½in) discs with a pastry cutter.

Place the dumplings over the contents of the pan. They will sit on top and steam, rather than sink into the sauce. Replace the lid and cook for a further 20 minutes. Serve immediately, straight from the pan.

Shoo Fly Pie

Americans love pies, and this one is particularly easy to make and uses only the simplest of store-cupboard ingredients.

Legend has it that flies are particularly fond of molasses (or treacle), hence the charming and evocative name.

For the pastry
170g (6oz) plain flour
Pinch of salt
85g (3oz) cold butter, cut into small pieces
4 tablespoons cold water
For the filling
170g (6oz) plain flour
110g (4oz) soft brown sugar
½ teaspoon ground cinnamon
¼ teaspoon ground ginger
¼ teaspoon grated nutmeg
55g (2oz) butter
6 tablespoons treacle
120ml (4fl oz) boiling water
½ teaspoon bicarbonate of soda

For the pastry, place the flour and salt in a mixing bowl and rub in the butter until it resembles fine breadcrumbs.

Mix in the water and, working quickly, bring the mixture together until it forms a smooth dough. Wrap in kitchen film, or place in a plastic bag and chill for about 30 minutes before rolling out. (This dough can be made in a food processor in seconds.)

Preheat the oven to 190°C/375°F, gas mark 5.

Roll out the pastry and line a loose-bottomed 23–25cm (9–10in) metal flan tin.

For the filling, sift the flour into a bowl and stir in the sugar and spices. Cut and rub in the butter as you would for making pastry to make a crumb mixture.

Put the treacle into another bowl, pour over the boiling water and mix in. Stir in the bicarbonate of soda, and about one-third of the crumb mixture. Pour this into the prepared pastry case, then sprinkle the rest of the crumb mixture evenly on top. Bake for 30–40 minutes or until firm but still a bit wobbly in the middle. Serve at room temperature, with whipped cream if liked.

MENU 2
SERVES 6
Boston fish chowder
Barbecued spare ribs
Corn bread
Succotash
Strawberry shortcake

Boston Fish Chowder

This recipe is loosely based on one written in 1884 by a Mary J. Lincoln, who ran a famous cookery school in Boston at the end of the 19th century. One of her pupils was a certain Fannie Farmer, who was to write a cookery book as influential to America as Mrs Beeton's were to England. The cream cracker crumbs used to thicken the soup are a descendant of the ships' biscuits that the early pilgrims used to thicken their chowders on the long sea journey to New England.

1 tablespoon vegetable oil
110g (4oz) smoked streaky bacon, sliced across into 1cm (½in) pieces
2 onions, chopped
450g (1lb) potatoes, peeled and cut into 1cm (½in) dice
1 teaspoon cornflour
1.2 litres (2 pints) full-fat milk
450g (1lb) skinned fillets of cod or haddock, cut into 1cm (½in) pieces
Salt and freshly ground pepper
3 cream crackers, reduced to powder in a food processor
Dash of Worcestershire sauce
30g (1oz) butter, cut into tiny pieces
Chopped parsley to garnish

Heat the oil in a heavy-bottomed saucepan and fry the bacon pieces over a low heat, or until they render their fat. Turn up the heat and fry until crisp, turning as necessary. Remove about half the cooked bacon with a slotted spoon and reserve.

Cook the onion in the remaining fat for 5–10 minutes or until softened but not browned. Add the potatoes and stir-fry for 1 minute.

Dissolve the cornflour in a little of the milk. Add the remaining milk to the potato mixture, then stir the cornflour mixture into this. Bring to the boil and simmer, over the lowest possible heat, stirring occasionally for about 10–15 minutes, or until the potatoes are completely tender.

Add the fish and season well with salt and pepper. Continue to simmer for 2 minutes and then stir in the cracker crumbs. Simmer for 2–3 more minutes or until thickened slightly. Add Worcestershire sauce to taste, and check the seasoning.

Serve in heated bowls and sprinkle with the butter pieces, the reserved crisped bacon, and chopped parsley if liked.

Barbecued Spare Ribs

Barbecued meat in America meant, and still often does mean, that the meat is cooked over charcoal and served with a spicy sweet and sour sauce. Nowadays, however, particularly in home 171 cooking, the meat is often cooked under a domestic grill or in the oven and either basted with or cooked in one of the countless variations of the ever-popular barbecue sauce.

The almost obligatory sweet element in this recipe is provided by maple syrup, which was the original sweetener obtained from the sap of the maple tree and used by the first settlers. Make sure to buy pure maple syrup, and not maple-flavoured syrup. It is available in this country from some supermarkets, health-food shops and delicatessens. The essential hot element comes from the Tabasco sauce which gives these ribs their real 'soul food' element. Tabasco sauce was originally created in 1869 by Edmund McIlhenny of Louisiana from his own hot pepper plant for the delectation of his family and friends. This same Tabasco sauce is now marketed worldwide by a company which is still run by descendants of the McIlhenny family.

1.8kg (4lb) 'American-style' pork spare ribs (available in large supermarkets)

For the sauce
1 tablespoon vegetable oil
½ onion, finely chopped
1 clove garlic, crushed
6 tablespoons tomato ketchup
2 teaspoons powdered English mustard
3 tablespoons Worcestershire sauce
2 tablespoons red or white wine vinegar
3 tablespoons maple syrup (see above)
½ –1 teaspoon Tabasco sauce (or more to taste)
Salt and freshly ground pepper
5 tablespoons water
To serve
Plainly cooked white rice

Strawberry Shortcake

Preheat the oven to 220°C/425°F, gas mark 7. Arrange the spare ribs in a roasting pan, cover with foil, and cook for 15 minutes. Remove the foil and pour off and discard any fat and watery juices.

Reduce the oven temperature to 180°C/350°F, gas mark 4.

Meanwhile heat the oil in a saucepan and cook the onion over a medium heat, stirring occasionally for 5–10 minutes, or until softened but not coloured. Add the rest of the ingredients, bring to the boil, turn down the heat and simmer for 2–3 minutes.

Pour the sauce over the ribs in the pan, tossing to coat well, then bake uncovered for 1 hour, basting every 10–15 minutes.

Serve immediately on plainly cooked white rice with any remaining sauce dribbled over. Do provide plenty of napkins or, even better, wet flannels, as the only way to enjoy these ribs is by eating them with your fingers.

Corn Bread

MAKES 1 LOAF

There are lots of recipes for different versions of corn bread in the United States. This is my version. It isn't authentic but it is quite delicious and takes only a few minutes to make. Most corn bread recipes use buttermilk, which is not easy to get in this country. This version uses ordinary milk plus yogurt as a substitute which works perfectly. Cornmeal is available from good supermarkets, ethnic grocers and health-food shops.

55g (2oz) butter, melted
110g (4oz) cornmeal
55g (2oz) plain flour
1 teaspoon salt
30g (1oz) caster sugar
1 tablespoon baking powder
A good pinch of bicarbonate of soda
225ml (8oz) low-fat natural yogurt
120ml (4fl oz) milk
2 eggs, beaten

Grease a 1.5 litre (2½ pint) loaf tin with a little of the butter.

Mix all the dry ingredients in one bowl and all the liquid ones in another.

Quickly, and using as few strokes of a spoon as possible, fold the wet ingredients into the dry. Pour into the greased tin and bake in a preheated oven at 200°C/400°F, gas mark 6 for 35 minutes or until a skewer comes out dry when pushed into the middle of the loaf.

Allow to cool, then slice.

Succotash

The name of this mixed vegetable dish comes from the American Indians, who invented the ingenious method of growing corn surrounded by bean plants. As the corn grew tall, the beans could grow up and use the stems as supporting canes. This dish brings together the two staple vegetables of the first native Americans.

You can of course vary the vegetables as you fancy, but the two essential ingredients are corn and beans. The Indians sometimes added meat to this vegetable 'stew' to make a complete pot dinner. This is succotash at its simplest and easiest. In season, you can of course use fresh vegetables instead of frozen, which will naturally make the dish taste even better and more authentic.

225g (8oz) frozen broad beans
225g (8oz) frozen sweetcorn kernels
30g (1oz) butter
4 spring onions, chopped
3 tablespoons double cream
Salt and freshly ground pepper

Cook the beans and corn according to the instructions on the packet. Meanwhile heat the butter in a saucepan and cook the onion over a medium heat, stirring for 2 minutes. Drain the vegetables and add to the onions in the pan. Stir in the cream and season with salt and pepper. Continue to cook, stirring until the cream is just heated through. Do not boil. Serve immediately.

Strawberry Shortcake

The shortcake in this all-time favourite American dessert is not like the sweet biscuit which we know as shortcake, but is a light sweetened scone-like confection. It is essential that it is served as freshly baked as possible, but this is not a problem as it is so quick and easy to make.

Some cooks make one big shortcake and serve it cut in wedges, but I think individual ones look nicer. Vary the berries with the season: a mixture looks and tastes good.

For the shortcakes

285g (10oz) flour
1 teaspoon salt
1 teaspoon baking powder
1 heaped tablespoon sugar
55g (2oz) butter
165ml (5½fl oz) milk
To serve
450g (1lb) strawberries, hulled and sliced
150ml (¼ pint) double cream, whipped with 1 tablespoon sugar and ¼ teaspoon vanilla essence

Preheat the oven to 230°C/450°F, gas mark 8.

Sift the flour, salt, baking powder and sugar into a bowl, then cut in the butter until the mixture resembles fine breadcrumbs. With a fork, mix in the milk and bring together to form a soft dough. (All this can be done in seconds in a food processor.) Knead on a lightly floured work surface for about 20 seconds, then pat out to a thickness of 1cm (½in). Make 8 biscuits, using a 7.5cm (3in) cutter, re-rolling the trimmings where necessary. Place on a greased baking tray and bake for 12 minutes. Allow to cool, or serve hot or warm.

Split the shortcakes horizontally through the 'equator' and place a 'bottom' on each plate. Spoon over some sliced strawberries, then some cream. Replace the 'lids' and spoon over more strawberries and cream, piling it as high as possible.

CHAPTER 17

COOKING WITH ALCOHOL

I n many a British kitchen, alcohol is a seasonal ingredient, lighting the Christmas pudding to the table in Will-o'-the-Wisp blue flames and soaking trifle sponges in a single week of festive licence. Perhaps those boozy trifles are to blame for the widely held misunderstanding about cooking with alcohol, a lingering suspicion that wine and spirits in sauces can make you tipsy.

Repugnance at the very opposite idea, of paying good money for drink and then cooking the alcohol out of it, is the justification for another common mistake. But cooking with undrinkable wine never made food good.

These are all very understandable errors in a country with a culinary tradition of whimwhams, trifles, syllabubs, and a famous, if half forgotten, repertoire of soporific nightcaps – brown Betty, rumfustian and negus to name three – and where tax adds a hefty percentage to the price of every bottle.

The primary use for wines, spirits and beer in the kitchen is as a flavouring, but the alcohol itself has properties which are employed for different purposes. It lowers the temperature at which ices freeze hard (see page 135), and it has germicidal attributes which, although refrigeration has reduced their usefulness, we do still use for preserving fruit (see page 146).

The acidity in wine, as opposed to the alcohol, helps to tenderise meat in long-cooked dishes, and to thicken cream in syllabubs.

The alcoholic strength of all intoxicating drinks is clearly written on labels and cans. In this country, and in Europe, it is expressed as a percentage of alcohol by volume. Spirits such as brandy, whisky, gin and vodka contain up to about 50 per cent pure alcohol; wines are usually around the 12–13 per cent mark, and fortified wines and aperitifs somewhere in between. Beers range from a high of around 9 per cent down to negligible amounts in low alcohol lagers.

In its pure form, ethyl alcohol, which is the alcoholic component of all alcholic drinks, boils at a temperature of 78°C (173°F) and evaporates into the atmosphere. The more it is diluted, the higher the temperature at which it boils. At the boiling point of water, 100°C (212°F), all alcohol, however dilute, will disappear in moments with the steam. So in dishes like the *carbonade* of beef (see page 70), cooked in beer, or the haunch of venison cooked in red wine (see page 71), alcohol presents no threat to anyone.

FLAMING SPIRITS

The most theatrical use of alcohol in cooking is to pour spirits over ingredients in a wide pan and set light to the vapour. Flambéeing enjoyed a much-derided vogue in restaurants where it was performed with relish and flamboyant gestures by waiters, not cooks, and with results that were mixed at best. *Nouvelle cuisine* spelled the beginning of the end of unbridled flambéeing, and pyrotechnics are back where they belong, in the kitchen.

Alcohol that is strong enough to set alight, generally spirits, can be incorporated at different stages of preparation. In casseroles of meat or game, it is added and ignited after the meat has been browned, and before the main body of cooking liquid goes in. Chefs disagree about what exactly blazing cognac does for, say, *coq au vin*. Some add cognac and don't set light to it, but nearly everyone agrees that, flamed or unflamed, the dish does not taste quite right without it.

The idea that flaming spirits burn off some of the fat in which the meat has browned must be a mistaken one, because the heat created by the burning alcohol is mainly above the flames, not under them. As alcohol vaporises at temperatures up to the boiling point of water, and fat burns at temperatures far higher, burning off fat can only occur if the flambéeing procedure is incorrectly executed. Visualise a chef setting light to the contents of a shallow pan by tipping one edge into the flames of a gas burner, and it is not hard to see how the fat might catch fire. But this is dangerous, and there are few nastier tastes than the bitter by-products of burned fat.

Even when correctly done, flambéeing is not without risk. Make sure that there is sufficient space above the pan for the alcohol to burn safely, and that hair is tied back. Measure out the small amount of spirits to be used before approaching the stove. When they have been added, light them with a match, *never* by tipping the pan into a gas flame. Then stand back and enjoy the show, and the rich smells which linger when the flames have died down.

The same procedure applies to recipes which call for spirits to be flamed towards the end of cooking – to finish a quick sauce for a steak, or to give crêpes Suzette a final flavour boost.

Crêpes Suzette

SERVES 4

> 12 crêpes (see page 94)
> 55g (2oz) unsalted butter
> 55g (2oz) caster sugar
> Juice and finely grated zest of 2 oranges
> 2 tablespoons Cognac
> 2 tablespoons orange Curaçao, Cointreau or
>   Grand Marnier

Melt the butter in a large frying pan on a low heat and stir in the sugar. Cook gently together until the mixture begins to caramelise, but do not let it darken too much or it will be bitter. Stir in the orange juice and grated zest.

Now work fast, and methodically, or the sauce will all be soaked up by the early crêpes before the last few are in the pan. Take a crêpe and lay it in the pan, best-looking side down. Fold it in half, then in half again to make a triangle, and push to one side of the pan. Repeat the operation until all the crêpes have been used up. Mix together in a small pan the Cognac and orange liqueur and warm them a little. Pour the liquid over the crêpes, stand back and set light to the alcohol immediately. Serve as soon as the flames die down.

FLAVOUR WITHOUT FLAMES

Herbs flavour many alcoholic drinks, not just sweet liqueurs such as Chartreuse and Benedictine, but dry vermouths which include wormwood; *pastis* perfumed strongly with aniseed; and gin with juniper berries. Used sparingly, vermouth or *pastis* can add fascinating complexity to sauces for fish, for example, or gin to any dish which might include juniper, such as a terrine of game.

Elizabeth David witheringly dismissed the idea of there being any incontrovertible orthodoxy about which particular drink must be used with this or that ingredient. In her own kitchen she confessed to resorting frequently to whisky, gin or rum in place of Cognac or Calvados. She claimed that the best sauce for lobster ever invented included *anisette* liqueur and soy sauce. Here is the recipe she provided in *An Omelette and a Glass of Wine*.

Lobster Courchamps

SERVES 2

For one freshly boiled, medium large (about 680g/1½lb) hen lobster or *langouste* (if you are boiling your own at home, you can always add the goblet of Madeira stipulated in the original recipe), the ingredients for the sauce are 2 small

175

shallots, a heaped teaspoon of tarragon leaves, 2 tablespoons of chopped parsley, salt, pepper, a scant teaspoon of strong yellow French mustard, 24–30 drops of soy sauce, approximately 6 tablespoons of mildly fruity Provence olive oil, the juice of half a rather small lemon, and 1 teaspoon of *anisette de Bordeaux*.

From the split lobster extract all the red and creamy parts. Pound them in a mortar. Mix with the finely chopped shallots, tarragon and parsley. Add the seasonings and the soy sauce, then gradually stir in the olive oil. Add the lemon juice and, finally, the *anisette*. Divide the sauce into two portions, and serve it in little bowls or squat glasses placed on each person's plate, so that the lobster can be dipped into it. The lobster meat can be cut into scallops and piled neatly back into the shells.

DEGLAZING WITH WINE TO MAKE QUICK SAUCES

Using wine to deglaze a pan in which meat or fish has been sautéed in a little fat, or dry-fried, is an excellent way to add flavour to a quick sauce based on the browned residues. Remove the cooked meat or fish to a warmed plate and keep it warm while making the sauce. Pour off any unwanted fat, being careful not to lose any of the well flavoured juices with it. Pour a splash of dry, or medium dry wine into the pan, and over the heat scrape up the browned residues, mashing and dissolving them into the liquid. The important step now is to reduce the wine well, down to a tablespoon or so of syrupy liquid which is not much more than a glaze on the bottom of the pan. There are now several different ways of finishing the sauce, depending on the quantity and style you require.

If only a little is needed, take the pan off the heat, and quickly swirl in a few cubes of cold butter, keeping the pan in motion until it is all incorporated. Season the sauce, add any juices which have run from the resting meat or fish, and serve at once.

Alternatively, fresh double cream or *crème fraîche*, which is slightly more acid, can be added to the reduction of wine and pan juices and simmered for a few moments, then seasoned and served.

Where a larger quantity of sauce is required, then stock, or better still in the case of a meat dish, meat glaze (see page 75), will increase the volume. Sauces extended in this way may need a thickener such as *beurre manié* (see page 79) or corn or potato starch, in which case the sauce should be cooked for a few minutes more after the thickening has been added.

PART TWO
INGREDIENTS

CHAPTER 18
VEGETABLES

In the *Cook's Oracle*, published in 1818, Dr William Kitchener said, 'I should as soon think of roasting an animal alive – as of boiling a vegetable after it is dead.' Who will disagree with him that freshness is the 'chief value and excellence' of vegetables? It is not improbable that fresher produce was available in the early 19th century when towns were surrounded by their own market gardens and supplies were sent daily to market. Then, each vegetable had well defined seasons and new arrivals were the cause of excitement and feasting.

Think again, and one realises how limited the selection must have been by the end of winter, how badly infested the vegetables were before science gave growers reliable methods of controlling pests, and how quickly those organically grown salad leaves must have wilted on their way to market in a horse-drawn cart.

Today we all eat designer-vegetables. They have had their seasons extended, and their colour and texture optimised by breeders and plant geneticists. Taste, too, is getting a look-in at last, as supermarkets realise that at least some of their customers are more interested in flavour than they are in price and appearance.

The choice of vegetables available to the cook has never been greater. We eat shoots, seeds, fruits, stalks, leaves, roots, tubers, and flower buds – all supplied year-round in tolerable condition. No one can doubt that gardeners have the advantage of the freshest vegetables, but improvements in packaging materials and an ever better understanding of storage temperatures and conditions have raised standards immeasurably.

STORING VEGETABLES

In centrally heated modern homes without cold cellars and cool larders, it can be difficult to provide many vegetables with storage conditions which suit them. Airborne moulds and enzymes within the vegetables themselves are important causes of spoilage. Dehydration is another.

Disposing of mouldy vegetables as soon as they are spotted, and washing storage bins are the best precautions against mould.

Enzyme action, which shows as browning and eventually sliminess, is accelerated by damage to the plant tissues. This may be caused by bruising, packing too tightly together, or by insects.

Dehydration is caused by dry air, but too *much* moisture encourages deterioration too. The salad drawers of refrigerators are designed to provide cool conditions without excessive moisture loss in the dry air circulating the shelves above them.

The ideal temperature for storing aubergines, beans, cucumbers, green peppers, squash and tomatoes is about 10°C (50°F). Most other vegetables, including cabbage, carrots and tomatoes, fare better at just above the freezing point of water. The salts and sugars in their cells will prevent them from freezing. Potatoes, however, turn sweet when chilled below 4°C (40°F).

Draughty hallways and cold spare bedrooms have their uses.

VEGETABLES – APPLICABLE COOKING METHODS

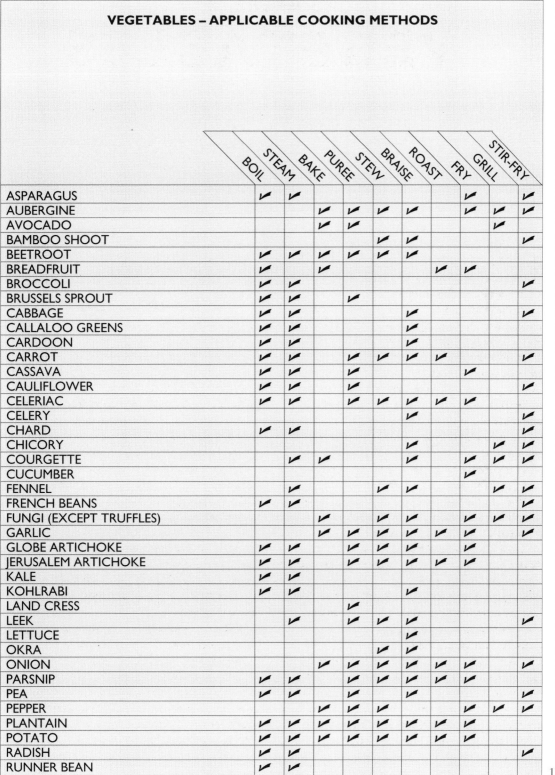

	BOIL	STEAM	BAKE	PUREE	STEW	BRAISE	ROAST	FRY	GRILL	STIR-FRY
ASPARAGUS	✔	✔						✔		✔
AUBERGINE			✔	✔	✔	✔		✔	✔	✔
AVOCADO			✔	✔					✔	
BAMBOO SHOOT					✔	✔				✔
BEETROOT	✔	✔	✔	✔	✔	✔				
BREADFRUIT	✔		✔				✔	✔		
BROCCOLI	✔	✔								✔
BRUSSELS SPROUT	✔	✔		✔						
CABBAGE	✔	✔				✔				✔
CALLALOO GREENS	✔	✔				✔				
CARDOON	✔	✔				✔				
CARROT	✔	✔		✔	✔	✔	✔			✔
CASSAVA	✔	✔		✔				✔		
CAULIFLOWER	✔	✔		✔						✔
CELERIAC	✔	✔		✔	✔	✔	✔	✔		
CELERY						✔				✔
CHARD	✔	✔								✔
CHICORY						✔			✔	✔
COURGETTE			✔	✔		✔		✔	✔	✔
CUCUMBER								✔		
FENNEL		✔			✔	✔			✔	✔
FRENCH BEANS	✔	✔								✔
FUNGI (EXCEPT TRUFFLES)				✔	✔	✔		✔	✔	✔
GARLIC			✔	✔	✔	✔	✔	✔		✔
GLOBE ARTICHOKE	✔	✔		✔	✔	✔		✔		
JERUSALEM ARTICHOKE	✔	✔		✔	✔	✔	✔	✔		
KALE	✔	✔								
KOHLRABI	✔	✔				✔				
LAND CRESS				✔						
LEEK		✔		✔	✔	✔				✔
LETTUCE						✔				
OKRA					✔	✔				
ONION			✔	✔	✔	✔	✔	✔		✔
PARSNIP	✔	✔		✔	✔	✔	✔	✔		
PEA	✔	✔		✔		✔				✔
PEPPER				✔	✔	✔		✔	✔	✔
PLANTAIN	✔	✔	✔	✔	✔	✔	✔	✔		
POTATO	✔	✔	✔	✔	✔	✔	✔	✔		
RADISH	✔	✔								✔
RUNNER BEAN	✔	✔								

VEGETABLES – APPLICABLE COOKING METHODS

	BOIL	STEAM	BAKE	PUREE	STEW	BRAISE	ROAST	FRY	GRILL	STIR-FRY
SALSIFY	✔	✔			✔	✔				
SAMPHIRE	✔	✔								✔
SORREL	✔			✔						
SPINACH	✔			✔						✔
SPROUTED BEANS	✔									✔
SQUASH	✔	✔	✔	✔	✔	✔	✔	✔	✔	
SWEDE	✔	✔			✔	✔	✔			
SWEETCORN	✔	✔			✔	✔			✔	
SWEET POTATO	✔	✔	✔	✔	✔	✔	✔	✔		
TOMATO			✔	✔	✔	✔			✔	✔
TURNIP	✔	✔			✔	✔				
WATERCHESTNUT					✔	✔				✔
WATERCRESS				✔						

A–Z OF VEGETABLES

ACKEE

(also Akee)

Scarlet oblong or egg-shaped fruit of a Caribbean tree, rarely seen fresh in Britain but available canned. Its soft, pale yellow flesh is often likened to scrambled egg. Another name for it is vegetable brains. Salt fish and ackee is a big dish in Jamaica. Under-ripe and over-ripe ackee are poisonous, so stick to the tinned variety unless you can call on expert opinion. Rinse off the canning brine and remove any pink parts before using. It will only need warming through.

ARTICHOKES

(see Globe artichokes and Jerusalem artichokes)

ASPARAGUS

May and June is the time for home-grown asparagus, the edible shoots of a member of the lily family. On the Continent, white and purple varieties are more highly esteemed than the green asparagus which has always been preferred in England. Imported asparagus from places as far apart as Thailand and South America can be found year-round. Asparagus still enjoys luxury status, although its price, in season, is now comparable with less exciting vegetables.

Asparagus is graded by the thickness of the stalk, and the condition of the bud. Assorted sizes, sold loose, are fine for soups. When buying bunched asparagus look for tightly closed buds and stalks of uniform thickness. Open buds and dry, soggy or woody-looking ends are all signs of staleness. Once cut, the flavour deteriorates quickly. Store asparagus, loosely wrapped, in the salad drawer of the refrigerator for as short a time as possible. Wilted asparagus is refreshed by standing the cut ends in cold water for an hour or two.

To prepare, trim the ends, and if the lower parts of the stalks are tough, remove the cuticle-like skin with a swivel potato peeler or sharp knife, working from the base towards the fragile bud.

Steaming is the most usual cooking method, though it can also be boiled, fried and stir-fried. Laid flat it is cooked over steam in a covered pan.

Alternatively it is tied in small bunches which are placed, cut-end down, in a small amount of boiling water so that the tender tips cook in the steam. Asparagus kettles, which have an interior basket to hold the spears upright, are tall, narrow, lidded pans made for the purpose. Using extra-wide kitchen foil it is a simple matter to improvise a high, domed lid for a saucepan of suitable size. Cooking times can range from 5–15 minutes depending on the size and variety, and how well cooked you like it. Test for tenderness near the base of a stem. Drain thoroughly before serving hot, cold or, best of all, warm, with melted butter or vinaigrette, or an emulsified butter sauce (see page 79).

AUBERGINE

(Brinjal, Eggplant)

This Asiatic relative of the tomato comes in a greater variety of shapes and sizes than most cooks may realise. We are all familiar with the glossy, deep purple types commonly grown under glass in northern Europe. Some other varieties, however, are as small and white as hen's eggs; others are rose pink, yellow, pale green and streaked. The range of shapes includes globes, pears, and more pointed and elongated forms.

Choose firm aubergines which have unblemished glossy skins without wrinkles. The stem end should look fresh too. Store them, loosely wrapped, in the salad drawer of the refrigerator.

They need little preparation. The skins are tender so they are rarely peeled. The varieties grown today are seldom bitter, and it is no longer necessary to salt slices of raw aubergine to draw bitter juices from the flesh. The practice of salting continues for another reason, because the spongy flesh absorbs less oil when it is 'degorged' before cooking. Use stainless steel knives to prevent the flesh discolouring. Aubergines may be frozen cooked, or raw in thick slices.

Aubergines are usually baked, fried, or mixed with other vegetables in dishes such as ratatouille. They are an essential ingredient of moussaka. A purée of char-grilled aubergine mixed with olive oil, salt and garlic is known as 'poor man's caviar'.

AVOCADO

(Avocado pear)

More than 500 varieties of this tropical tree fruit are grown. Some are no bigger than a human thumb, while in Caribbean markets they can reach a weight of several pounds each. Avocados may be pear or sausage shaped or round; smooth or rough skinned; and coloured green, flecked with yellow, red, greeny purple or almost black. The flesh, which contains at least 25 per cent fat, and more protein than any other fruit, is creamy or greenish yellow when ripe. The test for ripeness applies to all varieties. They should yield to gentle pressure applied to the stalk end.

Avocados are harvested unripe, and ripen best at temperatures between 15°C (60°F) and 21° (70°F). Don't refrigerate them until they are ripe, and then only for a day or two. Avocados are best eaten raw.

To halve an avocado, use a stainless steel knife to cut it lengthwise around the stone, then twist the two halves in opposite directions to separate them. Applying acid lime or lemon juice, or vinegar, to the cut surfaces helps to prevent the flesh blackening. Avocados do not freeze successfully.

Ripe avocado flesh is the basis of the Mexican dip *guacamole*. It is mashed together with salt, hot green chillies, lime juice and green coriander. Most avocados, however, are eaten with nothing more than salt or a spoonful of salad dressing. Halved avocados can be baked or grilled.

BAMBOO SHOOT

Not all types of bamboo have edible shoots, and some of the edible varieties are poisonous if incorrectly prepared. As canned bamboo shoots satisfy Chinese and Japanese cooks whose dishes are the ones we will need them for, the preserved variety is acceptable. They have little flavour and are used for their crisp texture.

BEAN SPROUTS

(see Sprouting beans and seeds)

BEETROOT

Strong malt vinegar has done a great disservice to the beetroot. Its qualities as a hot vegetable are generally unappreciated. Turned in butter and seasoned with black pepper, beetroot's sweet taste is excellent with red meat and game. Plant breeders have done much to improve its once earthy flavour, and small varieties ranging in size from hen's eggs to apples are gaining favour over larger varieties shaped like monster carrots. The cooked beetroot sold by greengrocers can be reheated. When buying raw beetroot look for firm, unblemished roots with fresh leaves.

To preserve their magnificent colour, beetroot are cooked in their skins. Trim the leaves and roots, leaving a good 2.5cm (1in) of both to prevent excessive 'bleeding' of the colour. Boil them whole until tender. The skins will slip off easily when they are cool enough to handle. They can also be steamed or baked.

Raw, grated beetroot makes a good winter salad on its own or mixed with grated carrot and parsnip, and dressed with oil, vinegar and fresh thyme, or mixed with soured cream and horseradish. Beetroot is an essential ingredient in the Russian soup *borsch*.

Beetroot for freezing should be fully cooked.

BREADFRUIT

The starchy fruit of a tropical tree, breadfruit can weigh up to 4.5kg (10lb). The greenish yellow skin and seed are usually removed before the cream-coloured flesh is baked, boiled, roasted or fried. Its bread-like flavour is slightly sweet. Breadfruit is never eaten raw.

BROCCOLI

(Calabrese, Sprouting broccoli)

This sprouting form of cauliflower repays the cook who treats it with the respect accorded to asparagus. Its flavour announces its origins as a member of the cabbage family. Regardless of its colour, which may be deep, blue green, purple or white, insist on tight buds, firm stems, and obviously fresh leaves in the looser varieties. It is rich in calcium and in vitamins A, B and C. These are best retained by storing it, refrigerated, for the minimum length of time. Cook as briefly as possible by boiling or steaming until tender.

BRUSSELS SPROUT

Small, perfectly formed miniature cabbages, Brussels sprouts quite literally sprout from the stout stems of their large parent plants. It used to be said that good sprouts only appeared after the first frosts of winter, but new breeds and foreign imports now ensure high quality produce for much of the year. Choose small, tight, bright green sprouts which feel hard and have no loose outer leaves. Store them, as briefly as possible, in the salad drawer of the refrigerator. Sprouts which are spongy or yellowing are not worth the trouble of cooking.

Evenly sized sprouts will take the same time to cook. Prepare them by trimming the bases. Making cross-cuts in the stem ends is not necessary and only encourages sogginess. Cook sprouts in plenty of rapidly boiling salted water until just tender. If they are really fresh, they will taste nutty and almost sweet. Staleness and overcooking both result in unpleasantly sulphurous cabbagey odours.

Brussels sprouts are frozen raw, after blanching.

BUTTERNUT SQUASH
(see Squash)

CABBAGE

The *brassica* family, to which cabbages belong, is a large one including cauliflower, broccoli, Brussels sprouts, kale and kohlrabi as well as the many types of cabbage itself. The Chinese vegetable *pak choi*, or spoon cabbage, is another member. In one form or another, cabbage is in season for most of the year. As a general rule the looser, darker-leaved varieties such as spring greens and well-flavoured Savoys with their honeycomb textured leaves, are best, nutritionally and aesthetically, when cooked briefly with as little water as possible. Hard hearted cabbages are more versatile, lending themselves to slow braising with spices or fruit, and to being eaten raw, grated or shredded in winter salads. Hard red cabbage keeps its colour without turning blue when braised in an acidic environment with apples, wine or vinegar.

Cabbage which has been fermented to make *sauerkraut*, or pickled as it is in the Korean speciality *kimchee*, keeps without refrigeration.

Choose fresh-looking, undamaged cabbages without wilting or yellowing leaves, or dried stems or bases. Prepare loose varieties like spring greens by rinsing and shredding the leaves. Denser varieties should be cut in quarters, and the hard core cut out before the leaves are shredded. If large leaves are to be used as wrappers for a stuffing, they should be pulled off whole and blanched.

Cabbage is a good source of vitamin C and contains some vitamin A. Loose varieties should be stored, refrigerated, for as short a time as possible. Hard cabbages keep well in a cool place – better still, wrapped, in the salad drawer of the refrigerator.

Young green cabbage can be blanched and frozen. Dishes made with hard cabbage also freeze.

CALLALOO GREENS
Caribbean cooks use the leafy green tops of various kinds of edible tuber as general-purpose greens and in a soup called *callaloo*, made with crab or salt pork, coconut milk and spices. Chard leaves or spinach can be substituted in recipes for *callaloo*.

CARDOON
A dish of cardoons is one of the thirteen courses in a traditional Provençal Christmas Eve dinner. The stalk-like leaf ribs of this member of the thistle family have a delicate flavour which is not unlike that of another relative, the artichoke. Only the pale, tender inner parts are used, cut into usable lengths and boiled until tender, about 30 minutes. They can be served with melted butter, or with a white or cheese sauce.

CARROT
Sweet, cheap and available all year round, carrots are a faithful ally in every kitchen. The home-grown spring crop begins in April; the main crop arrives in July. Selective breeding has produced carrots in all shapes and sizes from tiny globes and baby's fingers to long straight or tapering roots. The vigilance of supermarket buyers has virtually eliminated the big woody carrots that used to be sold in winter. Freshness is easy to spot when young carrots are sold in bunches complete with their feathery leaves. With or without the leaves, look for firm, smooth skinned car-

rots without damage. Sprouts at the trimmed stem end are a sure sign that they have been long out of the ground.

Carrots are best stored in cool, dark, dry and airy conditions. Much of the flavour and sweetness is near the skin, so scrub or scrape them, and trim the stem end. Carrots are good raw, grated and dressed with oil and lemon juice, or cut into batons and served with a dip. They are a versatile cooked vegetable, an essential ingredient in stocks, and suitable for boiling, steaming, baking in gratins, puréeing, braising, roasting and stir-frying. Cooking times will depend on variety, age and cooking method. The sweetness of carrots is exploited in fruit cakes and jams.

Carrots can be frozen whole, if small, or sliced or chopped.

CASSAVA
(Manioc, Yuca)
There are more than a hundred varieties of the tropical cassava plant grown for their large, starchy tubers which are a staple in parts of West Africa and Central America. Cassava may be bitter or sweet, but bitter types contain hydrocyanic acid and are poisonous unless well cooked. Peeled of its bark-like skin, the hard cream or yellow flesh can be cooked and eaten like potatoes. Tapioca, the dried meal *farhina* or *farine de manioc*, and *cassareep*, a bitter-sweet thickening agent used in Caribbean cooking, are made from cassava.

CAULIFLOWER
This useful member of the cabbage family lays down food stores in the thick stems of its tightly packed flowers which are known as curds. These may be white, cream, or green, or purple in the case of the variety known, confusingly, as Cape broccoli. Look for unblemished curd and fresh leaves with no sign of yellowing. Store, as briefly as possible, loosely wrapped in the salad drawer of the refrigerator.

The leaves of full-size cauliflowers weighing upwards of 500g (1lb 2oz) are discarded, and the curd broken into florets of even size before cooking. Miniature cauliflowers suitable for a single serving are cooked whole.

Steaming is a kinder treatment than boiling, 183

and better retains the shape and taste. Cheese sauce is an ever popular companion to cauliflower as a main dish, or to accompany meat. Indian cooks spice it imaginatively. It can also be stir-fried, deep-fried in batter, and made into creamy soups.

Florets of cauliflower are blanched for freezing.

CELERIAC

Its second name, turnip-rooted celery, accurately describes celeriac's unimpressive appearance, but not the sweet, celery flavour of its off-white flesh. This rather knobbly, starchy root has to be peeled deeply, a point to bear in mind when deciding how much to buy. The flattened, globe-shaped roots range in size from large oranges to large swedes. The flesh is very firm, but large roots may be woody or even hollow inside. Store in cool, dark, dry and airy conditions.

Celeriac is good raw or cooked. Cut surfaces brown in contact with the air, so use a stainless steel knife and put prepared celeriac into acidulated water. Its colour when boiled or steamed can be rather grey, but puréed with plenty of cream, or with mashed potato, it is an excellent accompaniment to meat, fish and game. Finely julienned (see Glossary) or grated celeriac, raw, or blanched in acidulated water, is excellent with a mustardy mayonnaise or vinaigrette. Celeriac can be substituted for celery in stocks, and is useful in casseroles and braises.

CELERY

Self-blanching varieties of celery have done away with the need to earth-up the stems to whiten them. It is a cleaner crop than it used to be, and even the outer stems have fewer tough strings. Stems that are crisp enough to snap are fresh. Bendy ones are not.

Top, tail and wash celery stems, which may be green or white with no appreciable difference in taste, and eat them raw with cheese or dips, or diced and mixed with fruit, nuts and mayonnaise in a winter salad. Braising, alone or with other vegetables such as onions and tomatoes, is the best cooking method. It is an essential ingredient for the stock pot.

Celery is blanched for freezing, after which it is unsuitable for eating raw but is still good in soups and casseroles.

CEP

(see Fungi)

CHANTERELLE

(see Fungi)

CHARD

(Leaf beet, Swiss chard)
This form of beet is grown for its leaf ribs, which are thick and creamy white, and for its deep green leaves which can be cooked and used like spinach. The delicately flavoured ribs are trimmed, cut into suitable lengths, then steamed and served like asparagus.

CHICORY

What we call chicory the French call endive, and vice versa. This is confusing, but understandable since they are close relatives within the chicory family. Forced, torpedo-shaped spears of Belgian chicory are the most widely available variety in this country. But chicory takes many forms. Straggly open green types such as frisée, escarole, and the many deep rose red and variegated varieties from Italy, shaped like cabbages, roses, torpedoes or multi-pronged tongs, are to be found in increasing profusion. Radicchio is the best-known of these.

Browning is always an indication of staleness. Forced spears should be tightly shut and firm. Other varieties can be tender, crisp or tough, depending on the breed. Bitterness is a characteristic of the chicory family, but modern varieties are rarely bitter enough to need special treatment. The darker, outer leaves of green varieties are a possible exception.

Store chicory as you would lettuce, loosely wrapped in the salad drawer of the refrigerator.

All the chicories are good salad vegetables, especially in winter. Spears and some of the fleshy red varieties can be braised, or wilted in olive oil with garlic.

CHILLI

All the hot capsicums are called chillies, and they range in size from about 1cm (½in) long up to

30cm (1ft). There are literally hundreds of varieties. Size, colour and shape are no guide to their heat, although red chillies are usually sweeter than green ones. The seeds and internal ribs are the hottest parts. Smooth, well-filled skins are signs of freshness.

Handle chillies with care. Wear rubber gloves, and wash knives and boards carefully after use. The heat in chillies is produced by the alkaloid capsaicin, which can cause really painful sensations of burning. Be particularly careful not to touch your eyes after handling chillies.

Habitual chilli eaters can tolerate larger amounts of capsaicin than those who eat them only occasionally. They can also distinguish differences in flavour which are lost on occasional heat seekers. Mexican and other foreign recipes sometimes call for quantities of chilli which would make occasional eaters quite ill. The cook who adds chilli with caution, until a comfortable heat is produced, is not being a wimp.

When a recipe calls for skinned chillies, hold them with tongs to toast them over a flame, or under a grill until the skin is charred on all sides. Leave them to sweat in a plastic bag for 5-10 minutes, then the skins will easily slip off.

COURGETTE
(Zucchini)
These miniature marrows are a big improvement on their full-grown relations. Yellow and pale varieties are sometimes found in addition to the more common green ones. Small is beautiful in terms of taste, and they can be eaten cooked or raw, thinly sliced and dressed simply with lemon juice, olive oil and salt. They are now available all year round. Choose firm, smooth-skinned, unblemished courgettes and store them in the salad drawer of the refrigerator. They need minimal preparation. Trim the stem end and steam, fry or stir-fry whole, or in slices if small. Larger courgettes can be stuffed and baked. They are an essential ingredient in ratatouille. Courgette flowers can be used as receptacles for stuffings.

CUCUMBER
Long, smooth cucumbers with dark green glossy skins are the type most often seen in shops and markets, although ridged and warty varieties are also grown. Short cucumbers are also cultivated for pickling. Fresh cucumbers are rigid, not bendy, and, closely wrapped, will keep for up to a week in the refrigerator if whole. Cut cucumber keeps less well.

Most cucumbers are eaten raw, in salads, but chunky batons of peeled cucumber flesh are very good cooked lightly in butter as an accompaniment to fish. Yoghurt, garlic and herbs with cool flavours such as mint, dill, fennel and coriander are the ingredients in various Middle Eastern and Indian salad dishes. Scandinavians slice cucumber thinly, salt it for an hour or so to extract some of the moisture, and dress it with a slightly sweetened mixture of wine or cider vinegar, water and finely chopped dill leaves.

CUSTARD MARROW
(see Squash)

DANDELION
Very young dandelion leaves are one of the earliest saladings of spring. Their slightly bitter flavour is best offset by a hot dressing which wilts the leaves. Fry finely chopped bacon in its own fat, then deglaze (see page 176) the pan with a dash of wine vinegar, mix with the leaves and serve at once. The hot bacon fat replaces the usual oil.

DUDI
(see Squash)

ESCAROLE
(see Chicory)

FENNEL
(Florence fennel)
The sweet aniseed taste and crisp, celery-like texture of fennel makes it a welcome addition to the range of vegetables now available throughout most of the year. The lower stems of the plant swell to form a closely interleaved bulb of palest green 'leaves'. The upper stems and feathery leaves have usually been trimmed before it gets to market. Choose fennel bulbs which are fat and well formed. The cut surfaces should look fresh, and the 'leaves' undamaged and tight fitting. Stored, closely wrapped, in the salad drawer of 185

the refrigerator, it will keep for several days.

Small fennel bulbs, braised whole, are good enough to serve as a vegetable course on their own, or as an accompaniment to fish, poultry or roast meat. Large ones are halved or quartered for braising. Sliced raw fennel adds crispness and flavour to salads. Diced fennel, mixed with apple, celery, nuts or raisins and mayonnaise or yogurt goes well with cold meats. Trimmings are a useful addition to fish or chicken stock.

FRENCH BEAN
(Green bean, Haricot vert)
Gardeners appreciate just how good fresh French beans can taste, and the great variety that can be grown. Pale yellow-podded beans are popular in France and the dark purple-podded types, which turn green when cooked, can be eaten raw in salads when very young.

Fresh French beans should be crisp enough to snap when bent. Store them, loosely covered in the refrigerator. Trim the ends and boil, steam or stir-fry them briefly. Lightly cooked beans which have been refreshed by plunging into cold water can be served as a salad. A vinaigrette dressing made with a proportion of hazelnut oil and slivered, toasted hazelnuts is particularly good.

FRISEE
(see Chicory)

FUNGI
Mushrooms and their kith and kin, including truffles, have some of the most fascinating smells and flavours at the cook's disposal. Many of the best can only be gathered in the wild, but an increasing number are being cultivated, as the selection now seen in the shops demonstrates. This is a welcome development because many wild species are poisonous, some fatally so, and identifying them is a skilled business. A competent adviser or a good field guide are indispensible companions to the interested amateur mushroom hunter. *Mushrooms and Other Fungi of Great Britain and Europe* by Roger Phillips (Pan Books), and *The Macdonald Encyclopedia of Mushrooms and Toadstools* by Giovanni Pacioni (Macdonald) are two detailed field guides with colour photographs.

As a general rule, wild mushrooms are more intensely flavoured and perfumed than cultivated ones. Prominent in the long list of esteemed edible species are ceps, chanterelles, shiitake, oyster mushrooms, pied de mouton, horn of plenty, beefsteak fungus, blewits, morels and straw mushrooms.

Whether cultivated or wild, mushrooms for the kitchen should look and smell fresh and pleasant. They should be firm and dry, free of insect damage or slime. Wild mushrooms should be eaten the day they are picked. Cultivated varieties can be kept for a day or two, covered loosely, in the salad drawer of the refrigerator.

To prepare mushrooms for cooking, cut off any gritty or woody parts of the stem, and wipe or clean with a soft brush, or cloth, to remove any grit. If necessary, they can be rinsed immediately before cooking.

Dried mushrooms are even more intensely flavoured than fresh ones and are a useful storecupboard ingredient for adding flavour to a wide range of dishes. Reconstitute them in warm water for about 30 minutes before using in soups, stews, sauces and casseroles.

All fresh mushrooms are delicious when gently fried in butter or good olive oil with garlic, salt and pepper, and finished with a little fresh lemon juice and chopped parsley. Wild mushrooms and game are traditionally paired because their seasons coincide. But morels, fresh or dried, are wonderful with chicken, in sauces, stuffings or casseroles. Ceps flavour a risotto fit for the gods. All have an uncanny affinity with eggs.

Fresh white truffles show off their astonishing, pheromone-like perfume best with simple dishes of eggs, potato, pasta or risotto. Good truffles are strongly perfumed, very firm, and not too knobbly. Preparation is minimal. They are brushed free of earth, then shaved wafer thin over the food.

Black truffles, which are chosen on the same basis, are usually cooked. They are used, sliced, in stuffings and sauces, and with eggs. They need to be peeled of their hard rind, but the peelings are recycled in wine or stock as a flavouring.

Black truffles are less headily perfumed than white, and both are best when truly fresh. Neither can be kept for more than a few days. Preserved truffles are pale shadows of fresh ones, though olive oil which has been scented with white truffles is very good as an instant, if expensive, dressing for pasta.

GARLIC

This most pungent member of the onion family is one of the most indispensable flavourings in the kitchen. Freshly harvested garlic, whether home grown or imported, is best of all. Each round bulb contains a number of individual cloves which are broken off and peeled as needed. In cool, dry, airy conditions whole bulbs keep well for many months. The exterior may be white, pink or even purple, but the flesh inside is greeny white. The strength of the flavour varies according to type, growing conditions and age, but any green shoots in the centre of the peeled cloves should be cut out as they can be unpleasantly pungent.

Raw garlic has a much stronger flavour than garlic which has been well cooked, which is why dishes like chicken with 40 cloves of garlic sound alarming but taste exceptionally good. Be careful when frying garlic, though, because it becomes acrid if browned too well.

Garlic hangs more strongly on the breath when it is raw. After you have handled it, washing with cold water removes the taint better than hot.

Where a recipe calls for crushed garlic, this is best done by setting the peeled garlic on a pinch of salt, laying the broad end of a cooking knife over it, and pressing firmly with the flat of your hand. Cleaning a garlic press thoroughly takes longer than wiping a board and a knife, and, if it is not cleaned well enough, stale residues may taint later dishes.

GLOBE ARTICHOKE

The flavour of globe artichokes is one of those distinctive tastes against which others are

---

PREPARING A GLOBE ARTICHOKE

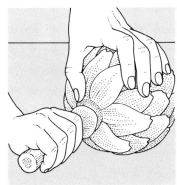

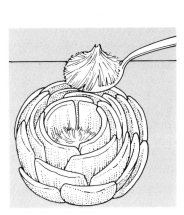

1. Just before cooking, break off the stem; this pulls away many of the strings. Pull off some of the tougher outer leaves. If only the base or *fond* is required, pare off all the leaves, and remove choke.
2. If serving the artichoke whole, you can trim the leaves as shown, if you like, as well as the top.

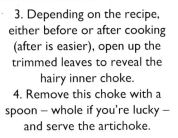

3. Depending on the recipe, either before or after cooking (after is easier), open up the trimmed leaves to reveal the hairy inner choke.
4. Remove this choke with a spoon – whole if you're lucky – and serve the artichoke.

defined. In the mouth they produce a sweet, slightly metallic aftertaste which is why wine is seldom drunk with them. Artichokes belong to the thistle family and are cultivated for their flower buds. Each one is a fleshy base closely surrounded by overlapping scaly leaves which protect a central bundle of threads called the choke. In some small, slender varieties, harvested when very young, the whole vegetable is eaten. In the more widely available globes, weighing up to 450g (1lb) or more, only the fleshy bottom part of the leaves and the base, or *fond*, are edible.

Choose firm, tightly constructed artichokes and try to use them the same day. Do not remove the stems until immediately before cooking; then break them off, pulling away some of the strings which attach them to the base. Apply lemon juice or vinegar to prevent blackening.

If only the bases are needed, cut them down (see page 187). If they are to be served as a course on their own, there is no need to trim the leaves unless required to fit the pan. Boil them in salted water, or steam until tender. This will take at least 30 minutes but is simple to judge by pulling off an outside leaf. It will come away easily when the artichoke is cooked. The choke also pulls out easily when the vegetable has been cooked. If serving them hot, wear rubber gloves to protect your hands while removing the chokes. Serve with a puddle of buttery sauce or dressing in the space left by the choke. Pull off the leaves one by one, dip in the sauce, and scrape off the fleshy base between the teeth.

JERUSALEM ARTICHOKE

These tubers, unrelated to globe artichokes except, tentatively, in flavour, are members of the sunflower family. Choose firm, undamaged tubers with as few knobs as possible. If they must be peeled before cooking, drop them into acidulated water to prevent discoloration. They are more easily peeled after they have been boiled or steamed until tender. They can be roasted with a joint, and used in gratins, soups and purées.

KALE

(Curly kale)
The dark, blue-green leaves of kale have a stronger flavour than most other members of the cabbage family. The leaves are cooked briefly, like spring greens.

KANTOLA

(see Squash)

KARELA

(see Squash)

KOHLRABI

(Turnip cabbage)
This member of the brassica family, which tastes something like a cross between a turnip and a cabbage, is nicest when very small, about the size of an eating apple. It is smooth, pale green, or occasionally purple, with leaves which spring from the sides of the globe (though these have usually been trimmed). The cut surfaces should look fresh and the vegetable be firm and unblemished. Steam or boil small kohlrabi whole until tender, 15 minutes or more. Serve buttered, with cheese sauce or gratinéed. Stir-fry thin slices.

LAMB'S LETTUCE

(Corn salad, Mâche)
Not a true lettuce, the sweet-tasting, fragile leaves of lamb's lettuce are becoming a popular year-round addition to the salad bowl.

LAND CRESS

When young, the leaves of land cress look and taste like watercress. It is easily grown, and a useful winter crop for soups and salads.

LEEK

This member of the onion family is indispensable for stocks and soups. Young leeks can be steamed whole and eaten like asparagus. Large ones can be served as an accompaniment to red meats and game, cut in short lengths and steamed. They also make an excellent purée. Leeks are easy to grow, and thinnings can be used in stir-fried vegetable mixtures.

The green tops of leek leaves are usually trimmed, and the cut surfaces are a good indica-

Braised fennel (see page 72) is a good accompaniment to plainly grilled meat, poultry or fish.

tion of freshness. Leeks continue to grow after they are cut. Heavily trimmed leeks bulging from the centre of a cut end are stale. Avoid leeks with a hard, central core. This develops as the vegetable begins to go to seed in summer.

To prepare young leeks, top and tail them. Older ones usually need washing to remove earth trapped in the leaves. Halve them lengthwise and rinse carefully. If they are to be cooked whole, slit only the green part, and wash.

LETTUCE

Although lettuces now come in an increasing variety of colours and shapes – green, red and chestnut, plain leaved, indented or madly frilly – differences in taste are relatively slight. Texture is more interesting, and ranges from soft to crunchy. Types such as Cos, Webb's Wonder and Winter Density combine the two with crisp ribs and softer leaves. Iceberg is crisp right through, and cabbage or butterhead lettuces are mainly soft. Frilly *lollo* lettuces can mop up indecent quantities of salad dressing. Always mix leaves and dressing at the last possible moment so that the leaves do not wilt.

Avoid lettuces which are wilted or damaged by insects or mishandling. Store lettuce, loosely wrapped, in the salad drawer of the refrigerator.

Lettuce hearts can be braised or stir-fried with Chinese oyster sauce.

MANGETOUT PEA

(see Pea)

MARROW

(see Squash)

MOOLI

(see Radish)

MORELS

(see Fungi)

MUSHROOMS

(see Fungi)

OKRA

(Bhindi, Gumbo, Ladies' fingers)

These ridged, tapering vegetables are edible seed pods. They have a mild, slightly earthy flavour, and an unctuous texture which is used to good effect in many Caribbean stews, and in much Indian cooking. These are the treatments that suit them best.

The name ladies' fingers is a good indication of their size. Choose okra which is firm, unblemished, and has a good green colour. Trim the stalk end without opening up the seed pod if they are to be cooked whole.

ONION

Onions and shallots are the plant's stored food supplies, and their pungent smell and ability to make our eyes water are their defence against attack. Onions are an essential ingredient of innumerable dishes worldwide. Most of those we buy have pinky gold skins, but white and purple varieties, both usually fairly sweet, are· also widely available. (The latter are usually called red onions.) Large Spanish onions are usually the mildest and sweetest of all. Chefs swear by the superior flavour of shallots.

All types should have clean, dry outer skins, and feel very firm. Softness indicates rotting, and any bruised or damaged areas may quickly succumb. Onions keep best of all the vegetables we buy when stored in a cool, dry, airy spot out of direct sunlight.

Except when baked whole in their skins, onions are peeled before cooking. Cutting releases the onion's defensive irritants which make us cry, and although the skins can be removed under water, the only way to chop them is on a board. If uneven chopping does not detract from the dish, they can be chopped in a food processor. Another ruse is to wear a pair of industrial or ski goggles. This is almost essential for dealing with large quantities for chutney. If you want to prepare chopped onions in advance, rinsing them in cold water before setting them aside helps to deodorise them. Leave them somewhere cool, but not in the refrigerator or they will taint its contents.

Any small, firm onions can be used for pickling.

OYSTER MUSHROOMS

(see Fungi)

PARSNIP

Like their relative the carrot, parsnips are a sweet tasting root vegetable with a distinctive flavour. They can be boiled, steamed, puréed, roasted, stewed, braised and made into fritters, soups and gratins. Choose firm, unblemished parsnips without rust spots. They will keep for several days in a cool, dry airy spot, or wrapped, in the salad drawer of the refrigerator. Peel parsnips thinly before cooking. Older parsnips may take longer than young ones. Freeze this winter vegetable for summer use.

PEA

Most peas are grown for freezing or canning, with the result that few of those which reach the market fresh are as young, sweet and full of flavour as those grown in the garden. But there are always exceptions.

Mangetout peas and snap peas, both eaten with their pods, and available, thanks to imports, for most of the year, are ever more popular. They taste as good as they look.

When buying peas for shelling, look for fresh, well-filled pods which are not so full that seem about to burst (this indicates fully ripe, and therefore starchy rather than sweet peas). Flat, mangetout pea pods should also be bright green, and crisp not flaccid. Snap peas, which have little peas inside which are eaten with the shells, should be crisp enough to do just that, *snap*.

For maximum sweetness, store peas as briefly as possible, loosely wrapped in salad drawer of the refrigerator.

Mangetout and snap peas are prepared by breaking off the stalk end and pulling it towards the tip, taking any side strings with the stalk.

Sweet young peas are best plainly boiled, with or without a sprig of mint, and finished with a pat of butter. Older peas can be braised with diced bacon and small onions, or used in soups or purées. Snap and sugar peas can be boiled, steamed or stir-fried.

All types of peas can be frozen.

PEPPER
(Bell pepper, Sweet pepper)
Large sweet peppers, the size of a large orange, are members of the same family as chillies. Red peppers are ripe green peppers, but the yellow, orange and black ones are bred for their colour. Black peppers cook, disappointingly, to dark green.

Look for unblemished peppers with well-filled shining skins. Wrinkling is a sign of staleness. Loosely wrapped, they keep well for up to a week in the salad drawer of the refrigerator.

Peppers can be stuffed and baked, or sliced and eaten raw in salads. Discard the seeds and interior membranes. The treatment that best brings out their flavour is simply blistering their skins until charred over a flame, or under a grill, before peeling, slicing and dressing them with olive oil and seasonings. This salad can be served hot, warm or cold and is especially good made with red peppers.

Peppers will freeze, though they are available all year round.

PLANTAIN

Not surprisingly, since they look like bananas, plantains belong to the same family. They are sold green and unripe, yellow and half ripe, or black and ripe. Sizes range from not much bigger than a large thumb to more than twice the size of a large banana. The taste, when cooked, is very varied, but comparisons with the finest new potatoes do not over-state the best examples. They tend to become sweeter as they ripen, but all require cooking.

Wherever they grow, deep-fried slices of plantain replace potato crisps. Chunks of plantain are excellent in stews and casseroles. They are usually peeled before cooking, and are best kept in a light airy place, not in the refrigerator.

POTATO

A single plant may produce several pounds of potatoes, underground tubers from which new plants are produced in the following season. Depending on the variety, and the point in its life when it is harvested, a potato can weigh anything from less than 30g (1oz) to about 450g (1lb). Some are round, most are oval or kidney-shaped, and some are long, even pointed. Skin colour ranges from almost transparent in newly formed potatoes, through pale golden brown and pink, to deeper pink, brown and nearly black. Skin texture may be smooth, or netted as in some melons, and the eyes, the points from the potato will sprout, may be deep or shallow. Seed catalogues make much of shallow eyes. The flesh inside may be any shade of white or cream, pinkish, pale or deep soft yellow. These are all characteristics that can be seen. What cannot be judged on sight is whether the flesh will be waxy or floury when cooked.

Increasingly, cooks demand to know. As a result, more and more potatoes are marketed by name, and, when packaged, with their cooking characteristics clearly explained. The best potatoes command premium prices. Old breeds which produce small crops of well-flavoured tubers are being more widely grown, and new varieties created.

Growers, both commercial and domestic, divide potatoes into earlies, second earlies and maincrop varieties, depending on the time they are harvested. Most new potatoes are earlies or second earlies, but maincrop varieties are also harvested when small and some never attain much size.

When buying new potatoes, look for skins which will rub off easily. In other types, firmness and well-filled, unblemished skins indicate freshness. Softening, greening and sprouting are all signs of staleness. Never buy or cook greening potatoes which contain poisonous alkaloids (see page 300).

Store potatoes in a cool, dark, airy place. It is vital to exclude light, or they may quickly develop green patches.

Potatoes are endlessly versatile, forming an accompaniment or background to any number of other flavours. They can be boiled or baked in their skins, or peeled and steamed, mashed, roasted or fried. Do not use a processor to make a purée. These machines are so powerful that they break up the starch granules and the result will be gluey.

The darkening, or blackening, which sometimes occurs when potatoes are cooked is caused by iron in the tubers themselves. Using a stainless steel knife or peeler, and adding a pinch of cream of tartar to the boiling water, should prevent discoloration.

Good all-rounders for most cooking purposes include King Edward, Cara, Kennebec, Maris Piper, Romano, Bintje, Desirée and Pentland Hawk.

Varieties which bake well include Marfona, Arran Pilot, Cara, Catriona, Estima, Golden Wonder, Maris Piper, Morag, Pentland Dell and Pentland Squire.

Well-flavoured potatoes which are good for salads because they keep their shape when cooked, are also ideal for inclusion in stews and casseroles. These include Asperge, La Ratte, Cornichon, Belle de Fontenay, Jersey Royal, Charlotte, Epicure, and Pink Fir Apple.

Potatoes which mash well include Pentland Dell, Pentland Ivory, Pentland Squire, Golden Wonder, Maris Piper, and Epicure.

Candidates for chips include Arran Pilot, Maris Piper, Pentland Dell, Spunta, Bintje and Maris Bard.

There is not much need to freeze potatoes, but lightly cooked new potatoes freeze successfully, as do recipes including mashed potato, such as croquettes.

PUMPKIN
(see Squash)

RADICCHIO
(see Chicory)

RADISH
The fast growing radish is every child's first gardening success. Freshness is easier to spot when they are sold in bunches with their leaves attached. Sprouting from trimmed ends, and softness, are sure signs of staleness. Their crisp texture and peppery taste is best appreciated when they are eaten with butter, salt and crusty bread as a simple hors d'oeuvre. White winter radish, or mooli, is a long, smooth and white root which has a similar flavour and can be eaten raw, or steamed or boiled and served like turnips.

ROCKET
(Arugula, Roquette, Rucola)
Rocket grows as fast as its name. Its leaves, eaten in a mixed salad, or with shavings of fresh Parmesan or Parma ham, have a hot, aromatic, peppery

taste which is either addictive or disliked.

RUNNER BEAN

Perhaps because they are so easy to grow, and crop so heavily, runner beans are a national institution despite their tendency to be stringy. When young and fresh, the newer stringless varieties are good, fresh-tasting and tender cooked or raw. Although they are usually cut in thin diagonal slices and boiled, more of the nutrients are retained if they are cut in longer pieces and steamed, or finely cut and stir-fried. Overgrown runners are more of a penance than a pleasure.

SALSIFY

Also called the oyster plant or vegetable oyster, the long tapering roots have creamy white flesh which can be cooked and served like turnips. Peel thinly or scrape the roots, and drop them into acidulated water to prevent discoloration. Scorzonera, which has a darker skin and is larger than salsify, is prepared the same way.

SAMPHIRE

(Glasswort, Marsh samphire, Sea asparagus)
Fishmongers sometimes sell samphire or sea asparagus from their slabs. Its succulent, branching stems taste of the sea. They need careful rinsing, and only the briefest of boiling in unsalted water. Serve buttered, as a course on their own, or with fish.

SHALLOT

(see Onion)

SORREL

Sharply astringent, lemony tasting sorrel leaves are fragile and melt as soon as they are heated. For this reason they are often cut in fine ribbons and added to sauces for fish at the last moment, and to omelettes. Puréed sorrel is usually thickened. The leaves are also eaten raw in salads. Sorrel contains oxalic acid and, like spinach, should not be eaten in large quanties.

SPINACH

Fleshy, dark green spinach leaves contain good amounts of vitamins A and C, but also of oxalic acid, so it should not be eaten in excessive quan-

tities. Young leaves can be served raw as salad greens. Larger leaves, stripped of their stems, are cooked briefly until just soft, in a covered pan in no more liquid than the washing water left clinging to them. A big pan of spinach cooks down to a surprisingly small quantity, so allow at least 225g (8oz) of raw spinach per person, and drain cooked spinach very thoroughly before serving.

Choose spinach which looks crisp and fresh, without insect or other damage. Keep it, for no more than a day or two, loosely wrapped, in the salad drawer of the refrigerator.

Spinach freezes well.

Use it in soups, quiches, omelettes, and as an accompaniment to fish, and grilled or fried meat or poultry.

Beetroot and turnip tops can be cooked like spinach. Spinach beet, a variety of beet grown for its leaves, is larger and coarser, with fleshy white ribs. The green portions are cooked as spinach.

SPINACH BEET

(see Spinach)

SPRING GREENS

(see Cabbage)

SPROUTING BEANS AND SEEDS

When seeds germinate, vitamins, especially C, are produced which are not present in the dormant seeds. Various types of peas, beans and other seeds are sprouted as foodstuffs. Most sprouts are eaten before they begin to form leaves, but some, such as mustard and cress, are grown on until they form stalks and two leaves. Mung, adzuki and soya beans, whole dried peas and chickpeas, lentils, wheat, alfalfa and fenugreek seeds are commonly sprouted. Bean and pea sprouts should be cooked, briefly, if they are to be eaten in any quantity, because they contain a substance which inhibits trypsin, one of the enzymes with which we digest their protein.

SQUASH

Pumpkins, gourds and squashes, melons, cucumbers and marrows all belong to the same family. Although some are more useful as decoration than as food, most are edible. Quick-growing summer varieties such as young marrows and 193 courgettes are thin skinned. Winter squash have a hard rind, firm flesh, and the hollow interior contains large numbers of seeds, usually hard. Pumpkins are the most commonly available type of winter squash, but other varieties such as butternut, acorn, Queensland blue, custard marrow and pattypan squash are increasingly available. The largest squashes are usually bought in pieces, unless the whole vegetable is wanted for a Halloween lantern, or to serve as a dramatic soup tureen for a winter party.

Choose unblemished specimens which feel heavy for their size. Uncut winter squashes keep well, some large ones for many weeks when stored in cool, dry conditions.

Most varieties tend to blandness when cooked, and are at their best when peeled, seeded, and baked in chunks brushed with oil or butter. They can also be boiled, steamed or puréed, and are often seasoned with spices such as ginger and cinnamon, and a little sugar to emphasise the sweetness of the flesh.

Vegetable spaghetti is boiled or baked whole until tender, at least 30 minutes, then the spaghetti-like interior is served with any pasta sauce. To prevent it bursting, make a small hole in it before cooking.

Other varieties include karela and kantola, which are slightly bitter, and blander types such as christophine (or chayote), and dudi. These can be cooked like courgettes.

SWEDE
(Neeps, Rutabaga)
The turnip flavoured swede is yet another member of the cabbage family. Its pale orange flesh can be used in any recipe for turnips, but it is at its best when steamed or boiled, well drained and puréed with generous amounts of butter and black pepper. It is also a useful addition to robust winter stews and casseroles.

Large swedes can be unpleasantly fibrous, and may even be bitter. The variety Garden Swede is sweeter than most. Like most roots, they keep well in cool, dark, dry, airy conditions.

SWEETCORN
(Maize, Corn-on-the-cob)
Only gardeners ever taste sweetcorn at its sweet-est. The moment it is picked, the sugars in its creamy yellow kernels begin to turn to starch so rapidly that there is a noticeable difference in taste even an hour after picking. Nonetheless, it is still a particularly sweet vegetable, best of all plainly boiled and buttered and stripped with the teeth. Salt them only after they are cooked, because salt toughens the skin of the kernels. Parboiled cobs can be grilled or barbecued, basted with a glaze of equal parts of honey and melted butter. Very tender young cobs can be barbecued inside their protective husks.

Biggest is not best. Choose cobs which are creamy in colour and well filled in preference to those with deep yellow kernels which are more mature but less sweet. Try to eat them the day they are bought.

Cooked corn stripped from the cobs can be mixed with other vegetables such as peas, and used in fritters and soups. Miniature varieties are cooked and eaten whole.

Whole cobs, cooked and dry-packed in tins, are a good standby for grills and barbecues. Sweetcorn can be frozen on or off the cob.

SWEET POTATO
This elongated tuber is best boiled or baked in its skin. Its yellow, white or pink flesh tends to discolour if peeled before cooking. Choose, store and cook as you would potatoes. Sweet potatoes can also be used in pies, bread and sweet dishes, and can be glazed with butter and sugar to emphasise their sweetness.

TOMATO
Good looks are deceptive. Public dissatisfaction with poorly flavoured tomatoes has been heeded by growers, who now offer better varieties – at premium prices, of course. Few tomatoes grown under glass match the superb flavour of the sun-ripened fruit we buy on Mediterranean holidays, but at least the choice is improving.

Big, pumpkin-shaped tomatoes are good for stuffing, and plum tomatoes have dense flesh which makes them useful for sauces and stews.

Not all tomatoes are red when ripe. Some varieties are yellow or orange. But all ripe tomatoes should be firm not soft. To peel them easily, use a sharp knife to cut out the calyx, taking the hard central core with it in a small cone. Drop the tomatoes into boiling water for about 30 seconds, then into cold water. Drain them, and the skin should peel off easily.

A salad of sliced tomatoes with salt, good olive oil and a few leaves of fresh basil is unbeatable.

Tomatoes can be frozen raw or cooked. Open freeze raw tomatoes in halves.

TURNIP

The fashion for baby vegetables has done a great service to the turnip, which, when young, is sweet and slightly peppery and can be steamed or boiled without peeling. Navets are a small, flattish French variety tinged with purple. Turnips belong to the cabbage family, and their leaves can be cooked like spinach.

Choose firm, small turnips no larger than apples. Store them for a day or two in a cool, dry, airy place.

Peel and quarter them to boil or steam. White or cheese sauce is good with turnips, which go particularly well with beef and most red meats.

TRUFFLES

(see Fungi)

VEGETABLE SPAGHETTI

(see Squash)

VINE LEAF

Blanched vine leaves have a slight astringency which makes them useful wrappings for small fish and game birds such as sardines and quails, and for stuffings of rice and cheese etc. Choose young, tender vine leaves and store them like salad greens. Brined vine leaves are available in packets and need to be soaked in clean water for half an hour or so before using.

Vine leaves have an extraordinary affinity with mushrooms. Line a casserole with vine leaves, fill with mushrooms, a whole clove or two of peeled garlic, and a little olive oil and seasoning, and bake covered until the mushrooms are tender.

WATER CHESTNUT

Chinese cooks put a greater emphasis on texture than their western counterparts, and water chestnuts, which remain crisp when cooked, are a valuable ingredient in stir-fries and *dim-sum*. They are usually found tinned. Fresh water chestnuts are peeled before being eaten raw or cooked.

WATERCRESS

Watercress grows wild in streams and lakes in this country, but it can be infected with liver fluke from sheep droppings and so farmed watercress is a safer bet.

Choose fresh, crisp dark green leaves with no signs of yellowing or slime, and keep for no more than a day. It deteriorates quickly.

Its peppery taste enlivens lettuce salads. It is also good in soups, sauces, omelettes and quiche.

ZUCCHINI

(see Courgette)

CHAPTER 19

FRUIT

Fruit is nature's vehicle for the distribution of seed. Evolution has ensured that it is appealing to man, bird and beast alike. With odd exceptions, such as rhubarb which is a stem, and crab apples and rowans which are not palatable, fruit can be eaten raw, as nature intended.

Ripening is a process which fruit alone undergoes. Once it is fully formed, a number of changes occur which increase its efficiency as a distributor of seed. Acidity and starch content reduce, and sweetness increases to make the fruit pleasantly edible. Skin changes from green to a colour which advertises the fruit's ripeness for all to see. A characteristic fruity perfume develops as a further attractant to the consumers who will unwittingly distribute the seeds.

Many fruits, if picked fully formed but not fully ripe, will continue to ripen in storage, becoming sweeter and less acid as they do so. Pears, for example, actually benefit from early picking, which prevents the deterioration in texture which affects fruit left on the tree. Exceptions include citrus fruits, melons and pineapples, which take all their sweetness directly from the parent plants. These will not become any sweeter after picking, although softening and the development of perfume may continue.

Shelf-life was not one of nature's considerations, but it is a prime concern of growers and distributors whose products must fly halfway round the globe and still look good when they arrive. Breeders have responded by developing strains which are firmer and less fragile than garden fruit. Some, there is no denying, are as disappointing as florists' roses – all show, and lacking scent and taste.

Not only is fruit engineered to meet the requirements of transport and display, too often at the expense of its quality on the table, but much of it is treated too. The skins of citrus fruits are usually waxed to retard dehydration, although unwaxed lemons are increasingly available, and Seville oranges for marmalade are not treated. Ethylene gas is used to accelerate ripening in fruits such as bananas which are shipped when they are still hard and unripe to minimise damage in transit. These treatments are believed to be harmless.

Science has provided great benefits too, as anybody will admit who is old enough to remember how tedious it was to examine every raspberry for maggots before effective pest control got the better of them. Good packaging is another boon, minimising the damage which accelerates deterioration.

Residues of pesticides and fungicides are a worry. Washing fruit before eating it is sensible. But washing damages fragile berries such as raspberries, so the decision – to wash, or not to wash – is a personal one.

Poisons within the fruits themselves are not a serious hazard, but a word of caution is necessary about the pips and stones of several common varieties. The pips of apples, pears and citrus fruits, and the seeds within the stones of peaches, nectarines, apricots, plums and cherries contain cyanogens, and should not be eaten in quantity. An occasional swallowed pip is not dangerous. Neither is there any hazard from a stone which has split within the fruit, or a kernel used to give a hint of bitter almond flavour to a compote.

The leaves of rhubarb are poisonous.

CHOOSING AND STORING FRUIT

When buying fruit, look for unblemished skin, well-filled and unwrinkled. Fruit that is juicy will feel heavy for its size. Berries and other soft fruits should be plump and dry. Fruit without bruises, splits or insect damage will keep much better than fruit which has been injured, and will be less vulnerable to mould spores and enzyme action. The adage about one rotten apple spoiling the barrel is just as true of the fruit bowl, or of the salad drawer in the refrigerator.

The ideal storage temperature for bananas, citrus fruit, melons and pineapples is about 10°C (50°F). Apples, pears and most hard fruits keep well in the refrigerator. Fruits with fragile skins – strawberries and raspberries, for example – suffer from condensation in the refrigerator which encourages mould. Left out, on the other hand, they rapidly dehydrate. Use them quickly.

Many of the exotic fruits imported from the tropics, or grown under glass nearer home, are damaged by extreme cold. Noting the temperature at which supermarkets display unfamiliar varietes can offer useful clues to ideal storage conditions.

A – Z OF FRUIT

APPLE

No fruit looms larger in the British culinary tradition. As a native species with good keeping qualities it was for many centuries the only fresh fruit available in winter, so generations of cooks have exercised their ingenuity on it. There are said to be more than 6,000 named varieties grown in this country alone, although only a tiny fraction of them are produced commercially.

The distinction between 'cookers' and 'eaters' or dessert apples is not a very useful one, except for identifying varieties such as Bramley's Seedling which are too sour to eat with pleasure. Another characteristic of most apples sold as cookers is that the cooked flesh collapses into a pulp. This is not at all what the cook wants for tarts and pies, but is just the job for a sharp apple sauce to serve with roast pork, duck or goose.

Well-flavoured dessert apples which also taste good, and do not collapse when cooked, include Blenheim Orange Pippin, Cox's Orange Pippin, Crispin, Egremont Russet, Granny Smith, Idared, Jonagold, Jonathan, Orleans Reinette, Ribston Pippin and Winesap.

Other aromatic and pleasingly crisp dessert varieties include Ashmead's Kernel, Discovery, Fiesta, Fuji, George Cave, Golden Delicious, Kidd's Orange Red, Lady Williams, Laxton's Fortune, Laxton's Superb, Lord Lambourne, Sunset, and Worcester Pearmain.

Apples can be stewed, puréed, baked, fried (very good with grilled duck breast, roast game, black pudding or hot *foie gras*), made into pies, tarts, fritters, ices, jellies and other preserves. Many northern French recipes with the suffix *à la Normande* combine apples, cream and cider – or Calvados, the spirit distilled from it – in dishes of poultry or game.

APRICOT

Velvet-skinned, pinky orange apricots are at their best when sun-ripened on the tree. Most imported apricots are picked before they ripen, and their taste can be disappointingly undeveloped. Cooking them with plenty of sugar, and a little lime or lemon juice if they are lacking acidity, intensifies the flavour. They are halved for poaching, baking, and making into pies or tarts. Cut round the fruit and twist the halves apart. Eat ripe apricots as they come, or in fruit salads.

ASIAN PEAR
(Nashi)
A crisp, juicy, yellow-skinned fruit which looks and tastes more like an apple, though its grainy texture is pear-like. Eat like apples, or use in fruit salads.

BABACO
This long, ribbed fruit is yellow when ripe, and 197

looks not unlike a blunt banana. The skin, which has a sheen, is edible. The fruit is related to the pawpaw, but its taste tends to blandness. Sliced in sections it looks pretty in fruit salads.

BANANA

The size, shape and flavour of the familiar banana varies considerably with variety and ripeness. The development of brown and black mottling on the skin is a sign that the fruit is sweet and ready to eat. Sliced bananas on breakfast cereal, and in trifle and fruit salad, are well entrenched. Fried bananas, sprinkled with lemon juice and brown sugar and flamed in rum, are worth a detour. They are also good in tarts, tea breads, sandwiches and fritters.

BLACKBERRY

(Bramble)

A single blackberry is not one fruit but several. Each of the drupelets, as the small spheres of juice round every seed are called, is a self-contained fruit in its own right. Cultivated blackberries tend to have more flavour as well as being larger than their wild counterparts. But this is by no means a rule. The best are tart and full of taste, the worst are boring on both counts. Pick them when they are ripe and all the drupelets are well filled, glossy and very dark purple in colour. When they are fully ripe the calyx and pithy centre will be left behind when they are picked.

Blackberries can be eaten raw with sugar and cream, or mixed with other fruits in summer pudding. Blackberry and apple pies and crumbles are family favourites. They are also used in ices and preserves. Bramble jelly is especially good.

BLAEBERRY

(Bilberry, Whinberry, Whortleberry)

These small, round, dark blue berries are gathered wild on moors, mountains and open woodlands in Britain, Europe and northern Asia in late summer. They are tart and sweet and well worth picking. Eat them raw in open tarts, or mixed with yogurt or in fruit salads. They can be cooked in pies, pancakes or fritters, and made into ices and preserves. In the Alps they are added to sauces for game.

BLUEBERRY

Cultivated blueberries are related to blaeberries, but are usually three or four times larger. There is nothing in their handsome appearance – smooth blue-black skins and plump shape – that offers a clue to their flavour, which may be sharp and sweet, or bland. In North America, where they grow wild, they are used in pies, cheesecakes, muffins, pancakes, ice creams and a variety of other recipes. They can be eaten raw or cooked in tarts, fruit salads and summer puddings.

CAPE GOOSEBERRY

(Chinese lantern, Physalis)

The name Chinese lantern picturesquely describes these small, shiny orange globes hidden in a papery husk. The garden variety is for decoration only. Cape gooseberries grown for eating have an intense flavour – not unlike passion fruit, but less sharp. Eat them raw, in one bite, after peeling back the husk. They make excellent fresh *petits fours* when dipped in melted fondant (see page 138) and very good ices.

CHERIMOYA

(see Custard apple)

CUSTARD APPLE

(Sweetsop)

A tropical fruit of the Americas, the custard apple, or sweetsop, has soft, custard-like flesh when fully ripe. The fruit is made up of multiple segments, with many seeds. The soursop is a larger, spiny variety of the same species. A third custard apple is the cherimoya, which has a green scaly skin, with pointed bumps. The flesh inside all three can be eaten with a spoon, discarding the seeds, or made into drinks and ices.

CHERRY

The distinction between sweet dessert cherries for eating fresh, and sour cherries used in cooking has been blurred by the creation of new multi-purpose varieties which exploit characteristics of both types. Many hundreds of varieties are cultivated and the colour range is vast – from pale creamy fruit tinged with pink, through every shade of red to deepest wine, almost black. Taste before buying loose cherries. Packaged fruit is generally sweet, and should be labelled. Look for plump, glossy, well-filled fruit. Stems which are fresh and green are a sign of freshness. Ripe cherries are very perishable. They should be treated as soft fruit, and stored briefly in a cool place.

For use in savoury dishes such as duck with cherries, or for jams and ices, some of the old sour varieties offer superior flavour. Use cherries to make pies, tarts and *clafoutis*. A cherry stoner has a cup like a ceramic Polo mint and a prong to push the pit through the hole.

CITRON

This is a large, sour, lemon-shaped member of the citrus family from which we get candied citron peel.

CLEMENTINE

This sweet, almost seedless, loose-skinned citrus fruit is a cross between a tangerine and a bitter orange. Look for fruit with good orange colour and bright, well-filled skins. Eat fresh, in segments or slices. Or use in ices or marmalades made with a mixture of citrus fruits. The preservative wax should be scrubbed off if you're using the peel in marmalade.

CRAB APPLE

These small, astringent wild apples are too sour to eat raw. They can be gathered in gardens and hedgerows. The fruits may be pale gold, tinged with pink, or bright, orangey red according to the variety. They make pretty pink and delightfully perfumed apple jelly to eat at breakfast or tea, or with roast pork or duck. Herb-flavoured jellies are usually based on crab apple.

CRANBERRY

The native cranberry, which grows wild on moors, is smaller than its closely related American counterpart which is grown commercially. The bright red berries, noted for their unusually good keeping qualities, are sour and astringent. Cranberry sauce to serve with roast turkey is an American Thanksgiving tradition which has been adopted here for Christmas. But cranberries have other uses too. They are high in pectin, and make good preserves, sometimes spiced or mixed with oranges. With plenty of sugar they can be used in pies and ices and drinks. Cook them till the skins burst before adding sugar because it toughens the skins when combined with raw fruit. In small quantities, cranberries add a tart note to sauces for game, and sweet meats such as lamb and pork.

CURRANT

Blackcurrants and redcurrants are more often seen than the white variety, which has almost transparent, greeny-white berries. When ripe, all types can be eaten raw but they will need sugar. Cooking alters and greatly intensifies the flavour of blackcurrants, which make wonderful jellies, ices and cordials. Redcurrant jelly is traditionally served with roast lamb and game, and melted to glaze the soft red fruits in open tarts. The easiest way to strip the berries from their branching stalks is to pull the main stalk of each bunch up through the tines of a fork, allowing the currants to drop into a bowl.

Currants are fragile, and so easily squashed that it is difficult to keep them. Preserves and dishes using cooked currants can be made with fruit which has been frozen.

CURUBA

(see *Passion fruit*)

DAMSON

These small, blue-black plums have a bloomed skin and once went under the name 'damascenes'. They are more often found wild in late summer than on sale. They are sometimes sweet enough to eat raw, but they are tart and the stone is large in relation to the amount of flesh. The flavour, when cooked and with added sugar, is excellent, and they make very good pies, tarts, preserves, ices and fools. Damson cheese, a preserve stiff enough to cut in slices, is eaten with cheese, or on its own.

DATE

Fresh, ripe dates, sold loose or on the stem, are much more luscious than the partially dried dates sold in pencil-case boxes, or the pressed dates in blocks that are gritty with sugar which has crystallised. Fresh dates have honey-like flavours. The skin may be golden brown or chestnut, smooth or slightly creased. They are eaten raw, just as they are, or the long, pointed stone can be removed and the cavity stuffed with cream cheese, marzipan, or a coarse nut filling.

DURIAN
This is the tropical fruit that smells so revolting that travellers are forbidden to carry it as cabin baggage in aircraft. It is large, weighing several kilos, and has a thick, spiky, greenish skin. The flesh inside is rich, aromatic and sweet, but not everyone can get it past their nose.

ELDERBERRY
The prolific elder grows wild all over Britain, in city parks and on waste ground as well as in hedgerows. Its flat, creamy white saucers of multiple flowers develop into heavy bunches of berries in late summer, when the birds feast on them, spattering red-black juice. The flowers are more fragrant than the fruit, which countrymen make into wine. They can be eaten raw, but are rather tart and better cooked. Combined with apple they add a novel note to crumbles and pies.

FEIJOA
(Pineapple guava)
Originally from Brazil, this winter import is now grown in New Zealand and the Mediterranean. The green skinned fruit is about 7.5cm (3in) long, wider at the stem end than at the tip. The flesh of the ripe fruit is paler than the skin, and its flavour is likened to strawberries.

FIG
The fig is a hardier tree than its mythic Mediterranean image suggests, and some varieties thrive in sunny gardens in Britain, fruiting generously over a long late-summer ripening season. Everyone who has been put off by dried stewed figs should try the fresh ones now widely available. Whether large and purple with a slight bloom, or small and green, or tinged with deep pink or purple, fresh ripe figs are a sweet delight. Once ripe, the skin splits easily, so choose unblemished fruit and do not try to keep them for more than a day or two.

The skin can be eaten or not, and the flesh is soft. In fresh figs the seeds are soft and are eaten too. Serve them alone, or with dark grapes, sweet plums and fresh dates as a dramatic, slightly sinister-looking dessert. They go well with thin slices of *prosciutto* as a first course. Or slit them from the stem end in quarters, but not right through to the base, and stuff them with ground almonds, mixed to a stiff paste with cream and a little fresh lemon juice.

GOOSEBERRY
Green gooseberries are one of the first home-grown fruits of the year, following rhubarb on to the market in May. Some are the cooking equivalent of apples; others are the unripe fruit of dessert varieties. They are inedibly astringent when raw, but have an inimitable flavour when cooked, and can be stewed to make a tart sauce for rich fish such as mackerel, or fatty meats such as roast pork. Sweetened with sugar they are traditionally made into pies, crumbles, tarts, fools and ices. Gooseberry jelly has a lovely pink gold colour and can be scented with elderflowers which bloom in the same season. Tie three or four heads of elderflowers in muslin and steep them in the sweetened juice after the sugar has been added and before boiling for a set (see page 147). The perfume is very strong, and steeping takes only 10 minutes or so.

Sweet dessert gooseberries can be pale green, yellow, pink or deep red, smooth or hairy. Leveller and Careless are varieties with particularly good flavour. Dessert varieties are best eaten raw. When cooked they do not have as much flavour as green gooseberries.

GRANADILLA
(see Passion fruit)

GRAPE
Crops from the southern hemisphere, where the seasons are the opposite of our own, allow grapes to be imported all year round. Distinctly different varieties are grown for wine-making and for the table. As with grapes for vinification, great differences in flavour and character are attributed to growing conditions, and a single variety grown in three different locations can

taste more like three different types of grape. Most dessert varieties are sweet and juicy when ripe, and colour makes no particular difference to flavour. Seedless grapes are increasingly popular, with Thomson and Flame among the favourites. For intensity of flavour there is no beating the highly scented sweetness of big, white Muscat grapes. Fragole, also known as Strawberry Grape, Siegerrebe and Black Hamburg are well flavoured dessert varieties grown in this country.

Use seeded or seedless grapes in open tarts, and serve them with soft and blue cheeses.

When peeled grapes are called for, dip them briefly in hot water and the skins should slip off easily. A hairpin can be used for hooking out the seeds without halving the fruit.

GRAPEFRUIT

Good breeding has greatly increased the sweetness and consequently the popularity of grapefruit. This juicy citrus fruit is available in a range of sizes and colours from pale green through yellow to pink. Sweetie is a green-skinned variety which is less tart than most. Grilled grapefruit halves enjoyed a vogue, but the fruit is best eaten raw, scooped from the cut halves or in segments. To prepare good-looking segments, use a really sharp stainless steel knife to cut away the skin and underlying pith. Then cut cleanly between the membranes to release the segments. Work over a bowl to catch the juice. Fresh grapefruit has a surprising affinity with smoked fish served as a cold hors d'oeuvre.

GREENGAGE

For flavour the greengage is a prince among plums – sweet and juicy when fully ripe, and with a matchless flavour when poached in syrup, or cooked in pies, jams and ices.

GUAVA

A heady and pervasive perfume is the guava's strongest suit. The fruit, grown in tropical and sub-tropical climates, is pear shaped and looks much like a quince. When ripe the flesh can be pink or creamy white, and the texture is grainy, like pear but more so. The seeds are soft enough to be edible. Once ripe they are highly perishable and should be eaten quickly. Halve them and scoop out the flesh with a spoon. The flavour is caught very well in ices, jams and jellies, which are the best ways to preserve them.

HAW

Hawthorn berries ripen in September and can be gathered until early winter. They are tart, but edible, and can be made into wine and jelly.

HIP

The scarlet fruits, or hips, of wild or garden roses can be gathered after the first frost and before winter. They are a very rich source of vitamin C, but the hairy seeds inside the fruit are choking and can irritate the gut. This is why hips are traditionally made into jelly, cordial syrup and wine.

KIWI
(Chinese gooseberry, Kiwi fruit)
The rough, light brown skin of the kiwi belies the tart, sweet flesh inside, which has a texture that is both crisp and tender. Some kiwis are boringly bland, but appearance offers no clue. Peeled, and sliced across the rings of tiny black edible seeds, its bright green flesh is an attractive addition to fruit salads. Kiwis can also be halved and eaten like boiled eggs with a spoon. Savoury uses are heavily promoted by the growers.

KUMQUAT

Although not technically a citrus fruit, the kumquat looks and smells like one, and is related to the citrus family. The whole fruit, which resembles an elongated miniature orange, can be eaten raw, skin and all, though some are too strongly flavoured to give much pleasure. Like citrus fruits the skin contains highly perfumed essential oils. Preserving them in equal parts of heavy syrup and spirits (brandy or vodka) mellows them.

LEMON

No fruit has a more important place in the kitchen than the lemon. In addition to its value as a flavouring for every kind of sweet recipe, the juice has a quite extraordinary capacity to bring out the flavours of other ingredients. A few drops 201 can transform flat flavours into vibrant ones. Think of the sharp juice as a flavour enhancer to be used, like salt, in savoury dishes as well as on fruits with low acidity.

Lemons are imported all year round from Mediterranean countries and further afield. The main distinction is between those which have thin skins with little underlying pith, or are thick-skinned and pithy. Thin skins are generally an indication of juiciness, and nicer for slicing for drinks. When the zest is wanted, thick-skinned lemons should have more of the highly flavoured essential oils, and are best for marmalade and some preserves. Choose lemons that feel heavy for their size, and avoid any that are dull-skinned or puckered. Supermarkets sell unwaxed lemons which do not have the protective fungicidal coating routinely applied to citrus fruits.

Lemons are used to flavour puddings of every type from hot soufflés to ices. Make lemon meringue pies, lemon tarts, jellies, creams, sponge cakes and biscuits. Fresh lemon curd and lemonade are heaven. Use the finely pared zest to flavour sugar. Lemons preserved with salt take on a new dimension, and are an essential ingredient in many North African dishes.

Lemon juice can replace vinegar in salad dressings, and, like vinegar, can be used to prevent browning when applied to the cut surfaces of fruit and vegetables.

LIME

This tropical and sub-tropical member of the citrus group is smaller than the lemon, sour and with a thin, bright green skin. The zest is highly aromatic and there are marked flavour differences between limes grown in different parts of the world. Limes can be substituted for lemons in most recipes. Although smaller, their flavour is stronger, so expect to use the same number or fewer.

The acidity of lime juice has the capacity to coagulate proteins in raw fish, to 'cook' without heat, and is used for this purpose in the South American speciality *ceviche*.

LIMEQUAT

Limes and kumquats were crossed to produce this small, green and very sour fruit. Use it as a flavouring in recipes, and in preserves.

LOGANBERRY

This is a hybrid cross of raspberry and blackberry. It can be eaten raw or substituted in recipes for either. The berries are a deep, soft red, larger and longer than raspberries, and equally variable in flavour. Choose dry, undamaged fruit and use it quickly. The berries are too fragile to keep well.

LONGAN

(see Lychee)

LOQUAT

(Japanese medlar)

Although related to the European medlar, loquats, which grow round the Mediterranean as well as in the Far East, are eaten when freshly ripe and not allowed to ferment as medlars are. The ripe fruit has a downy yellow or apricot coloured skin and juicy, slightly crunchy flesh which is both sweet and tart.

LYCHEE

(Litchi)

This sub-tropical native of southern China keeps well in the fridge for several weeks, making it a useful buy for the once-a-week shopper. Lychees have an intense grapey taste, combining acidity with sweetness in flesh which is juicy and tender. Ripe fruit are the size of quail's eggs, or a little bigger, with a pink-tinged brittle casing which peels off easily. Inside is the translucent white flesh and a single, inedible seed. Lychees are best eaten raw, but can be served peeled in a light syrup.

The smaller and less distinguished longan is related to the lychee. Rambutans are another relative with shells covered in soft, hairy spines.

MANGO

A ripe mango of a good variety is indisputably one of the world's best fruits. Size and colour are poor indicators of quality and ripeness. The smooth, inedible skin may be green, yellow, brightly flushed with pink or red like an apple, or red all over. Unripe fruit are hard. Ripe mangoes give a little when gently pressed. Size ranges from a few ounces to the better part of a pound. What they all share is a large stone to which the flesh clings tenaciously. The flesh colour is usually pale or dark apricot. Its texture is luscious and, in the mouth, feels almost oily. The flavour and perfume are intense and unique. Analogies to tinned peaches and the smell of warm pine woods pale beside the fruit itself.

Ripe mangoes make excellent ices, mousses and fresh fruit sauces, and are good in fruit salads. Slightly unripe ones can be served with smoked fish or meat. Unripe mangoes are best made into chutneys, but ripe fruit, especially if fibrous, can be used too.

MANGOSTEEN

No relation to the mango, the mangosteen looks rather like a hard, dark brown apple. Inside the tough rind are translucent white segments of sweet, fragrant flesh which are usually eaten raw.

MEDLAR

This native fruit is becoming a rarity, to be found in old gardens and growing wild, although medlar trees are still being planted by curious cooks and gardeners. Rough and russet-skinned medlars look like immature apples with a large calyx. Even when ripe, in late October when they are picked, the fruit is too hard and astringent for eating. But kept until it is so ripe that the flesh has fermented to a purée, a practice known as 'bletting', the fruit sweetens. Medlar jelly is a traditional preserve.

MELON

Melons come in all shapes and sizes – round, oval and long, small enough for a single serving and large enough for several families. Colour ranges from dark to pale green and every shade of gold. Some of the best, such as Galia and Pineapple melon, have skins which, because of their roughened markings, are described as 'netted'.

A good melon is heavy for its size. If its fragrance is pervasive even before it is cut, then it will taste good. The flesh will be ripe if the stalk end has a little give when gently pressed. Cut large melons in halves and scoop out the seeds, saving the juice. Melons small enough to make a single serving can be topped like boiled eggs, the seeds removed, and the lid replaced. Highly flavoured melons need no embellishment. Less well-endowed melon flesh can be improved with a little fresh lime or lemon juice, which is a much better treatment than dried and powdered ginger. For taste, the varieties Ogen, Galia, Charentais, Cantaloupe and Pineapple melon are among the best. Inexpensive Honeydew melons are often tasteless.

Watermelons, which have crisp, sweet red flesh, are enjoyed more for their texture and refreshment value than for their taste, which is elusive.

All types of melon are best eaten chilled. Highly scented ones need to be well wrapped if they are not to taint everything else in the refrigerator.

PREPARING A MANGO

Cut lengthwise along the two sides of the flat stone to form three slices, two with rounded bases and flat tops. Make criss-cross cuts in the flesh of these

slices and turn inside out to make a hedgehog shape. Don't forget to peel the central slice and nibble the flesh off the stone.

203

MULBERRY

Ripe mulberries drop from the tree, staining not only the ground but anything or anyone they come in contact with. The deep purple berries are fragile, multiple fruits like raspberries, and never appear in the shops although they grow in old gardens and parks, often neglected. Mulberries can be used for jam and substituted for blackberries in recipes. They are excellent raw, served with cream or sweetened mulberry juice. White mulberries are rarer than purple.

NECTARINE

(see Peach)

ORANGE

There is no telling from its weight and obvious freshness whether an orange will be well-flavoured and sweet, or whether the membranes inside will be coarse and the flesh dull. Disappointment is likelier in summer than in winter when the Mediterranean crop arrives in the shops, but good oranges can usually be found for most of the year. Navel oranges should be particularly sweet, and blood oranges with their ruby juice are essential for *sauce maltaise* (see page 82). For marmalade-making, bitter Seville oranges are the ones which produce the true taste of English breakfast marmalade, though all types of citrus fruit can be mixed and matched in preserve recipes. Sevilles are also the oranges to use in sauces for duck and other savoury recipes. They can be frozen, whole, to provide year-round supplies. When grated zest is needed, take it from the hard-frozen oranges, then let them thaw to extract the juice.

Freshly squeezed orange juice, scented with essential oils from the zest, remains a treat.

Classic Mediterranean salads combine slices of orange with raw sweet onions and black olives.

Try using freshly grated orange zest in place of candied peel in cakes and puddings. As a change from slices of orange served with caramel syrup, add a little orange flower water to a plain syrup. Use small pieces of orange zest, fresh or dried, to casseroles of meat or game.

Ortaniques, which are an orange/tangerine cross, can be used as oranges. Ugli fruit are an orange cross too (see page 208).

PASSION FRUIT

These egg-shaped, egg-sized fruit are a better investment than the high prices make them appear. The little flesh there is inside the purple-brown skin is highly scented and strongly flavoured, so only small quantities are needed. It is not necessary to wait until the skin is deeply puckered. Passion fruit are ripe when the skin colour is rich and deep.

Inside is a mass of edible seeds which are coated, like tomato seeds, with a clinging layer of flesh. The fruit can be opened and eaten with a spoon, or the seeds can be sieved out and the flesh used in mousses, ices, soufflés and sauces. With or without the seeds, passion fruit is an excellent addition to fruit salads.

The yellow-skinned curuba and larger orange granadilla can be used in the same ways.

PAWPAW

(Papaya)

The pawpaw is one of the most widely grown and prolific of the tropical fruits. Its tender, highly perfumed flesh is denser and more melting than melon, and is a deep, soft orange. Most of the pawpaws sold in Britain are of moderate size, weighing 450g (1lb) or less, although much larger examples are found in places where it grows. The shape is pear-like and sometimes irregular, and the skin, which is inedible, turns from green to yellow as the fruit ripens. A ring of yellow at the stem end of an unripe pawpaw is said to indicate a fruit which will ripen if kept. The cluster of seeds inside looks like caviar.

Slices of pawpaw sprinkled with fresh lime juice are a traditional breakfast in the tropics. The fruit makes a good addition to fruit salads.

PEACH

Nectarines are smooth-skinned varieties of peach, without the down that gives peaches their special complexion. Both are dessert fruit par excellence. Small white-fleshed peaches win top marks for flavour, although yellow- and pink-fleshed varieties run them a close second. Some have stones which cling tenaciously to the flesh, while in others the stone is barely attached and comes out easily. This, like the tenacity of the skin, cannot be judged by appearance. To release the stone, cut round the line of the crease and twist the two halves apart. Some peaches peel with little trouble, others don't. Dipping them briefly in hot water works with some, not with others. Obstinate ones are better peeled, if you must, with a very sharp, stainless steel knife.

Choose fruit which is firm but not hard, and undamaged. Peaches are easily bruised, which is why they are picked before they are fully ripe. Any that fail to ripen satisfactorily can be cooked, but ripe peaches are at their best raw, with or without cream.

Ripe peaches and nectarines are excellent in tarts, fruit salads and ices. Ripe or under-ripe fruit can be used in pies, compotes, preserves and chutneys.

PEAR
The trick with pears is to catch them the day they reach the peak of ripeness, after which they deteriorate rapidly. They continue to ripen after picking and can be bought while still firm enough to travel. Once ripe, they can be refrigerated for a day or two, no more. Of the 5,000 or more named varieties, many have a grainy texture, or poor flavour. Appearances are not much help. Good-looking pears can be very disappointing, and uninvitingly rough looking fruit can taste wonderful. When named varieties are offered, good dessert choices include Beurré Superfin, Comice, Doyenne du Comice, Packham's Triumph, Red Bartlett, Red Williams, and Williams Bon Chrétien, which is the Bartlett pear of canning fame. Good cooking pears include Beurré Dumont, Forelle, Napoleon, and Vicar of Winkfield. Dual purpose eating and cooking varieties include Anjou, Beurré Hardy and Beurré Bosc, Conference, Pitmaston Duchess, and Nelis.

Ripe dessert pears go well with cheese, especially with blue and goats' milk cheeses. Poach pears with vanilla, or with red wine and spices. They are good in tarts, ices and a variety of puddings.

PERSIMMON
(Sharon fruit)
The Sharon fruit is a variety of persimmon bred to popularise a fruit rarely seen on sale in this country. Both resemble flattened, rather square,

orange tomatoes. The difference is that while the true persimmon is inedibly astringent until so ripe that it looks ready to burst, the less luscious Sharon is ripe when it reaches a more conventional degree of softness. The flesh is sweet, soft, and has little perfume.

PINEAPPLE
The statuesque pineapple is the emblem of hospitality carved in stone on the gate finials of country houses. There is a lot of waste involved in stripping off the deeply-faceted skin, but its continuing popularity is ensured by the fact that its taste fully lives up to the promise of its dramatic appearance. When ripe, the fruit is strongly perfumed and a leaf from its handsome plume can be pulled out. Fresh-looking leaves are the best indication that the pineapple is not stale.

Use fresh pineapple in ices, fruit salads and creamy desserts, but not in recipes which include gelatine. This reacts with the fruit's pepsin enzymes and does not set. It is this enzyme which makes the fibrous flesh unexpectedly digestible.

Savoury recipes which combine fresh or cured pork with pineapple are much nicer made with fresh fruit than with oversweetened tinned pineapple.

PLUM
Although good dessert plums are well worth eating raw, the flavour of plums is intensified by cooking, and sour varieties or under-ripe plums cooked with sugar are often better than the fresh fruit. Plums make particularly good pies, tarts, and compotes. They are also good in casseroles of game, and Chinese cooks use them to make a variety of sweet-sour sauces. They also make excellent preserves.

Colour ranges from the true green of gages, through the yellow Mirabelle varieties beloved of French pastry-cooks, through every shade of red and purple to the blue-black of damsons. The shape may be round or oval, but fresh plums will always have well-filled skins, often with an attractive bloom. Cooking plums with good flavour include Belle de Louvain, Czar, Godshill Blue, and Pond's Seedling. Well-flavoured dessert varieties inclue Coe's Golden Drop, Curlew, Denniston's Superb, Mirabelle de Nancy and Oullin's Golden Gage.

POMEGRANATE

The pomegranate is the exact opposite of fast food. Beneath its tough burnished skin lie hundreds of little bladders of scarlet juice, each containing an astringent seed. It is fiddly to eat, or to prepare, but the juice is well worth extracting for long drinks or to use in marinades for poultry, game or lamb. Both the seeds and pips are full of tannin, hence their astringency. To extract the juice without damaging the seeds and thus releasing too much of the tannin, press them firmly but not too fiercely over an orange or lemon squeezer.

Pomegranate juice is the basis of the sickly-sweet French cordial Grenadine.

POMELO

(Shaddock)

The largest member of the citrus tribe is less well flavoured and juicy than the grapefruit, which is probably descended from it.

PRICKLY PEAR

(Barbary fig, Cactus pear, Indian fig)

Not a fruit that is worth searching out, but sweet and edible. As befits the fruit of a cactus, it has sharp spines which are not only painful but difficult to remove from the skin. When offered for sale it is stripped of spines, but should still be treated with care in case any have been missed. The flesh is sweet and may benefit from a few drops of lime or lemon juice.

QUINCE

A cook's fruit, the quince cannot be eaten raw but makes exceptionally good preserves, jellies to be served as jam, and stiffer jellies to be eaten as sweets. When ripe, the fruit, which can be the size and shape of apples or stubby pears, is a pale yellow and covered with greyish down. A bowl of ripe quinces will perfume a room. The fruit contains large amounts of pectin, especially in the seeds, which makes it ideal for preserves. Add pieces of peeled quince to casseroles of poultry or game, or make into a sauce to serve with roast pork or goose.

Japonica apples or quinces, the smaller fruit of the flowering shrub, can be used in same ways as larger quinces.

RAMBUTAN

(see Lychee)

RASPBERRY

There never seem to be enough raspberries to make jelly and jam as well as raspberry tarts, summer puddings and hazelnut meringues and still have enough left over for breakfast. Pick-your-own farms are the best places to find affordable raspberries, and although they go in for heavy cropping varieties with lesser flavour, all raspberries make good preserves.

Raspberries make the best of ices (see page 136) and fruit sauces. Unsweetened raspberry vinegar, made by steeping raspberries in red wine vinegar, is especially good in dressings for salads made with less than brilliant tomatoes.

Choose fruit which looks fresh and dry, with well-filled drupelets and preferably with no juice dripping from the bottom of the punnet. Some of the raspberries bred for air-freighting from North and South America keep better than home-grown varieties. Store them for the minimum time, in a cool place or the refrigerator.

Frozen raspberries soften and bleed when thawed, but are fine in summer puddings, fools, mousses, soufflés and sauces, or added to apples in pies or crumbles.

Loganberries and tayberries are raspberry and blackberry crosses.

RHUBARB

Forced spring rhubarb is the first fruit crop of the year. It is grown in darkened sheds and picked by candlelight to prevent the unfurled leaves from greening. The slender pink stalks are good cooked in pies or crumbles, poached with sugar and a piece of vanilla pod, and in ices. Outdoor rhubarb, available in late spring and early summer, is coarser in texture, even sourer, and has less flavour. Nonetheless, it makes very acceptable pies and crumbles.

Strawberry ice cream (see page 136) with soft summer fruits and a fruit coulis *(see page 84).*

Rhubarb or rhubarb and ginger jam are homely preserves, but will need extra pectin if made with forced rhubarb.

Rhubarb can also be cooked without sugar as a tart accompaniment to rich meats, or fish.

ROWANBERRY

The orangey red berries of mountain ash or rowan trees are made into a jelly that is traditionally served with game, especially grouse and venison. The berries are not sold commercially but the tree is grown in suburban gardens and municipal parks as well as growing wild in the Scottish highlands and English moors. Birds are the rowan's only other consumers.

SAPODILLA

A tropical fruit, also called a tree potato, which describes its appearance pretty accurately. Sapodillas are about the size of new potatoes and, when ripe, have soft, sweet flesh. They are usually eaten raw, peeled and without the black, shiny seeds. Unripe fruit are grainy and astringent, but will ripen in a warm room. Ripe fruit can be refrigerated.

SATSUMA

A loose-skinned variety of orange, originally from Japan. The skin is paler than other oranges. Peel and eat them as dessert fruit, or use them, alone or in combination with other citrus fruits, in marmalade.

SLOE

These small blue-black fruits of the blackthorn are a hedgerow crop and related to plums. The fruit is too sour to eat, but can be made into jam. The best known use for it is to flavour gin. Fill a bottle with sloes, picked after the first frost if you are to save yourself the trouble of pricking each one, and top up with gin. Close tightly and leave for two or three months to mature. Use as a liqueur.

STAR FRUIT

The starriest attribute of this fruit is the five-pointed shape of its slices, which look pretty in fruit salads. Star fruit have deeply ridged sides and are pointed at both ends. The edible yellow skin has a waxy sheen, and the flesh is fresh tasting but unexciting. It is invariably eaten raw, and the seeds discarded.

STRAWBERRY

These are the most popular of the summer fruits, widely grown in gardens and allotments, on patios and city balconies. Modern strawberries, which have seeds sunk in the surface rather than on top of the flesh, all derive from American varieties first imported in the 17th and 18th centuries. Cultivated varieties of our native wild strawberry are now called Alpine strawberries and *fraises de bois*. The honey flavoured, tiny fruit, occasionally seen in very classy shops and grown commercially in France, is descended from an eastern European species.

Ripe strawberries of every kind are painfully perishable, and the best indication of flavour is their smell. Most are picked under-ripe and are never quite as good as fruit picked when ready to eat. Another regrettable trend are the varieties, now widely grown, which have a firm, pale protrusion at the stalk end. They are difficult to hull, and the pale section is often still hard when the the rest of the fruit has ripened.

Strawberries are best washed (if they must be) before they are hulled, and served just as they come, or with sugar and cream, or wine. Their place in tarts, and cream-filled cakes or meringues, is unassailable. Little Scarlet is the prime variety for jam.

TANGERINE

The name covers a variety of loose-skinned oranges including mandarins. The fragrance of the peel and flesh is markedly different from close-skinned oranges. But they are eaten and used in the same ways. Mineolas and tangelos are tangerine and grapefruit crosses.

TAYBERRY

(see Raspberry)

UGLI FRUIT

The ugly duckling of the citrus family is a hybrid cross of three fruits – grapefruit, orange and tangerine. Treat it as a sweet, loose-skinned grapefruit.

CHAPTER 20

MEAT, POULTRY AND GAME

Like all our foodstuffs, meat is changing. The beef which our grandmothers served when they were young was slaughtered when the animals were up to six years old. Now beef cattle are butchered at two. Not only are they younger, they are leaner. Both farming and processing techniques have changed.

It is still possible to buy meat from traditional breeds of animals and birds which have been reared out of doors and doctored only when they are sick. Organically produced meat and poultry is gastronomically as well as aesthetically pleasing, and growing numbers of people are prepared to search it out and pay premium prices.

Economics affects every stage of meat production, including butchery. Hanging carcasses in controlled conditions improves both flavour and tenderness. But reduced hanging time means reduced costs, so most meat is hung for the minimum period.

Tenderness and flavour also depend on which parts of an animal the meat is cut from. Muscles in the forequarters of grazing and foraging species have to work harder than those at the rear. Hard-working muscles have more and stronger connective tissue, so they are tougher – but they also develop more flavour.

BUYING AND STORING MEAT

How much meat to buy depends on the dishes to be made, and the appetites of the diners. Eighteen-year-old sportsmen eat a whole lot more than ladies of a certain age who subscribe to the dictum that a woman cannot be too rich or too thin. When buying lean meat without bones, think in terms of allowing 100–170g (3½–6oz) per serving. For meat on the bone, allow 225–340g (8–12oz).

Market forces dictate what is available, and what it costs, and variations even locally can be surprising. In areas where demand for prime cuts is strong, the price of meat for stewing and braising may be very reasonable. Conversely, strong demand for budget cuts may push their prices up. These differentials are being reduced, however, by a change in wholesale practices. Increasingly, butchers buy parts of carcasses, rather than whole ones, to suit their trade. Another factor is health and hygiene legislation which restricts the forms in which some types of meat (offal, for example) can be supplied.

When thinking about economy, bear in mind that cuts of meat which will need long cooking often take longest to prepare too, as well as using more fuel. Shrinkage is another consideration. A fillet steak, cooked quickly to medium rare, shrinks less than an equivalent weight of braising beef cooked to well-done.

Always choose meat that looks and smells wholesome. Avoid anything that looks dry, or excessively wet.

The keeping qualities of meats are variable. As a general rule, the larger the piece the better it keeps. Minced and chopped meat is more perishable than chops or steaks, which in turn are more perishable than large joints. Supermarkets put helpful use-by dates on their packaging, and instructions about whether the contents are better left in their wrappings or taken out before refrigerating at home. As a general rule, red meat – beef, lamb and mutton – can be kept in the refrigerator for 3–5 days, pork and veal for 2–4 days. Minced meat and offal of all types are best used within a day of purchase.

Always store meat low down in the coldest part of the refrigerator, and make sure that it cannot contaminate any other foodstuffs with leaks or drips (see page 300).

MEAT PREPARATION AND HYGIENE

Thorough cooking destroys bacteria, and here the cook faces a conflict of interests. To be absolutely safe, all meat should, ideally and theoretically, be cooked to an internal temperature of at least 70°C (160°F). This means the meat will be well done, which of course is not to everyone's taste. The flavour of rare beef and lamb are widely liked, and in dishes such as steak tartare the meat is eaten raw. Veal and pork are invariably cooked thoroughly because they taste better that way. Stringent inspection ensures that the pork we buy in this country is very unlikely to be infected with trichinella cysts, but memories are long, and most people still feel happier eating pork which has been well cooked.

In practice, the dilemma is not insoluble. Healthy adults with a taste for rare beef, lamb and game, can choose to take greater risks than are advisable for young children, invalids and the elderly. Casseroles, stews, braises and pot roasts are all cooked more than well enough to destroy bacteria, and present no threat unless carelessly reheated. Joints of meat roasted in one piece should also be safe. Even if the interior of the joint is rare, the meat nearer the outside will be thoroughly cooked. Note, however, that this is not the case with boned and rolled joints. Any surfaces contaminated during preparation can end up in the centre of the piece, so rolled joints should be thoroughly cooked.

BEEF CUTS

Standardisation has not yet eliminated wide regional variations in cutting methods and in the names given to the pieces. These are the most common British cuts.

BARON OF BEEF

A very large roasting joint cut from the sirloin and rump. *Roast.*

BRISKET

This cut, from the underside of the forequarter, is sold on or off the bone, and may be rolled. It can be fatty, but the flavour is good. Brisket is excellent for making salt beef. *Boil, or braise in pieces as a pot roast.*

CHUCK OR BLADE BONE

This is taken from the top of the forequarter, and is usually sold boned, as chuck, blade or braising steak. The meat has some marbling of fat through the muscle. *Stew or braise.*

CLOD AND NECK

These are fairly lean cuts from the neck end of the forequarter, usually sold ready cut up for stewing, or minced. *Stew or braise.*

FILLET

Taken from the underside of the lower spine, this is a muscle which has had very little work to do. It is the most tender and quickly cooked cut of beef, better served rare to medium than well-done. Good fillet has a light marbling of fat. It can be roasted or cut into *filet mignon, tournedos*, or *Châteaubriand* steaks. This is the cut to use for beef Wellington. *Roast, grill, fry.*

LEG AND SHIN

These are the lean leg muscles – shin from the forelegs, and leg from the hindquarters. Flavour is their strong suit, and they need long, slow cooking to melt the high proportion of gelatinous connective tissue. *Stew, braise, or use in stock.*

MINCE

This can be made with various cuts and trimmings, and once the beef has been put through

Rare roast fillet of beef served with a tarragon-scented béarnaise *(see pages 35 and 82).*

the mincer its provenance is undetectable. Pale colour usually indicates a high fat content. Supermarkets generally offer the option of extra-lean mince with a stated fat content. Buying any of the cuts sold for stewing, then mincing them at home, is another choice. ***Stew or make into hamburgers, meatballs, cottage pie, meat loaf and sauces.***

RIB

Rib cuts are confusingly named. Back rib comes from nearer the front of the carcass than forerib. The distinction matters. Although the joints look rather similar, forerib is the better cut for fast-roasting at high heat, preferably on the bone. Back rib is more suited to slow-roasting, or, when boned and rolled, braising as a pot roast.

Rib steaks, and single ribs on the bone, taken from the forerib, are excellent for grilling.

Wing rib, or prime rib joints, are cut from the sirloin, and are the tenderest of the rib cuts.

Thick rib is a shoulder cut best suited to slow-roasting and braising.

Thin rib is the lower portion of the ribs. The meat is inter-layered with fat and has good flavour. It can be braised, on or off the bone, or minced. ***Forerib: roast or grill. Back rib: roast, or braise as a pot roast. Wing or prime rib: roast. Thick rib: roast or braise. Thin rib: braise.***

RUMP

This is the rearmost section of the animal's back and is usually boned and cut across the grain of the meat into rump steaks, which are fairly tender and have good flavour. ***Grill or fry.***

SILVERSIDE

Taken from the upper area of the back leg, this is lean, coarse-grained meat with good flavour. It is usually boned and rolled. Although it can be slow-roasted, it is better suited to braising or salting. ***Braise as a pot roast, or salt and boil.***

SIRLOIN

The long upper back section between the ribs and the rump. It includes the last three ribs (see Rib, above), and the fillet which is often separated from it (see Fillet, above). Sirloin is prime, tender meat, and when cut into joints, on the bone or boned and rolled, is fast-roasted on high heat. It can also be divided into a variety of steaks. Sirloin and entrecôte steaks are boneless. T-bone and porterhouse steaks include some bone. ***Roast, grill, fry, dry-fry.***

SKIRT

This is a name applied to various internal muscles which are lean and coarse-grained, but which have excellent flavour. Goose skirt, some-

BEEF

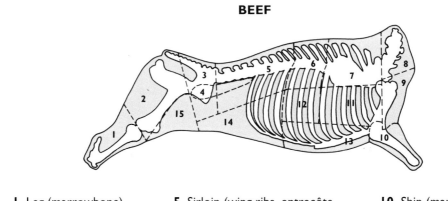

1. Leg (marrowbone)
2. Topside, silverside and aitchbone cut
3. Rump
4. Fillet (*filet mignon*, tournedos and Châteaubriand)
5. Sirloin (wing ribs, entrecôte, porterhouse and T-bone steaks)
6. Foreribs
7. Chuck and blade and back ribs
8. Neck
9. Clod (marrow bone)
10. Shin (marrow bone)
11. Thick rib
12. Thin rib
13. Brisket
14. Thin flank and skirt
15. Thick flank or top rump

times called flank steak, can be grilled or fried provided it is kept rare. ***Grill, fry, braise or stew.***

TOP RUMP

A lean cut of fine-grained meat from the inside section of the rear leg. ***Braise as a pot roast, or roast.***

TOPSIDE

This is the uppermost section of the hind leg. The meat is lean, fine-grained, and usually made into rolled joints. ***Braise as a pot roast, or roast.***

BEEF OFFAL

OX HEART

Tough and fibrous. ***Braise or stew.***

OX KIDNEY

Strongly flavoured and best cooked slowly, as in steak and kidney puddings. ***Braise or stew.***

OX LIVER

Strongly flavoured and best slow-cooked with other robustly flavoured ingredients. ***Braise or stew.***

MARROW BONES

These are the leg bones, containing a rich central core of luscious marrow fat which is used to enrich sauces, or as a delicacy in its own right. The bones are poached or roasted, and the marrow scooped out and served on toast. ***Roast, poach, or use in stock.***

OXTAIL

Richly flavoured and very gelatinous. ***Braise.***

TONGUE

This is sold either fresh or salted. A single tongue can weigh more than 1.8kg (4lb). It requires long, slow cooking and can be eaten hot or cold. ***Boil.***

TRIPE

This is the lining of the first three stomachs. Old recipes call for tripe which was prepared by scraping and washing only. But the tripe sold now is bleached and pre-cooked, and needs only another hour or so's cooking. ***Braise.***

VEAL CUTS

Calves fed on milk produce paler veal than those which have eaten grass. Most parts are lean and tender. In fact the lack of marbling fat through the muscles means that particular care must be taken to ensure that veal does not become dry.

BEST END AND BEST END OF NECK

A forequarter joint from behind the shoulder, which includes the upper section of the ribs. It is sold as a roasting joint, or divided into chops or cutlets. ***Roast, grill or fry.***

BREAST

Cut from the underside of the forequarter, this is usually boned and rolled for roasting or braising. It is a well flavoured and relatively economical cut. ***Roast or braise as a pot roast.***

ESCALOPES

These are thin slices cut across the grain of the meat. The best come from the topside of the leg. Good escalopes are also cut from the underside of the leg, and coarser ones from silverside. Escalopes from the shoulder are less tender. ***Fry.***

FILLET OF VEAL

An exceptionally tender cut which can be roasted whole or cut into medallions and fried. ***Roast or fry.***

KNUCKLE AND SHIN

These are the lower parts of the legs. They are gelatinous, well flavoured pieces which are excellent for stock. Cut into short lengths they are sold as *osso buco* (see overleaf). ***Braise.***

LEG

Leg provides escalopes of various grades, the best being cut from the cushion or topside. The leg is usually divided into its three main muscles – cushion, silverside and thick flank – any of which may be roasted or braised in a large piece, or sliced thinly into escalopes. ***Roast, braise or fry.***

LOIN

This is the cut which lies between the best end and the rump. It can be roasted whole, on or off the bone, or divided into chops, or boned into medallions, for grilling or frying. A whole loin may or may not include the fillet. *Roast, grill or fry.*

MIDDLE NECK AND NECK

These are boned and chopped for pies, or minced. With the bones they are used for stock. *Stew, braise, or use in stock.*

MINCED VEAL

Made from a variety of secondary cuts, its gelatinous quality is particularly useful in combination with other meats in meat loaves and terrines. Use slow-cooking methods unless you have selected a prime cut for mincing, in which case the meat can be grilled or fried. *Fry, grill, braise, etc., depending on quality.*

OSSO BUCO

The meatiest *osso buco* is cut from the hind leg or knuckle, but the front leg or shin is also used. The meat is gelatinous and well flavoured. *Braise.*

PIE VEAL

This is diced veal from a variety of secondary cuts. Use in pies and casseroles. *Stew or braise.*

RIBS

Central section of the rib cage. *Braise or poach.*

SCRAG

Scrag is boned and chopped as pie veal, or minced. With the bones it is used for stock. *Stew, braise, or use in stock.*

SHOULDER AND CHUCK

A whole shoulder can be roasted, on or off the bone, or divided into smaller roasting or rolled braising joints of varying degrees of tenderness. Escalopes cut from this forequarter section are not top quality. *Roast or braise.*

STEWING VEAL

Secondary cuts suitable for stewing and braising, usually offered in larger pieces than pie veal.

VEAL OFFAL

Calves' brains and sweetbreads are no longer sold in this country.

CALF'S FOOT

Only occasionally available, but marvellous for giving stock a rich, gelatinous unctuousness.

HEART

A hard-working muscle which needs tenderising, it is good for stuffing and braising.

VEAL

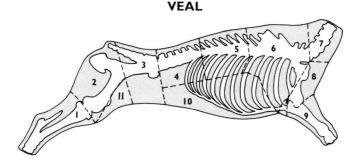

1. Knuckle or hind leg (*osso buco*)
2. Leg (cushion or topside, and silverside or undercushion)
3. Rump
4. Loin and fillet
5. Best end
6. Shoulder and middle neck
7. Neck
8. Clod
9. Shin or foreleg (*osso buco*)
10 Breast and ribs
11. Thick flank

KIDNEY

Calf's kidney is a great delicacy, and expensive. Brief frying so that it remains a little pink and juicy is the best treatment whether it is served with or without a sauce.

LIVER

Calf's liver has a fine texture and flavour, and, like kidney, is best lightly cooked. Fry thin slices lightly in butter or olive oil. If grilled, particular care must be taken to ensure that it does not dry.

LAMB CUTS

Lamb is the meat of young sheep up to a year old. New season's English or Welsh lamb, available for Easter, is one of the shrinking number of truly seasonal treats, producing small roasting joints that are particularly sweet and tender. Mutton is the meat of mature sheep. The breed of the sheep governs the size of the joints, and the meat is darker, less tender and more strongly flavoured than lamb. Mutton is not widely available, so although cuts of mutton are the same as those for lamb, suitable cooking methods differ. Those given here refer to lamb.

BEST END OF NECK

Also called rack of lamb, this is a versatile joint from the forequarter between the neck and the loin. A best end comprises six or seven small ribs, which are sold in the piece or cut into chops or cutlets. A well trimmed rack is one of the few pieces of meat that makes a good roast for two people. A guard of honour roast is made by joining two racks, face to face, with the fatty layer to the outside. For a crown roast, two or three racks are joined in a circle, fat side towards the centre.

The central eye of meat, boned and trimmed of all fat, can be cut into noisettes, which may be grilled or fried. *Roast, grill, fry, braise.*

BREAST

A fatty cut from the underside of the forequarter, usually boned and rolled. It can be stuffed. *Roast or braise.*

LEG

Leg of lamb (known in Scotland as gigot) is the most popular roasting joint. A long leg includes the chump. Half legs are sold as smaller roasting joints. The upper part is also cut in thick slices called gigot-chops with the bone, and leg steaks when boneless. *Roast, fry or grill.*

LOIN

This is the tenderest cut of lamb, taken from the saddle area between the best end of neck and the chump. The most magnificent roasting joint is a saddle of lamb – a cut which includes both sides of the loin, plus the upper part of the chump and the tail, all in one piece. The loin and chump can also be cut into separate roasts, to be cooked on or off the bone; or they may be cut into individual loin and chump chops, or double loin chops called butterfly chops.

The eye of the loin can be boned and trimmed to be roasted in a piece, or cut into noisettes for frying. These are usually dressed with a thin layer of fat. *Roast, grill or fry.*

MIDDLE NECK AND SCRAG END

These are bony pieces from the neck end of the forequarter, used mainly for stews and braises. The meat is sweet and rather fatty.

Neck fillet, sold separately, is a tender piece which can be cut in small pieces for kebabs, or fried in one piece before slicing.

Slices across the neck itself are bony pieces called neck cutlets. *Stew and braise. Fillet: braise, fry or grill.*

SHOULDER

An economical roasting joint which is fatter and sweeter than leg, but more awkward to carve. It can be boned and stuffed in a variety of shapes, of which a pumpkin-shaped ball is the most eye-catching. The meat is also boned and minced, or cut into pieces for casseroling or kebabs. *Roast, grill, or braise.*

LAMB OFFAL

BRAINS

These are a great delicacy. They are firmed by blanching, then fried. Deglazing the pan with vinegar or lemon juice provides an instant sauce. 215

HEART

Lambs' hearts are inexpensive and full-flavoured. Stuff and braise, or casserole in slices. Allow one per serving. ***Stew or braise.***

KIDNEY

Whenever possible buy lambs' kidneys in their suet casings, when they will keep for 2 days in the refrigerator. Allow 3 or 4 kidneys per serving. Strip off the suet and thin membrane, then halve the kidneys and cut out the central core. Lightly grill or fry to serve a little pink. Overcooking or adding salt before cooking toughens them. ***Fry or grill.***

LIVER

Lambs' liver is economical and well-flavoured. It is best lightly fried. ***Fry, grill or braise.***

SWEETBREADS

These are an unfashionable delicacy. They are blanched, then as much of the skin and membrane as possible is picked off, before being cooked until tender. They can be fried or, better still, cooked gently in a *blanquette*-style velouté sauce. ***Fry or stew.***

TONGUE

Lambs' tongues are usually sold fresh, but can sometimes be bought salted. Allow 2 or 3 fresh tongues per serving. Simmer them in water or stock until tender before skinning and removing the root bones. They can be pressed for serving cold, or reheated in a *blanquette*-style velouté sauce. ***Fry or stew.***

KID AND GOAT

The meat of goats – or, more often, of their kids – is increasingly available as goats' milk cheeses grow in popularity. Most of the kid meat sold comes from the young males. The meat of mature animals has a reputation for pungency, but kid meat can be substituted for lamb in most recipes. It is tender and very lean, so extra care is needed to ensure that it does not dry out. Roasts should be basted and cooked slowly. Braising is the safest choice for all but the most juvenile animals. The offal is comparable with lambs' and can be used in the same ways.

PORK CUTS

Pigs today are bred leaner and slaughtered younger than they used to be. Its youth ensures that the meat is tender, but, being leaner, care is needed to ensure that some cuts are not dry.

BELLY

Also called streaky or flank, this is cut from the

LAMB

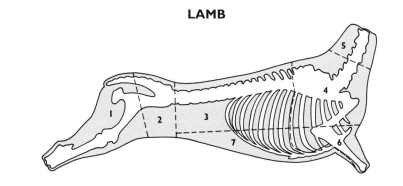

1. Leg (fillet end and shank end or knuckle)
2. Chump
3. Loin (saddle), fillet and best end of neck (rack of lamb)
4. Shoulder (blade side or end) and middle neck
5. Scrag
6. Shoulder (knuckle or shank end)
7. Breast

underside of the animal with layers of fat and lean in almost equal proportions. Thick rashers are sold for frying, and it is the ideal piece to mince or chop for terrines. The bones with some of the meat attached are sold as spare ribs. *Grill, fry, mince.*

BLADE AND SHOULDER

These provide a selection of cuts – among them the sparerib (not to be confused with spare ribs from the belly), which can be braised in one piece, or cut into chops for grilling or frying. The fatter blade joint from the neck end is slow-roasted or braised whole, or cut into chops. *Roast, braise, fry or grill.*

HAND AND SPRING

This is the front leg and shoulder area above and behind it. It is sold in one piece, or two, is fairly fatty and very well flavoured. *Roast or braise.*

LEG

A large, prime joint which can be roasted whole, on or off the bone, but is more usually divided into two roasting pieces. The upper section can be cut into leg chops for braising or grilling. *Roast, grill, or braise.*

LOIN

This is a long section along the back of the pig,

and the prime end is nearest the tail. It is cut into roasting joints which can be cooked on the bone, or boned, rolled and stuffed. The aptly named tenderloin is the fillet, which is available separately and can be cut into medallions for frying, or roasted or fried in one piece.

Loin chops are cut from the foreloin, chump chops from the end nearer the tail. Pork chops will curl when grilled or fried if the skin and fat are not slashed at intervals (or use kitchen scissors). *Roast, grill or fry.*

PORK OFFAL

FAT

Back fat is rendered down to make lard. Sliced into sheets it is used to cover lean joints, and for larding (see page 71). Caul fat, a net-like web of fat from the stomach area, is invaluable, if you can get hold of it, for wrapping kebabs, home-made sausages, faggots and *crépinettes*, and for lining terrines.

HEART

This can be stuffed and slowly braised.

KIDNEY

Pig's kidney is less delicate than lamb's or calf's. *Grill or fry.*

PORK

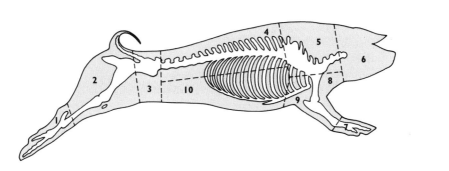

1. Trotter (hind foot)
2. Leg (fillet end and knuckle end; *cured as ham and gammon*)
3. Chump

4. Loin (fore loin, middle loin and fillet or tenderloin; *cured as back bacon*)
5. Shoulder or neck end (sparerib and blade; *cured as collar bacon*)

6. Head
7. Trotter (fore foot)
8. Hock
9. Hand and spring
10. Belly (thick, thin end and spare ribs; *cured as streaky bacon*) 217

LIVER

This is very good in terrines. The flavour is stronger than lamb's or calf's liver, and less widely liked. It is therefore inexpensive. ***Fry or braise.***

TAIL

The adage about eating every part of the pig, except its squeak, is true.

The tail is rich in gelatine and makes a very good stockpot ingredient.

TRIPE

The tripe from pigs is the main ingredient in chitterlings (*see Glossary*).

TROTTERS

These have already been blanched when you buy them. They provide good quantities of gelatine for the stock-pot. The well-cooked trotters can then be split lengthwise, breadcrumbed and fried. A love it or hate it delicacy.

BUYING AND STORING POULTRY

The range of poultry available today is wider than ever. Although the production of capons (castrated chickens) is no longer permitted in this country, and boiling hens can take some tracking down, an increasing variety of chickens, ducks, turkeys and other breeds of poultry is sold. One reason for this is a growing preference for white,

as opposed to red meats. Another, which is very good news for cooks, is that demand for free-range poultry has expanded. The lower prices of chickens produced in broiler houses ensure that these retain a lion's share of the market, but the superior flavour of slower-growing free-range poultry, which is slaughtered when several weeks older, has won it increasing popularity in the marketplace.

Most poultry is sold oven-ready, which means it has been plucked and cleaned and is ready to cook. In traditional butchers and poulterers, poultry which has been hung with the guts still inside to develop its flavour is weighed after plucking but before cleaning, and with the head and feet still attached. The oven-ready bird will be about one-third lighter.

All fresh poultry should look fresh, plump and cleanly plucked, and smell fresh. When it is sold packaged, either fresh or frozen, the packaging should be undamaged.

For refrigeration at home, poultry is taken out of its wrappings. If it has giblets, these should be put in a covered dish and refrigerated separately. Set the bird on a shallow dish, cover it loosely, and store it in the coldest part of the refrigerator. Cook within 3 days.

Frozen poultry must always be thawed completely before cooking. Open one end of the bird's wrappings, and set it on a dish so that the melt-water cannot drip on to other foods. Cook thawed poultry as soon as possible, and do not reheat it.

TRUSSING A BIRD

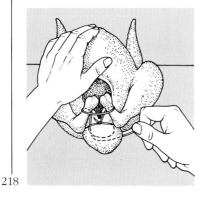

1. Tie one end of a long string round tail. Pass around drumsticks and back again round tail. Pull tight to draw drumsticks and tail over vent.
2. Turn bird on its breast and bring string around between thigh and body on one side. Loop around wing, across neck flap, and round other wing. Tighten and bring end of string, back to tail. Tie.

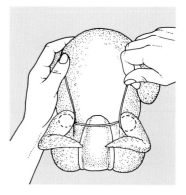

POULTRY PREPARATION AND HYGIENE

Poultry poses a higher risk of salmonella food poisoning than any other foodstuff, and so particular care is needed when handling and cooking it. Hands should be washed before and after touching raw poultry, and knives and boards and all work surfaces should be thoroughly cleaned after use.

The bacteria are destroyed by cooking, which is why poultry should always be thoroughly cooked to an internal temperature of at least 70°C (160°F). This is not difficult to judge. Use a pointed knife or skewer to pierce the flesh, aiming for the centre of the thickest part. The juices which emerge will be clear and almost colourless when the meat is cooked. If they are tinged with pink, continue cooking and test again until they do run clear. When cooking a whole bird, test the thickest part of the thigh, near the point where it joins the body.

CHICKEN

Chicken is the most adaptable of meats, taking well to a wide range of cooking methods and additional flavourings. A variety of styles and sizes of birds are produced.

BROILER OR ROASTING CHICKEN

These are the least expensive, factory-farmed birds, reared in broiler houses and slaughtered at about 7 weeks old, by which time they will weigh 1.4–2kg (3–4½lb). Larger birds are available in good quantity around Christmas and Easter. Broilers are sold oven-ready, fresh and frozen, whole and in pieces.

The flesh is reliably tender and succulent, and suitable for most purposes. *Roast, fry, grill, poach, steam, braise, stew, or stir-fry.*

DOUBLE POUSSIN

These are young broiler chickens weighing around 1kg (2lb 3oz). They tend to lack flavour, but butterflying them – cutting out the backbone and pressing the birds flat – makes them a suitable shape for grilling with herbs and other flavourings (see page 46). *Roast, fry or grill.*

POUSSIN

The smallest of the broiler chickens, weighing in at about 450g (1lb), give or take an ounce or two. The flesh is meltingly tender but lacks flavour. *Roast, grill or fry.*

BOILING FOWL

These are mature birds, usually former laying hens, weighing 2.3–3.2kg (5–7lb). They are full of flavour, very inexpensive, and the best choice for stock and soups. They are unsuitable for roasting but ideal for slow-cooked casseroles and for poaching whole with vegetables in a classic *poule au pot* (see page 12). *Poach, braise, stew or use in stock.*

CORN-FED CHICKEN

A diet of maize gives the skin of corn-fed chickens an attractive yellow colour and improves the flavour of the flesh. The usual size range is 1.4–2kg (3–4½lb). Cook simply. *Roast, fry, grill, poach, steam.*

FREE-RANGE CHICKEN

Some chickens are more free-range than others. The minimum requirement for free-range status is 28 days, during which the birds have access to the open air and can feed at will. These are usually slaughtered at 8–10 weeks, and, being more mature, have better flavour than broiler birds. The best free-range birds are traditionally reared, with access to the open air throughout their lives. They receive no routine medication and are slaughtered at 10–12 weeks old. Slower maturation produces chickens which combine tenderness with excellent flavour, suitable for all cooking methods. *Roast, fry, grill, poach, steam, braise, stew, stir-fry.*

DUCK

Technically speaking, a duckling becomes a duck when it develops its mature plumage at about 2 months old. Commercially produced ducklings are usually slaughtered at about 7 weeks, when, depending on the breed, they will already weigh as much as 3.2kg (7lb) after cleaning.

Ducks and ducklings can be bought fresh or frozen, whole or in pieces. Except when buying 219 boneless duck breast, allow a minimum of 450g (1lb) per serving. Choose plump birds with plenty of meat on the breast.

AYLESBURY DUCKLING

This is the most widely available type – a white-feathered breed with a generous covering of fat. ***Roast, braise, stir-fry.***

BARBARY DUCK

This descendant of the Muscovy duck is bred in France and becoming much more widely available in this country. It is a plumper bird with far less fat than an Aylesbury duckling, and even better flavour. The size range is large, from about 1.4–3.2kg (3–7lb). The boned breast meat can be grilled or fried like a steak. ***Roast, braise, grill, fry, stir-fry.***

GRESSINGHAM DUCKLING

A home-produced cross-breed which is leaner than an Aylesbury duckling but not as lean as a Barbary duck. ***Roast, braise, stir-fry.***

GOOSE

Fresh geese are available from September to December, and frozen birds all year round. The young geese available in the autumn weigh 4–6kg (9–13lb). By Christmas they will have reached up to 8kg (18lb). A large part of the weight is accounted for by the frame, so you need to allow a minimum of 450g (1lb) per serving. Cold roast goose makes very good eating so, if in doubt, buy more rather than less.

Goose is a fatty bird and its fat is prized for cooking *confit* (see page 143) and general frying. For this reason whole birds are almost always roasted. Pieces of goose are made into *confit* and *rillettes*. ***Roast.***

GUINEA FOWL

Domesticated guinea fowl combine the tenderness of poultry with some of the flavour of game. The meat is a little darker than chicken, and can be dry if not carefully cooked. Guinea fowl are usually sold oven-ready and most are a suitable size for two at a weight of about 1.1kg (2½lb). ***Roast or braise.***

QUAIL

Farmed quail are tiny birds with a surprising amount of well flavoured and succulent meat on their sparrow-like frames. Ready for the oven they usually weigh only 110–140g (4–5oz), although slightly larger ones can sometimes be found. They are sold fresh or frozen all year round. Allow one or two per serving. ***Roast, grill, fry, braise.***

SQUAB

Young pigeons bred for the table are very different in flavour and texture from wild ones. The

---

STUFFING A CHICKEN UNDER THE SKIN

With the chicken breast up, and starting at the neck end, slip your fingers between the skin and flesh of the breast on one side. Work your fingers in to

loosen the flesh along to the tail. Be careful not to break the skin. Do the same to the other side of the breast, then slip in the stuffing on both sides.

flesh is dark pink, tender and succulent, and the flavour excellent. Oven-ready birds are usually sold fresh and weigh about 340g (12oz) each. Allow one squab per person. *Roast, grill, fry, or braise.*

TURKEY

Fresh and frozen turkeys are available all year round. A majority of the birds produced are white-feathered varieties, though some turkeys with black plumage are also available. While these turkeys, described as bronze, are produced by less intensive methods, they are not necessarily free-range.

Most turkeys are slaughtered, plucked and cleaned in one continuous process to conform to European legislation. But it is still possible to buy birds which have been hung after slaughter, and this means a more distinctive flavour. These are labelled 'traditional farm-fresh' and are sold 'clean plucked', in which case a weight allowance has to be made for dressing, or oven-ready. Traditional farm-fresh turkeys are usually much more expensive.

Frozen turkeys are the cheapest. They need slow and lengthy thawing to ensure that their meat will be both safe and tender.

Self-basting turkeys have been treated to keep them moist when they are roasted. This usually includes flavourings as well as butter or vegetable oil, and most cooks will prefer untreated birds.

Turkey joints and pieces are also available all year round and can be substituted for chicken in many recipes. *Whole birds: roast. Turkey pieces: roast, grill, fry, braise, poach, steam, stir-fry.*

GIBLETS

Giblets is the collective name of all edible poultry offal. The neck and gizzard and heart can be used for stock, or finely chopped in stuffings.

Poultry livers make particularly fine eating, provided that care is taken to cut away any parts which have been stained a greenish colour by the gall bladder. The stained areas will taste bitter and should always be discarded.

The livers of all types of poultry can be lightly fried or grilled to make a snack or quick meal. All are excellent in terrines and pâtés.

BUYING AND STORING GAME

For game, read 'wild', although some game, pheasants for example, are not as wild are they used to be. Farmed and freed is a more accurate description of their pampered lifestyle. Venison and boar are now farmed too.

Traditionally the term covered all furred and feathered meat. Without stringent laws laying down when it may be shot, there would not be much of it left. Some species, like the now rare capercaillie, hardly ever appear on the open market. The shooting seasons are designed to ensure that the birds and animals breed in sufficient numbers. Although all types are available in autumn and early winter, each variety has its own particular season.

The characteristics of game meat are its depth of flavour and lean-ness. The hanging question looms large in the public mind, thanks to tales of people who like to eat their game 'high'. Hanging improves the taste and texture of game meat. Game which is sold oven-ready is very seldom high because licenced game dealers know that most of their customers will not buy long-hung meat. But it can be ordered by those who do not want to take the alternative course of hanging their own small game in the fur or feather.

Game birds are best plucked as close to the time they are cooked as is practicable. Young birds will usually have pointed flight feathers at the tips of their wings, soft, pliable feet, and downy feathers on the breast. These are best for roasting, but older birds are still excellent when carefully braised or cooked in pies or steamed suet puddings. They can also be made into pâtés and terrines.

Choose game that has been well shot. Avoid birds which have bloody patches on the breast, and birds and animals with broken limbs (they can contain nasty splinters of bone).

Game freezes quite well, although there is some loss of flavour and succulence. Store it, well wrapped, as you would other types of meat and poultry.

221

GROUSE

This is the earliest bird in the game calendar, at its best in the first half of the season (August 12th to December 10th). Its diet of young moorland heather shoots gives it an especially fine flavour, and it is best roasted rare or medium rare. Nearly all the meat is on the breast. The legs are usually slightly bitter. Stock made from the carcasses is also bitter, even when liberally sweetened with vegetables. If you want gravy, therefore, you will have to rely on stock made from other game. A grouse is just enough for two at a pinch.

PARTRIDGE

Red-legged partridge, known as 'Frenchmen', are slightly larger than the native English grey-legged partridge, and their flavour is less highly regarded. The season runs from September 1st to February 1st, and the birds are at their best in October and November. Partridge have succulent, finely flavoured meat which is better briefly hung than high. Allow one bird per serving.

PHEASANT

This is the most widely available of the game birds and its flavour can vary considerably depending on what it has been eating. The season runs from October 1st to February 1st, and they are at their best from the opening until Christmas. Most of the oven-ready supermarket birds have not been hung long enough to develop their flavour, so they can be disappointingly bland. Hen pheasants, which are slightly smaller and plumper than the cocks, have a reputation for finer flavour. Smaller birds will feed two; large ones will stretch to four. But pheasant presents the cook with a problem: in an ideal world, the light breast meat and darker flesh on the legs would be cooked by different methods. Roasting suits the breast meat very well, but the legs are best braised. Separated before cooking, one pheasant will make two meals for two. Lightly fry the breasts for one meal, and casserole the legs for another. When roasting, prevent the breast from drying by basting frequently.

WOODPIGEON

Too common to need the protection of a shooting season, woodpigeon are available all year round. They are best in summer, especially after the harvest when they have eaten their share of corn. They are meaty birds with dense, dark, well flavoured flesh which is easily dried by over-cooking. When roasted they are best eaten fairly rare. Those who prefer well-done meat would do better to braise pigeon or eat it in pies or steamed suet puddings. Pigeon breast, lightly fried in clarified butter (see page 239) is very good. Allow one bird per person.

SNIPE AND WOODCOCK

These are related species with distinctive long beaks. Snipe weigh only about 100g (3½oz) dressed weight, and are in season from August 12th to January 31st. The larger woodcock weighs about 285g (10oz) and is in season from October 1st to January 31st. It is customary to roast either bird complete with the head and innards. The innards, known as the trail, are scooped out and spread on a croûton of bread, placed beneath the roasting bird in the oven to catch the juices.

WILD DUCK

Mallard, widgeon and teal all make good eating. The wild duck season runs from September 1st to February 20th. The flavour of the meat is strong, and they are very much leaner than their domesticated cousins. The smallest is widgeon, which will serve one. Teal will serve one or two. Mallard will serve two or three. All are best roasted slightly pink. The meat toughens and dries when cooked further, and is better braised for those who prefer it well done.

HARE

Although hares may be shot all year round (except on Sundays and Christmas Day), they may not be sold from March to July, and make the best eating from October to January. A young hare, or leveret, will serve four; an older hare up to eight. Young hares can be roasted whole, or the saddle and hind legs treated separately. The legs of mature hares are better braised, but the saddles can be roasted. The meat of both is best roasted to rare or medium, and should be well-basted to prevent it from drying and hardening.

For jugged hare you will need the blood

reserved when the hare was hung. It is prevented from coagulating by stirring in a teaspoonful of wine vinegar, then refrigerated separately to be added to the sauce in the last few minutes of cooking.

Hare meat is full of flavour and relatively inexpensive. It can be made into sauces and stuffings for pasta, and any number of braised and casseroled dishes.

RABBIT

Most of the rabbit offered for sale has been farmed, but wild rabbit is also available. Both are sold year round. Farmed rabbit can be used in most recipes suitable for chicken, but wild rabbit is lean and benefits from careful cooking to ensure that it does not dry or harden. It is best braised or casseroled, although it can be fried, grilled or roasted. Rabbit is not usually hung.

VENISON

All types of deer meat are called venison, and in this country four types are available. These are the meat of roe, fallow, red and Sika deer, and all may be wild or farmed. The seasons vary according to breed, sex and locality, and frozen and farmed venison are available all year round.

Venison is close-textured, dark, lean meat, tender when taken from young animals, and more fully flavoured from older ones. Mature animals are hung for up to 3 weeks.

Prime cuts for roasting include the haunch, or hind leg, and the saddle, which includes the fillet. Haunches of older animals and shoulders are usually braised or cut up for stewing or pies. The neck and flank are stewed, braised or minced for sausages.

Chops and medallions of tender young venison can be fried or grilled.

WILD BOAR

Wild boar and cross-bred animals are farmed in this country. The meat is exactly what you would expect a gamey version of pork to be – darker and denser than meat from long domesticated species. Like pork, the prime cuts can be roasted and grilled. The harder worked muscles are better braised or stewed. Boar meat is lean and should always be well cooked.

BACON AND HAM

In Britain and across the western world, a taste for cured pork has persisted long after the necessity for curing as a method of preservation. As a consequence, the salting, smoking or drying processes that pork undergoes are, in many cases, far less drastic than they used to be. Indeed, factory-produced bacon is so mildly cured that it cannot be kept without refrigeration.

Bacon is made from the sides and back of the pig. Gammon is bacon-cured pork from the hind legs. The traditional method of dry-curing over a period of weeks gives old-fashioned bacon its rich flavour. It has been largely superseded by much speedier brining in tanks. The streamlined modern process involves injecting brine directly into the meat instead of letting it soak in gradually. Green or unsmoked bacon is simply salt-cured. Smoked bacon, which has a recognisably darker rind, is smoked after dry-curing or brining.

Ham production has a greater number of variations. Curing, by dry-salting or brining, is a slower process and may include additional flavouring ingredients such as treacle, vinegar or beer. Once cured, the ham is air-dried, or smoked in the fumes of aromatic woods such as apple, hickory, juniper or oak.

Bacon, and some but not all hams, must be cooked. Bacon rashers are grilled or fried. Joints of bacon, made from the leaner parts such as the gammon, shoulder, back and collar can be boiled, braised or baked. Suitable methods and timings are governed by the way the pork has been cured, and it should be supplied with the appropriate instructions.

Some of the finest hams, such as Italian *prosciutto di Parma* (see page 112), Swiss *jambon de Grisons* and French *jambon de Bayonne*, are cut in paper-thin slices and eaten raw. Home-produced air-dried hams intended for eating raw include Denhay ham from Dorset, and Woodall's Cumbria Mature Royal.

Survivors from a distinguished line of home-produced hams which require cooking include Bradenham hams from Wiltshire, and York hams.

Some whole hams which have been lightly cured can be baked with no further ado. More traditionally cured hams will need soaking for 24 hours to remove excess salt, before being simmered until tender. The skin is then removed and the ham coated with sugar or syrup before being baked in a hot oven for about 20 minutes to glaze it. Detailed advice on soaking and cooking times will be supplied by the producer or retailer.

SAUSAGES AND SALAMI

From French *andouillette* to Polish *zwyieka*, there is a sausage, or several, for every letter of the alphabet. For practical purposes they can be divided into those which require cooking and those which do not.

Fresh cooking sausages can be made from meat of every kind. Pork sausages are by far the most popular, followed by beef, but excellent sausages are also made with lamb and venison. Fresh sausages are usually fried or grilled after pricking the skins to prevent bursting. They aren't called bangers for nothing.

Uncooked fresh sausages are highly perishable and should be stored for no more than a day or two in the refrigerator. They should always be well cooked. Pre-cooked varieties such as black puddings and frankfurters can be kept for several days in the refrigerator and will only need heating through. *Salami* and similar cured sausages which have been air-dried or smoked, keep for long periods if they are uncut and stored in cool, dry conditions. Once sliced, they quickly dry and should be stored for a day or two only, closely wrapped in the refrigerator. Vacuum-packed slices will have a use-by date.

FRESH PORK SAUSAGES

Many butchers still make their own sausages, and the recipes vary greatly. Some are pure pork with seasonings; others contain greater or smaller proportions of cereal fillers. The meat may be minced coarsely or finely. Sizes range from continuous lengths of Cumberland sausage to tiny cocktail sausages, with standard British banger size, and the slimmer chipolatas, in between. French *andouillettes*, which contain tripe as well as pork, meaty *saucisses de Toulouse*, a definitive ingredient of *cassoulet*, and Spanish *chorizos*, distinctively flavoured with paprika, can sometimes be found. ***Fry or grill.***

FRESH BEEF SAUSAGES

These are similar to pork sausages, but the beef gives them a rosy colour. ***Fry or grill.***

BLACK PUDDINGS

These have significant regional variations. In Scotland they are made with sheep's blood. In the north of England pig's blood is usually used. Fat, cereals, onions, spices and herbs go into black puddings. French *boudin noir* and Irish *drisheen* are similar. Although black puddings are already cooked, they are usually reheated. ***Fry or grill.***

WHITE PUDDINGS

The British varieties are not meaty at all. They are made with oatmeal or pearl barley, suet, leeks, herbs and spices. The several varieties of French *boudin blanc* are very different. These may contain veal, chicken, pork or rabbit, finely minced and mixed with cereal, milk or cream, and seasonings. ***Fry or grill.***

HAGGIS

Haggis is a large, often round, sausage unique to Scotland, made with oatmeal, sheep's offal and seasonings, all packed into the 'pluck' or stomach of a sheep. ***Boil or steam.***

SMOKED SAUSAGES

This group includes frankfurters, *bockwurst*, *knackwurst*, and *wienerwurst*. ***Poach.***

SALAMI AND SAUCISSONS SEC

These are salt-cured and air-dried or smoked for long keeping. They are seldom cooked, and are eaten thinly sliced. The range of factory-made and rustic varieties is vast. The Italian *salami* described by Valentina Harris (see page 113) are the best known and most highly regarded. Good French *saucissons sec* include peppery *saucissons d'Arles*, and garlicky *saucissons de Lyon*.

SLICING SAUSAGES

These are the cooked varieties sold from delicatessen counters. Again there are many different types, from pale, smooth Italian Mortadella and ever-popular garlic sausage to dark *zungenwurst* from Germany.

CHAPTER 21

FISH AND SHELLFISH

I n this age of dietary correctness and nutritional right-thinking, fish is a paragon. It is low in calories and high in protein. Even rich fish like herring and salmon score high marks because their fats are good ones – that is to say unsaturated – and their calories fewer than meat or poultry. Fish is quickly cooked, and invariably tender. In fact it could have been designed as a fast food to meet the demands of busy cooks.

Freshness is all. The first hurdle of fish cookery, buying good fish and shellfish, is the highest. Shoppers in Hong Kong's markets buy live prawns one or two at a time and carry them home in plastic water-bags like goldfish won at a fair. So insistent are the Chinese on freshness that they have a special word, *hsin teem*, to describe the particular sweetness of truly fresh fish. This is the peak of freshness to insist upon when making Japanese *sushi*, or any of the other raw fish dishes such as Scandinavian *gravlaks* or South American *ceviche* (see Glossary).

With the exceptions of salmon, trout and mussels, which are likely to be farmed, most fish and shellfish are caught or gathered in the wild. Vagaries of weather, and of fish stocks, ensure that supplies are unpredictable and prices erratic, sometimes astonishingly so. At the fish counter it can pay to be flexible and adventurous, to buy what is freshest and least expensive because it is plentiful, rather than what is most familiar.

Most of the fish we eat in Britain still comes from the cold waters of the North Atlantic and from the seas around our shores, although Mediterranean fish and more brightly-coloured species from the Indian Ocean and the Caribbean have become commonplace.

FISH

Most cooks can recognise salmon and trout, but how many of us these days would know a cod from a haddock if presented with the whole fish? Precious few, probably, though as everything on the fishmonger's slab is likely to be clearly and accurately labelled, it possibly doesn't matter. Choosing the right species is important, for on this depends flavour, richness and texture. Size and shape will also help determine cooking method, preparation and choice of recipe.

Fish come in two basic shapes, round or flat. Round fish have an eye on each side of the head and swim with the dorsal fin uppermost. Flatfish are adapted for life on the seabed. Their eyes are sited asymmetrically on the upper surface of the fish, the side which has dark skin beautifully camouflaged to blend with its environment. The size range of both round and flat fishes is vast, from anchovy to shark, dab to halibut.

Spanning both categories are some species with cartilaginous frames instead of bones. A disconcerting characteristic of these fish – the rays, skates and sharks – is that when freshly caught they smell of ammonia. This is caused by the breakdown of urea, a constituent of the flesh which helps the fish to retain its body fluids against sea-water's tendency to draw them out by 225 osmosis. The smell wears off after a day or two, and disappears completely when the fish is cooked.

Another distinction is between salt-water fish and those that live in lakes and rivers. Two of the best freshwater species, salmon and sea trout, spend periods in both environments.

BUYING FISH

Fresh seafood smells of the sea – a salty, sea-breeze smell with a hint of iodine. Fish or shell-fish that smells fishy is not fresh. The exceptions are ray, skate and shark (see above). Fish that are fresh have brilliantly shiny scales or skin, bright bulging eyes, and red or bright pink gills. Fresh fish are firm to the touch. Dull, sunken eyes, limpness, dullness and easily shed scales are all sure signs of staleness.

The freshness of fish that has already been filleted, and possibly skinned as well, is more difficult to judge. Smell and the reliability of the source are the best indicators.

While high-street fishmongers are an endangered species, supermarkets are becoming more adventurous outlets for wet fish. Shops of both types will prepare fish to customers' requirements, usually at no extra cost. They will gut, scale, trim and skin fish to order, and prepare fillets, cutlets and pieces for particular dishes. They are also an invaluable source of advice.

STORING FISH

Fish is the most perishable of commodities. Whole fish keep better than fillets or cutlets, but should be cleaned – ie gutted – before storage. Ideally, fish should be bought and eaten on the same day. It can be stored, covered, in the refrigerator for short periods.

Freezing does not improve fish, but when there has to be a choice between frozen fish or stale fish, then freezing is by far the better alternative.

PREPARING FISH

Fins and tails are trimmed for aesthetic reasons, except in the case of fish with spiky fins when they are removed for safety's sake. Cut them off with kitchen scissors.

If they are to be eaten with their skin on, fish with large scales need to be de-scaled. Do this by scraping the body with the edge of a knife from the tail towards the head. To stop the scales flying all over the kitchen, work in a sink of water and rinse the fish afterwards.

Gutting, or eviscerating, round fish is done most quickly and efficiently through a slit in the belly (see below). However, if the fish is to be stuffed, or cooked and served whole, it will look better if it is gutted through the gills (see below).

The combination of sharp knife and slippery fish needs special care when skinning or filleting. Work on a non-slip surface and use a dry cloth or kitchen paper to help take a firm grip on the fish.

Flatfish are skinned before filleting (see opposite), and round fish afterwards. Flatfish have well defined skeletons and are easy to fillet (see

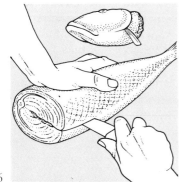

GUTTING A ROUND FISH

Remove fins and scale if necessary. To gut through belly, cut off head (if required) behind gills. Using a sharp knife, cut down belly towards vent. Remove innards.
To gut through gills, hook index finger through gill opening on one side of fish and draw out innards in one piece, along with gills.
Wash briefly in cold water.

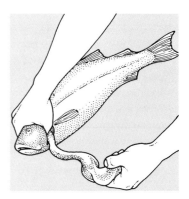

overleaf). Round fish can be boned through the back to make fillets, or through the belly if the fish is to be served whole (see overleaf). Other methods of boning round and flat fish are designed to leave the fish whole but with a pocket for stuffing.

COOKING FISH

Fish is more akin to eggs than to meat in terms of the heat needed to cook it. Fish flesh is fully cooked at 60°C (140°F), well below boiling point. This is the temperature at which the muscle proteins coagulate. Because the muscle fibres in fish are short, and their connective tissues delicate, further cooking beyond this point leads to dryness or disintegration.

Obviously there are cooking methods, frying for example, which generate very much higher temperatures. In the case of frying, the fish is protected from drying out and falling apart by a coating of crumbs or batter. Other techniques rely on basting, or additional ingredients such as sauces or stuffings to protect the fragile flesh.

Cooking times for fish are shorter than those for meat or poultry. Think in terms of 5–10 minutes for thin fillets, 15 for thicker cutlets. No matter what method of cooking is used, the way to determine whether the fish is done remains the same. Insert the point of a knife into the thickest part and check to see if the flesh has changed from translucent to opaque. As soon as the fish is opaque it is cooked. A further indication is that it separates easily from the bones. When cooking a whole fish or thick cutlets, test next to the bone. Fish with coloured flesh – salmon or sea trout, for instance – are easiest of all to judge because the colour lightens as it becomes opaque.

Frying Shallow- and deep-frying (for method, see page 60) are suitable for nearly all varieties. Only very rich, oily fish such as mackerel, sturgeon and tuna are unsuitable. Any fish small enough to make a single serving – trout and sole, for example – and very small fish such as whitebait can be fried whole. Fillets or cutlets of larger fish are fried too. A coating of flour, egg and breadcrumbs or batter protects the fish from drying and makes an appetisingly crisp shell. Oil, butter, lard or bacon fat can be used as the medium for frying.

Dry-frying without fat in a non-stick frying pan is a good technique for cooking seasoned escalopes of, say, salmon, which has some fat of its own.

Grilling Most small fish and cutlets from large ones can be grilled successfully (for method, see page 42). Oily fish are particularly good cooked in this way, as are flatfish. Choose other methods of cooking for cartilaginous fish (see above) and cod's poor relations.

Poaching and steaming No method shows off really good fish better, or does less to disguise fish that is dull or stale. So it is best used for well-flavoured fish, such as salmon, halibut or turbot, although, with the exceptions of tuna and the herring family, most types of fish can be poached or steamed successfully. For general guidance on

SKINNING A FLAT FISH

Lay the fish, dark side uppermost, on the work surface. Make a cut across where the tail joins the body, and use the point of a knife to work a skin flap from the flesh. Hold the tail end firmly with one hand, using a cloth; with

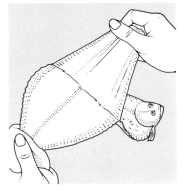

the other take hold of the flap of skin. Pull the skin firmly towards the head and remove. If Dover sole, turn the fish over, and holding it by the head, continue pulling the white skin of the other side off. This is optional.

poaching and steaming, and how to steam fish between two plates, see Chapter 2.

Braising Cooking fish in a small amount of liquid in a pan with a tightly fitting lid is a method well suited to large pieces of fish which might otherwise be in danger of drying before being cooked through. Whole monkfish tails and cutlets of halibut, the largest of the flatfish, are good.

Casseroling Robust, meaty fish such as tuna and monkfish make excellent casseroles (see page 68).

Baking The method of wrapping fish in paper or foil and baking it in the oven can be used for large fish to be served whole, as well as for single servings. Fish baked *en papillote*, as this method is called, are often stuffed. Baking suits all but the smallest and boniest fish.

BONING A ROUND FISH THROUGH THE BELLY

 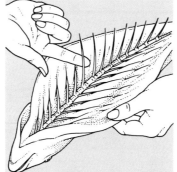 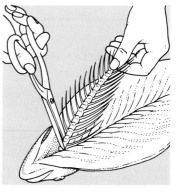

1. Gut, then extend opening to tail. Hold fish open to expose ribs. With a small knife or your finger, pull each rib free.

2. Run a knife or your finger along the backbone to free it from the flesh, and cut from the tail end.

3. Grasp the severed end and pull out the bone, working towards the head. Snip it free as near to the head as possible.

FILLETING A FLAT FISH

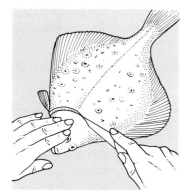 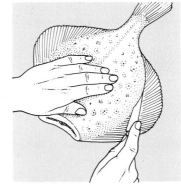 

1. Place fish on work surface. Hold securely with one hand. With the other, cut off head just behind gills. Remove, taking innards out too.

2. Firmly holding fish, slice around one side, between body and fins. This loosens the edge of one of the fillets. Do this for all four fillets.

3. Slide knife into flesh along middle of fish, and cut lengthwise. Then saw gently, moving towards fins, keeping knife flat, to remove fillets.

HERRING AND COD

TEXTURE ★★★ = EXCELLENT
★★ = GOOD
★ = FAIR

FLAVOUR ☆☆☆ = FIRM & SUCCULENT
☆☆ = GOOD
☆ = POOR

	TEXTURE	FLAVOUR	BAKING	BRAISING & CASSEROLING	POACHING & STEAMING	GRILLING	FRYING
HERRING FAMILY							
ANCHOVY	★★	☆☆☆				✔	✔
HERRING	★★	☆☆☆	✔			✔	✔
PILCHARD/SARDINE	★★	☆☆☆	✔			✔	✔
SHAD, ALLIS SHAD	★	☆☆	✔			✔	✔
SPRAT	★★	☆☆				✔	✔
WHITEBAIT	★★	☆☆					✔
COD FAMILY							
COD	★★	☆☆☆	✔		✔	✔	✔
COLEY, SAITHE, COAL FISH	★★	☆☆	✔	✔	✔		✔
HADDOCK	★★★	☆☆☆	✔	✔	✔	✔	✔
HAKE	★★	☆☆	✔	✔	✔		✔
LING	★★	☆☆	✔	✔	✔		✔
POLLACK	★★	☆☆	✔	✔			✔
WHITING	★	☆☆	✔		✔		✔

FLAT FISH

TEXTURE ★★★ = EXCELLENT
★★ = GOOD
★ = FAIR

FLAVOUR ☆☆☆ = FIRM & SUCCULENT
☆☆ = GOOD
☆ = POOR

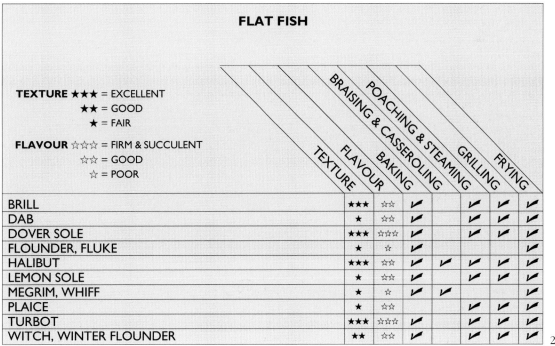

	TEXTURE	FLAVOUR	BAKING	BRAISING & CASSEROLING	POACHING & STEAMING	GRILLING	FRYING
BRILL	★★★	☆☆	✔		✔	✔	✔
DAB	★	☆☆	✔		✔	✔	✔
DOVER SOLE	★★★	☆☆☆	✔		✔	✔	✔
FLOUNDER, FLUKE	★	☆	✔				✔
HALIBUT	★★★	☆☆	✔	✔	✔	✔	✔
LEMON SOLE	★	☆☆	✔		✔	✔	✔
MEGRIM, WHIFF	★	☆	✔	✔			✔
PLAICE	★	☆☆			✔	✔	✔
TURBOT	★★★	☆☆☆	✔		✔	✔	✔
WITCH, WINTER FLOUNDER	★★	☆☆	✔		✔	✔	✔

FRESHWATER FISH

TEXTURE ★★★ = EXCELLENT
★★ = GOOD
★ = FAIR

FLAVOUR ☆☆☆ = FIRM & SUCCULENT
☆☆ = GOOD
☆ = POOR

	TEXTURE	FLAVOUR	BAKING	BRAISING & CASSEROLING	POACHING & STEAMING	GRILLING	FRYING
CHAR, OMBLE CHEVALIER	☆☆	★★★	✓			✓	✓	✓
BROWN TROUT	☆☆☆	★★★	✓		✓	✓	✓
BREAM	☆	★	✓	✓		✓	✓
BURBOT	☆	★	✓				✓
CARP	☆☆☆	★★	✓	✓	✓		✓
CATFISH	☆☆	★★	✓				✓
EEL	☆☆☆	★★★		✓		✓	✓
ELVERS	☆☆	★★★					✓
GRAYLING	☆☆☆	★★★	✓		✓	✓	✓
GUDGEON	☆☆	★★					✓
PERCH	☆☆	★★	✓		✓	✓	✓
PIKE	☆	★★	✓		✓		✓
PIKE-PERCH, ZANDER	☆☆	★★	✓		✓		
RAINBOW TROUT	☆☆☆	★★	✓		✓	✓	✓
SALMON	☆☆☆	★★★	✓	✓	✓	✓	✓
SEA TROUT, SALMON TROUT	☆☆☆	★★★	✓	✓	✓	✓	✓
ST PETER'S FISH, TILAPIA	☆☆☆	★★	✓		✓	✓	✓
STURGEON	☆☆	★★	✓	✓	✓	✓	✓

BONITO & SWORDFISH, MACKEREL & TUNA

TEXTURE ★★★ = EXCELLENT
★★ = GOOD
★ = FAIR

FLAVOUR ☆☆☆ = FIRM & SUCCULENT
☆☆ = GOOD
☆ = POOR

	TEXTURE	FLAVOUR	BAKING	BRAISING & CASSEROLING	POACHING & STEAMING	GRILLING	FRYING
BLUEFISH	★★	☆☆	✓	✓	✓	✓	
BONITO	★★	☆☆	✓	✓		✓	✓
MACKEREL	★★	☆☆☆	✓			✓	✓
SCAD, HORSE MACKEREL	★	☆				✓	
SWORDFISH, MARLIN	★★	☆☆☆	✓	✓		✓	✓
TUNA	★★★	☆☆☆	✓	✓		✓	✓

MIXED CATCH

TEXTURE ★★★ = EXCELLENT
★★ = GOOD
★ = FAIR

FLAVOUR ☆☆☆ = FIRM & SUCCULENT
☆☆ = GOOD
☆ = POOR

	TEXTURE	FLAVOUR	BAKING	BRAISING & CASSEROLING	POACHING & STEAMING	GRILLING	FRYING
BARRACUDA, BECUNE	★★	☆☆	✓			✓	✓
BASS, SEA BASS, SEA PERCH	★★	☆☆☆	✓			✓	✓
BREAM, SEA BREAM, PORGY	★★	☆☆	✓	✓		✓	✓
CATFISH, WOLF-FISH	★★	☆☆	✓	✓	✓	✓	✓
CONGER EEL	★★★	☆☆	✓	✓	✓		✓
DOLPHINFISH, DORADE, MAHI-MAHI	★★	☆☆	✓		✓	✓	✓
GARFISH, GREEN BONE	★★	☆☆	✓			✓	
GREY MULLET	★★	☆☆	✓			✓	✓
GROUPER	★★★	☆☆☆	✓	✓		✓	✓
GURNARD	★★	☆☆	✓			✓	✓
JOHN DORY	★★★	☆☆☆	✓	✓		✓	✓
MONKFISH, ANGLER FISH	★★★	☆☆	✓	✓		✓	✓
POMFRET, RAY'S BREAM	★★★	☆☆	✓			✓	✓
POMPANO	★★	☆☆	✓			✓	✓
RABBIT FISH, RAT FISH, SPINE FOOT	★★	☆☆	✓			✓	✓
REDFISH, OCEAN PERCH	★★★	☆☆	✓	✓		✓	✓
RED MULLET, GOATFISH	★★	☆☆☆	✓			✓	✓
SCABBARD	★★	☆☆☆				✓	✓
SNAPPER	★★★	☆☆☆	✓			✓	✓
WRASSE	★	☆☆			✓		✓

SHARKS, SKATES & RAYS

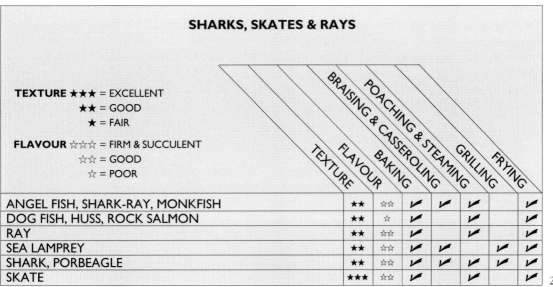

TEXTURE ★★★ = EXCELLENT
★★ = GOOD
★ = FAIR

FLAVOUR ☆☆☆ = FIRM & SUCCULENT
☆☆ = GOOD
☆ = POOR

	TEXTURE	FLAVOUR	BAKING	BRAISING & CASSEROLING	POACHING & STEAMING	GRILLING	FRYING
ANGEL FISH, SHARK-RAY, MONKFISH	★★	☆☆	✓	✓	✓		✓
DOG FISH, HUSS, ROCK SALMON	★★	☆	✓		✓		✓
RAY	★★	☆☆	✓		✓		✓
SEA LAMPREY	★★	☆☆	✓	✓		✓	✓
SHARK, PORBEAGLE	★★	☆☆	✓	✓	✓	✓	✓
SKATE	★★★	☆☆	✓		✓		✓

CRUSTACEANS

In an ideal world, all the crustaceans – lobsters, crabs and their many and varied shrimp relations – would be sold alive. Where this is possible, it is always the best way to buy them, although to most of us they are usually only available ready-cooked. Whichever way you buy them, choose with care.

LOBSTERS

The European lobster has large claws, is blue-black when alive and turns coral red when cooked. The spiny lobster may be red, greyish or blue when alive, and red when cooked. Very large specimens of either type, say over 1.5kg or 3lb, are impressive but may be tough. Both types shed their shells as they grow, and the best time to catch one for the table is just before it moults. Then the shell will be rock hard and well filled. Immediately after moulting the shell is pliable and the flesh inside it waterlogged and far from its best. Whether buying lobster alive or cooked, look for a hard shell and a tail which springs back to the curled position when pulled out straight. Uncooked, frozen lobster tails must be taken on trust.

The consensus on the most humane way to kill and cook a lobster is to immerse it for 2 minutes in boiling salted water or *court bouillon* (see page 77), then to simmer, covered, for 12 minutes for the first 450g (1lb), 10 minutes for the next, and 5 minutes for every 450g thereafter.

For recipes that require raw lobster, such as lobster thermidor (see Glossary) and lobster *à l'armoricaine*, the creature is killed by severing the spinal cord. Nature provides a target in the cross-shaped mark behind the lobster's head. Use a heavy, pointed knife to pierce the target mark decisively, then split the lobster in halves lengthways, or cut it into sections.

CRABS

The hard-shelled edible and spider crabs are usually sold ready-cooked. Choose crabs that feel heavy for their size. Males have larger claws, smaller tail-flaps and a higher proportion of white to brown meat. Expect crabs to yield about one-third of their cooked weight in edible meat. The cooked meat can be served cold, or incorporated into other dishes, hot or cold.

To kill a live crab humanely use a large awl – the Universities' Federation for Animal Welfare sells a specially designed instrument. Killing crabs by drowning them in fresh water is not thought to be humane. Plunging them in boiling water is not unkind but causes them to shed their claws, allowing water into the main cavity and spoiling the meat.

To cook freshly killed crabs immerse them in briskly boiling salted water for about 20 minutes, or more if they are large. To stop the cooking process plunge them into cold water for a few minutes before draining and leaving to cool.

Small swimming crabs and shore crabs are edible too, although usually only harvested immediately after the moult, when they are known as soft-shell crabs. Because the new, soft shells harden in a matter of hours, these crabs are usually sold prepared and frozen. Preparation involves cutting away the face and apron. The crabs are then floured and fried in clarified butter (see page 239), or to flavour soups and stews.

DUBLIN BAY PRAWNS

Dublin Bay prawns – or scampi, or *langoustines* – look more like mini-lobsters than prawns. Uncooked, shelled tails without golden crumb coatings can be bought from good fishmongers. Otherwise they are usually sold in their shells, ready cooked. To extract the tail meat, break open the underside of the carapace with your thumbs and prise out the meat.

FRESHWATER CRAYFISH

This little aristocrat is seen more often in restaurants than in shops. It is another mini-lobster with a deep red shell when cooked, and esteemed for the delicacy of its flavour.

SHRIMPS AND PRAWNS

From the cook's point of view, the distinction between shrimps and prawns is mainly a matter of size. Most are sold cooked, shelled and frozen, although the severed tails of large raw prawns are increasingly available for stir-frying and similar recipes. The dark, thread-like gut that runs along the tail should be removed whenever possible from the raw or cooked meat.

SHELLFISH

A much wider variety of shellfish is edible than ever appears on the fishmonger's slab. The bivalves, those with two shells such as oysters, mussels, scallops and clams, can be eaten raw or cooked, while the gastropods, single-shelled creatures such as periwinkles and whelks, are usually cooked.

The bivalves feed by filtering seawater and are vulnerable to contamination by sewage and other pollutants which are undesirable, even dangerous, in foodstuffs, and especially in shellfish that are eaten raw. The first safeguard against seafood poisoning is to ensure that supplies come from a reliable source. The second is to check that they are alive and well, even if they are to be cooked. If they don't close when tapped they are dead or dying. Discard any that are doubtful. Although shellfish will live for several days in cool damp conditions, it is best to eat them on the day they are bought.

Most oysters and mussels sold in Britain are farmed and should not require cleaning. Clams and scallops, which may be farmed or dredged, can be brushed under cold running water then put in cold salted water (110g/4oz salt to 3.5 litres/7 pints of water is about right) for an hour or two to expel any particles of mud or sand

Bivalves cooked in their shells – mussels and clams – should open when cooked. If they remain closed, discard.

OYSTERS

There are literally hundreds of varieties of oyster grown all over the world. Most of those eaten in Britain are European varieties grown in English or French waters and served raw. Famously good varieties include flat-shelled natives such as Colchester Pyfleets and Whitstables. French trenchermen conjure with names like Belons and Armoricaines, which refer to oyster-growing areas in Brittany. They also talk of *plates* and *creuses*, flat and rougher shelled Portuguese varieties, and of *fines de claire*, which are oysters cultivated in special basins.

The custom of not eating native oysters during their summer breeding season, when there is not an R in the month, is made unnecessary by varieties with different breeding habits.

European oyster varieties are seldom cooked.

Shucking or opening oysters with a knife is not without hazard. Even experts hurt themselves. If possible, use an oyster knife, which has a guard that offers some protection in case of slips.

SCALLOPS

Fresh scallops taste exquisitely sweet and are at their best lightly and simply cooked. Open them raw and separate the edible cushion of white muscle and the orange coral from the rest of the body, which is usually discarded.

MUSSELS

Farmed mussels are an inexpensive delicacy and little trouble to prepare. Wash them in cold running water and pull off the beard, the tuft of fibres with which they anchor themselves to the growing-site. They require very brief cooking and quickly toughen if overdone.

CLAMS

When travelling abroad, the British eat *palourdes* in France, *vongole* in Italy and clam chowder in New England. At home for some reason clams are neglected and exported to France. They can be eaten raw, but are generally cooked. Larger varieties are typically baked on the shell with a layer of buttered and herbed crumbs. Small clams are good in soup, and in sauce for spaghetti.

SQUID, OCTOPUS AND CUTTLEFISH

These are all members of the cephalopod family, and all have firm, well flavoured flesh which lends itself to stews and casseroles rather better than most other kinds of fish. They do not have bones, as such, and their bag-like bodies could have been designed for stuffing. Squid ink can be used to give a black colour to risotto sauces and pasta. Ink which has become granular through freezing can be reconstituted with a little hot water.

Octopus may be large and require tenderising and longer cooking than squid or cuttlefish, which are more widely available. All can be pre- 233 pared by the fishmonger, or at home (see illustrations below).

SMOKED, DRIED AND SALTED FISH

Salting, smoking and drying are preserving methods which, thanks to refrigeration, are no longer strictly necessary. They persist because we like the tastes they produce, and, in the case of smoked salmon, the whole world agrees. All smoked fish are salted before being smoked over hot or cold smoke. As a rule, cold smoked fish such as finnan haddock and kippers need further cooking, and hot smoked fish such as buckling do not. Salmon, which is cold smoked, is an exception and is eaten raw. Where possible, avoid smoked fish which has been artificially dyed.

Buckling, bloaters and kippers are all herrings smoked to different recipes. Arbroath smokies and finnan haddock are both smoked haddock. Smoked eel is rich and filling, as is smoked mackerel, both of which are set off well by horseradish cream, a traditional accompaniment to smoked trout.

Smoked sturgeon, swordfish, halibut and salmon trout are usually sold thinly sliced and eaten like smoked salmon.

Salmon nowadays is more lightly salted and smoked than it was when preservation was the principal purpose. For some tastes, the fashion has gone too far. Irish smoked salmon is often more robustly cured than Scottish. The London cure is the least assertive.

Salmon cured only with salt and dill is *gravlaks* in Norway, *gravad lax* in Sweden. It is an increasingly popular first course.

Tarama or *botargo*, two names for the salted and cured roe of grey mullet or smoked cod's

---

PREPARING SQUID

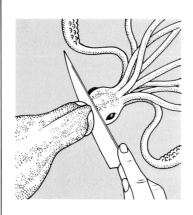

1. Cut off the head and tentacles where they meet the body. Cut the tentacles from the head, and remove and discard the beak. Discard the head.
2. Pull the quill-shaped pen (the transparent bone) from the pouch, along with the innards. Discard the pen and innards.

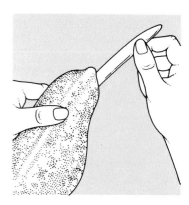

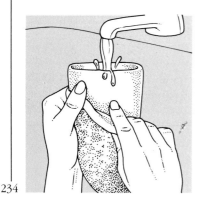

3 Peel off the skin and rinse the pouch of the fish under cold water. Pull off and skin the triangular fins on either side of the pouch.
4. Cut the pouch into slices if wished. Cook the pouch, the tentacles and fins.

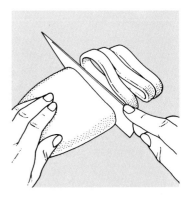

roe, are the basis of the Greek *taramasalata*.

Dried salt cod, or *bacalao*, needs soaking for up to 48 hours in several changes of cold water before it can be used to make the Spanish and Basque recipes in which it figures. Stockfish is dried cod which has not been salted, an ingredient in Scandinavian and Italian recipes.

Salted anchovies canned in oil are used mainly as a seasoning or relish. Another strongly-flavoured delicacy is bummaloe fish – salted, dried, fried to a crisp and better known as Bombay duck.

Salted herrings in their many forms are a Scandinavian passion eaten on their own or with bread, usually rye, or potatoes. They are widely sold in Britain in tins or jars.

Caviar is the roe of various species of sturgeon found in the Caspian and Black Seas. It is usually dark grey in colour and is at its best when fresh and lightly salted. Most of the caviar sold in Britain has been pasteurised. Beluga caviar, from the beluga sturgeon, is the rarest, the most expensive and the most popular in Britain. Oscietra is preferred in France and the United States. Sevruga caviar is more plentiful, therefore cheaper, but not necessarily less good. Eat caviar on the day the tin is opened. Serve it on ice with freshly made toast or *blini* (see page 00).

Other types of fish eggs are made into caviar of a sort. Lumpfish roe, dyed red, orange or black, is undistinguished, inexpensive, salty and inclined to stain other foodstuffs with its colour. Caviar from red-gold trout or salmon roe is good when it is tender and not over-salted. Capelin caviar is the off-white roe of an Arctic fish with a mild flavour and slightly gritty texture.

CHAPTER 22
DAIRY PRODUCE AND EGGS

Milk, cream, cheese and eggs are such basic, familiar foodstuffs that it is easy to take their virtues for granted. Despite the food-poisoning scares of recent years over salmonella in eggs and listeria in soft cheese, dairy produce retains an image of wholesomeness. The advice to avoid raw, or lightly cooked eggs, and soft cheese, if we are vulnerable by reason of extreme youth, old age, illness or pregnancy, has been heard and heeded. Eggs have been banished from that pretty bowl in the kitchen to the safer haven of the refrigerator. Conscientious cooks have checked that the temperature in their fridges is as low as it should be (see Chapter 27), and take care to wrap foods correctly to prevent cross-contamination.

Whether enough is being done at government level to eliminate these hazards is a question that remains.

The evidence of earlier success in fighting the formidable forces of the microbial universe is apparent in the many forms of dairy produce which are pasteurised. Before the 19th-century French chemist Louis Pasteur invented the heat treatment that took his name, and in the process founded the science of microbiology, milk itself was a health hazard, and cheese-making a far more hit-and-miss business than it is today.

MILK

Fresh cows' milk is sold in a number of different forms, all of which are used in cooking, and keep for three or four days in the refrigerator.

PASTEURISED MILK

Pasteurised milk has been heat-treated to kill harmful bacteria, which does not, of course, prevent its subsequently becoming contaminated. This all-purpose milk contains about 4 per cent fat, which rises to the top of bottle or carton.

HOMOGENISED MILK

Homogenised milk has been mechanically treated so that the cream is permanently dispersed through the liquid and does not rise to the top. It has also been pasteurised, contains about 4 per cent fat, and is a general-purpose milk in the kitchen.

SEMI-SKIMMED MILK

Semi-skimmed milk is a reduced-fat milk and contains less than 2 per cent fat. It tastes less rich than full-cream milk.

SKIMMED MILK

Skimmed milk contains less than 0.3 per cent fat and is noticeably less rich than full-cream milk. It is unsuitable for babies because most of the fat-soluble vitamins A and D have been extracted.

Skimmed milk fortified with vitamins A and D, plus skimmed milk solids is also available.

CHANNEL ISLANDS AND JERSEY MILK

Channel Islands and Jersey milk – the richest milks of all – contain between 4 and 8 per cent fat which rises to the top in a rich yellow, creamy layer.

RAW, UNPASTEURISED MILK

Raw, unpasteurised milk from herds certified as brucellosis free, is untreated, and is the only type of fresh cows' milk which has not been pasteurised.

CULTURED BUTTERMILK

Cultured buttermilk is pasteurised skimmed milk which has been treated with a culture which ferments to produce its characteristic acidity. It is particularly useful in baking for soda bread and scones. Cultured buttermilk is not the same thing as buttermilk produced as a by-product of butter-making.

UHT OR LONGLIFE MILK

UHT or longlife milk is homogenised cows' milk which has been heated to well above boiling, then rapidly cooled and packed in sterile conditions. This treatment alters the flavour of the milk, but gives the cartons a shelf-life of many months without refrigeration. Once opened, store and use longlife milk as fresh.

EWES' MILK

Ewes' milk is not widely available. It is very rich, white, and slightly sweet, and can be substituted for cows' milk in recipes.

GOATS' MILK

Goats' milk is becoming more popular. It has a stronger, livelier taste than cows' milk, and can be used in the same ways.

POWDERED DRIED MILK

This is a useful standby which can be used in cooking when re-constituted according to the instructions on the packaging. Non-dairy creamers and whiteners are intended only for use in hot drinks.

CREAM

Cream is the butterfat content of cows' milk in its liquid form, which has been separated from the milk. Most of the fresh cream on sale has been pasteurised, although raw, untreated cream can be found, and has a particularly excellent flavour. Cream which has been subjected to the high heat UHT treatment carries a longlife label.

Matching appropriate styles of cream to particular uses in the kitchen requires an understanding of their very different properties and limitations.

Resist the temptation to substitute lower fat types unless you are sure they will work in the planned dish. Single cream, for example, cannot be whipped to a semi-solid state.

Cream can be expected to keep for three or four days in the refrigerator, and will carry a use-by date.

DOUBLE CREAM

Double cream contains about 48 per cent butterfat and can be whipped. To obtain the optimum volume of whipped cream, add 1–2 tablespoons of milk or water per 150ml ($\frac{1}{4}$ pint) of cream straight from the fridge. Do not do this if you want to use the cream as a decoration. Do not overwhip cream or it will turn to butter.

Double cream can be used to enrich sauces and soups, but may separate or curdle if boiled, or combined with acid ingredients. It is usually a last-minute flavouring addition to dishes.

WHIPPING CREAM

Whipping cream contains about 39 per cent butterfat and whips best straight from the refrigerator.

WHIPPED CREAM

Whipped cream is sold ready whipped and contains stabilisers to maintain its volume. It has the same fat content as whipping cream and may be sweetened.

SINGLE CREAM

Single cream contains about 19 per cent butterfat and has been homogenised. It cannot be whipped and is used for pouring, and for enriching soups. It will not thicken sauces.

HALF CREAM

Half cream is homogenised and contains about 13 per cent butterfat. It cannot be whipped. It can be used to enrich milk puddings and home-made yogurt, but not for sauces.

CLOTTED CREAM

Clotted cream is the richest of all with a butterfat content as high as 63 per cent. It is already almost solid, so it cannot be whipped or poured. Spread on scones it is an essential element of a West Country cream tea.

EXTRA THICK DOUBLE CREAM

Extra thick double cream has been homogenised and is intended for spooning on to desserts straight from the carton. It has the same fat content as double cream but does not whip.

SPOONING CREAM

Spooning cream is a homogenised cream used only for spooning. It will not whip, and thins when heated.

SOURED CREAM

Soured cream has a pleasantly acidic taste which is produced by adding a souring culture to homogenised cream in the manufacturing process. It has a butterfat content of about 20 per cent, and its principal uses are for dips and enriching soups and sauces.

SMETANA

Smetana is made from skimmed milk which has been enriched with cream and treated with a souring culture. It has a lower fat content than soured cream, about 10 per cent, and is used to enrich soups and sauces which should not then be boiled.

YOGURT

Yogurt is milk which has been subjected to a controlled souring process using one or more of the bacteria which occur naturally in untreated milk, most commonly *Lactobacillus bulgaricus* and *Streptococcus thermophilus*, which produce a particularly agreeable flavour. All yogurts are 'live' except those which have been pasteurised or UHT treated *after* the milk has been turned into yogurt. These are longlife products which can be kept, unopened, without refrigeration. All other yogurts should be refrigerated and will have a use-by date on the packaging.

Unsweetened and unflavoured varieties without the added starch, gelatine or preservatives found in many dessert yogurts are the ones which interest the cook.

These plain or natural yogurts are made in several styles which vary widely depending on whether they are made with whole or skimmed milk, or from cows', ewes' or goats' milk. They are used in soups and sauces, dips, marinades, dressings, relishes and drinks.

When used in cooking as a low-fat alternative to cream, yogurt has the disadvantage of curdling when boiled unless it has been stabilised.

TO STABILISE YOGURT

To stabilise yogurt for cooking mix 1 tablespoonful of cornflour with 1 tablespoonful of water and stir it into 600ml (1 pint) of natural yogurt in a saucepan. Bring it almost to the boil and simmer for 10 minutes. Use as required.

NATURAL OR PLAIN YOGURT

Natural or plain yogurt is milk to which yogurt cultures have been added. It may be set or churned, and either type can be used as a starter for home-made yogurt.

LOW-FAT YOGURT

Low-fat yogurt is made from skimmed milk and has a fat content of between 0.5 and 2 per cent.

GREEK YOGURT

Greek yogurt and Greek-style yogurt are thick and creamy. Although traditionally made with ewes' or goats' milk, it is now also made with cows' milk. The fat content ranges from about 6–10 per cent.

GOATS' MILK YOGURT

Goats' milk yogurt can be used in cooking without first being stabilised.

Home-Made Yogurt

MAKES 1 LITRE (1¾ PINTS)

The tartness and thickness of home-made yogurt will depend on how it is incubated and on the type of milk used. Yogurt cultures will not grow at temperatures below 32°C (90°F), and are destroyed by temperatures above 46°C (115°F). The optimum incubation temperature is between 40–43°C (105–110°F). An electric yogurt-making machine takes care of temperature control.

To make yogurt without a machine involves finding a way of keeping the mixture of milk and starter culture warm until it has set. This can be done by placing a covered bowl in a warm airing cupboard, or on top of a cooker pilot light or central-heating boiler, or pouring it into a vacuum flask, closing it tightly, and leaving it for about 8 hours. Whichever method you choose, the yogurt must not be jogged, stirred or disturbed while it is incubating. If it is, it will separate. Refrigerate yogurt immediately it has set, and preferably for several hours before serving.

1 litre (1¾ pints) full-cream milk
1 tablespoon natural yogurt

Heat the milk in a saucepan until almost boiling. Remove it from the heat and set it aside until it has cooled to 40–43°C (105–110°F). Stir in the yogurt and whisk lightly together.

Pour the mixture into clean jars or bowls, cover and incubate, undisturbed, maintaining the same temperature for 6–8 hours, or until set. Refrigerate immediately.

BUTTER

Butter can be made from the milk of many animals, the contrary camel being a notable exception, but the butter we buy in this country is invariably made from the cream of cows' milk. The cream is churned until it separates into solid yellow fat, and thin, pale buttermilk.

Butter is the basis of many classic sauces such as *beurre blanc* and hollandaise sauce, and softened butter, flavoured with finely chopped herbs and seasonings, then chilled again, is served in small pats which melt over grilled meat, fish and poultry, and freshly cooked vegetables.

Butter's superior flavour makes it the finest fat to use for cakes, pastry and biscuits.

As a frying medium, butter is problematic because it contains milk solids which burn at normal frying temperatures. Butter cannot be used for deep-frying. Adding a small proportion of vegetable oil to butter for shallow-frying reduces, but does not eliminate, its propensity to burn. A better solution is to use clarified butter, or concentrated butter (see below) which contain fewer milk solids and less water.

Two distinct types of butter are widely available. Most British butter is made with pasteurised cream which is described as sweet. In France, Holland and Denmark, lactic butter is made from pasteurised cream which has been ripened with a culture which gives it its distinctive taste. Both types of butter are available with or without added salt. Salting butter was, historically, a means of preserving it, and the taste for salted butter has persisted.

For most cooking purposes, salted and unsalted, sweet cream and lactic butter can be used interchangeably, and the choice will be governed by individual taste. Fine sweet cream butters, usually unsalted, are made in northern France, which are especially good eaten with bread, and for making puff pastry. When baking with unsalted butter, consider adding a pinch of salt to bring out the taste and balance the flavours of the other ingredients.

Butter should be stored in its wrappings in the refrigerator. Because it easily picks up flavours from other foods, it is best stored in a separate, closed compartment.

CLARIFIED BUTTER

Clarified butter is used for shallow-frying and can be made at home. It is worth processing a pound or two at a time, because it keeps well. It is made by heating any fresh butter to boiling point then allowing it to separate into almost pure fat and a milky mixture of solids. Strain off the fat and discard the solids. Store clarified butter in the refrigerator.

CONCENTRATED BUTTER

Concentrated butter is commercially produced clarified butter which is sold for cooking. It is not used as a spread. It has a higher butterfat content and contains less moisture than fresh butter, and recipes will need to be adjusted to accommodate it. Expect to use about 10 per cent less concentrated butter and a very small amount 239 of compensating additional liquid.

GHEE

Ghee is a form of clarified butter used in Indian cooking for which clarified or concentrated butter can usually be substituted. It is also available in a vegetarian form made from vegetable oils.

WHIPPED BUTTER

Whipped butter is a mixture of butter and liquid which have been beaten together and aerated to increase the volume and make it easier to spread when cold. Use only as a spread, or to dress vegetables.

NON-DAIRY FATS

These include the many forms of margarine and low-fat spreads, suet, lard, and meat and poultry dripping.

CHEESE

Cheese is an elemental foodstuff in its own right as well as a valuable ingredient in the kitchen. The range of farm-produced and factory-made cheeses is vast. There are over a thousand named varieties, but no satisfactory way of classifiying them. One reason is that the texture of many cheeses changes radically as they ripen. Another is that although obvious categories such as hard, semi-hard and soft are useful, they must be modified by considerations such as whether the raw material was cows', ewes', buffalo or goats' milk, and whether that milk was raw or pasteurised. There are further sub-divisions between cheeses ripened by bacteria only, by moulds, and by organisms growing on the surface and their enzymes, or by a combination of these, or none, as in the case of fresh cheeses which are not ripened at all.

Cheese relies for its existence on the fact that the protein in milk will coagulate to form a curd of casein when it is treated with rennet. The incomparable array of tastes produced depends on many factors, from the pasture the animals were grazed on to the particular bacteria, moulds and enzymes which ripen it, and the many chemically complicated changes it undergoes.

Most cheese sold in Britain today is pre-

FATS AND OILS

Fats can be divided into two types, unsaturated and saturated. Saturated fats are usually of animal origin and will remain solid at room temperature. These include butter, dripping, and suet. Saturated fats of vegetable origin include coconut oil, palm oil and cocoa butter. Hard margarines are also saturated, even when they are based on oils which are unsaturated. This is because the hardening process, hydrogenation, converts unsaturated fats into saturated ones. Unsaturated fats are subdivided into mono-unsaturated and poly-unsaturated types, both of which are usually soft at room temperature, or oils.

packed, and of a very reliable standard. But this is not true of the finest cheeses, and whenever possible it is better to buy cheese from specialist suppliers who will always encourage their customers to taste before they decide. To anyone who has not tasted the best Cheddar produced on a farm in the traditional way and matured for two years or more, the experience will be a revelation. Another surprise to those who have looked no further than the supermarket for their cheese, will be the choice and diversity of farm-produced cheeses now made in this country. The renaissance of British cheese-making that has taken place over the last 20 years is nothing short of glorious.

Wherever cheese is made, the locally distinctive cheeses are used in cooking. So when making traditional recipes it is these cheeses which will give the dishes their authentic flavours. The ready availability of an ever-increasing variety of esoteric foreign and home-produced varieties is a boon to the cook.

Cheese of all types can be eaten as it is without cooking. Cheeses which are commonly used in cooking tend to be those which are fresh and uripened, and those which are hard and mature. Ripened soft cheeses, such as Brie and Camembert, and semi-hard cheeses are used only occasionally in recipes and are, for the most part, eaten as a course on their own.

BUYING AND STORING CHEESE

Fresh cheeses such as cottage and cream cheese, Italian Mozzarella and Mascarpone, are best bought from suppliers with a high turnover, stored in their packaging in the refrigerator, and used by the date shown on the pack.

Mould-ripened cheeses such as Brie, Camembert, the soft blues and Roquefort-style cheeses, are also best stored at a temperature of 5°C (41°F), which is the advised temperature for domestic refrigeration. This is the temperature at which they are matured by the makers. In the case of Brie and Camembert avoid buying cheese which has a chalky layer through the centre as this is a sign that the cheese has not been correctly matured. The chalky layer will not soften with further keeping.

However, the refrigerator does not provide an ideal environment for mature hard and semi-hard cheeses such as Cheddar, although it will probably be the best place most homes can offer. The optimum storage temperature for these cheeses is 11°C (52°F), so the ideal place is a cool larder or cellar, or in winter an unheated room.

Matured cheese starts to deteriorate from the time it is cut, and is best bought in quantities which can be used within a few days. A combination of greaseproof paper covered with a layer of foil provides a good wrapping. Stretchy plastic wraps are not advised because cheese has a high fat content, but they do achieve the best defence against drying. Other forms of plastic encourage sweating or condensation. However pre-packed cheese, which is packaged under controlled conditions, is best stored unopened until needed.

If you can offer traditionally made hard cheese a larder or cellar, it will be possible to cover its cut surfaces and leave the rind open to the atmosphere. Allowing the rind to breathe in this way improves the cheese's keeping qualities.

Cheeses which have rinds which have been washed as part of the production process ideally need different conditions again. This group contains some of the greatest dessert cheeses including French Reblochon, Epoisses, Livarot and Pont l'Evêque, Irish Milleens, and Belgian Limburger. The ideal storage temperature for these cheeses is 14°C (58°F), but the EC would like to see retailers and their customers refrigerating them. The discussion continues.

COOKING WITH SOFT CHEESES

Fresh, unripened cheeses make regular appearances in recipes for sweet and savoury pastries, cheesecakes and desserts.

Cottage Cheese Cottage cheese is made with skimmed cows' milk and has large, soft curds and a clean, bland flavour. It is low in fat, and its granular texture can be smoothed by processing or sieving for use in cheesecakes and other recipes.

Cream Cheese Cream cheese is a cows' milk cheese made from single or double cream. It is soft and smooth and has a rich, buttery taste. Full-fat soft cheese is similar but has a less rich flavour and lower fat content.

Crowdie Crowdie is made from unpasteurised skimmed cows' milk enriched with cream. It is similar to cottage cheese, but is smoother and sharper.

Curd Cheese Curd cheese is a soft, cows' milk cheese with a tart flavour produced by souring the milk with a lactic starter.

Feta Feta is a firm white cheese preserved in brine which is traditionally made in Greece from ewes' milk. Feta-style cheeses made with cows' milk are also available.

Fromage Frais Fromage frais is made from skimmed cows' milk and may be enriched with cream. The fat content varies from negligible up to about 8 per cent, and the texture from floppy to firm.

Mascarpone Mascarpone is a light, Italian soft cream cheese made from cows' milk. It has a smooth creamy taste and is eaten as a dessert (see page 119).

Mozzarella Mozzarella is traditionally made in Italy from the milk of water buffalo, and this *Mozzarella di Bufala* has a softer, less rubbery texture than the cows' milk Mozzarellas more widely sold in this country for topping pizzas and eating in salads. Most is sold in packets containing some of the whey to keep the balls of cheese moist. Dry packed blocks of Mozzarella are also available. It has a bland, slightly creamy flavour, and melts into strings when cooked.

Quark Quark is a soft curd cheese made in Germany from cows' milk. It has a slightly tart 241 flavour, and may taste more or less creamy according to the fat content of the milk used to make it.

Ricotta Ricotta is an Italian cheese made from whey. In its fresh, unripened form it has a bland, almost sweet flavour, and soft texture. It is the basis of many stuffings for filled pasta and is also eaten as a dessert.

COOKING WITH HARD AND SEMI-HARD CHEESES

Hard and semi-hard cheeses are used for sauces, gratins, and fondues, in stuffings, tarts, flans, breads and soups, and on vegetables, pasta and grills. In British cooking, Lancashire and Cheshire are noted for their melting qualities when heated, and Cheddar is used, universally, in its own right, as well as appearing as the ubiquitous substitute for almost every hard foreign cheese required in recipes. Think of how many different strengths and flavours are represented by the range of Cheddar cheeses sold in a large British supermarket, and next time you read a recipe which calls for Italian Pecorino, Dutch Gouda, Swiss Gruyère or Spanish Manchego, translate that diversity into an appreciation that the specification of the 'right' cheese may be lamentably imprecise.

Over-cooking hard cheese will cause it to separate into tough strings or curds and oily melted fat. Use gradual and gentle heat when cooking hard cheese, except when using it to make an appetisingly crusty topping on dishes browned under the grill. Take care not to overdo the browning. Few foods taste or smell more unpleasant than burned cheese.

Gruyere-style Cheeses Gruyère-style cheeses are made with unpasteurised full-cream cows' milk and share the provenance of being produced, traditionally, in high Alpine pastures. As with Cheddar, there are factory and farm versions, and the best of the cheeses made in the old way can be very fine indeed. *Gruyère*, made in Switzerland, and *Beaufort*, *Comté* and *Cantal* from France, are comparable cheeses which share a rich, nutty flavour with flowery overtones and similar cooking qualities.

Parmesan Parmesan is a hard cheese made in northern Italy from semi-skimmed, unpas-

teurised cows' milk. It has a granular, slightly gritty texture and a powerful, piquant and spicy flavour. A little Parmesan goes a long way. Authentic Parmesan will have the words *Parmigiano Reggiano* branded on the rind, which becomes very hard as the cheese ages. Three or four year old mature Parmesan is the best choice for grating finely for pasta dishes. Buy it in the piece and grate it freshly as required. *Grana Padano*, also from northern Italy, is similar to Parmesan.

Pecorino Pecorino is the generic term for the many ewes' milk cheeses made in central and southern Italy. On its home territory, mild fresh, and slightly stronger young Pecorino cheeses are available. But when Pecorino is specified in recipes it will usually mean one of the mature varieties which are pale, dry and sharply flavoured. The best known hard varieties used in cooking are *Pecorino Romano* and *Sardo*.

Sbrinz Sbrinz is a hard Swiss cheese made from unpasteurised cows' milk. It has a strong, piquant flavour and good flavouring qualities in cooking.

Manchego Manchego is Spain's best known cheese. It is made with ewes' milk, and when well aged has a rich, nutty flavour.

EGGS

Without the magical chemistry performed by eggs, a large part of the cook's repertoire could not exist.

They are used to aerate cakes and soufflés, to thicken custards and soups, and to create the stable emulsions that make mayonnaise, hollandaise and many other sauces possible. They are also, of course, eaten for themselves, boiled, poached, fried, coddled, scrambled, and in omelettes.

BUYING AND STORING EGGS

Eggs can be contaminated by bacteria at any stage of their production, even before they are laid if the hen has been infected with salmonella, as well is in their subsequent handling. Whether free-range or battery-farmed, all types of eggs must now be treated with caution.

Egg shells look impermeable, but are in fact porous. This means that they can pick up smells from other foods as well as bacterial contamination. They should be stored in their boxes in the refrigerator, pointed end downwards, for no more than two weeks, or the date advised on the packaging. Discard any eggs that are cracked or broken.

Freshness can be judged in two ways. A new-laid egg placed in cold water will sink to the bottom and lie on its side. A week-old egg is more buoyant, and its broader end will tilt upwards in water because the air-pocket inside the egg will have expanded. As the egg ages, the air-pocket continues to expand until after two or three weeks the egg is buoyant enough to stand on its tip in water, or even to leave the bottom.

An alternative way of testing for freshness involves breaking an egg on to a plate. If it is new-laid, the yolk will be plump and central, surrounded by a thick, cushion of white, and only a small quantity of runny white. As an egg ages, the white becomes progressively runnier until, in a two to three week old egg it flattens out completely, and the yolk moves further from the centre of the white.

COOKING WITH EGGS

The only disadvantages of extreme freshness are that when boiled in their shells, very fresh eggs are difficult to peel, and that the raw whites are more difficult to beat into meringue than those from eggs which are a few days old.

It has long been noted that more stable foams are produced when egg whites are beaten in copper bowls. Although copper bowls have been used for over 200 years, an adequate explanation for the practice is quite recent. It appears that metal ions in the copper bind with one of the many proteins in egg white to create molecules which are less easily unravelled by overbeating, and the presence of a proportion of these metal-protein molecules stabilises the whole body of foam.

Another puzzle is the greenish grey line that sometimes appears round the yolks of hard-boiled eggs. This is a harmless discoloration caused by a build-up of ferrous sulphide and it is less likely to occur if the eggs are very fresh. Boiling them only until the yolks are sufficiently set, cooling them rapidly in cold water and peeling them immediately, are strategies designed to minimise discoloration.

The increase of salmonella in eggs is a more recent worry. Heating to a temperature of 70°C (160°F) destroys salmonella bacteria. Egg white sets at a temperature of 60°C (140°F), and egg yolk at 70°C (160°F). This is why soft-boiled eggs, runny omelettes, home-made mayonnaise and lemon curd, all of which contain eggs which are either raw or heated to less than 70°C (160°F), involve a degree of risk which vulnerable groups are advised not to take.

HENS' EGGS

There is no difference in taste or nutritional value between brown and white-shelled eggs. Shell colour is determined by the breed of the hen, not by its feed. Nor is there any difference in nutritional value between eggs produced by battery birds and free-range hens, or those reared in any of the other categories of husbandry in between. Aesthetic and cost considerations govern the choice.

Hens' eggs are graded by weight into seven size groups. Size 1 eggs weigh 70g or over (approx. 2½ oz); size 2 weigh 65–70g (approx. 2¼–2½ oz); size 3 weigh 60–65g (approx. 2–2¼ oz); size 4 weigh 55-60g (approx. 2 oz); size 5 243 weigh 50–55g (approx. 1¾–2 oz); size 6 weigh 45–50g (approx. 1½–1¾ oz); size 7 weigh under 45g (1½ oz).

Eggs produced by fancy breeds of hens, including pullets which produce smaller eggs, can sometimes be bought. Only their size needs consideration when calculating how to cook them.

DUCK EGGS

Duck eggs have a distinctively rich flavour, preferred by some people to hens' eggs. They are usually larger than hens' eggs and should always be well cooked in case they contain salmonella bacteria. Duck eggs are very good for baking.

GOOSE EGGS

Geese are still seasonal layers, so their eggs are only seen in spring and early summer. Their eggs are considerably larger than hens' eggs and are excellent for baking. They should always be well-cooked.

GULLS' EGGS

Seagulls' eggs are collected from rocky cliffs and are sometimes sold by traditional game dealers. Their flavour is, not surprisingly, slightly fishy. They are smaller than hens' eggs, dull grey green with darker spots, and are usually sold already hard-boiled.

QUAILS' EGGS

Quails' eggs are becoming more widely available and are a delicacy. The pretty grey-brown eggs are variously mottled with darker spots and are eaten hard-boiled with celery salt. They can also be soft-boiled and served hot or cold. They are so small that dropped into a pan of simmering salted water, they are soft-boiled in 1 minute, hard-boiled in 2.

CHAPTER 23

RICE, PULSES AND GRAINS

Rice, pulses and grains are the staple foods of most of the world's population, and they are cooked in ways that are as numerous and varied as the peoples who depend on them. Countless recipes have passed, unchanged, down through generations of cooks, perpetuating practices which are in some cases no longer necessary, and in others inadvisable.

Modern methods of cultivation, harvesting, processing and packaging produce grain and pulses which by the time they appear on supermarket shelves are ready to cook with no further ado.

RICE

Some 90 per cent of the world's rice crop is grown in monsoon Asia. Europe's largest producer is Italy, and some rice is still grown in Spain where it was first systematically cultivated by the Moors. America has been exporting rice to Europe since the 18th century.

Over the years Britain has imported recipes as well as the rice to make them with. Many well entrenched dishes such as Indian pilaus were brought home from former colonies. Foreign holidays have given us a taste for paella and risotto, and for each of these dishes there is an appropriate variety of rice and a particular way of cooking it which shows it off to best advantage.

ARBORIO

This is the risotto rice most easily found outside Italy. Other types suitable for risotto are Baldo, Carnaroli and Roma. The plump white grains absorb large quantities of liquid, becoming tender and creamy without losing the essential bite characteristic of freshly made risotto. (For more information on risotto rice, see *The Cooking of Italy* on page 116.)

BASMATI

Lives up to its name, which means fragrant, and is the preferred Indian rice for *pilaus* and *biryani* dishes. Its grains are small and slender, and cook faster than most other types. Separate grains are no problem with basmati, which is well worth its premium price.

BROWN

Both long- and short-grain rice are available in this unrefined form. Brown rice is a popular wholefood choice because only the husk has been removed and the bran is retained. It has a nuttier flavour and a chewier texture than white rice, takes longer to cook and absorbs more liquid. Brown basmati cooks fastest.

CAROLINA

Usually known as American long-grain rice, this is a versatile, general-purpose variety suitable for both sweet and savoury dishes.

GLUTINOUS

Has medium to short grains and cooks to a tender, slightly sticky fluffiness. It is used in oriental dishes eaten with chopsticks. The unrefined version of glutinous rice is described as black, but looks brown.

PATNA

A long-grained Indian variety with grains that stay separate in dry dishes, stuffings and salads. Usually sold simply as long-grain rice.

PUDDING

This, obviously most used for puddings, has the capacity to absorb large quantities of liquid. Its short grains become almost spherical and its texture creamy and soft.

THAI FRAGRANT

A long-grain white rice grown in Thailand. Its texture is tender and fluffy, with just enough stickiness to eat easily with chopsticks.

VALENCIA

This is the choice for paella. The grains are short and become tender without stickiness.

WHITE

This is the generic term for rice which has been refined to remove the husk and bran, and then polished. It may be described no more specifically than long-grain or short-grain, or it may be identified by variety, say basmati or arborio.

WILD

This is not a true rice but an aquatic grass once gathered by the North American Indians and now cultivated. The slender, dark brown grains can absorb up to four times their volume of liquid, and take at least 45 minutes to cook. The final texture is chewier than true rice, and its nutty flavour much stronger.

BOILED RICE

Any long-grained rice can be cooked by this method without pre-soaking, or rinsing or drying out when cooking is complete. The grains will be separate and none of the nutrients wasted. Allow about 55g (2oz) uncooked rice per serving. The same technique works for brown rice, and for wild rice, although both will take longer to cook, and will absorb more liquid (see Chart). Check the volume of the rice in a measuring jug before putting it in a pan with a heavy base and tight-fitting lid. Add the measured amount of water to rice (see Chart) and a little salt. Bring to the boil, reduce the heat and cover the pan tightly. Cook on a very low heat for 15–20 minutes (see Chart) until all the water has been absorbed and each grain is tender and separate. Let the pan stand, covered, off the heat, for 5 minutes before opening it.

If all the liquid is absorbed before the rice is tender, add more water by sprinkling it over the top of the rice with your hand. Cover the pan and continue cooking until the rice is ready. Fluff up the rice with a fork and serve.

Leave the pan undisturbed for the whole of the suggested cooking time, and if further cooking is necessary avoid uncovering the pan too often. The worst that can happen is that a layer of rice will stick to the base of the pan, or that it will take longer than expected to cook.

Saffron Pilau

SERVES 4–6

If you use saffron strands, soak them in a tablespoon of hot water for a few minutes before adding them with the rest of the liquid. Powdered saffron is stirred straight into the rice.

> 450g (1lb) basmati rice
> 30g (1oz) clarified butter (see page 239) or fresh butter
> 6 whole cloves
> 6 whole cardamom pods
> 10cm (4in) cinnamon stick, broken in pieces, or ½ teaspoon ground cinnamon
> About 450ml (¾ pint) cold water
> A pinch of saffron strands or a scant ¼ teaspoon powdered saffron
> Salt

Melt the butter in a heavy-based pan with a tight-fitting lid and add the cloves, cardamoms and cinnamon. Fry the spices for a few moments, taking care not to burn them. Add the rice and stir to coat every grain.

Add the water, saffron and salt. Bring to the boil, stir once, lower the heat and cover with a tightly fitting lid. Cook the rice on a very low heat for 15 minutes, or until all the water is absorbed and each grain is tender and separate.

Risotto alla Parmigiana

SERVES 4

The special creamy texture of a well-made risotto is produced by stirring the rice constantly for 20–30 minutes while it cooks. This is a leisurely stirring action, nothing frantic. Making risotto, drinking a glass of wine and chatting are all compatible activities. (See also Valentina Harris, page 110; recipe for Risotto con Gambaretti, page 117).

> *About 1 litre (1¾ pints) chicken stock (see*
> *   page 76)*
> *55g (2oz) butter*
> *2 tablespoons olive oil*
> *2 tablespoons finely chopped shallot or*
> *   onion*
> *310g (11oz) arborio rice*
> *Salt and freshly ground black pepper*
> *55g (2oz) Parmesan cheese, freshly-grated*

Heat the stock and keep it simmering gently. In a heavy-based pan heat together half the butter and all the oil. Add the shallot or onion and cook until it is transparent. Add the dry rice and stir it around until every grain is coated. Pour about 150ml (¼ pint) of hot stock over the rice, and cook, stirring, on a medium heat until the liquid has been almost completely absorbed. Add another ladleful of stock, and cook, still stirring, until that too has been absorbed.

Go on adding stock, a ladleful at a time, and cooking and stirring until each grain of rice is swollen and tender but still has a little bite in the centre. Take the pan off the heat and season the rice to taste with salt and pepper, and stir in the remaining butter and grated Parmesan. Serve immediately with, if you like, a little extra grated Parmesan.

Leftover risotto cannot be reheated successfully but it can be recycled in deep-fried croquettes (see page 158).

Cream of Rice

SERVES 6

This is a creamy, cold rice pudding, set almost solid with a little gelatine, which enjoyed long popularity with members of the Bath Club. The recipe is from *Arabella Boxer's Book of English Food*, a rediscovery of British food from before the Second World War. Looked at afresh, it makes a pleasant low-fat alternative to whipped cream.

> *900ml (1½ pints) milk*
> *110g (4oz) pudding rice*
> *2 tablespoons caster sugar*
> *7g (¼oz) or ½ envelope of powdered gelatine*
> *1 egg yolk, beaten*
> *3 tablespoons lightly whipped cream*

Bring the milk to the boil and shake in the rice. Bring back to the boil and cook for 20 minutes, half covered. Add the sugar and cook for another 20 minutes, then turn into a basin, keeping back about 4 tablespoons of the hot milk. Pour this into a cup and dissolve the gelatine in it. Once melted, stir it into the rice, mixing well. Then stir in the beaten egg yolk and leave to cool. When it has reached room temperature, fold in the whipped cream and turn into a serving dish. Chill for a few hours, or overnight.

RICE COOKING TIMES

Type of rice	Ratio of water to rice	Approx. cooking time
Brown rice	2–3:1	25–45 minutes
White rice	1½–2:1	15–20 minutes
Wild rice	4:1	45–60 minutes

The liquid measures and cooking times given here are approximate. It may be necessary to add more water, using the method described in Boiled Rice, or to extend the cooking time.

Serve very cold, with a dish of lightly cooked fruit still slightly warm or at room temperature.

WHEAT – SEMOLINA, COUSCOUS AND BURGHUL

WHOLE WHEAT GRAINS

These, newly harvested, are the principal ingredients of frumenty, a long-cooked porridge made with milk, sugar and spices. They can also be cooked in savoury, risotto-style dishes.

BURGHUL OR BULGAR

This is made from whole wheat grains which have been partially cooked and then cracked. It needs no further cooking and is ready to eat after soaking in cold water for about 20 minutes. The most popular dish made with bulgar is *tabbouleh*, a fresh-tasting Middle Eastern salad. The cereal is squeezed dry and mixed with lemon juice, olive oil, chopped onion and tomato, salt and lavish quantities of parsley and mint.

SEMOLINA

This is milled from hard wheat and contains a high ratio of protein to starch. It is used commercially for making pasta, and at home for making gnocchi (see page 116) and in baking, as well as in nursery milk puddings.

COUSCOUS

Couscous is a granular cereal based on semolina. It is the staple of North African cooking and the basis of a colourful repertoire of one-pot meals. Traditional and instant varieties are available. A couscoussière is a specialised two-tier pot in which the couscous steams over water or a stew of meat and vegetables bubbling beneath it, but any steamer with a closely fitting lid will do.

MAIZE – CORNMEAL AND POLENTA

The dried kernels of maize are ground to various grades of fineness to make cornmeal. Polenta is a cornmeal made from yellow corn. Cracked hominy and hominy grits are made with corn which has been treated with strong alkalis to remove its tough outer layers. Mexican *tortillas* and *tamales* are made with lye-treated cornmeals.

OATS

Oatmeal, as opposed to rolled oats or oat flakes, is used to make real Scots porridge. Good fresh oatmeal needs only a little salt to bring out its flavour. Serve the porridge with milk and, optionally, sugar. The traditional measure is a handful of oatmeal to a breakfast cupful of water – about 35g (1¼oz) oatmeal to 175ml (6fl oz) water. Bring the water to the boil and trickle in the oatmeal in a steady rain, stirring constantly.

Simmer for about 20 minutes, adding a pinch of salt about half-way through cooking. The exact timing will depend on the grade of oatmeal used.

Oatmeal is also used to make oatcakes, biscuits and a coating for fried herrings.

PULSES

The renowned flatulence-inducing properties of pulses are little affected by cooking in any particular way since they are due to a molecule which the human body lacks the right digestive enzymes to process. The guilty molecules pass undigested into the lower gut where they provide rich pickings for bacteria which stage a population explosion, giving off uncomfortably large quantities of gas in the process. Moderate bean consumption is the only sure preventative.

SOAKING

There is no apparent advantage in soaking beans for longer than about 4 hours, although it may be more convenient to soak them overnight than for the times indicated in the Chart (see opposite).

COOKING

Boil then simmer is the rule. Some pulses, including red kidney beans, black beans and lima beans, contain toxins which are safely neutralised by rapid boiling for about 10 minutes. But because one variety of bean may have several different names, and confusion can easily arise between varieties which look very similar, it is a good idea to boil all whole pulses, vigorously and uncovered, for the first 10 minutes of the suggested cooking time. There is no need to change the water before continuing the cooking process because any toxins present will have been vapourised and driven off.

Soya beans contain a substance which is not harmful, but which inhibits the body's ability to absorb their valuable vegetable protein. Boiling them rapidly for the first hour of cooking overcomes the problem.

After the initial period of boiling, beans and peas to be used whole should be simmered, and salt added towards the end of the expected cooking time. If cooked at a continuous rolling boil they will jostle together, splitting their skins and spoiling their looks. If peas and beans are salted at the start of cooking, they never become as tender as if salt is added when newly cooked.

Recipes for bean-based dishes invariably call for the pulses to be cooked until tender, or nearly so, before the flavouring ingredients are added. Even those for long-cooked dishes such as *cassoulet* and baked beans are assembled with cooked beans. The reason is a useful one for the innovative cook to understand. It is that in a sufficiently acidic cooking environment – in sauces with wine and tomatoes, for example – the pulses will soften very little more and will keep their shape despite continued cooking and even reheating.

Dried pulses can be kept for months, even years, though keeping them for more than 12 months is not recommended. Long-stored peas and beans will take longer to cook, and this introduces an element of unpredictability into the suggested cooking times.

SOAKING AND COOKING TIMES

Variety of pulse	Soaking	Boiling	Simmering
Aduki beans	4 hours	10 minutes	1–1½ hours
Black beans	4 hours	10 minutes	1–2 hours
Black-eyed beans	4 hours	10 minutes	1–1½ hours
Borlotti beans	4 hours	10 minutes	1–1½ hours
Broad beans	4 hours	10 minutes	1–2 hours
Brown beans	4 hours	10 minutes	1–2 hours
Butter beans	4 hours	10 minutes	1–2 hours
Cannellini beans	4 hours	10 minutes	1½–2 hours
Chickpeas	8 hours	10 minutes	2–3 hours
Field beans	8 hours	10 minutes	2–3 hours
Flageolet beans	4 hours	10 minutes	1½–2 hours
Haricot beans	4 hours	10 minutes	1–1½ hours
Lentils – Puy	None		½–1 hour
green	None		½–1 hour
red	None		20–30 mins
brown	None		½–1 hour
Lima beans	4 hours	10 minutes	1–1½ hours
Mung beans	4 hours	10 minutes	½–1 hour
Navy beans	4 hours	10 minutes	1–1½ hours
Peas – split	1 hour		¾–1 hour
whole	4 hours	10 minutes	1–1½ hours
Pinto beans	4 hours	10 minutes	1–2 hours
Red kidney beans	4 hours	10 minutes	1–2 hours
Soya beans	8 hours	1 hour	2–4 hours

The Cooking of France

by RAYMOND BLANC

We tend to lose sight of how vast a country France is. Significantly, though, we never forget the diversity of its cuisine.

Raymond Blanc, of Le Manoir aux Quat'Saisons, Oxfordshire

From the Mediterranean warmth of Provence to the Atlantic climes of Brittany, from the Alpine majesty of Franche-Comté to the wine-steeped richness of Burgundy, France offers a melting-pot of food and culture – regionally so diverse yet always unmistakeably French. To eat well in France is a universal right – the realistic expectation of the majority, not the privilege of the few.

I do not pretend, however, that all is rosy in the land of my birth. Good bread baked twice or three times daily by artisan *boulangers* is no longer something to be taken for granted, or necessarily even easily found. Overfishing is having a disastrous effect on both the quality and availability of a major natural resource. In France as in Britain we are having to face the cost of bad management and greed. *Le fast food* is as ubiquitous in Lyon, proud heartland of Gallic gastronomy, as it is in London or New York.

The EC imposes bizarre controls in the name of hygiene which make a nonsense of culinary traditions – not least the threat to stock-making in professional kitchens and the proscribing of raw eggs. Foul things bubble beneath the surface, erupting from time to time in national scandals like Bovine Spongiform Encephalopathy, the hellish consequence of feeding diseased animal protein to herbivores. France is no safer than Britain from the malpractices of industrial food producers. Horrible things are done in the name of animal husbandry as the financial pressures from giant supermarkets squeeze the margins of food producers. Corners are cut in the drive to be ever more cost-effective. And gradually but perniciously the rot sets in. A standard slips here, another small family business slides into insolvency, and intensive rearing techniques erode decency as well as quality of life.

There is much to be concerned about, and no French person can afford to be complacent about the food he eats. Yet all is not lost. We still have so much to be proud of, so much to emulate.

To love food and wine is not an indulgence, for devotion to eating well is not the same thing as greed. A *gourmet* is not a *gourmand*. We must eat to live, but all the more reason to make eating well a way of life. There is an old French saying that you never grow old at the table. Watch the extended French family lunching in a restaurant on a Sunday. The grandparents are as enthusiastic as their children and their children's children. They eat together, they discuss the merits of the food, the techniques employed in its transition from raw ingredients to harmonious dish. The wine goes down. There is laughter, relaxation, a pleasure shared across generations. This is reaffirmation of life, something wonderful that transcends the depressing concept of food as fuel. The occasion may be special for a dozen different reasons: a birthday, a christening or confirmation, a wedding feast. But the reason need not be very grand in the overall scheme of things. An omelette and a glass of wine, as Elizabeth David said. A bowl of soup and a piece of good bread. A piece of good bread alone, for the pleasures of the table do not have to be extravagant. *'Faites simple,'* said Escoffier.

Another great proselytiser of the table, Curnonsky, said that

Tarte au Fromage Gruyère de Comté (Gruyère tart from the Franche Comté)

with cooking, as with all art forms, simplicity is the sign of perfection. We may argue that cooking does not need to aspire to art, and that to describe it in such terms is pretentious. But the recognition of mastery implicit in the award of Michelin stars suggests that food can be elevated to the sublime. Let there be no confusion, however. Good food can be perfect new potatoes dressed with a little olive oil and sea salt as it can also be a *grande bouffe*. There are pinnacles and there are plains. The secret is to enjoy them both.

The story of food in France is

as long as history, and it rests on a tradition which is both regional and seasonal. Unlike Britain, which has long imported much of its food from overseas, France has always been an essentially agrarian and self-supporting society. The industrial revolution never had the same cataclysmic effect that it did in Britain. Of course France has great cities and bustling ports, but it also has the luxury of land mass. Drive out of any city and you will enter true countryside.

Food is grown and eaten locally, as it always has been. Much bitter debate takes place 251 within the EC about the level of subsidy to small farmers in France, but it is the very continuance of the small farm which is the life blood of the rural community. Hens are still raised outdoors and taken live to market. A stallholder displaying twenty small goat cheeses will have made them herself. The *primeurs*, baby vegetables, will have been pulled that very morning. When the grower has sold his bunches of carrots and tiny, sweet beets, then he will pause for a glass or two with his friends before cycling home.

The local market – with its wild produce picked or hunted for sale – is an expression of an even more distant past, when men gathered and hunted before they learned to farm. Honey and berries were gathered long before they were cultivated. Today wild mushrooms and truffles are there in the woods for the taking if you know the old ways, and a surprising number of people still do. Every French chemist is a mushroom expert, able to pronounce on the edibility of any specimen brought for his or her sanction – a considerable responsibility given the toxic nature of many fungi.

The French are great hunters and, it must be said, poachers. Those *Chasse Privée* signs tell their own story, and there are more shotguns in French village communities than ever you'll find in Britain. People go shooting as a right.

The flavours of the wild feature in much great cooking, and make timely punctuation marks on a food calendar that stretches the seasons at both ends: Provence is revelling in spring as early as February, while spring produce is still growing in Normandy towards the end of May.

Obviously food is transported throughout France, but there are still some things that can never escape their seasons. *Foie gras* and ceps spell autumn; lamb, salmon and asparagus mean spring; chanterelles and an abundance of fruit and vegetables will always taste of summer, while the barely simmering one-pot dishes of beef and chicken – the daubes, *pots au feu* and *poules au pot* – bring warmth to cold winter nights.

It is these last, the so-called *plats mijotes*, that remind us of the pivotal role of the farmhouse kitchen. These are the dishes of folk memory. Did we really remember those daubes of yesteryear, the beef shin slowly absorbing the flavours of garlic and herbs as the broth enriches, the meat grows ever more succulent and the rich, satisfying smell permeates the house? Or did we read about it, imagine it and then create the effect for ourselves?

It doesn't matter. The importance is not what was, but our expectation of what should be. It is important to draw from the examples of the past, but more important still to redefine it. Food is not a shibboleth, nor is it inflexible. The kitchen is not an exclusive club with a coded entry key but a place where we can all exercise rights. While it is true that there is nothing entirely new in cooking, it is essential to explore with an open mind. I am entirely self taught and therefore do not accept much of the received wisdom that has dominated cooking and stifled imagination.

My roots are in the real food of everyday France, in the history of its cuisine and in the endless reinterpetation of ideals within a regional and seasonal framework. All history is revisionist,

and the history of food is no exception. Every generation finds in the past what it chooses to imprint on the future. In fact the French farmhouse kitchen tradition did exist, still does exist, and is a hugely important influence on the food we enjoy today. Visitors to my restaurant, Le Manoir aux Quat' Saisons, may feel the food we serve has come a long way from those simple farmhouse roots, but the emphasis on the best of what is in season, on quality and on integrity of flavour, are philosophically much closer to *la vraie cuisine de bonne femme* than the surface glamour of a sophisticated restaurant may at first suggest.

The farmhouse encapsulates so much of what is good in French food that it is both a starting point for the serious cook and symbolically representative of a state of the culinary art. The farmer and the farmer's wife are meshed in work, life and food. The farmer raised cows for milk, cattle for beef and pigs for pork. Out of these came *charcuterie*, long-keeping items forming an extraordinarily rich legacy that continues to play a key role on bistro, brasserie and café tables. The chickens scratching in the yard delivered eggs first, meat for the pot second. Ducks and geese were raised for sale.

They still are. Force fed on maize, they yield delicious *foie gras*. Salted and poached in their own fat, they produce *confit*, a taste that truly defines Périgord. The farmhouse saw the development of pickling and preserving, the precursor to canning. And what could be more quintessentially French than farmhouse cheeses from cow's, goat's and sheep's milk? The unpasteurised Brie and Camembert, Reblochon and Pont l'Evêque, the Gruyère of my childhood.

The farmhouse is an icon, and the idea of a self-contained unit providing all that is needed to live in comfort is attractive. But methods change, even in Arcadia, and the French farmer, like everyone else, is looking for bigger yields. Small and organic appeals to the aesthete and romantic in us all, but is less attractive to the practical farmer who is also a contemporary businessman. The 20th century has not generally been good for farm produce, yet the French still excel at establishing and maintaining quality standards for which the consumer is prepared to pay a premium.

A good example of this is the *poulet de Bresse*, a five-star chicken indeed, though probably no better than those from Bourbonnais and Le Mans. These superior birds are killed at four months, after a life spent in green open spaces. For the last two weeks of their lives they are fattened on oats, corn and skimmed milk. They are delicious, if frighteningly expensive. The next category is the label *rouge fermier*. These do spend some time out of doors to build muscle, and are fattened for thirteen or fourteen weeks on cereals, usually getting a last week in the condemned cell on skimmed milk. These birds are from selected breeds including Landes, which have a yellowish flesh, and the black plumed chickens of the south-west from Mayenne, Périgord, Loue and Challans. The most elegant chicken of all is the *poulet au torchon*, which is fattened for forty days and sold wrapped in a dazzling white cloth. For one of these you take out a mortgage with the butcher.

The French acceptance that quality always carries a higher price has until recently had no parallel in Britain, where the word quality may be used increasingly by marketeers but the reality in the shops still seems as far away as ever. We have no equivalent here of *présalé* Pauillac lamb, *poulet de Bresse*, *lentilles de Puy*. This is not to say you cannot buy them if you search determinedly enough and know what you want, but British suppliers still have a long

The story of food in France is as long as history, and it rests on a tradition which is both regional and seasonal.

road to travel before quality and service are the rule rather than the exception. It is difficult not to be jingoistic when comparing, for example, a French butcher with his high-street counterpart here. Of course Britain has excellent meat, but the way it is generally cut up and presented makes me wince. I am happy to say that this is starting to change, but it is a painfully slow process. Fish, too, is badly treated and most British fish shops are disgraceful, really shaming for an island nation. This will continue to be the case until people are prepared to make demands. You are the buyer and can dictate the terms. The shopkeeper will benefit because only by giving extraordinary service can he score over his supermarket rival.

Ask any visitor to France what he or she loves about the place and the answer will almost always include the joys of eating

out – not necessarily in the most expensive restaurants but sampling the huge diversity of bistros, brasseries and cafés. France is truly a café society. People with very little money will still pay the price of a perfect cup of coffee, still lunch on a *prix fixe* menu, and will not hesitate to take their families out to supper. Consequently you can still find small, family-run bistros offering a bill of fare that satisfies and pleases: *rillettes*, *jambon persillé*, Toulouse sausage and *frites*, rare seared *onglet* (the butcher's piece) and a salad, omelettes, a *tranche* of lamb and *flageolets*, *lard salé* and lentils. Such menus offer quality and value, flavours in abundance and satisfaction guaranteed. In larger towns and cities you find splendid brasseries, often with Alsatian credentials, for many of them once brewed their own beer. *Sauerkraut*. *Plateaux de fruits de mer*. People watching, taking their time.

Of course this spills over into the way people cook at home, while helping shape a cultural framework in which food is enjoyed honestly and as a right. It also creates a demand for ready-made items to buy and take home, like the salads and pork products of the *charcutière* and stunning *pâtisserie*.

The bistro produces dishes which can be cooked at home, so it offers not just an aspirational template but also an achievable model. Classic bistro cooking includes slow cooked daubes and *hochepots*, *sautés*, simple roasts and grills as well as *charcuterie* and simple blanched vegetables. Here, in a nutshell, are the principal procedures of the professional kitchen often conducted in full view of the dining room. The process is therefore 253

demystifying. There is nothing to be afraid of.

Even though some of the delineations are little more than cartographic conveniences, French cooking is essentially local and it is well worth identifying the principal regions. Champagne and the north of France includes the Ardennes, Artois and Picardie. Beer features in the cooking here, influenced by its proximity to Belgium and Germany. Blood sausage, *potée* and herring are typical fare. Think of Normandy and you think of fish, *beurre blanc*, pork and cider. Butter, not olive oil, is the emulsifying agent. Apples feature everywhere. Tripes are cooked *à la mode de Caen*. And of course there is Camembert, arguably the world's most famous cheese.

Brittany is close by but has its own traditions and fierce independence. *Pré-salé* lamb, shellfish, *crêpes* and *fars* (baked sweet Breton puddings). Artichokes are everywhere, and cider and Calvados are more commonly drunk than wine.

Alsace Lorraine abuts Germany and Switzerland and looks the part. The wine is Riesling, but the *sauerkraut*, sausages and dumplings are lighter and more refined than those of Germany. Who has not heard of quiche Lorraine?

Paris is at the centre of the Ile de France, an area defined by a 50km radius drawn from the heart of Notre Dame. No city is richer in its restaurants, *pâtissiers*, *boulangeries*, *charcuteries* and *traiteurs*.

The Loire is the longest river in France and has many beautiful châteaux. Fish understandably take pride of place in the cooking of the Loire valley. Plums and

**Boeuf à la Gordienne
(slowly braised beef)**

prunes figure widely. The Loire is home to Muscadet, the perfect wine partner for fish. Sologne is noted for its game while Pithiviers gives its name to the centres of gastronomy in Dijon and Lyon. Bresse chickens come from here and Charolais beef. Lyon is widely regarded as the capital of *charcuterie*.

The great rivers of the Rhône and the Saône run through Burgundy, home to some of the world's finest vineyards – Chablis, Macon, Beaujolais. The Massif Central shapes the centre of France with Berry, Bourbonnais, Limousin, Cantal and Auvergne. This is an area famous for its hams, dishes featuring cabbage like *potée* and *aligot*, the heavy potato and cheese purée made with Cantal cheese. Perrier and Vichy have their sources near Clermont.

Périgord with its truffles and *foie gras* is to the south west along with the wine centre of Bordeaux and a long, Atlantic coastline. *Entrecôte bordelaise*, oysters and all manner of seafood, walnuts and pâtés abound, as do shallots, garlic and parsley. The wines of the region are stunning. Heading towards Spain we come to the Pyrenees and Gascony. Hot peppers, *pipérade*, hake with green sauce, tuna, swordfish and sardines. *Garbure* is a rich soup meal with goose and ham. Red is the local colour, the heat of the south. Languedoc produces more *vin de table* than any other region with Corbières, Roussillon and Minervois. Languedoc is home to *cassoulet*, that wonderful dish of beans, lamb and pork to which Carcassonne, Castelnaudary and Toulouse all lay claim.

Provence is a beautiful land of ancient perched villages, cypress

trees and the most vivid colours of the Mediterranean. This is the most Italian part of France with its *pissaladière*, pasta, olives, first pressing oil, anchovies, tomatoes and basil. Fish soup is puréed and served with *rouille*, a spiced garlic mayonnaise. Garlic abounds and the sun shines from Marseilles in the west to Nice and Cannes in the east.

Finally, my lightning cook's tour brings me back to my birthplace, Franche-Comté, where the Alps provide the natural boundary between France, Italy and Switzerland. As a child I revelled in the mountains, gathering wild mushrooms, hunting for frogs, fishing for trout. Life revolved around mealtimes, and I learned to respect all the rituals and customs of the table. But it was not until I was nineteen that I discovered my calling, one warm summer's evening in Besançon. Suddenly I saw, as if for the first time, an elegant restaurant, its terrace illuminated by gas lamps and candles. I drank in the diners, the sense of occasion, the gleaming cutlery and sparkling glasses. I marvelled at a capon presented to a table, black truffles showing through its crisp brown skin, surrounded by the brightest red crayfish. It was a moment of revelation. At last, without any doubt, I knew where I was going as surely as I knew where I had come from.

Franche-Comté is perhaps the part of France least touched by the 20th century. It is a land where there are still peasants living as their forefathers did, a place where the annual killing of the family pig has an almost mystical significance. There are no great restaurants in Franche-Comté, only the same good, honest food you eat in people's homes. This seems far removed 255 from the world of *nouvelle cuisine*, but I see them as inextricably linked, for there are dangerous misconceptions about *nouvelle cuisine*. It should not be dismissed as a short-lived fad in which chefs lost sight of their roots and the integrity of the food to paint pictures on plates. *Nouvelle cuisine* is only a logical extrapolation from the food of the past, a movement where our pursuit of lighter techniques and the purity of flavour is driven by our knowledge of food chemistry and nutritional value as much as by a desire to revolutionise the kitchen. Revolutions are fired by anger, the drive to impose change for its own sake, and mistakes are the inevitable consequence. This should not lead us to reject the essential message of *nouvelle cuisine*, for by embracing more from the diet of the southern Mediterranean, with its emphasis on fish, olive oil and vegetables, and by rejecting animal fat and excessive salting, we can continue to take pleasure at the table while reinforcing our joy in life.

MENU I: FOOD AND WINE FROM FRANCHE-COMTÉ
SERVES 4

Tarte au fromage Gruyère de Comté
L'Etoile, 1984, Domaine de Montbourgeau, Jean Gros
Poulet aux morilles et vin d'Arbois
Arbois Savagnin, 1986, Puffeney
Le plateau de fromages Franche-Comté
Chateau Chalon, 1979, Jean-Claude Peftier
Iles flottantes 'façon Maman Blanc'
Domaine de Montbourgeau, Jean Gros

Tarte au Fromage Gruyère de Comté (Gruyère tart)

For the pâte brisée
125g (4½oz) unsalted butter, cut into small dice, at room temperature
255g (9oz) medium strong flour
Pinch of salt
Just under 60ml (2fl oz) water
For the filling
250ml (8fl oz) milk
250ml (8fl oz) double cream
4 whole eggs
Salt
6 turns freshly ground white pepper
2 pinches freshly grated nutmeg
255g (9oz) Gruyère cheese, grated

Preheat the oven to 230°C/450°F, gas mark 8.
To make the pastry Place the diced butter, flour and salt into a large bowl. It is important not to use butter directly from the fridge as it will be too hard to mix with the flour. Neither must it be creamy, however, or it will mix too intimately with the flour and create a harder dough. It must be of a *workable* texture. With the tips of your fingers mix the ingredients very lightly until you have a sandy texture. This is important. The flour and butter must be barely mixed together until you reach a fine crumb stage. If you over-mix it the dough will become too elastic and unworkable and the pastry will retract during cooking.

Add the water and mix with the flour and butter. The purpose of the water is to add moisture to the dough in order to homogenise it. Work quickly: if you work the dough too much the gluten in the flour will develop and the pastry will be hard and will retract.

Turn on to a lightly floured

table and knead briefly until you have a smooth dough. Place on a small tray and cover with cling film or a teacloth and leave to rest for a minimum of 30 minutes. This allows the total absorption of the water by the flour so that the dough will be easier to work and less elastic.

Have ready a 20cm (8in) diameter tart tin with a removable base.

On a lightly floured table roll out the dough to a circular shape about 3mm (⅛in) thick. Roll the dough around the rolling pin and line the tart tin. Press it into the tin, cut the edges and thumb the dough up the sides so that it is 2–3mm (⅛in) above the top. There is always some shrinkage of the pastry in cooking, and by this means you will prevent any leakage of the egg filling.
To prepare the filling In a bowl mix together the milk, double cream, eggs, salt (2 small pinches will be enough: the Gruyère itself is high in salt), pepper and nutmeg, and whisk thoroughly so that it is well mixed together.

Spread the grated cheese on the bottom of the tart and pour the mixture over it. Place the tart at the bottom of the preheated oven, and bake for 30 minutes. Serve warm.

Poulet aux Morilles et Vin d'Arbois (Sauté of chicken with morels and cream in Arbois wine)

The smoky taste of the Arbois wine in this dish is a perfect match for the morels, and creates a most special flavour. If you cannot find Arbois wine, use dry sherry instead. The total preparation and cooking time is approximately 1 hour. The dish can be prepared a few hours in advance and reheated.

1 good corn-fed chicken,
1.35kg (3lb)
30g (1oz) dried morels or 200g
(7oz) fresh
Salt and freshly ground pepper
55g (2oz) plain flour
110g (4oz) unsalted butter
200ml (7fl oz) Arbois wine or
dry sherry
500ml (18fl oz) double cream
1 teaspoon Marc de Jura or
Marc de Bourgogne
(optional)

Ask your butcher to cut the chicken into six pieces – two breasts on the bone, two legs and two thighs. Ask him to keep the bones for you; these can be used to make soup.

If you are using dried morels (available from most good delicatessens), cover them with water to rehydrate and leave to soak for 20 minutes. Drain, then wash well in plenty of running water. If you are lucky enough to have found fresh morels, wash them two or three times in plenty of water – they contain a lot of sand and other particles. If morels are large, halve or quarter them.

Season the chicken with salt and pepper. Sprinkle flour over it and shake off any excess. On a medium heat melt the butter in a cast-iron pan large enough to hold the chicken pieces in a single layer. When the butter is hot but not brown, add the chicken pieces. Cover the pan and cook slowly for about 20 minutes, turning the chicken pieces after 10 minutes. The chicken should be seared, not coloured (this would discolour the sauce and make it too strong).

Remove most of the butter from the pan and add the morels. Sweat them for 1 minute to intensify their flavour.

Add the wine, and bring it to the boil for 30 seconds. This removes most of the alcohol, but do not allow it to boil longer or the sauce will lack acidity and character. Add the cream and, if using it, the Marc de Jura (it will add depth). Let the sauce simmer, very slowly, on a gentle heat for about 20 minutes. At this stage you must not cover the pan or the evaporated moisture will drip back into the dish and may well split the cream.

An ideal accompaniment for this dish would be *pilau* rice or fresh pasta.

Iles Flottantes 'Façon Maman Blanc' (Floating islands – my mother's way)

The whole dessert can be prepared well in advance (1 day) and the caramel 1–2 hours before.

For the meringue
6 egg whites
255g (9oz) caster sugar
For poaching the meringue
1litre (1¾ pints) milk
2 vanilla pods
For the vanilla cream
10 egg yolks
85g (3oz) caster sugar
The milk used for poaching the
egg whites
For the caramel
60ml (2fl oz) water
100g (3½oz) caster sugar

For the poaching milk Split the vanilla pods in half lengthways and with a teaspoon scrape out the insides. Chop the pods very finely. Place the milk,

vanilla pod and seeds in a large shallow pan and bring to the boil. Whisk to disperse the vanilla into the milk, then reduce the heat, just to simmering point, for 5 minutes.
For the meringue Beat the egg whites at medium speed in an electric mixer until they make light peaks, then add the sugar. Increase to full speed and whisk until firm peaks are achieved (3–4 minutes). Do not over-beat or the whites will collapse and separate.

With a large spoon scoop out six large chunks of egg white and poach them in the simmering milk for 2–3 minutes. Turn them over and poach for a further 2 minutes. Remove with a slotted spoon and leave to drain on a small tray. Repeat with the remaining egg whites. The heat should be adjusted to barely cook the eggs and create a perfectly textured meringue. Do not allow the milk to boil. Do not cover the pan.
To make the vanilla cream In a bowl whisk the egg yolks and sugar together. Pour the hot vanilla milk over the egg mixture, whisking constantly. Pour into a clean pan and place over a medium heat. Stir continuously with a wooden spoon until the vanilla cream begins to thicken and coats the back of the spoon. Strain into a container and stir it from time to time (the residual heat may still be enough to cause curdling). Leave to cool down.

Pour the cream into a glass serving bowl, up to two-thirds full. Pile up the poached meringue on the top of the cream and refrigerate for a minimum of 4 hours.
To make the caramel Pour the water into a straight-sided saucepan and add the sugar.

257

Cook over a medium heat to a rich dark caramel (blond would be too sweet). Dip the bottom of the pan into tepid water for a few seconds to cool (but not solidify) the caramel slightly, then pour a coating on to the poached meringues and refrigerate.

To serve, place the bowl on the table and let everyone help themselves (children first!).

Note The vanilla cream can be used to accompany a wide range of desserts. Adding coffee essence, Kirsch, Grand Marnier, caramel or grated lemon zest will create a variety of flavours. You can also make a lovely ice cream from it, and it can be used in *bavarois*.

MENU 2: FOOD AND WINE FROM PROVENCE
SERVES 4

Soupe au pistou
Palette, 1988, Château Simone, René Rougier
Boeuf à la Gordienne
Bellet Rouge, 1986, Château de Crémat, Charles Bagnis
Tarte au citron
Muscat de Lunel N.V., Coopérative de Lunel

Soupe au Pistou (Vegetable soup with pistou)

This soup is one of the most popular of all Provençal dishes and can be a whole dinner in itself. The name *pistou* came from the verb 'pista', meaning to crush. All sorts of vegetables can be added, so please feel free to interpret the recipe in your own way.

125g (4½oz) dried butter beans, soaked in water for 1 day
Salt and freshly ground pepper
1 onion, sliced
1 small leek, sliced
4 tablespoons olive oil
4 tomatoes, seeded and chopped
55g (2oz) French beans, cut into 2.5cm (1in) lengths
1 small potato, cut into dice
1 small carrot, cut into dice
1 courgette, cut into dice
4 lettuce leaves, roughly chopped
2 sprigs thyme
4 sprigs savory
1 bay leaf
55g (2oz) vermicelli, broken up into pieces
For the pistou
4 cloves garlic, peeled and chopped
13 basil leaves
75g (2½oz) Parmesan cheese, grated
3 tablespoons olive oil

Drain the dried beans, and cook them in salted water to cover for 40 minutes. Sweat the onion and leek in the olive oil, without colouring, about 4–5 minutes. Add the tomatoes and cook for a further 5 minutes. Add all the other vegetables, along with the drained dried beans and the herbs, and cover with water. Season with salt and pepper. Boil, skim, and add the vermicelli. Cook for a further 10 minutes at simmering point.

The traditional way of making *pistou* is to use a pestle and mortar. Pound the garlic and basil until you have a paste. Add the Parmesan and olive oil gently. Season with salt and pepper. If you haven't got a pestle and mortar you may use a liquidiser.

Pour the soup into a large tureen and serve the *pistou* separately.

This dish can be served with garlic croûtons.

Boeuf à la Gordienne (Slowly braised beef)

800g (1¾lb) silverside of beef, cut into 8 large chunks
120ml (4fl oz) olive oil
2 shallots, finely chopped
For the marinade
¾ bottle Provençal red wine
2 tablespoons red wine vinegar
1 onion, finely sliced
1 carrot, finely sliced
2 cloves garlic, crushed
1 sprig each of savory, thyme and parsley, 1 sage leaf, 1 bay leaf and 1 piece of orange zest, all tied together

Mix together all the marinade ingredients and leave the beef in it for 24 hours. Drain the meat and vegetables in a colander, retaining the liquid. Pat meat dry.

Heat the oil in a pan, then colour the meat for about 5 minutes. Remove the fat.

Add the shallots to the pan and colour lightly. Add all the vegetables and the herbs from the marinade and cover with the marinade red wine. If necessary, add some more red wine so that the meat is entirely covered.

Cover the dish with the lid and leave in a gentle oven (150°C/300°F, gas mark 2) for 3–4 hours. Serve the finished dish in the casserole as it is. A purée of potatoes enriched with olive oil would accompany this dish very well.

Tarte au Citron (Lemon tart)

The sweet shortcrust pastry should be prepared at least 6 hours in advance and refrigerated. The dish can be prepared a few hours prior to your meal. The acidity of the lemon juice in this recipe means you should use only stainless steel equipment.

For the sweet pastry
255g (9oz) plain flour (medium
    strong), sifted
85g (3oz) icing sugar
2 egg yolks
125g (4½oz) unsalted butter,
    creamed
2g (½ coffeespoon) baking
    powder
Pinch of salt
2 tablespoons water

For the lemon cream
375ml (13fl oz) lemon juice
12 egg yolks
6 eggs
310g (11oz) caster sugar
255g (9oz) unsalted butter, in
    pieces

Preheat the oven to
375°F/190°C, gas mark 5.
To make the sweet pastry In a
large bowl mix together the
icing sugar, egg yolks, creamed
butter, baking powder and salt.
Add the flour to the butter
mixture and rub together with
your fingertips until the texture
becomes sandy. Then add the
water, mix and press together.

Lightly flour your work
surface and place the dough on
it. Knead with the palms of your
hands until it is well blended,
then knead vigorously for a few
seconds more. Wrap in cling
film and chill for at least 6 hours.

Remove the dough from the
fridge 30 minutes before you
intend to use it. Lightly flour the
work surface and roll the dough
out into a circle 3mm (⅛in)
thick. Rest for 2–3 minutes.

You will need a tart tin with a
removable base, 25–28cm
(10–11in) in diameter, 3cm
(1¼in) high. Butter the sides
using a pastry brush and extra
butter. Roll the pastry around a
rolling pin, and line the tin.
Press in the sides. Trim off the
excess from around the edge,
then thumb it up to about

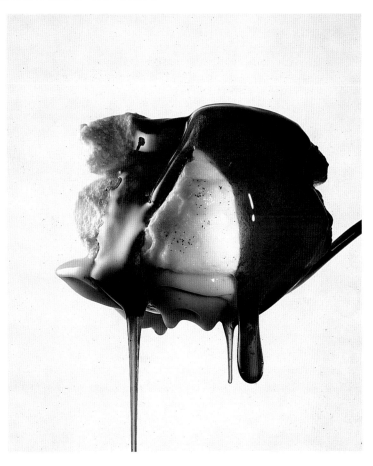

**Iles Flottantes 'Façon Maman Blanc' (floating
islands, my mother's way)**

2–3mm (⅛in) above the top.
Chill for a minimum of 30
minutes.

Line the inside of the pastry
case with aluminium foil or
greaseproof paper and fill with
baking beans. Transfer the tin to
the preheated oven to blind-
bake. After 20 minutes remove
the foil or paper and baking
beans, and cook for a further 10
minutes to obtain a beautifully
coloured crusty pastry.

To make the lemon cream
Bring the lemon juice to the boil
in a saucepan. Cream together
the egg yolks, eggs and sugar in
a bowl, then pour in 100ml (3½fl

oz) of the hot lemon juice.
Whisk until well blended, then
add the remaining juice. Place in
a pan, and bring to the boil,
whisking all the time, until the
cream is smooth and binds
together. Remove from the heat
and add the butter progressively,
whisking all the time until the
cream is smooth and binds
together. Pour into a deep tray
to allow it to cool down to room
temperature.

To serve, pour the lemon mixture into the pastry case and
smooth the top with a palette
knife. Refrigerate for 2 hours
before serving.

CHAPTER 24

HERBS AND SPICES

Herbs and spices have been used to give flavour to food since before the dawn of civilisation. Throughout the centuries they were also cultivated and processed for medicinal use, and many of today's so-called alternative therapies – aromatherapy, herbalism, homeopathy – are still dependent on the properties and essential oils of herbal and spice plants. With just a selection of herbs in a window-box, and a few jars of dried or whole spices, the cook has an armoury of flavours with which to complement each and every dish prepared.

HERBS

Herbs are annual or perennial plants which grow mainly in temperate to hot climates – the Mediterranean is thought to be the place of origin of most herbs used in European cookery. (An exception is the tropical lemongrass.) Many herbs therefore can be grown in gardens in the UK, where they can be decorative as well as useful. As a general rule, grow plants of Mediterranean origin – thyme, marjoram, oregano, rosemary and sage, for instance – in sunny spots, and the juicier green species such as chives, mint, chervil and parsley in partial shade, or where the sunlight is dappled.

Most herbs can be grown in containers inside or out, although larger plants, such as dill, fennel and lovage, are better in the garden. Grow plants with the same sun and watering needs in the same containers if liked. Be careful with some herbs, whether in container *or* garden, as they have invasive root systems and can take over. These include the mints and tarragon.

Some herbal plants produce both herb *and* spice, among them coriander, dill and fennel.

In cooking, fresh herbs are generally better than dried. The flavour of most is altered by the drying process (see page 145), some subtly, some less happily. Tougher, fleshier herbs, those whose essential oils can survive the drying process, are most successful – lovage, marjoram, mint, sage and savory etc. Bay, rosemary and thyme dry well, but they are evergreen so are available all year round.

If buying dried herbs, use them quickly; if they become musty, throw them on the compost heap or sprinkle into indoor plant pots as an instant herbal 'feed'. Keep all dried herbs in a dark, cool place, and when using in cooking always spoon them out of the jar rather than shaking them directly over the dish; steam could be absorbed by the herbs left in the jar and they could become damp. And lastly, never forget that the flavour of herbs concentrates when dried, so use only one-third what you would fresh.

Chop fresh herbs at the last minute to prevent loss of essential flavouring oils: use a sharp knife, scissors or, in the case of basil, simply tear.

Freezing is a good way of preserving some herbs, particularly those delicate ones which cannot be dried so successfully – basil, chives, chervil, dill, fennel, parsley and tarragon. Freeze whole or finely chopped (in an ice-cube tray with water for an instant herbal stock-cube).

One of the best ways of preserving the flavours

of herbs is by steeping them in oils and vinegars to be used in cooking. For herb oils, use a bland oil – rich extra virgin olive oils need no flavour additions – and add a good 2 tablespoons crushed herb per 300ml (½ pint) oil. Leave for at least 10 days, in sunlight, if possible. The oil is ready when it tastes and smells strongly of the herb – a little on the back of your hand should be enough to tell you. When strained, add a sprig of the same fresh or dried herb, and use lavishly. Suitable herbs are bay, basil, coriander, fennel, marjoram, oregano, rosemary, sage, savory, tarragon and thyme.

For vinegars, use a good 3 tablespoons herb leaves and stalks, slightly crushed in 1 litre (1¾ pints) mild wine or cider vinegar. Leave in a dark place for at least 10 days. Strain as above.

CULINARY HERB MIXTURES

The most widely used is the bouquet garni, a fragrant and aromatic bunch of fresh or dried herb sprigs, leaves and stalks tied together and composed especially for the dish. The classic combination is a bay leaf, a sprig of thyme and some parsley stalks; if the stalks are long enough, simply tie together with string for ease of removal. More complicated combinations, sometimes with added spices or lemon peel, can be tied with a celery stalk, or in a leek leaf. Dried chopped herbs and spices can be wrapped and tied in a small square of muslin.

Fines herbes is a traditional French mixture of four more subtle herbs – chervil, chives, parsley and tarragon. It is particularly good sprinkled at the last moment on to omelettes.

Herbes de Provence is a flavourful mixture of dried Provençal herbs – marjoram, oregano, rosemary, savory and thyme – sometimes with fennel seeds as well.

SPICES

Spices come principally from tropical parts of the world, and their botanical origins are far more diverse than those of herbs. Many are berries, seeds or fruit of trees, shrubs and vines (juniper, cardamom, nutmeg, mace and pepper among them); some are flower buds (cloves) or fruit pods (vanilla, star anise, tamarind); some are tree barks (cassia and cinnamon) and a number are derived from rhizomes or roots (galangal, ginger and turmeric).

Most spices have to be imported and bought rather than grown, and therefore can be as expensive as they were in medieval times.

Whole or fresh spices are generally better, as their essential oils quickly fade when ground. Some cannot easily be ground at home – cloves and cinnamon, for instance – so buy powdered if necessary. Use a mortar and pestle for seed or berry spices such as coriander, cumin and juniper, or a special spice mill (a coffee grinder can be used, but wash carefully afterwards). Always crush and grind at the last minute. Store ground spices in a dark place.

Some spices need to be, or are improved by, a dry-roasting before use. Roast them in a dry frying pan just until the flavour is released, and be careful – *over*-toasted spices must be thrown away, as they will be too bitter.

Some spices can be used to flavour oils and vinegars. Chilli oil can be bought, but a couple of dried red chillies will quickly imbue a mild oil with their heat, as will a knob of fresh ginger. Spiced vinegars can be made with peppercorns, mustard seeds, bay leaves, allspice berries etc.

CULINARY SPICE MIXTURES

The most famous and familiar blend of spices is the Indian curry powder or *masala*, which varies according to region, dish or major ingredient. Basics are usually dried red chillies, coriander seeds, mustard seeds, black peppercorns, fenugreek seeds, dried ginger and turmeric. Curry powders are best when home-made.

Some traditional English spice blends are still available commercially: whole pickling spices; dried ground mixed spice, used primarily for cakes and desserts; and the French *quatre épices* (black peppercorns, cloves, nutmeg and ginger).

The Chinese five-spice mixture, available whole or ground, consists of star anise, cassia, fennel seeds and cloves, plus an eastern spice known as anise pepper.

Ras-el-hanout is a variable North African mixture which can contain as many as twenty spices, and is used to flavour couscous and the long-cooked *tajines* or stews of Morocco.

261

A–Z OF HERBS AND SPICES

HERB/SPICE	CHARACTERISTICS	USES
ALLSPICE (S) *Pimenta officinalis*	Whole large brown berry of a tropical myrtle tree, available whole or ground. Warm spicy flavour, like an amalgam of peppery cinnamon, cloves and nutmeg.	Use whole in pickles, marinades for meats, poultry, game, fish, and in long-cooked dishes such as stews. Ground in pâtés, cakes, and fruit puddings.
ANGELICA (H) *Angelica archangelica*	Fresh leaves, shoots and stems are highly and sweetly aromatic. Stems available crystallised; seeds and leaves dried.	Use the fresh leaves in salads, and cooked with tart fruit. The stems can be cooked as a vegetable. Candied or crystallised stems can be used to decorate cakes, trifles etc.
ANISE(ED) (S) *Pimpinella anisum*	Small pale brown seeds, available whole or ground. Leaves fresh. Strongly aromatic, sweet and pervasive (as in pastis, Pernod, ouzo etc.).	Use sparingly, whole in stocks, marinades and sauces for fish, poultry and pork, and in chunky sauces and curries. Also whole or ground in sweets, creams and breads.
ANNATTO (S) *Bixa orellana*	An orange colouring and flavouring obtained from the tiny triangular seeds of a South American tree. Seeds whole or ground. To colour cooking oil or lard, macerate seeds over gentle heat. The flavour is subtle.	Used in South American cooking, and by the Chinese to colour meats. Good with red meats and chicken as well as fish, shellfish, vegetables, pulse and grain dishes, especially rice. Colours red cheeses such as Leicester and Cheshire.
ASAFOETIDA (S) *Ferula asafoetida*	The sap of a giant eastern fennel, available as resin or powder. It smells foetid but, when used in small quantities in food, is very savoury.	Use sparingly, in fish dishes, and Indian spice mixtures, for vegetables particularly.
BASIL (H) *Ocimum basilicum*	Fresh or dried leaves. Fresh is best, addictively and warmly aromatic (dried can be curry-like in flavour).	Best with tomatoes, aubergines, courgettes (*ratatouille*). Good whole in salads, fish, chicken or veal dishes, and with eggs. Pounded leaves make the Italian pasta sauce *pesto*, and the French *pistou* for soup.

262

HERB/SPICE	CHARACTERISTICS	USES
BAY (H) *Laurus nobilis*	Fresh or dried leaves. A sweet resinous and balsamic scent, slightly bitter-tasting in fresh leaves.	Traditional in *bouquet garnis*, in stocks, court bouillons, stews and many sauces. Sometimes used fresh in milk puddings, and with fruit dishes. Burn on barbecue coals for fragrant smoke.
BERGAMOT (H) *Monarda didyma*	Flowers fresh, and leaves fresh and dried. A member of the mint family, both leaves and flowers are vaguely minty in flavour.	Add leaves to salads, stuffings for pork or poultry, to wine and fruit drinks. Crystallise or candy the vivid red flowers. This was the plant used for Oswego tea by US settlers at the time of the Boston Tea Party.
CARAWAY (S) *Carum carvi*	Sickle-shaped, striped seeds, and fresh leaves. Pungent and musky in flavour, popular in Central European cooking.	Use leaves in salads or as garnish. Seeds in, and on, cakes and breads; in vegetable dishes (cabbage and *sauerkraut* particularly), and in and with sausages, rich meats like pork, duck and goose, and some stews (*goulash*). Good with cheese too.
CARDAMOM (S) *Elettaria cardamomum*	Related to ginger and turmeric. It is the seed pods of the plant that are used, and these are available as pods, loose seeds and ground seeds. The flavour is warm, soft and fragrantly spicy. Green, brown and white pods are available, the green most prized in India. Crush pods and add whole, or crush and remove seeds, and use whole or ground.	Essential in *pilaus*, curries and Indian spice mixtures, and also used in Indian ice cream. A flavouring of Scandinavian buns, breads and pastries, and Middle Eastern sweetmeats. Good in meat dishes and *charcuterie*, with fish, and many sweet sauces and fruit desserts.
CELERY SEED (S) *Apium graveolens*	Seeds of the vegetable plant, available whole or ground, or in celery seasoning (ground seeds and salt). The seeds are tiny, taste strongly of celery, and are slightly bitter.	Use in salads, fish stocks and dishes, soups, stews, bread doughs, on top of breads or biscuits, or in egg dishes.

HERB/SPICE	CHARACTERISTICS	USES
CHERVIL (H) *Anthriscus cerefolium*	Leaves fresh and dried. Delicate aniseed flavour which is best fresh and raw.	Good in green salads, with eggs, cheese, poached fish, chicken, vegetables, meat, and in delicate butter sauces. Use lavishly, as parsley.
CHILLI (S) *Capsicum spp*	For fresh, see page 184. Dried whole or chopped. Ground chillies available as chilli powder or seasoning (often mixed with cumin), either hot or mild, or cayenne pepper, hot and piquant. Also in chilli pastes and sauces (Tabasco) and in chilli oil.	Use dried in hot sauces, meat, fish and chicken curries, and many eastern dishes, but sparingly as they will still contain the hot seeds. Cayenne is good with many vegetables, and can spice up mild cheeses, eggs, bean and pulse dishes.
CHIVES (H) *Allium schoenoprasum*	The smallest member of the onion family, with a delicate onion flavour. Stalks are available fresh or freeze-dried.	Use snipped (with scissors) as a last-minute garnish for egg dishes, new and baked potatoes (with soured cream), with many vegetables, in salads, soups, soft cheeses, and with fish, chicken and lamb dishes.
CINNAMON/CASSIA (S) *Cinnamomum spp*	The bark of eastern trees, with similarly sweet, fragrant and aromatic scents. Cassia is slightly coarser. Available in rolled sticks, quills, and ground. Cassia leaves (the Indian bay) and buds.	Use whole cinnamon or cassia quills in pickles, *pilaus*, meat and poultry stews and curries. Pick out afterwards. Ground in cakes, biscuits, puddings, baked foods, stewed and fresh fruit dishes. Use cassia leaves and buds as bay and cloves.
CLOVE (S) *Eugenia caryophyllata*	The nail-shaped flower buds of a tropical evergreen tree, available dried whole, or ground. Spicy vanilla, peppery and carnation-like in flavour.	Use whole in *bouquet garnis*, in meat, game and poultry stews, marinades and stocks, in *pilau* rice, to stud onions for stock/sauce (bread sauce), to stud baked hams, whole with cooked fruits (remove before serving). Ground in sweet puddings, cakes, breads, pickles etc.

HERB/SPICE	CHARACTERISTICS	USES
CORIANDER (S) (H) *Coriandrum sativum*	Leaves fresh (commonly in bunches with roots still on), and dried. Fresh warm, musky and faintly aniseedy. Seeds whole or ground, warm with orange overtones.	Use fresh leaves in salads, soups, meat, poultry, game and fish curries and stews, vegetable dishes, fresh green Indian chutneys and relishes. Seeds whole or lightly crushed in vegetable dishes, pickling mixtures (Greek olives), curries; ground in curries, sauces, meatballs and kebabs.
CUMIN (S) *Cuminum cyminum*	Seeds, whole or ground. Seeds resemble caraway in shape, but flavour is quite different: warm, musky and aromatic. In Indian culinary terminology, two types are clearly defined: black or true, and white.	Use whole or ground in meat and poultry curries, and other hot dishes such as chilli con carne (ground cumin often flavours chilli seasoning), sausages, vegetable dishes and salads (in Morocco), and cheese.
CURRY LEAVES (S) *Murraya koenigi*	Small shiny leaves, fresh or dried, of a tropical tree, with a pronounced curry flavour.	Used in many curries. Chop, then fry in oil to release flavour before adding the other ingredients.
DILL (S) (H) *Anethum graveolens*	Leaves fresh or dried; seeds whole or ground. All parts of the plant are aromatic, with a sharp but sweet aniseed taste. Seeds are more bitter, leaning towards caraway.	Use fresh leaves in salads, with soft cheeses and egg dishes, with oily fish marinades (*gravlaks*), in fish sauces, with potatoes, and, with seeds, in pickles of cucumber. Seeds in breads, braised vegetable dishes, vinegars.
FENNEL (S) (H) *Foeniculum vulgare*	Leaves fresh and dried; seeds dried. All parts of the plant barring the roots are aromatic, with a unique sweet anise flavour. Stalks are used fresh or dried as well. Related to Florence fennel (see page 185), the frondy leaves of which may also be used as a herb.	Use fresh leaves and stalks with egg dishes, seafood baked, grilled or poached. Fennel is said to be *the* fish herb. Put a few dried stalks in and under barbecued fish, meat or poultry. Leaves also in salads, dressings, sauces, soups and vegetable dishes. Seeds on breads, in curries, vegetable dishes and an Italian *salame*.

265

HERB/SPICE	CHARACTERISTICS	USES
FENUGREEK (s) *Trigonella foenum-graecum*	Irregularly shaped seeds of an annual plant, available whole dried or ground. Whole seeds can be sprouted. Seeds need to be carefully roasted to release their bitter-sweet flavour. Fresh leaves are bitter when raw, curry-sweet when cooked. Dried leaves available too.	Seeds are used in curries of all kinds, curry mixtures, chutneys and pickles. Sprouted seeds (see page 193) and very young fresh leaves in salads. Older leaves as a vegetable. Dried leaves to flavour and colour meat and poultry curries, or ground, in *tandoori* marinades.
GALANGAL (s) *Alpinia spp*	Two types, the greater and lesser, are roots related to ginger. Available whole fresh or dried, ground and pickled. The flavour is peppery, less hot than ginger.	Used widely in the cooking of south-east Asia, especially Thailand. In curries, stews, with chicken and seafood.
HYSSOP (H) *Hyssopus officinalis*	An ancient herb, one of the flavourings of Chartreuse liqueur. Fresh or dried leaves, which have a bitter, minty flavour.	Use a few fresh leaves in green salads, with cheese, in rich duck, goose or lamb dishes, with vegetables like peas, and even in some stewed fruits and fruit pies.
GINGER (s) *Zingiber officinalis*	The underground rhizome or tuber of a tropical plant, ginger is available as whole fresh rhizomes; whole dried; whole syrup-preserved, crystallised or pickled; and ground. Fresh has a clean, fresh, spicy and peppery flavour.	One of the most important spices of the Orient, fresh especially. Peeled, then sliced, chopped, grated and used in Indian curries or Chinese stir-fries. Fresh is also good with some fruits, and vegetable dishes. Dried must be bruised before use; good with fish, poultry and red meats. In the west, ground ginger is used primarily in sweet things.
JUNIPER (s) *Juniperus communis*	The purplish berry of a small temperate evergreen shrub or tree. Berries fresh or dried. The flavour is spicy, camphory, with a hint of pine or resin. It is the essential 'botanical' flavouring of gin.	Cook with game, or with milder meats to make them more gamey in flavour. Use in marinades, sauces, stuffings, pates and sausages. Wonderful, crushed with rock salt and garlic, with cabbage.

HERB/SPICE	CHARACTERISTICS	USES
LEMON BALM (H) *Melissa officinalis*	Fresh or dried leaves, sweet and lemon-scented. Used in the making of Benedictine and Chartreuse liqueurs.	Use a few fresh leaves in a salad, sauce for fish, or game, poultry or meat stuffings. Good in dishes using lemon juice or lemongrass, egg mixtures, custards, stewed fruits, white wine cups.
LEMONGRASS (H) *Cymbopogon cytratus*	A fragrant tropical grass, available as whole fresh stalks, dried stalks, and ground. The flavour of the fresh is very pronounced lemon with a hint of heat (substitute, if difficult to find, with a little fresh ginger and lemon peel, which contains the same essential oils). Dried must be soaked before use, and is less lemony, more peppery.	The essential flavouring of south-east Asian cookery, especially in Indonesia, Malaysia and Thailand. Used whole fresh in curries, soups, especially of poultry, pork and seafood. Bruise fresh stems before adding to food, and retrieve when dish is cooked.
LEMON VERBENA (H) *Lippia citriodora*	Lemon-flavoured leaves, fresh or dried.	Use sparingly in fruit salads, with melon, in punches and refreshing drinks. It can also flavour custards, jams, sauces for fish, and replace lemongrass in recipes.
LOVAGE (H) *Levisticum officinale*	Fresh leaves are celery-like in appearance, and taste like a meaty amalgam of celery and curry. Dried leaves retain the flavour well. Seeds are dried, and can be sprinkled on bread and biscuits before baking, or ground as a savoury seasoning.	Use young leaves in salads; more mature leaves in soups, meat, poultry and game stews, stuffings, and to add meaty flavour to vegetarian dishes. The stems can be cooked as vegetables or crystallised like angelica.
MARJORAM (H) *Origanum spp*	Leaves fresh or dried. There are several types, primarily sweet (*O.majorana*) and pot (*O.onites*). The flavour of both is camphory, warm with pepper, basil and thyme overtones; sweet is generally considered the finest as it is mildest in flavour.	A meat herb, to be used in pâtés, sausages, stuffings, marinades, *bouquet garnis*, stocks. Good with fish and chicken too. Add fresh towards the end of cooking to vegetable and pulse dishes, fresh tomato sauces, soups or stews. Good sparingly in salads as well.

HERB/SPICE	CHARACTERISTICS	USES
MINT (H) *Mentha spp*	The leaves of many varieties — spearmint, apple mint, peppermint, pennyroyal etc. — are available fresh or dried. Spearmint and apple mint are the types most commonly grown for kitchen use, but most can be used similarly. The basic flavour is menthol cool.	Use fresh in English mint sauces for lamb, Middle Eastern yogurt and cracked wheat salads (*tabbouleh*), Indian yogurt chutneys. Cooked with many vegetables, especially new potatoes, peas etc., and good with fish and chicken. The herb most used in sweet dishes — in ice creams, sorbets and mousses, with fruits and as a garnish. Sprigs decorate and flavour drinks — mint juleps and Moroccan sweet mint tea, for instance.
MUSTARD SEED (S) *Brassica spp*	The condiment, whether made mustard or powdered, is the result of grinding the seeds of three related plants, black, brown or white. The last is very much less pungent, and is the one grown for the seedling mustard of mustard and cress.	The spice seeds, of black mustard particularly, are important in eastern curries, spice mixtures and pickles. Brown are used to flavour rice, dhal and vegetable dishes. Mustard oil is the cooking oil of North India. Made and powdered mustards are good as meat condiment, mixed into sauces such as mayonnaise. Also good with some fish, and with cheese. Add made or powdered mustard to a cooked dish at the last moment, and heat very gently.
NIGELLA (S) *Nigella sativa*	Tiny black seeds, available dried whole or ground, of a plant related to the garden flower, love-in-the-mist. A complex, mild flavour, aromatic and peppery.	Although known as black cumin, the spices are not similar. Nigella is used in eastern spice mixtures such as the famous *panch phoran*, curries, pickles and vegetable dishes. Good as a pepper substitute in many pulse dishes, sauces, stews etc. It is occasionally seen sprinkled on breads in the Middle East.

HERB/SPICE	CHARACTERISTICS	USES
NUTMEG AND MACE (S) *Myristica fragrans*	Mace is the orange aril covering the nutmeg kernel of a tropical evergreen tree fruit. Mace is available in 'blades' or ground. Nutmeg comes as whole kernels or ground. Nutmeg is warm, sweet and nutty in flavour; mace is similar but more delicate.	Ground mace is good in delicate milk puddings, and traditional in western potted meats and fish, and sausages. Whole is used in eastern rice dishes. Nutmeg is grated freshly and at the last minute into white sauces, mashed potatoes, pale meat dishes, vegetable dishes, cakes, pies and puddings.
OREGANO (H) *Oreganum vulgare*	The 'wild' version of marjoram. Leaves available fresh or dried. The flavour is much more coarse, robust and pungent than marjoram. It dries well, and is the *rigani* of Greece.	Important in Italian cooking: the flavour of many pizzas, spaghetti sauces, and salads of Mozzarella cheese and tomatoes. It flavours Greek Feta cheese salads and kebabs. Good with many meat, poultry, game and vegetable dishes, and grilled fish.
PAPRIKA (S) *Capsicum tetragonum*	Ground powder of a dried red, sweet rather than hot, pepper (which is occasionally available fresh). It is very much milder than chilli seasoning or cayenne (see Chilli). A similar powder is sold in Spain, *pimientón*.	Most used in Hungarian cooking, in *goulash* and other meat stews. There the heat of the spice can vary, and hot or mild varieties are available. Used in Spanish sauces and sausages. Adds red colour and piquancy to egg dishes, and pale sauces. Use in vegetable and rice dishes.
PARSLEY (H) *Petroselinum spp*	Available fresh or dried. Fresh flat-leaf parsley is more flavourful and robust than the curly variety. Parsley stalks are full of flavour as well, and should be saved for stocks and *bouquet garnis*.	The most common and usable of herbs, as it goes with almost any food, from the garlic and pepper amalgams of the south to the cod and potatoes of the north. Use in court bouillons, in a *bouquet garni*, as last-minute garnish, either in sprigs or finely chopped. Mix with butter and garlic for a savoury butter for snails, mussels and many other fish and vegetable dishes. Good with eggs and cheese dishes.

HERB/SPICE	CHARACTERISTICS	USES
PEPPER (s) *Piper nigrum*	The seeds of the tropical pepper vine are available whole, crushed, ground and, in the case of green, fresh or pickled. Black, white and green peppercorns come from the same plant: green are immature; black are sun-dried green; white are the mature seeds stripped of their ripe red coating. Pink or red peppercorns are the berries of a tropical tree. Green is mildest in flavour; white are hot, but less fragrant than black.	The king of spices, and used as condiment all over the world. Use crushed green and red for fish, green in sauces, savoury butters, and with beef; ground white in sauces and stews where a light colour is needed. Whole white or black peppercorns can be used in stock, marinades and court bouillons; coarsely ground black to coat steaks. Black pepper is said to be good with strawberries.
POPPY SEED (s) *Papaver somniferum*	Seeds of the opium poppy, available whole and ground. The tiny, round blue-black or 'white' seeds have a subtle nutty flavour. They can be sprouted.	Seeds are used widely in Asia in meat, vegetable and rice dishes, and in spice mixtures. In Europe the whole black seeds are commonly used on breads. Good in many baked dishes, on pastries, in creamy dressings, or as a garnish.
ROSEMARY (H) *Rosmarinus officinalis*	The needle-like, tough leaves of an evergreen flowering shrub, available fresh or dried. The scent is highly aromatic, camphory and honey-like. Use in sprigs to be removed, as the leaves are unpleasant to eat.	Has a great affinity with pale and red meats, game and chicken (tuck sprigs into or under a roasting joint, or burn on barbecue coals). Add a sprig to butter or oil in which potatoes or meat are to be cooked. Add to a *bouquet garni*, stocks and jellies.
SAGE (H) *Salvia officinalis*	Leaves of several varieties of an evergreen shrub are available fresh or dried, or ground. The flavour is powerful, harsh and dry, but fragrant, with overtones of camphor. It dries well, but takes time as the leaves are fleshy.	Use sparingly, as the flavour is very strong. Fresh in salads, in soups, stuffings (sage and onion), in sausages, as garnish for eggs, tomato and cheese dishes (it flavours the English Sage Derby cheese). Used in many Italian dishes (*saltimbocca*), or leaves fried in oil and butter for cooking veal or calf's liver.

HERB/SPICE	CHARACTERISTICS	USES
SAFFRON (S) *Crocus sativus*	The stigmas of a variety of crocus, available in deep red threads or ground. Both are very expensive as more than ½ million crocuses are hand-harvested for just 450g (1lb) spice. Threads are a better buy as ground can be adulterated. The flavour is bitter, yet pungently sweet. Add ground directly to dishes. To get the deepest colour and fullest flavour from the threads, grind them slightly in a mortar and pestle, then infuse in warm water or stock before adding to a dish.	Use in dishes where the colour as well as flavour is appreciated – most notably in *paella*, *pilaus*, risotto and other rice dishes; in fish soups and shellfish dishes; with chicken and lamb dishes; and in sweet breads and biscuits.
SASSAFRAS (S) *Sassafras albidum*	The product of an aromatic North American tree of the laurel family. The spice consists of dried ground leaves or dried bark, in pieces or ground. The ground leaves are also known as filé powder.	Used for thickening rather than flavour, particularly in Creole and Cajun cooking – the famous gumbo is thickened with filé powder. Good with red meats, pork, chicken, duck, goose, fish and vegetables.
SAVORY (H) *Satureja spp*	Two varieties – summer (*S.hortensis*) and winter (*S.montana*) – are available as fresh and dried leaves. Both are aromatic, pleasantly bitter and a little like thyme in flavour; winter savory is sharper.	Known in Europe as the 'bean herb' – good with beans and pulses, as well as cooked vegetable, meat, rabbit and poultry dishes, and roast meats and sauces. Use sparingly as it is powerful fresh *and* dried.
SESAME SEED (S) *Sesamum indicum*	The seeds, white, brown and black, of an Asian annual plant. Available whole or ground. A nutty flavour is enhanced by dry-roasting. They are pressed for their oil, which is very strongly nutty, and widely used in Chinese cooking. The seeds can be sprouted.	Used whole in and on breads, rolls, cakes and biscuits, in vegetable, rice and noodle dishes, as a garnish. Used extensively in Asian cuisine, whole or ground in sauces, desserts and soups. The Middle Eastern *tahina* paste, used in making *hummus*, and the sweet *halva* are both made from sesame seeds.

271

HERB/SPICE	CHARACTERISTICS	USES
STAR ANISE (S) *Illicium verum*	The pretty star-shaped dried seed pods of a tropical tree of the magnolia family, available whole, in pieces, ground and seeds. Strong licorice flavour, coarser than anise (and is the flavouring of Pernod and *anisette*).	An important flavouring in China and Vietnam, used ground in spice mixtures, and whole in braised dishes. Good with fish, shellfish, duck, chicken, pork and the best and tastiest baked Chinese spare ribs.
SWEET CICELY (H) *Myrrhis odorata*	Available as fresh leaves and long green-black seeds. Also known as anise chervil, its taste is somewhere between anise and licorice, fragrant and sugary.	Said to be the sugar-saver herb, because it cuts down the amount of sugar required in sweet recipes. Use leaves with fruits like apples and rhubarb, in fruit salads, and green salads. Chop the seeds and use similarly.
TAMARIND (S) *Tamarindus indica*	The spice comes from the pulp surrounding the seeds in the fruit pod of a tropical tree. Pods available fresh and dried, as dried slices, in a solid block and as a concentrate. Sour and fruity, it enhances other flavours. Concentrate is easiest to use; with all others, soak in hot water then press through a sieve for a souring juice. Tamarind is one of the constituents of Worcestershire sauce.	Best in Indian curries, chutneys, rice and lentil dishes, and in other East Asian dishes. Good with poultry and beef, in marinades and soups, and in cooling drinks.
TARRAGON (H) *Artemisia spp*	Leaves fresh and dried. French or 'true' tarragon (*A.dracunculus*) is superior to Russian (*A.dracunculoides*) because of its delicate anise flavour and the tingle it gives to the tongue. It is better frozen than dried.	Very important in French cuisine, and particularly associated with chicken and egg dishes, classic butter sauces such as *béarnaise* (see the photograph on page 211), and savoury butters. Good with fish, shellfish, red meat. Add fresh to green and potato salads, salad dressings and vegetables. White wine vinegar flavoured with tarragon has many uses (see page 261).

HERB/SPICE	CHARACTERISTICS	USES
THYME (H) *Thymus spp*	Leaves, fresh and dried, of at least two varieties most used in the kitchen: garden or common (*T.vulgaris*) and lemon (*T.citriodoris*). An intense, warm and clove-like flavour, which is retained in the dried leaves. Lemon thyme is obviously lemony.	A basic constituent of the *bouquet garni* and used in stocks, marinades, slow-cooked meat dishes, roast meats and poultry, tomato sauces and dressings. Lemon thyme is good with fish and superb in pork and veal stuffings (replacing lemon peel), and can flavour vegetables and desserts, particularly of fruit.
TURMERIC (S) *Curcuma longa*	An underground tropical rhizome related to ginger, turmeric is available whole fresh and dried, and ground. It has a warm, earthy and spicy flavour, and is a bright yellow. Use fresh or dried whole rhizomes as ginger; ground can be added directly to the dish.	Often used as a cheaper substitute for saffron, but there is no comparison in flavour. Used for the colour in curry powders, pickles (piccalilli), and many Indonesian and Malaysian dishes. Adds colour and mild flavour to fish, chicken, meat and vegetable dishes.
VANILLA (S) *Vanilla planifolia*	The seed pod of a South American climbing orchid, vanilla is available as whole pods, or as essence or extract. The flavour is not sweet, but full, warm and reminiscent of the best caramels and ice cream. Split pods lengthwise and scrape out seeds into a custard for instance; or store pods in a jar of caster sugar which will absorb the flavour.	Best in sweet dishes – those made with chocolate and coffee (and the drinks themselves), in ice cream, custards and other sweet sauces, and with many fruits. It can be used in fish and shellfish dishes.

The Cooking of India

by RAFI FERNANDEZ

India has always been known as the land of spice. Sailors entering the Indian ocean would taste it on the breeze. From Roman times, perhaps even earlier, it was cardamom and cinnamon, saffron and cloves, pepper and nutmeg that brought the explorers and merchant-traders hurrying to India's shores.

Rafi Fernandez, of Rafi's Spice Box, Sudbury, Suffolk

'Curry' is the best-known of India's culinary exports, but the curry-powder and flour-thickened preparations of Anglo-India are a sad travesty of the real thing. A genuine Indian curry is prepared from a cornucopia of spices, condiments and coconut, freshly grated, sautéed in *ghee* (clarified butter) or vegetable oil so that no rawness remains in the taste, and cooked slowly so that the sauce thickens while cooking and no extraneous thickening agent is needed. To this *mirch masala* (spice mixture) is added

chicken, fish, meat or vegetables as one wishes.

There are almost as many varieties of curry in India as there are people – a rich legacy of the diverse national and racial groups who have been attracted there. India has fifteen officially recognised languages, plus several dialects and, of course, English, which is still widely spoken in a variety of regional accents. The cuisine is an amalgam of many regional styles and techniques, and you will find local differences in every village and city.

The word *curry* is a product of the Raj and derives from the original south Indian *kari*, which means something in a spicy sauce. But the traditions of Indian cuisine go much further back than that, to the founding of Hinduism, the religion of some 85 per cent of India. Hindu beliefs, unlike other world religions, did not develop from a central founder or a single scripture, but from the fusion of two cultures. The fair-skinned Aryan people of Central Asia invaded northen India in about 2000 BC, displacing some of the dark-skinned original inhabitants, the Dravidians (who fled to the south). The Aryans settled, commingled with the remaining natives, and the earliest Hindu texts, the *Vedas* (Aryan hymns), date from about 1500 BC, centuries before any of the other major world religions.

It was the Aryans who first introduced rules of personal hygiene which it would be hard for any modern physician to fault. Mouth, hands and feet had to be washed before and after eating or drinking, and food which one person had sampled could never be touched by another except between husband and wife, mother and children. These are culinary and eating practices still observable in India today. Drinking cups were never allowed to touch the lips: the liquid had to be poured straight into the mouth – a rule still followed by strict Brahmins, the highest caste (originally priests) of Hinduism. The concept of reincarnation lies at the heart of Hinduism, which demands a respect for all forms of life, and a policy of non-hurting of life (*ahimsa*). It is for this reason that most Hindus are vegetarian; Hindus also revere cows, and will not eat their meat.

After the Hindu Brahmins, the next major religious influence was Buddha. Born the prince of a north-eastern Indian state in c. 563 BC, he was so appalled by the sorrow that his wealth and power caused to others that he renounced his birthright and the tenets of Hinduism. Thereafter he devoted himself to the achievement of perfect spiritual enlightenment through extreme asceticism. His diet is believed to have finally consisted of no more than he could hold in the palm

Naan (leavened bread)

of one hand – and only vegetarian food at that. Buddhism is now one of the major world religions, and strict Buddhists are vegetarian.

Similar philosophies were propounded by the sage Mahavira, founder of another 'breakaway' Hindu sect, Jainism, in the 6th century BC. The *ahimsa* of Jainism resulted in a vegetarian diet so strict that the Jains were not even allowed root vegetables in case they harmed insects as they pulled them from the ground. It is primarily because of these religious influences that, of the 700 million or so who live in India, some 75 per cent are vegetarian.

Other influences were brought by the many colonisers and raiders who were attracted

to India by their hunger for spice. Many of these simply returned to their own countries with their loot; others stayed and tried to Indianise themselves by marrying and converting to Hinduism. They were only partially accepted, however, so that new social and religious groupings were formed as a result.

One of the most significant of these were the Zoroastrians, from Persia, who arrived in about AD 785 and were required by the ruler of the kingdom where they landed to adopt his language and respect the Hindu laws. Over the centuries they became an established part of the cultural mix and began to call themselves Parsees. They settled in the main around Bombay, on the west coast. Their contributions to Indian culture have included some of the most distinctive features of its cuisine. For instance, the meats, nut and dried fruit combinations of much Indian cooking is very Persian or Middle Eastern in concept. Other famous Parsee dishes are *dhansak*, a stew of lamb, lentils and vegetables, and *patio*, a sour, sweet and hot sauced seafood dish, usually of prawns.

Christianity had already arrived with St Thomas the Apostle in the first century AD. A small community of Syrian Christians later established itself on the Malabar Coast on the west, and European powers arriving in the 16th century strengthened Christianity's hold – especially in the Portuguese enclaves of Goa, Daman and Diu. British colonial rule in the 19th century accelerated the process. Most Christians in India still eat fish on Fridays and do not eat food before receiving communion on Sunday. They are the only people in India who eat pork.

The impact of Islam was twofold. Founded in Arabia in the 7th century by the prophet Mohammed, Islam was extended by Muslim armies to west and east, eventually reaching the north of India. The Moghuls, an Indian Muslim dynasty descended from the Mongol ruler, Genghis Khan, reigned chiefly in the north between the 12th and 18th centuries. They established a new *haute cuisine*, known as Moghlai cooking, one of the greatest cuisines in the world. With origins in Persia and the Middle East, it is rich in meat, rice, fruit, nuts and sugar. To these have been added Indian herbs and spices, including a great deal of garlic. (The Hindus eschewed garlic, maintaining their use of *hing* or asafoetida, a

pungent and highly smelling spice.) Moghlai cooking is spicy, not hot, and famous dishes include creamy *kormas*, subtle *biryanis* and *pilaus* (which are very similar to the Persian *polos* and *pilafs*). The Moghuls served their dishes with great pomp and garnished them with *warq* (thin wafers of beaten gold and silver) – a habit copied by Hindu princes anxious to prove themselves equal.

The other lasting Moghul influence was the introduction of sweet dishes. As a result, India's appetite for sickly sweets – mostly made from milk – is at least the equal of the western world's appetite for chocolate.

By the time of the last Moghul, Aurangzeb, who reigned from 1658–1707, the Moghul Empire stretched from the north right down to the Deccan plateau in the south. A large Tamil Muslim community still exists there. They live in obedience to Koranic dietary law, eating *halal* food and eschewing pork and alcohol. A lot of these Tamil dishes are searingly hot.

The final strand in the cultural weave came in the late 15th century with the founding of Sikhism, a combination of Hindu and Islamic ideas, in the Punjab in the north-west. The Sikhs were warriors who liked plenty of protein. Today they are mainly farmers, but old habits die hard, and although most are vegetarian, many still eat meat.

Modern India is a secular state in which all these influences survive and add their flavour to the mix. For the bulk of India's enormous population the realities of life have changed little over the centuries. Most castes join freely in family festivities – marriage, childbirth etc – and dietary restrictions do not stand in the

way of social relationships. It is a fact of Indian life: each caste at a festival will prepare and eat its own food, without any risk of compromise to its rules.

It is true that Hindus have always refused to dine with Muslims; but then neither do all Hindus dine with each other. In Bihar, bread fried in ghee may be eaten even if it has been touched by a man of another caste (for *ghee* is the purest food, being a product of the sacred cow), though not if it is baked on fire; but this is not so in Bengal. Some vegetables may be eaten only if cooked without salt. Taboos like these differ from province to province and caste to caste, and are beyond the understanding of anyone who has not been brought up with them.

Disparate and varied as the origins of Indian food may be, there is one common factor that binds them all together – spicing.

Masala, the blending of various spices, is the cornerstone of all Indian cookery. Indian practitioners of the art will emphasise that it does not matter *which* spice you use, but rather *how* you use it, for it is through spicing that you express your individuality as a cook. That is why there are so many variants of even the best-known dishes. No two cooks achieve identical results, since each follows an individual spicing ritual which even now is largely handed down by word of mouth. Certain ingredients must be ground fresh for certain dishes, chopped for others, sliced for yet others; or spices must be dry-fried or fried in oil before a major ingredient is added, in order to release aroma. For it is *flavour* rather than heat that most Indian cooks aspire to achieve: despite the association of curry in western minds and palates with fiery chilli heat, the chilli only became part of the Indian culinary canon after the discovery of the New World in the 16th century. (Before this, mustard seeds and black pepper provided the heat in cooking.)

For centuries the favoured Indian cooking vessel has been the *handi*, a stewing pot which comes in many shapes, sizes and materials. Copper and brass were most favoured, but these had to be covered on the base with a fine coating of tin by the *kalai-wallah*, whose familiar trade-call still echoes in the memory. In the cities, however, we have taken to using *handis* made from aluminium and steel. Terracotta ones are used for dishes which include ingredients corrosive to metal. To this the Moghuls added the *tandoor* (clay oven), and much later came the *karahi*, a heavy pan for frying, the shape of which was influenced by the Chinese wok, and the *tava*, a metal plate used for cooking unleavened breads.

Tandoori and *karahi* foods were essentially fast-cooked, but most traditional Indian curries were and are cooked by long slow simmering in *handis*. The Moghuls soon took to and elaborated upon this process of culinary integration, and their most famous dishes are rich, unhurried, and flavoured with almonds, raisins and scented saffron. The *biryanis* especially – meat or fish and rice dishes for festive occasions – display the classic elements of *dum* or steam cooking. The *handi* with its fragrant layered contents was placed on burning embers and the top sealed with a washer of dough to let it simmer in its own steamy heat.

Rice is the staple food of India, but features particularly in the food of the south. In the north, breads are more popular as a meal basis, and they are made from a variety of cereals. Wheat is commonest – and we all know of *naan*, *chappati*, *paratha* and *puri* – but lentils, rice, millet and maize are also used. A Bengali favourite, *batura*, which is becoming more familiar in the UK, is made from strong white flour, in layers rather like puff pastry; a south-

Disparate and varied as the origins of Indian food may be, there is one common factor that binds them all together – spicing.

ern speciality is *dosai*, a combination of fermented rice and black gram flour.

Other staples in the Indian diet are dried lentils, beans, peas and chickpeas, which contribute nitrogen-rich proteins to the millions of non-meat eaters. When whole they are collectively known as *gram*; when split, they are often called *dhal*, also the name of the lentil curry served as a side dish. There are many different varieties of pulse, but the best-known in the UK are Bengal gram or *channa* (related to the chickpea), black gram or *urad* (a lentil), green gram or *moong* (the mung bean), red lentils or *masoor*, red gram or *tuvar* (split pea), black-eyed beans or *lobia*, red kidney beans or *rajma*, and chickpeas or *kabuli channa*.

The *handi* dominated the kitchens of the south, where the equatorial climate demanded

replacement of body fluids and a high element of digestives. The south's *rasam* (pepper water) and *sambhar* (lentil curry) are virtual soups compared with the thick rich sauces of the north. In addition to its role as a vehicle for other foods, rice in the south is used in special dishes. The most popular of these are *puliyadori* (tamarind rice), *tayyir sadam* (rice in curd) and *payyasam* (rice pudding).

The food of southern India includes the *shat rasas* or 'six flavours': sweet, bitter (asafoetida), salty, sour (tamarind), pungent (very hot chilli) and astringent (raw fenugreek). Cooking is also subservient to the Hindu religion. Most of the chefs are strict Brahmins, which prevents them from handling meat in any form, and many chefs will not allow anyone who is not a vegetarian into their kitchens. If they are *touched* by a meat-eater, they will take a ritual cleansing bath.

The eastern delta lands of Bengal favour sweet, sour and bitter tastes. A true Bengali will eat fish daily, but on festive occasions three or more fish dishes will be served. They fry their delicate seafoods from the Bay of Bengal in open *handis* to seal in the flavours before adding their sauces, covering and allowing the food to slowly simmer. Two very famous Bengali dishes cooked in this style are *shukto* and *labda*. Bengalis mostly use mustard oil in their cooking, to which it imparts a unique taste and aroma. They are also very partial to sweets – *gulab jamun*, *rasogolla* and many more.

On the west coast the vegetarian Gujeratis prepare specialities like *dhokla* – a dough of rice and lentils flavoured with yogurt, fresh herbs and spices. This is 277 leavened with baking soda and steamed after proving overnight. Another Gujerati blend of rice and lentils was the origin of what became the Anglo-Indian kedgeree. Gujeratis are also famous for their snacks, *farshans* – *kachori, chevda, dahi vada* etc. – and their *shaks*, dry vegetable curries. They love to combine sweet and sour, through using jaggery (raw cane sugar) and tamarind.

Also on the west coast are the *bhoras*, Shia Muslims who are renowned for their love of food. They were originally Hindus from Gujerat, and their native tongue is still Gujerati. Their most famous dish is *dhabba gosht*. Lightly seasoned and boiled meat (the *gosht*) is packed in a small *handi* (the *dhabba*) and topped with beaten raw eggs. Hot oil is poured in to quick-cook the topping, then the small *handi* put inside a larger one and immersed to its rim in boiling water, rather like a *bain-marie*. The finished dish tastes like a delectable meat loaf.

Indian gourmets insist that food is most delicious when eaten direct from the *handi*, as subtle flavours become lost in the transfer to serving dishes. Today, the Balti cuisine which is becoming so popular, particularly in the Midlands, is proving this. The food is served in the *karahi* in which it was cooked.

A survey of Indian restaurant menus in Britain would show that most offer their version of Moghlai cuisine, but as western palates are becoming more educated they are getting more demanding. If many of the restaurants are to survive they will have to re-think. Parts of Britain where the Indian population is dense – Southall, Brad-

ford and Manchester – are spoilt for choice. Elsewhere, sadly, many still have to make do with the second-rate, or travel long distances to enjoy something more traditional.

I think the reason for this mediocrity is a loss of love. When I cook for my family or friends I do it with love, and this should be felt by the diners. There are about 75,000 Indian restaurants in the UK alone, and I implore them to make more effort to achieve a home-cooked taste. We have the knowledge and techniques, so why not share them?

The Indian cook's shelf contains some 25 spices, which can seem daunting to the beginner. But there is no problem obtaining them. Indian spices are readily available even in supermarkets, with clearly descriptive labels. To those embarking for the first time on a 'curry', a few simple guidelines should be kept in mind. Most curries require spices to be crushed or ground to a paste. In India the traditional grinding stone is still preferred. In Britain we can achieve the same textures with the help of a good food processor, though a pestle and mortar is better for small quantities.

It is best to buy spices whole, and they should be dry-roasted before grinding. Whole spices have a longer shelf-life if they are correctly stored, in airtight jars in a cool dark place. Several brands of very good curry powders and *masala* pastes are available, and they can save you a great deal of time. But never forget: the best results are achieved by blending ingredients individually.

For a first attempt it is wise to choose only one or perhaps two dishes. Once you have become confident in your handling of the spices, you will find Indian cuisine offers great flexibility, and

you can vary the amounts of spice – especially the chilli heat – to suit your taste.

Given a good recipe book and a little perseverance, anyone can produce Indian food. Almost all of them unravel the mysteries of the spices and techniques which Indian cookery requires. These are the most essential:

BAGHAR

Spices, usually whole ones, are fried in hot oil or ghee. The reaction of the spice to the heat varies enormously. Some will gently brown; some swell up; others pop all over the place. The resulting infusion is poured over pulses, vegetables and a few meat dishes, then covered and rested till the aromas have seeped into the dish.

DRY-ROASTING SPICES

Spices are roasted in a hot but dry frying pan to bring out their flavours and aromas. They are then cooled and used either whole or ground into powder. Sometimes even 'wet' ingredients like onion, garlic, ginger, chillies, coconut and coriander leaves are treated in this way. They are then ground with the other whole spices to make a paste. This method makes naturally thick sauces: Indians never add flour.

Whatever your level of expertise, it is always wise to assemble all your ingredients before you start to cook. The early stages of a dish will require a constant flow of activity and careful control of the heat: you don't have time then to hunt for things you have forgotten. The result of inattention will be undercooked or – worse – burnt spices. Once

Gucci Pilau (fragrant rice with mushrooms)

you burn a curry there is no way back. You have to throw it all away and start again.

These cautions are not designed in any way to deter you, but rather to demonstrate that a little appropriate reading can make all the difference between success and failure. Better still is to watch a practical demonstration. Words often make techniques sound more complicated than they really are, whereas a good demonstration can have the clarity and lasting impact of a photograph.

MENU I: A VEGETARIAN MEAL FROM SOUTHERN INDIA
SERVES 4–6
Payyasam (Green gram and rice pudding)
Kuttu (Tamil mixed vegetables)
Alu bhat (Dry potato curry)
Aviyal (Mixed vegetables cooked in yogurt)
Sambhar (Lentil curry with vegetables)
Rasam (Pepper water with tomato juice)
Sadam (Plain boiled rice)
Pacchadi (Yogurt salad)

Vegetarian eateries in South India, mainly Brahmin, are called by various generic names – *Udipis, Vihars, Bhavans, Vilas, Tiffins* – and have remained totally impervious to the changing world. What characterises them is an atmosphere quite unlike that of any other restaurant, and service so super-efficient that there is never a lapse of more than a few minutes between the moment you place your order and your first taste.

There will be a plantain leaf and a glass of water already set out for you at your table, and the

waiter will deliver the menu orally at a rate of 120 words per minute. Unfold your leaf and sprinkle it with a hand-scoop of water from the glass. The food will not be served until this cleansing ritual is completed.

The meal begins with a small amount of *payyasam* (rice, lentils and nuts cooked in sweet thickened milk) or some other sweet, served as a *prasadam* (offering to the deity).

As you finish the sweet, the waiters begin appearing like unsummoned genii. One serves salt, hot pickles and salads; another brings at least two vegetable *karis*. Contrary to the popular belief that all south Indian dishes are tongue-curlingly hot, you will find that the food is cooked with curds, coconut or tamarind and seasoned so skilfully that the original flavours of the vegetables are enhanced rather than smothered by the condiments. Chutneys arrive next with *pacchadi* – tomato, onion and cucumber drenched with yoghurt.

Freshly steamed rice is served four times, each time to be eaten with a different course. When the first helping of rice is served, the waiter will pour some hot ghee over it – a purifying ritual that has been practised since Vedic times. The second serving is eaten with *sambhar*, a speciality made with *tuvar dhal* and *channa dhal*, vegetables and tamarind, and the other vegetable *karis*. The third is eaten with *rasam* – a thin, highly spiced broth made from lentil water with an addition of either tamarind, tomato or lime. This was the basis from which developed the Anglo-Indian 'mulligatawny', which means 'pepper water'. The final helping of rice is served with *thayyir* yoghurt).

Payyasam (Green gram and rice pudding)

85g (3oz) pudding rice
55g (2oz) split green gram (moong dhal)
350ml (12fl oz) water
400ml (14fl oz) evaporated milk
6 tablespoons sugar, or to taste
½ teaspoon grated nutmeg
½ teaspoon ground cardamom seeds (elaichi)
1 tablespoon rose water
6–8 strands saffron, soaked in 1 tablespoon warm milk
30g (1oz) each of almond flakes, pistachios and cashew nuts

Wash the rice and gram and drain. In a large pan soak them in the measured water for 1 hour. Bring to the boil and then simmer until the grains are nearly cooked, about 20 minutes. Add the remaining ingredients and simmer for a further 20 minutes, until the texture is that of a rice pudding. Serve hot or cold.

Kuttu (Tamil mixed vegetables)

110g (4oz) husked black gram (urad dhal)
250ml (8fl oz) water
1 teaspoon ground turmeric (haldi)
450g (1lb) mixed vegetables
2 tablespoons vegetable oil
1 teaspoon cumin seeds (zeera)
55g (2oz) fine desiccated coconut
Salt to taste
For the Baghar (final fry)
2 tablespoons vegetable oil
1 teaspoon mustard seeds (rai)
¾ teaspoon ground asafoetida
3 whole dried red chillies, seeded (lal mirch)
6–8 curry leaves (kariyapath)

Wash and drain the gram. Place in a heavy pan with the water and turmeric. Bring to the boil. Reduce heat, cover and simmer until soft but not mushy. Keep aside.

Meanwhile prepare the vegetables, cutting them into bite-size pieces. In a wok or large pan heat the oil and fry the cumin seeds and coconut until the coconut is golden brown. Add the vegetables and salt. Cover and cook until the vegetables are done but still crunchy, about 10 minutes. Add the lentils and mix well. Leave on a low heat.

In a small frying pan heat the *baghar* oil until smoking hot, and fry the *baghar* ingredients until the chillies turn dark and the mustard seeds crackle. Pour all the spices and oil over the lentil and vegetable mix, cover and rest for 5 minutes to infuse the aromas. Serve hot.

Alu Bhat (Dry potato curry)

2 tablespoons vegetable oil
1 teaspoon mustard seeds (rai)
¼ teaspoon nigella seeds (ajwain)
½ teaspoon each of fennel (sonf) *and cumin seeds* (zeera)
4 large dried red chillies, seeded (lal mirch)
1 large onion, finely chopped
3 cloves garlic, crushed
1 teaspoon ground turmeric (haldi)
15g (½oz) dry fenugreek leaves (methi)
200g (7oz) tinned chopped tomatoes
Lemon juice to taste
Salt to taste
30g (1oz) fresh coriander leaves, chopped (dhania)
450g (1lb) potatoes, peeled, cubed and boiled

Heat the oil and fry the mustard, nigella, fennel, cumin seeds and red chillies until the mustard seeds crackle. Add the onion, garlic, turmeric and fenugreek leaves, and fry on a low heat until the onion is translucent. Add the tomatoes, lemon juice, salt and coriander leaves. Bring to the boil. Fold in the potatoes, and serve hot.

Aviyal (Mixed vegetables cooked in yogurt)

1 onion, chopped
2 cloves garlic
4 tablespoons desiccated coconut
4 green chillies (hari mirch)
2 tablespoons coconut oil
1 teaspoon cumin seeds (zeera)
6 curry leaves (kariyapath)
1 tablespoon husked black gram (urad dhal)
110g (4oz) white Dutch cabbage, sliced
55g (2oz) frozen peas, thawed
110g (4oz) carrots, diced
1 red pepper, chopped
110g (4oz) white radish, sliced
1 green or partly unripe mango, sliced (optional)
175ml (6fl oz) natural yogurt
Salt to taste

In a food processor blend the onion, garlic, coconut and green chillies to a semi-coarse paste. Heat the oil and fry the cumin seeds, curry leaves and gram until the gram is golden brown. Add the processed paste and fry until the oil separates. Add the vegetables and mango and mix well. Cover and allow the vegetables to cook until nearly done, about 20 minutes. Cool until tepid and fold in the yogurt and salt. Mix well. Reheat without covering to avoid the yogurt curdling. Serve hot.

Sambhar (Lentil curry with vegetables)

*110g (4oz) red gram (*tuvar dhal*)*
*55g (2oz) Bengal gram (*channa dhal*)*
2 teaspoons sambhar powder
1 teaspoon ground turmeric (haldi)
500ml (18fl oz) water
55g (2oz) okra, tops sparingly trimmed
225g (8oz) cauliflower florets
10 shallots, peeled and left whole, or 10 small pickled onions, drained
2 tablespoons tamarind juice (imli pani)
1 teaspoon soft brown sugar
Salt to taste
4 unripe tomatoes, quartered
30g (1oz) deep-fried onions (readily available), for garnish
30g (1oz) fresh coriander leaves, chopped (dhania), *for garnish*

For the Baghar (final fry)
4 tablespoons vegetable oil
½ teaspoon mustard seeds (rai)
2 whole dried red chillies
½ teaspoon cumin seeds (zeera)
¼ teaspoon asafoetida (hing)
8 curry leaves (kariyapath)
4 cloves garlic, finely sliced

In a large pan place the two types of gram, the sambhar powder, turmeric and water. Bring to the boil then lower the heat and simmer until the lentils are cooked and all the water has evaporated. Lentils tend to boil over, so keep a watch or leave the pan slightly uncovered.

When the lentils are cooked and most of the water has evaporated, mash them with the back of a wooden spoon. Add the vegetables, tamarind juice, sugar and salt and mix well. Gradually add hot water until

281

Place the red gram, water, turmeric and oil in a large heavy pan and bring to the boil. Simmer until the lentils are soft and mushy. Pass through a sieve and add more hot water to obtain the consistency of a broth.

Meanwhile, dry-roast the spices in a hot frying pan until the mustard seeds crackle. Grind in a food processor or mortar and pestle. Add to the broth, along with all the remaining ingredients and bring back to the boil. Simmer for about 10 minutes to allow all the spices to infuse. Serve hot with all the spices in it, or strain and reheat before serving.

This broth should have a distinctive sour taste, so adjust with lemon juice if necessary.

Sadam (Plain boiled rice)

225g (8oz) patna, long-grain or
  basmati rice
350ml (12fl oz) water
1 teaspoon butter, ghee or oil
½ teaspoon salt

Wash the rice in three or four changes of water or until the water remains clear. Soak the rice in fresh water for about 20 minutes, as this will give a better yield when cooked. Drain the rice thoroughly and place in a pan with a tight-fitting lid. Add the measured water along with the butter, *ghee* or oil and salt. Bring to the boil, immediately reduce the heat to the lowest setting, and cover the pan. Allow to simmer for about 15–20 minutes.

Peep in to see if there are steam holes on the surface of the rice. If there are, the rice is cooked. Turn off the heat, replace the lid and allow the rice

Pacchadi (yogurt salad)

you have the consistency of a thick soup. Simmer until the vegetables are done, about 10 minutes. Add the tomatoes and keep warm.

In a small frying pan heat the oil and fry the *baghar* ingredients until the garlic slices are golden brown. Pour the oil and spices over the lentils and vegetables, and cover the pan to retain the aromas. Garnish with the deep-fried onions and coriander leaves and serve hot.

Rasam (Pepper water)

85g (3oz) red gram (tuvar dhal)
600ml (1 pint) water
½ teaspoon ground turmeric
  (haldi)

2 tablespoons vegetable oil
2 cloves garlic, crushed with the
  skin
6 curry leaves (kariyapath)
4 tablespoons tamarind juice
  (imli pani)
¼ teaspoon asafoetida (hing)
Salt to taste
½ teaspoon sugar
55g (2oz) fresh coriander
  leaves, chopped (dhania)
Ingredients to be dry-roasted
  and ground
10 black peppercorns (kali
  mirch)
1 teaspoon each of cumin seeds
  (zeera), *mustard seeds* (rai)
  and coriander seeds (dhania)
1 dried red chilli (lal mirch), *or*
  2 teaspoons ready-made
  rasam masala *(readily*
  available)

to rest for about 5 minutes before serving.

When serving, remove the rice in sections by pushing a flat spoon right down to the base of the pan instead of scraping it out in layers. Once you have transferred the rice to a serving platter, gently loosen the grains. Serve hot.

Pacchadi (Yogurt salad)

3 firm red tomatoes, chopped
1 small onion, finely chopped
½ small cucumber, finely
  chopped
2 green chillies, finely chopped
¼ teaspoon sugar
30g (1oz) fresh coriander
  leaves, chopped
Salt and chilli powder to taste
425g (15oz) natural yogurt,
  beaten
A few mint leaves, left whole

In a large bowl gently mix all the ingredients except the mint leaves. Chill in the refrigerator and garnish with the mint leaves before serving.

MENU 2: DINING AT HOME IN RESTAURANT STYLE
SERVES 4–6

Murgh tikka (Chicken tikka)
Naan (Leavened bread)
Raitha (Yogurt and cucumber salad)
Gucci pilau (Fragrant rice with mushrooms)
Kalmino patio (Parsee-style king prawn curry)
Balti gosht (Succulent lamb curry)
Tarka dhal (Mildly spiced lentils)
Lassi (Buttermilk drink)

This menu has been designed with the help of the Indian restaurants in the UK who have introduced most of you to Indian cuisine. These are my recipes, which perhaps have a more home-oriented flavour. Restaurant menus often list a hundred or more dishes. They work by preparing batches of basic sauces to which they add the extra ingredients necessary to fulfil individual orders. Restaurant sauces are made in huge cauldrons, so a small error in the amount of a particular ingredient is not usually detectable. Should this happen with a family-size batch, however, the result can be disastrous.

If you still prefer to eat at a restaurant, allow me to guide you on a few points. I find that if you are dining with a party, each person tends to order a dish of his or her choice with either rice or *naan* to accompany it. They then eat only what they have ordered, imagining it to be bad manners to try anyone else's dish. But the real fun is in ordering a selection and sharing it. Try and eat with your fingers if possible (remembering to use only the right hand, as the left is considered unclean). Rice might prove difficult at first but *naan* is easy. Break off small pieces and use them as scoops to lift the food. Someone remarked recently that eating Indian food with cutlery is like making love through an interpreter. Most Indian restaurants offer hot, wet and scented towels for you to clean your hands when you have finished eating.

You will usually have to wait 20 minutes or more before your food arrives. Use the time to nibble on *papadums* or crispy fried pieces of Bombay duck (*bomil* – dried fish – which is an acquired taste), and have something modest to drink, such as a glass of dry wine.

Desserts are not usually served in India, so the selection is often limited. Best is fruit, or try the famous *Kulfi* – Indian ice cream.

Indians generally end their meal with a *paan* – a betel leaf filled with sweet and bitter ingredients folded into a triangular shape and sealed with a clove. We believe it aids digestion and refreshes the mouth. Indian restaurants in Britain offer *paan* only in areas where the Indian population is dense. As a gesture of gratitude, it is customary to raise the fingers of your right hand to the forehead before accepting a *paan*.

Murgh Tikka (Chicken tikka)

4 tablespoons tikka paste
  (readily available)
110g (4oz) natural yogurt
Salt to taste
1 teaspoon sugar
4 chicken breasts, skinned,
  boned and left whole

Mix the tikka paste, yogurt, salt and sugar. Prick the chicken breasts with a fork to tenderise them, then marinate them in the yogurt mixture for about 2 hours. Skewer each breast and grill under medium heat, resting the skewers on the mesh grid. Baste and turn the skewers until the chicken is fully cooked with a few burnt spots, about 30 minutes. Remove, cut into bite-size pieces and serve hot with salad ingredients and *naan*.

If you like, the juices that have collected in the grill tray can be used to prepare a dip. Transfer all the juices to a small pan and bring to the boil with 60ml (2fl oz) water. Cool and fold in 120ml (4fl oz) double cream and 1 teaspoon sugar. Serve in a separate bowl.

283

Naan (Leavened bread)

1 teaspoon sugar
1 sachet dried active yeast
120ml (4fl oz) warm water
*225g (8oz) strong white plain
    flour*
*225g (8oz) white self-raising
    flour*
Salt to taste
*85g (3oz) ghee or unsalted
    butter, melted*
*1 egg beaten with 2 tablespoons
    milk*
*½ teaspoon each of poppy or
    onion seeds and sesame
    seeds, mixed* (khas khas *or*
    kalonji *and* til)
*30g (1oz) fresh coriander
    leaves, chopped* (dhania)

Place the sugar, yeast and water
in a bowl and mix well. Rest
until it turns frothy. Sieve the
flours and salt into a large
mixing bowl. Make a well in the
middle and pour in the yeast
and ghee. Mix together with
your fingers. Grease your palms
and knead the mixture until you
have a soft and pliable dough.
Rest, covered, in a warm place
until the dough has practically
doubled. This takes a few hours
or overnight depending on
temperature.

Divide the mixture into six or
eight portions and roll each on a
floured surface into a circle or
teardrop shape about 5mm
(¼in) thick. Place them on
greased baking trays and brush
them with the egg mixture.
Sprinkle on the seeds and a little
chopped coriander. In a
preheated oven (160°C/325°F,
gas mark 3) bake the *naans* for
about 10 minutes or until they
have puffed up and have brown
spots. Serve immediately.

Naans can be kept warm
wrapped in tinfoil in the oven, or
wrapped in a cloth kitchen towel
and heated in the microwave.
One piece will require 1 minute
on full power.

Raitha (Yogurt and cucumber salad)

225g (8oz) natural set yogurt
Salt and pepper to taste
1 teaspoon sugar
1 tablespoon mint sauce
¼ teaspoon chilli powder (lal
    mirch, *optional*)
*½ teaspoon freshly ground
    cumin* (zeera) *or fennel*
    (sonf)
*½ small cucumber, finely
    chopped*
*30g (1oz) fresh coriander, finely
    chopped* (dhania)

Beat the yogurt with salt,
pepper, sugar, mint sauce, chilli
powder and cumin or fennel
powder. Fold in the cucumber
and fresh coriander. Chill for 2
hours and serve.

Gucci Pilau (Fragrant rice with mushrooms)

*225g (8oz) basmati rice, washed
    and soaked for 20 minutes*
2 tablespoons ghee, butter or oil
*2.5cm (1in) cinnamon quill
    (dalchini)*
4 green cardamoms (choti
    elaichee)
4 cloves (laung)
2 bay leaves (tejpatta)
*½ teaspoon black cumin seeds
    (shahzeera)*
*225g (8oz) tiny button
    mushrooms, washed*
55g (2oz) frozen peas, thawed
*4 tablespoons green masala
    paste (readily available)*
6–8 strands saffron (zafran),
    *soaked in 2 tablespoons
    warm milk*
Salt to taste

350ml (12fl oz) water
*30g (1oz) deep-fried onions
    (readily available), for
    garnish*
30g (1oz) fresh coriander leaves
    (dhania), *for garnish*

Drain the rice and keep aside.
Heat the ghee gently and fry the
cinnamon, cardamoms, cloves,
bay leaves and black cumin
seeds until the cloves swell. Add
the rice and remaining
ingredients, except the garnish,
and mix well. Bring to the boil,
then reduce the heat to a
minimum setting, cover and
cook for about 20 minutes.

Toss well before serving, and
garnish with deep-fried onions
and coriander leaves.

Kalmino Patio (Parsee-style king prawn curry)

*450g (1lb) raw king prawns,
    shelled and de-veined*
2 tablespoons lemon juice
1 onion, chopped
6 cloves garlic, peeled
4 dry red chillies, seeded
*1 teaspoon ground turmeric
    (haldi)*
*1 teaspoon ground cumin
    (zeera)*
2 tablespoons vegetable oil
*4 tablespoons tamarind juice
    (imli pani)*
2 tablespoons demerara sugar
Salt to taste
*30g (1oz) fresh coriander
    leaves, chopped* (dhania)
Mint leaves, for garnish
*1 firm red tomato, chopped, for
    garnish*

Pat dry the prawns and then rub
them with the lemon juice and
keep aside. In a food processor
purée the onion, garlic, chillies,
turmeric and cumin until you
have a smooth paste. Heat the

oil and fry the ground paste until the raw smell disappears and the oil rises above the *masala* or mixture. Add the prawns and the remaining ingredients, except the garnish, and stir-fry on a medium-hot heat until the prawns turn a pinkish-orange colour, about 10 minutes. Garnish with the mint and tomato, and serve hot.

Note If you are unable to obtain raw prawns, use cooked ones but add at the very end, then stir, garnish and serve. To de-vein the raw prawns, make a shallow slit along the back of each and remove the black thread-like vein.

Balti Gosht (Succulent lamb curry)

1 large onion, sliced
2 cloves garlic, crushed
5cm (2in) piece fresh ginger, peeled and crushed
4 green chillies, chopped
2 tablespoons oil
2 tablespoons bhuna masala paste (readily available)
1 teaspoon ground turmeric (haldi)
15g (½oz) dry fenugreek leaves (methi)
1 teaspoon freshly ground cumin (zeera)
450g (1lb) lean lamb, cubed
200g (7oz) tinned chopped tomatoes, drained
Salt to taste
30g (1oz) fresh coriander leaves, chopped (dhania)

Gently heat a frying pan and dry-roast the onion, garlic, ginger and chillies until the onions become soft and slightly brown. When cool, grind them in a food processor until you have a smooth paste. Heat the oil and fry the ground paste, *bhuna*

masala, turmeric and fenugreek leaves until the oil rises above the spices. Add the cumin powder and lamb, and on a high heat fry well for about 2 or 3 minutes. Reduce the heat, cover and allow to simmer until the lamb is nearly done, about 35 minutes. If the gravy is too thick add a small quantity of hot water. Mix in the tomatoes, salt and coriander. Serve hot.

Tarka Dhal (Mildly spiced lentils)

110g (4oz) red gram (tuvar dhal)
55g (2oz) Bengal gram (channa dhal)
350ml (12fl oz) water
1 teaspoon ground turmeric (haldi)
2 whole green chillies
1 onion, sliced
30g (1oz) fresh coriander leaves (dhania)
200g (7oz) tinned chopped tomatoes
Salt to taste
For the Baghar (final fry)
3 tablespoons vegetable oil
½ teaspoon each of mustard (rai) and cumin seeds (zeera)
¼ teaspoon asafoetida (hing)
2 cloves garlic, sliced
6 curry leaves (kariyapath)
2 dried red chillies, seeded

Place the two types of gram, water, turmeric, green chillies, onion and half the coriander in a heavy pan and bring everything to the boil. Then allow to simmer, covered, until the lentils are mushy and all the water has evaporated, about 20 minutes. With the back of a wooden spoon mash the lentils until smooth. Add the tomatoes, remaining coriander leaves and salt and mix well. If too thick,

add a little boiling water to obtain the consistency of tomato soup.

Heat the *baghar* oil in a frying pan and fry all the *baghar* ingredients until the garlic slices are brown. Pour the oil and spices over the lentils and cover immediately. Rest for about 5 minutes, mix well and serve hot.

Sweet Lassi (Buttermilk)

250ml (8fl oz) natural yogurt
350ml (12fl oz) water
4 tablespoons sugar (or to taste)
½ teaspoon freshly ground black pepper
1 teaspoon each of freshly ground cumin (zeera) and fennel (sonf)

Put the yogurt and water in a large bowl, and whisk with an electric whisk until the two ingredients have blended well. Add the remaining ingredients and whisk again for about 2 minutes. Chill and serve.

Savoury Lassi

250ml (8fl oz) natural yogurt
350ml (12fl oz) water
Salt to taste
¼ teaspoon freshly ground black pepper
½ teaspoon freshly ground cumin (zeera)
1 green chilli, finely chopped
1 small onion, finely chopped
A few mint and coriander leaves, finely chopped

Put the yogurt, water, salt, black pepper and cumin in a large bowl and whisk with an electric whisk until all the ingredients have blended well. Add the remaining ingredients and fold in with a fork. Chill and serve. 285

CHAPTER 25

THE STORECUPBOARD

The storecupboard is a very personal piece of territory, a domain that reflects a cook's style as well as the practical demands of an individual's life. Whether the tins you fall back on are filled with baked beans or *foie gras*, everyone needs stores, not only to feed those unexpected guests who populate the pages of cookery books, more frequently perhaps than the lives of their readers, but for everyday use.

A cool, dry walk-in larder is the ideal food storage area. In larder-less modern kitchens, warmer storage conditions will dictate the list of supplies that can be kept without refrigeration.

DRY AND DRIED INGREDIENTS

COFFEE

Instant coffee for flavouring ices, iced drinks, icing and puddings.

DRIED HERBS

Some herbs dry much more successfully than others. Whenever possible, use herbs grown and dried in the sunshine of Provence for their extra sweetness and aroma. Thyme, rosemary, tarragon,and bay are particularly useful.(See also Chapter 24).

DRIED FRUIT

Dried apricots, peaches, apples, and pears and prunes make excellent compotes. Raisins, sultanas and currants are baking basics, together with glacé cherries and candied peel.

DRIED MUSHROOMS

Dried ceps, labelled *porcini* if they are imported from Italy, and morels are two of the best flavoured. They are expensive, but keep for a year or more if stored in an airtight jar, and a very small quantity will perfume a whole dish. Dried shiitake mushrooms are used in Chinese cooking for their meaty flavour.

FLOURS

Plain flour is indispensable for sauces, batters, pastry, and dusting on meat before browning; self-raising flour for cakes. Bread and pasta demand strong flour. All can be white, bleached or unbleached, or brown, containing more or less of the whole wheat grain. Flours made from barley, buckwheat and rye, add variety to breads. Arrowroot, cornflour or cornstarch, and potato flour, also called *farina* and *fécule* are useful for last-minute thickening.

All flours, but especially wholemeal varieties, deteriorate if kept too long. Note the best-before or use-by date on the packaging.

GELATINE

Unflavoured gelatine, in powdered or leaf form, can be used to set aspic as well as fruit-flavoured jellies and mousses.

GRAINS AND MEALS

Couscous, polenta, and bulgar (see Chapter 23) are staples to build meals around. Keep semolina for rolling pasta, as well as for baking and puddings. Oatmeal is a good coating for frying, especially herrings, as well as for porridge and baking. Cornmeal makes an instant coating alternative to breadcrumbs for frying.

INSTANT POTATO

Shop around for a good brand. Flavour instant mash with saffron or with plenty of finely chopped fresh chives to accompany grilled fish or poultry.

MUSTARD POWDER

Strong English mustard is best made freshly from mustard powder. Use it too for breadcrumb and herb coatings for roast rack of lamb.

NUTS AND SEEDS

Shelled nuts, and seeds, are best kept in cool conditions and used by the date shown on the packaging. Off flavours are caused by the fats in them turning rancid. To the usual list of almonds, pecans, walnuts, hazels and pistachios, add pine kernels, for making pesto sauce for pasta, or to toast and sprinkle on salads. Sesame and poppy seeds are used in baking, and caraway seeds for baking and flavouring braised cabbage. Toast sunflower seeds to sprinkle on yogurt or salads.

PASTA

Top quality dried pasta made from durum wheat keeps for more than a year. Spaghetti, cannelloni tubes for stuffing, lasagne sheets and macaroni for baking, and one of the small shapes for soup, make a basic selection. Egg noodles are useful as an accompaniment to meat or poultry.

PULSES

Dried beans, peas and lentils are the basis of innumerable economical and sustaining casseroles and soups (see also Chapter 23).

RICE

Basmati is the most quickly cooked, as well as one of the best-flavoured varieties for general use. Stock arborio for risottos, and round-grain rice for puddings (see also Chapter 23).

SPICES

Whenever possible buy them whole and grind your own. The provident cook takes care not to run out of black and white peppercorns, cloves, cinnamon, vanilla pods and juniper berries (see also Chapter 24).

SUGAR

Caster is the most useful general purpose variety because it can be used for creamed cake mixtures and sprinkling on fruit or cereal as well as for drinks. Coarser grained granulated sugar is a cheaper option for sweetening drinks and making preserves. Keep icing sugar for icing and for *coulis* (see page 84), and brown sugars for general sweetening and extra flavour in baking, confectionery and preserves.

SUN-DRIED TOMATOES

Sun-dried tomatoes have an intense tomato flavour. Add them to casseroles, or soften them in good olive oil and use them on salads or with pasta.

TEA

Traditional scented teas such as Earl Grey and jasmine are useful for soaking dried fruits and making iced drinks.

BOTTLES AND JARS

CAPERS

The immature flower buds of a Mediterranean shrub only develop their astringently peppery flavour when pickled, usually in salt and vinegar. They are sometimes dry salted or preserved in oil. Only pickled capers are available in Britain. Keep them, covered in their pickling liquid, to use in a tartare sauce, and in *tapenade*, the Provençal paste of capers, black olives and anchovies served as an hors d'oeuvre. In traditional English cooking they are used in a sauce for mutton; they are also good with fish.

CHUTNEYS, PICKLES AND RELISHES

Every family has its favourites. Try mixing a little hot lime pickle with mayonnaise for a tuna salad. Dress cold chicken with mayonnaise flavoured with sweet mango chutney. Keep a good dark chutney to eat with cheese.

ESSENCE

Vanilla and almond essences are the two most often used. Look for genuine natural extracts in preference to artificial flavourings. Specialist confectionery suppliers can offer a fascinating selection of flavourings for fondants and ices.

EXTRACTS

Beef and yeast extracts, Bovril and Marmite, can be used as savoury spreads, hot drinks, or to add savour to soups, stews and casseroles.

FLOWER WATER

Use orange-flower water and rosewater to perfume moist cakes, puddings, ices and fruit salads.

HONEY

Not just for tea, highly perfumed honeys flavour ices and make instant desserts spooned over thick yogurt or *fromage frais*. Use honey to sweeten tisanes, salad dressing and fruit compotes.

HORSERADISH

Creamed horseradish is a little less fiery than the plain variety, both sold in jars, and the traditional accompaniment to roast beef. Horseradish, well diluted with cream, goes particularly well with smoked trout, mackerel and eel.

JAM, JELLY AND MARMALADE

The cook's standbys are sieved apricot jam for sticking marzipan on to cakes, and raspberry, redcurrant or strawberry jelly for glazing soft fruit tarts. Redcurrant jelly goes well with lamb, duck or game, and rowan jelly is traditional with game. Marmalade cakes and steamed sponge or suet puddings are really old-fashioned treats.

MAYONNAISE

Pasteurised egg yolk is used in commercially made mayonnaise so it is the safe choice for those who prefer not to take the risk of eating uncooked egg. Find a brand you like and ring the changes on it with fresh herbs, or extra lemon juice, cream or yogurt.

MUSTARD

Whole-grain mustard and French Dijon mustards are used in salad dressings as well as eaten in their own right with grills and roasts.

OIL

Reserve fruity extra virgin olive oil for salad dressings and pasta, and have good but less expensive olive oil for frying. Groundnut oil (also labelled peanut oil or *huile d'arachide*) and grapeseed oil are lighter flavoured oils for deep-frying, and for dressings. Walnut and hazelnut oils are excellent for salad dressings, and need to kept cool after they are opened if they are not to turn rancid.

OLIVES

Olives add flavour to dark stews and casseroles, as well as to salads. Choose varieties with plenty of flavour. Small, black Niçoise olives have a high ratio of stone to flesh, but a particularly fine flavour. Keep them in oil flavoured with Provençal herbs.

SAVOURY SAUCES

Soy sauce has worked its way from oriental to British kitchens as a marvellous flavour enhancer, especially of fish and chicken. Naturally fermented varieties are more subtle. Oyster sauce is useful in Chinese dishes; and *nam pla*, a sauce made from fermented fish, adds authenticity and enormous flavour to any Thai-influenced dish.

Mushroom ketchup and anchovy essence can be used to add depth of flavour to stews, braises and sauces. Worcestershire sauce, tomato ketchup, and fiery Tabasco sauce are used in marinades, stews, braises, and sauces.

Jars of basil-flavoured pesto sauce make an instant meal with pasta. Tomato sauces for pasta can be personalised with fresh herbs and a splash of good olive oil.

TAHINI

Tahini, or sesame paste, flavours *hummus*. In small amounts it is also good in salad dressings.

VINEGAR

Balsamic and sherry vinegars have complex, mellow flavours. Keep them for salad dressings, adding to stews, casseroles and sauces, and for deglazing pan juices to make instant sauces for dry-fried poultry, meat or fish. White and red wine vinegars, and cider vinegar can be used in the same ways, and for making preserves. Vinegars flavoured with fruit or herbs are good for sauces and salad dressings (see page 261). Distilled malt vinegar is used mainly for preserving.

YEAST
For an impromptu loaf or pizza, keep a tin or packet of granular dried yeast, or easy-blend yeast. Use by the date shown on the packaging.

TINS

ANCHOVIES
Salted anchovies in olive oil are indispensable for pizza, salad Niçoise, and can be mashed in warm olive oil as a sauce for pasta or grilled vegetables. Slivers of anchovy sandwiched in offcuts of puff pastry go well with a glass of dry sherry or white wine.

CORNED BEEF
Corned beef hash makes a quickly prepared meal.

FRUIT
Tinned peaches and apricots are so different from the fresh fruits as to be an ingredient in their own right. Drain halves of fruit, fill the cups left by the stones with brown sugar, butter and cinnamon, and grill them until hot.

HAM
Keep a small tin of good ham and you can always make a quiche, or ham omelette.

PULSES
The increasing variety of beans and lentils now sold in tins can be called upon for casseroles and salads when there is no time to soak and cook dried pulses. Keep chickpeas to make *hummus*, the Greek dip flavoured with garlic and *tahini*, sesame paste.

SARDINES
Good sardines packed in olive oil can be mashed into an instant pâté, or spread on toast, and grilled as a snack or savoury.

TOMATOES
Whole or chopped, skinned, tinned tomatoes can be be used in sauces for pasta, pizza toppings, stews and casseroles, soups and sauces.

Small tins of concentrated tomato paste give a more intense flavour without adding extra liquid.

TUNA
Top quality tuna canned in olive oil is a delicacy in its own right, and the best variety for salads. Tuna canned in other vegetable oils or brine can be used in salads, flans and pasta sauces.

MISCELLANEOUS

CHOCOLATE
Top quality dark chocolate (see also Chapter 13) gives the best flavour to mousses, ices, baking and sauces. Keep it cool.

STOCK CUBES
Chicken, beef, fish and vegetable stock cubes must be kept dry. Used sparingly, they are a standby for soups, stews, and casseroles when there is no time to make stock.

UHT MILK AND CREAM
Longlife milk and cream can be used in soups, sauces and baking. Once opened, treat as fresh.

VINE LEAVES
Packets of brined vine leaves can be used as wrappings for stuffings such as goat's cheese, or to protect delicate fish and poultry from the fierce heat of the grill.

CHAPTER 26

WINE

by JOANNA SIMON

The amount of enjoyment you draw from a bottle of wine is up to you. You can regard it as a mere lubricant, an unheeded backdrop, like background music, for more important things, or you can take notice of it, think about it, savour it, really take pleasure from it. You don't need to go in for the full-blown chewing, sucking and spitting rite of the working wine-taster, but you do need to do a little more than merely swig and swallow.

Start by glancing at the colour: tip the glass at a 45-degree angle against something white and look down on the surface, especially near the rim, to see if it tells you anything about the wine's age, provenance or grape variety (see Colour Code, page 292). Then give a quick twirl of your glass so that the wine swirls and releases its volatile aromas. With nose in or at the top of the glass, sniff decisively and then take a reasonable-sized sip. Savour the flavours and textures in your mouth as well as the taste that lingers after you've swallowed (the 'aftertaste'). The whole procedure will be over in a minute and the outward display will have been minimal, but you will have derived a great deal more from one mouthful than you would have done if you had swallowed a whole glass without any thought.

When tasting is done as a prerequisite to buying, it takes on a slightly different function and some additional elements, because the aim is to compare several wines (whether twelve Chardonnays or a mishmash of styles from Italy) in order to pick those you think best – most tasty, best value, or perhaps having the most potential.

This is where the chewing, sucking and slurping comes in. It quite simply amplifies the various smells and flavours – but you have to be prepared to feel silly at first.

Take a sip of wine, roll it round your mouth to make sure it reaches all the tastebuds, particularly the sensitive ones on either side at the back of the tongue, and then open your lips a fraction and draw in some air (yes, the noise is you). This aerates the wine (in the same way as that preliminary twirl of the glass) and sends the volatile compounds up from the back of your mouth to your nose – or, to be precise, to your olfactory bulb, a much more perceptive and discriminating organ than your tongue. This enables you to taste the wine – nose and tongue working as a team.

Tastebuds on their own, despite their name, don't perceive many actual flavours (pinch your nostrils shut and you will see what I mean), but they do perceive some of the non-volatile elements such as sugar and tannin. Thus the tongue detects sweetness, especially at its tip, sharpness, especially at the sides, and bitterness, especially at the back. The tongue also 'feels' the wine: it senses its astringency, roughness or harshness, and smoothness; it gauges its 'weight' (light, medium or full-bodied), through the alcohol, glycerol, tannin, sugar and all the other non-water elements that together are known as 'extract'; it feels the 'length' of the wine – the length of time the flavours last; and it plays a key role in perceiving the 'balance' – the harmony, or not, of sugar, acid, tannin and alcohol levels.

The final stage in the serious tasting routine is of course spitting. Disgusting as it sounds, bizarre as it looks, it is polite – indeed essential – to spit at wine tastings. (The non-spitter is the one with the beaming smile and rosy glow buying more than he or she intended of wines that will appear less wonderful in the cold light of the next day's slight hangover and next month's bank statement.) Spitting is also easy: all you have to remember is that you do it every day cleaning your teeth. By all means put in some practice, but rest assured that there is no virtue in being able to spit from great distances. Bearing in mind that not everyone is aim-perfect, don't wear your best cream silk or primrose shoes to wine tastings, and, on a similar practical note, if you are standing rather than sitting, hold on to, or pin back, ties, scarves, necklaces, long hair etc. Finally, go easy on the pongy scent or aftershave, if only for the sake of other tasters, and, for the same reason, never smoke.

Having mastered the mechanics, you come to the taste itself – and immediately understand why wine tasters so often resort to a basketful of fruit and vegetable comparisons. With the exception of wines made from the Muscat grape, very few wines smell or taste of grapes. And yet they do smell fruity. In fact, if it didn't sound so daft you would say there was a distinct whiff of blackcurrants . . . or raspberries, strawberries, gooseberries, apricots. . . . It may appear pretentious, but it isn't. Apart from the fact that you and your brain are quite at liberty to interpret an aroma from wine in any way you like – apricots, carnations, carpet or condoms – science is on your side.

As well as the alcohols, esters and acids that account for most of the aromatic content in wine, around 500 other volatile compounds have been identified. These are derived from the grapes themselves, the production process (especially fermentation) and changes that occur with age. Each grape variety has its own combination of such compounds and therefore its own aromatic personality, and the environmental conditions of each vineyard then exert a further influence. Thus wine from the Sauvignon Blanc grape may be gooseberry-like, rather more like new-mown hay, or more asparagus flavoured.

The scientifically minded might like to know that it is the combination of fatty acids that are often responsible for the grassy smells in Sauvignon and other wines, that pyrazines give Cabernet Sauvignon its green pepper aromas, that terpenes make Muscat grapey, that ionones give floral aromas and that the hundreds of esters yield a multitude of fruit aromas. I could, in fact, list the compounds that give aromas of honey, butter, caramel, coconut, carnations, celery, *sauerkraut*, garlic, goat, mouse, horse sweat or horse urine and many others. I shan't, but you should now feel less inhibited and more confident about your own tasting abilities and the notes you make. The crux is that your tasting notes or memories mean something to you: don't fall into the trap of writing gooseberry and grass because it sounds right, if the wine actually reminds you of garlic and goat – but do use my Aroma Code (see page 292) as a prompt.

With your olfactory bulb in the right frame of mind, you are ready to face the fact that wine is a complex animal, made so by hundreds of chemical compounds. While some wines taste very distinctly of, say, blackcurrants and mint, most are less obvious. The finer the wine the more subtle and complex its smell and flavours, and the older it is the less distinct many of the fruit flavours become. Even so, you should always feel that there is fruit at the heart, although it may be mellow and autumnal – more plumped-up, spiced, dried fruits than juicy, fresh youthful fruit.

In most cases you should also feel that the smell is appealing – but there are some significant exceptions, particularly among old wines, just as there are some ferociously smelly, but sumptuously tasty cheeses. Mature red burgundies can pong of pigsties and decay; claret can be mushroomy; you still find the occasional old-style Australian Hunter Valley Shiraz with a 'sweaty saddle' smell; and among young wines the smell of cat's pee is ascribed to both Müller-Thurgau and Sauvignon.

Differentiating between a strange smelling wine and one that is off can be difficult. If you can't sniff out any pleasant aromas at all then the wine is probably bad and will taste so. With an old wine, if you sense that, however strong the pong, there is an underlying richness (as in a 291 smelly cheese), that is a positive sign. And with a young cat's pee white, you should feel that the overall smell (sometimes called the bouquet, but perhaps inapt in this case) is crisp and fresh rather than stale.

The other way to tackle the 'off' dilemma is to run through a checklist of no-hopers: vinegary aromas; a strong sherry-like smell; a dank, musty, mouldy stink that doesn't diminish at all, meaning the wine is corked (if the smell begins to clear when the wine is swirled in the glass, it is harmless 'bottle stink' – stale air trapped between wine and cork that soon disappears); strong sulphurous smells like struck matches, bad eggs, or burnt rubber.

You can also use your eyes. Begin by sizing up any foreign bodies. Bits of cork are harmless (they do not mean the wine is corked), as are small glass-like crystals (tartrate deposits) and bitty or muddy sediment in red wine, although the latter should certainly not have been poured into your glass. Bad signs are hazy or cloudy white wine, often allied to a vinegary nose; and, usually with a stale, sherry-like (oxidised) smell, brownish-yellow tinges, indicating that the wine is too old. Vinegary red wines may not be apparent from the colour, but past-their-best, oxidising reds will be pale brick-tawny, especially at the rim.

Finally, if a wine looks and smells satisfactory, but then seems to taste horrible, the chances are that the acidity, sugar or tannin and acid levels are not as you were expecting. It may be that it is not the style of wine you would like – too sweet, too dry, too big and tannic. But it may also be that the wine is too young and that key components need to mellow and harmonise. High tannin in red wines and high acid in whites are actually essential if the wines are to be laid down. That's not much consolation if you opened the bottle to drink tonight – but now you know you could always buy another to lay down.

COLOUR CODE

Age: white wines start pale and go darker, more yellow and eventually brown with age; red wines do the reverse. They start dark, with purple tints, and become paler, going from ruby to brick to over-the-hill tawny.

Climate: cool regions tend to produce paler wines – both white and red. German whites may be almost colourless, hinting at green, when young. Although warm climates give deeper colours, a strong yellow could also mean a good Sauternes or a cool climate dry white that is past its best (smell should tell you in both cases).

Grape variety: Cabernet Sauvignon, Syrah and Nebbiolo produce very deep purple-red wines, but Nebbiolo loses its purple and becomes garnet-brick more quickly. Pinot Noir gives relatively pale, never very purple wines.

Production process: ageing in oak makes white wines yellower; and red wines paler if prolonged – red Rioja is an example.

AROMA CODE

Almond: usually Italian, e.g. Soave and Valpolicella.

Apple: many whites – when particularly aromatic, may be German Riesling.

Apricot: Condrieu and other Viogniers.

Asparagus: Sauvignon Blanc, especially Californian Fumé.

Banana: young inexpensive whites and Beaujolais.

Biscuit: Champagne.

Blackcurrant: Cabernet Sauvignon, including claret.

Bread: Champagne.

Butter: oak-aged Chardonnay, including Burgundy.

Cat's pee: Sauvignon Blanc and Müller-Thurgau.

Cedar or Cigar box: claret.

Cherry: Burgundy, Beaujolais and many Italian reds.

Chocolate: many good reds, often young.

Eucalyptus: New World Cabernet, some claret, some Shiraz.

Game: mature Hermitage, Shiraz, red Burgundy.

Grape: Muscat.

Grass: Sauvignon Blanc, e.g. Sancerre and New Zealand.

Green pepper: Cabernet Sauvignon and Cabernet Franc, e.g. Chinon and Bourgueil.

Gooseberry: Sauvignon Blanc.

Honey: sweet wines, but also dry Chardonnay and Sémillon.

Lemon: many young whites.

Licorice: reds, often young and fairly full.

Lime: Australian Riesling.

Lychees: Gewürztraminer.

Mint: Cabernet Sauvignon and some Shiraz, especially New World.

Nut (hazel or walnut): white Burgundy, Champagne, other Chardonnays.

Oak: any wine fermented and/or aged in oak, e.g. Rioja and many Chardonnays.

Pears/peardrops: young whites, often Italian.

Pepper (freshly ground): Châteauneuf-du-Pape, Côtes-du-Rhône, dry white Austrian Grüner Veltliner.

Petrol: mature German Riesling.

Plums: many reds, e.g. Burgundy.

Raspberry: red Burgundy, red Loires, Châteauneuf-du-Pape, Beaujolais.

Rose: dry Alsace Muscat, Barolo.

Smoke: full-bodied reds (especially Syrah), Pouilly-Fumé, Alsace Pinot Gris.

Spice: many reds, e.g. Rhône and Shiraz, and Alsace whites.

Strawberry: Beaujolais, red Rioja, red Burgundy.

Tar: Barolo.

Tobacco: many reds, especially claret.

Toast: Blanc de Blancs Champagne and any wine that has been in new oak barrels (especially Chardonnay).

Vanilla: any wine that has been in oak, especially American oak, e.g. Rioja.

OLD OR NEW?

Little more than a dozen years ago, choosing a bottle of wine in Britain was a simple business. There were the French classics – the names everybody knew, led by claret, Burgundy and Champagne – and then the rest. If you decided to learn about wine, you needed only to address yourself to French wines, with a passing nod to the hocks (Rhines) and Mosels of Germany.

You didn't have to bother with Italian, Spanish, Portuguese, Hungarian, Yugoslavian or Austrian wines – they were all essentially plonk or household brands (often one and the same). Nor did you need to consider Californian wines: they were either plonk in carafes or avant garde, esoteric little numbers referred to as 'boutique'

wines. Australian wines, so far as they existed in the UK, were almost invariably marketed with joky names such as Kanga Rouge and Wallaby White. Bulgarian wines had still to make an impact in 1980. South African wines were mostly fortified 'sherry' types, and countries such as New Zealand and Chile might as well have been on another planet.

Nowadays high-street shelves groan with bottles from all these countries – alongside wine from Argentina, Canada, China, Slovakia, India, Israel, Lebanon, Oregon and Romania. In theory this ought to have made wine an extraordinarily complicated subject, but in one crucial way the newcomers have actually simplified it. They have given us varietals – wines made from, and named after, single grape varieties such as Chardonnay. This turned out to be a clever marketing device, but it emerged simply because the new producers took as their models the classic French wines – and then took as their starting point the individual grape varieties. They planted Chardonnay if they wanted to make a white Burgundy style; Cabernet Sauvignon if they wanted 'claret'. They then equipped their wineries with all the latest machines and started making wine, paying scant attention to climate – just so long as it was mild, sunny and not too wet – and even less attention to soil type.

To start with the grape variety might seem unexceptional, but it was, and is, quite different from the French approach. The French believe unswervingly in the supremacy of *terroir* - the complete package of soil and sub-structure, climate, slope and altitude peculiar to each particular site. And it is not the grower but the *terroir*, as represented in the regulations of each *appellation contrôlée*, that governs the grape varieties of a French wine (so much so that it is strictly forbidden to grow, say, Chardonnay in Bordeaux or Cabernet in Burgundy).

In the new wine world, growers still plant what they like where they like, but the mood in recent years has changed to a more French way of thinking. There is still a lot of scepticism about the potential of minerals and microbes in soil to influence the taste of the wine which comes from it, but there is a great deal of searching after perfect, cooler 'microclimates' – the new world 293 word for the particular climatic and environmental conditions of a specific site, and not unlike the concept of *terroir*.

The result is two worlds of wine – the great French classics and their modern counterparts – both equally valid, but still interestingly different and entirely complementary. This is how the best of them compare:

RED BORDEAUX

Red Bordeaux – claret to the British – is the most copied red wine of all, although it is seldom as closely copied as the other classics for the simple reason that it is made from a blend of grapes – Cabernet Sauvignon, Merlot, Cabernet Franc and occasionally one or two others. It is these that give the best wines their deep colour and special taste: a complex mixture of blackcurrants, green pepper, cigar boxes, cedar, sandalwood, lead pencils and, in young wines, new oak; with shades of dark chocolate, tobacco-leaf, mint, minerals and green olive sometimes not far behind; and hints of woodland undergrowth and dried fruit compote in the old wines.

The new producers did not see the point in planting and blending more than one variety, so they mostly opted for the aristocratic Cabernet Sauvignon, which predominates in most of the illustrious French châteaux from Lafite, Latour, Mouton and Margaux downwards (the Merlot-dominated exceptions are all in Pomerol and St-Emilion). Very generally, the result is simpler-tasting wines, with riper, more intense blackcurrant flavours (enhanced by the warmer climates) and often a more obvious vanilla or coconutty oak character (from the new oak barrels used to mature the wine). Mint is often a distinctive flavour, particularly in Australian Cabernets, while in some Californians there is a suggestion of eucalyptus. Californian Cabernets also tend to be rather tannic and tough.

Good Bulgarian Cabernets often have an attractive spice-and-tobacco character, whereas New Zealand Cabernets often show their cooler climate origins in fresh, more herbaceous flavours. The best Chilean Cabernets have deep, scented cassis fruit married with oak. Burgeoning Hungarian and Romanian Cabernets are ones to watch, as are *Vins de Pays* from the vast Languedoc-Roussillon area. In northern Italy, both Cabernet and Merlot tend to be lightweight and herbaceous, but Tuscany produces some richer, more exciting wines and there are also good, full-bodied Cabernets from the Penedés in Spain.

Merlot on its own, mainly grown in Chile and California, produces a wine that is quite similar to Cabernet, but softer and juicier.

RED BURGUNDY

While Cabernet Sauvignon has happily put down roots nearly everywhere, the Pinot Noir grape has frustrated most attempts to reproduce it outside its native Burgundy. It is one of the wine world's fussiest varieties. It doesn't like the heat and it doesn't like the cold and most of the new climates were too warm for it. The result was stewed, jammy flavours instead of Burgundy's heady scents, breathtaking fruit, velvety textures and strange, decaying richness. In recent years, however, the Californians have been discovering some ideal spots, particularly those cooled by sea breezes. Carneros, Santa Barbara County and Russian River have all come up trumps.

Outside California, regions such as Oregon (US), Yarra (Australia), Martinborough (New Zealand) and Walker Bay (South Africa) have also begun to produce impressive results. In the Old World, warm years give fairly light, but appealing results in Alsace, Sancerre and, in very limited quantity, Germany.

WHITE BURGUNDY

The white grape of Burgundy, Chardonnay, is as easy to handle as Pinot Noir is difficult, which is why Chardonnay is now being cultivated in almost every wine-producing country. Considering the full and fruity character of most Chardonnay wines, it is surprising to learn that it is not a variety with a strong personality. Yet that is its virtue: it gives wine-makers numerous options. It can be packed with tropical fruit flavours, with or without oak, buttery or nutty, or with some of the distinctive Burgundian vegetal character. The lean, dry, savoury Chablis style is the only one so far to have evaded the new wine world.

Which style the wine-maker chooses is usually a question of cost, related to his intended market, more than a question of regional or national style. To get the complex, creamy, nutty flavours of fine Burgundy, he needs not only to mature the wine in very expensive, small, new French oak barrels and leave it there on its lees (yeasty sediment which gives flavour), he must also ferment it in these barrels rather than in gigantic, easily monitored and maintained stainless steel tanks. Nonetheless, many Californian producers do make these investments in oak and time, as do top producers in Australia, New Zealand and South Africa. American oak is a useful, cheaper, less subtly-flavoured alternative; oak chips are cheaper again. These are suspended in stainless steel tanks of wine to give a tasty dash of oak to cheaper Australian Chardonnays.

Chilean Chardonnays improve every year and, in the Old World, there are good examples in Spain, Italy and among French *Vins de Pays*.

SANCERRE AND POUILLY FUME

If ever there was a grape with a strong personality, it is the Sauvignon Blanc of Sancerre and Pouilly Fumé. Lean, green and grassy with an appetising, crunchy gooseberry flavour at best, it tastes of tinned asparagus/peas/beans at worst. It is not as difficult to satisfy as Pinot Noir, but it does need the right climate – cool, but not so cool that the wine is aggressively tart. It doesn't like to be moulded and manipulated by the winemaker and seldom takes well to oak.

The California style of Sauvignon, or Fumé, is rather heavy, and Australia seldom does well with the variety, but New Zealand, particularly around Marlborough, makes stunning wines. South Africa and Chile are beginning to produce some attractive, inexpensive, if not very intensely flavoured versions. Back in France, the Sauvignons of Haut-Poitou are very satisfying, as are the best of Touraine, Bergerac and Côtes de Duras.

CHAMPAGNE

As if Chardonnay did not contribute enough to the wine world, it is also one of the three main constituents of Champagne, alongside Pinot Noir and the less refined Pinot Meunier. Because it is easy to handle, Chardonnay is the variety most favoured by Champagne's imitators in California,

Australia, New Zealand and even India, although the serious copyists don't stint on Pinot Noir. No-one overseas has yet matched a really great Champagne, but there is plenty, especially from Australia, now challenging the dismal lower echelons of Champagne – and at keen prices. The Champenois steadfastly maintain that it is not enough to reproduce, in a similar cool climate, the Champagne method (in which the wine ferments for a second time – hence the bubbles – and matures with the flavour-giving lees in the bottle). Their unusual chalk soil is critical, too, and will hold them aloft, they say, though occasionally I have my doubts. It may be New Zealand that catches them out.

In the Old World, Crémant de Bourgogne, Saumur, Vouvray and the best Spanish Cavas are worth considering.

STORING AND BUYING

Drinking wine out of a paper cup will do nothing to enhance its bouquet and flavours, but it won't actually harm it. Storing wine badly will. That doesn't mean a traditional purpose-built cellar is an absolute prerequisite to laying wine down, but you do need to know the optimum conditions and how far your circumstances meet them.

The ideal cellar has a constant cool temperature (about 45–55°C/7–13°F). It is dark, damp (about 55–70 per cent humidity), free of vibration and equipped with racks or bins for holding bottles horizontally.

● In practice you can get away with a temperature up to 20°C (68°F), so long as the temperature is *steady*, and so long as you bear in mind, when referring to vintage charts, that your wines will mature more quickly.

● Ultra-violet light and sunlight spoil wine quickly (although dark glass bottles offer some protection), but it is a simple matter to cover exposed bottles with a blanket.

● The main role of humidity is to stop the cork drying out and letting air in, but laying bottles horizontally helps prevent this. Kitchens, though often humid, are usually too warm.

● Constant shaking is bad for wine, but ordinary city household noise and vibrations are fine. *Persistent* and *heavy* vibrations from traffic or trains

295

could be problematic.

Many people find that their understairs cupboard is just about cool enough all year to store wine in, but if you don't have one, or if yours (like mine) is too warm or variable, look for nooks and crannies such as disused fireplaces, especially along north-facing walls. If you choose an unheated spare room, remember that occasionally heating it to 21°C (70°F) is not good for wine, and bear in mind that temperatures in garages, lofts and outside loos tend to fluctuate because of poor insulation.

If you cannot find a suitable spot at home, and you buy wine by the case for laying down, buy from a wine merchant who will store it (for an annual fee). Commercial cellars (as opposed to wine merchants) in which private individuals can rent space are rare, but worth looking out for. Alternatively, there are some expensive home options: purpose-made temperature-controlled wine cabinets, rather like fridges, that come in various sizes from about 50 bottles (normal fridge-size) to 500; and the Spiral Cellar, a 2-metre diameter, 2–3-metre depth, cylindrical cellar, with a spiral staircase, that you can dig into a convenient ground floor.

If you cannot store wine in reasonable conditions, it really is better not to try. Enjoy, instead, buying your supplies on a little and often basis.

For those who have cellar conditions, these are points to consider when choosing wines to lay down.

● The wine has to be good and have been made to mature. Cheap wines are not made to be kept and, while some wines at about £5 will keep well for more than 2 or 3 years, most will not. As a very rough guide, you should probably think in terms of £7 per bottle minimum for a wine that will improve over more than 5 years. (That doesn't mean, of course, that all wines costing over £7 are made to be laid down.)

● Far more red wines are made to mature than whites, and reds generally last longer. Among whites, good German Riesling, fine sweet wines such as Sauternes and Loires, and top white Burgundies last many years.

● Despite the impressive quality and flavour of many New World wines, the wines with a proven cellaring track record are still almost entirely the great European classics – claret, Burgundy, northern Rhônes such as Hermitage, Barolo, port, vintage Champagne and the whites mentioned above. Some Australian Shiraz-based wines and Hunter Valley Sémillon, and some California Cabernets and Zinfandels, do age well.

● Only lay down good vintages. Indifferent ones (like 1984 and 1987 for claret) will not have the ageing potential. It is worth remembering that 1988, 1989 and 1990 were an exceptional trio of fine vintages in most of the classic French regions, and also in Germany, where 1991 was also good. 1989 and 1990 were good for Barolo, 1988 and 1990 for Tuscan wines, and 1991 for vintage port.

● Some regions, particularly in Spain and Portugal, mature their wines and release them when they are ready for drinking.

● We tend to talk about a wine's peak, but the peak is, in fact, a plateau of optimum maturity which means that you have an extended period during which to enjoy it at its best. The better the wine the longer the plateau (and the slower the decline).

● Choosing highly regarded producers and estates is as critical as getting the right vintage. Poor wine-makers make disappointing wines even in splendid years (probably more true of Burgundy than anywhere else).

● If you think it is possible that you may want to sell any of your wine in the future, you must buy and keep in dozens and you should stick to recognised top names.

PART THREE
THE PRACTICAL KITCHEN

CHAPTER 27

FOOD HYGIENE AND SAFETY

gainst the backdrop of food-poisoning scares, it is no easy thing to find a middle course between neurotic preoccupation with safety and old-fashioned common sense. Some people fear they take their lives in their hands every time they approach a raw egg, or minced beef, or cold chicken, or unpasteurised soft cheese.

None of this is surprising, given the publicity surrounding the salmonella-in-eggs-and-chickens fright, listeria in chilled foods and soft cheeses, botulism in hazelnut yogurt and the nightmare threat of BSE, the so-called mad cow disease. On the whole, however, food poisoning is extremely rare and most of us approach the matter of kitchen hygiene in a strangely haphazard fashion. Obviously it would be better to know what the real dangers are, and then perhaps disregard them as a calculated risk, than to carry on in ignorance.

You should be particularly concerned if your household contains babies, infants under two, pregnant women, invalids or elderly people. All these groups have weaker immune systems than normal healthy adults and are more susceptible to illnesses caused by poor hygiene.

THE BACTERIA

If you remember to wash your hands, keep your knives and chopping boards well scrubbed, put clean tea towels out *every day*, and keep cooked foods away from uncooked, then you should not have to worry too much about bacteria. The four

things that bacteria need in order to multiply are food, moisture, warmth, and time. To avoid risk, food should be kept either hot (minimum 63°C/145°F) or cold (under 5°C/41°F), and should never be left lying around at room temperature. About 1½ hours is the maximum time that *any* dish should be left at room temperature. Hence the joke among environmental health inspectors that the best way to get a stomach upset is to go to a summer wedding.

Jill Rowley, a food hygiene consultant at Leith's School of Food and Wine, admits that the 1½-hour rule makes a mockery of the poached salmon slowly cooling in its cooking liquid, and of the professional cook's stock pot. But at least home cooks are not bound by commercial regulations and can make their own decisions about how strict they want to be.

LISTERIA

This is present in all sorts of places. Normal healthy people can carry it without knowing. Unpasteurised milk, soft cheese, pre-cooked chicken and pâté are all potential breeding grounds, as is soft-whip ice cream from machines that aren't properly maintained and cleaned. Hard cheese, processed soft cheese and manufactured block ice cream are considered safe.

SALMONELLA

Infection is often caused by food not being cooked properly (to a minimum 70°C/158°F throughout), or by cross contamination. You only have to cut some pre-cooked or uncooked food with a knife that has already chopped raw meat, or put it on a board where you have done the same. The bacteria from the raw meat will transfer. This is why commercial kitchens often have colour-coded knives and chopping boards.

BOTULISM
This is very nasty but also very rare. It results usually from damaged food containers, or food that has not been properly reheated. If you avoid dented cans or vacuum packs which have blown, you should be all right. A 10-minute blast at 80°C (176°F) kills the toxin.

STAPHYLOCOCCUS AUREUS
This lurks in wounds and the human nose, and in saliva. Thus it is important always to keep cuts covered with dressings, to wash your hands and wash any spoons that you have dipped into food for tasting.

BACILLUS CEREUS
Something few people may have heard of, but it thrives in boiled rice that is left too long at room temperature. For this reason it can often be found in fried rice – which, after all, is only old rice that has been given a short acquaintance with the frying pan, too short sometimes to kill bacteria.

BUYING THE FOOD
Even at the supermarket you can be thinking about safety. All the large foodstores are now required by law to provide 'Use by' and 'Best before' dates so that you can buy according to your planned weekly menu. Don't keep food beyond the dates given. Freezer food is labelled with stars (one star usually means it keeps for a week, two means a month, three means three months) though ice cream is different (one star usually means a freezer life of a day, two stars gives it a week, and three stars means a month). Old ice cream loses its texture and develops gritty crystals, though this doesn't mean it is unsafe to eat.

Supermarkets really ought to put all the chilled and frozen foods at the ends of the aisles nearest to the check-outs. These items should always be picked up last, so that they have less time to warm through or melt as you stand in the checkout queue.

Pack all the frozen and chilled foods in the same bag so that they help keep each other cold on the way home. If you have a long journey, or if it is a very hot day, then a cool-bag with ice-blocks in it will make a good portable fridge.

Microbiologists say that a single salmonella cell in chilled food can multiply to a million cells if left in a warm car for 3-4 hours.

AT HOME
Most of the perishable food you buy in supermarkets will have been kept according to strict, temperature-controlled regimes designed to keep it fresh and prevent contamination. It is when you get it home and unwrap it that the dangers *really* begin to multiply.

PESTS
The kitchen is a gastronomic wonderland not just for its human owners but also for a whole host of winged and other pests attracted by food and warmth. No-one should tolerate mice in the kitchen, though they're often easier to spot and deal with than that other nocturnal scourge, the cockroach. There's no mistaking a cockroach if you see one – like a sort of flattened grasshopper without the jumping legs – but the trouble is they hide during the daytime, and the first warning you may have of infestation is the smell they give to contaminated food.

All insects should be discouraged from the kitchen: bluebottles and houseflies, like cockroaches, can carry human diseases. The scientific name of one of the most common varieties of bluebottle, *Calliphora vomitoria* (the other is *C.vicina*), offers a fair summary of its character. What it's looking for as it comes buzzing in through the window is a nice juicy bit of meat to lay its eggs in. The common housefly, *Musca domestica*, feeds by partially liquefying its food – *your* food – with saliva, which it then sucks back up into its mouth. Often as it does this it regurgitates part of its previous meal – a particularly efficient way of passing on germs to human diners. As it is attracted as much by dirt as by sweetness, 299 its feet are none too wholesome either.

The only way to avoid this is scrupulous attention to hygiene. *Always* keep food covered. *Never* leave scraps lying around. *Always* wipe away spills.

THE REFRIGERATOR

The fridge is our greatest weapon against food going off. To get real control of the thing, however, you need a proper fridge thermometer, which should always show a reading of below 5°C (41°F). Most of us otherwise have no idea how cold our fridges really are. Once the temperature is down below 5°C (41°F), the bacteria in most foods will multiply only very slowly. Listeria is harder to combat than most, and will let rip even at a modest 10°C (50°F).

COOKED MEATS AND LEFTOVERS

It is important to cool leftovers as quickly as possible, remembering the 1½-hour rule. While they are cooling, cover them with cling film, or another dish, or one of those lovely old-fashioned wire domes.

The bottom shelf, where the fridge is coldest, should be reserved for raw meat. Put it on a flat plate so that it cannot drip and contaminate anything else. Cooked meats should always be kept away from raw, preferably on a higher shelf.

The colder your fridge, the more water is lost – so if you don't want the food to dry out or the flavours to travel from one dish to another, they should be well wrapped.

EGGS

Before we all stopped eating eggs and then started eating them again, people used to keep them quite happily in straw baskets in their kitchens without any fear of salmonella. They do have their own most elegant packaging, coated with a natural oily preservative. This protective film is damaged by water so it is always important to keep eggs dry, even if they are crusted with straw and dung and look as if they need a good wash. The fridge is the best place for them, and Moira Bremner in *Supertips* suggests that they should rest with the pointed end down so that the yolk will rise to the top instead of languishing in the air sac at the bottom.

What to do with cracked or damaged eggs? You might think there would be no harm in using a newly damaged egg in a cake, where it would be subjected to high heat for long enough to kill the bacteria, but the current wisdom is quite simply that you should never use any cracked or damaged egg at all.

CHEESE

This is where the tensions between gastronomy and hygiene are at their greatest. Cheese has a much better flavour if it isn't stored in the fridge. In former times it would have been wrapped in a vinegar-soaked cloth and stored in a cool larder. But the fridge these days is usually the obvious place for it, and the best compromise is to get it out at least 2-3 hours before eating it so that the flavour can grow. Whole rounds should be turned so that they don't develop soggy bottoms.

THE CAT

It may be nice for it to curl up in the kitchen, but there is the risk of Toxoplasmosis in the faeces and the litter which spreads to vegetables and undercooked or raw meat. Keep the beast off the kitchen surfaces, and make sure you wash your hands and the vegetables before handling.

POTATOES

Once they start to turn green and grow whiskers it is time to say goodbye. The Food Safety Advisory Centre says it is no good just cutting off the green bits: the toxin solanine builds up throughout the potato.

WRAPPINGS

Cling film is wonderful stuff, but it really shouldn't come into direct contact with food, particularly if the food has a high fat content. Its magic lies in its molecules – they are coiled and kinked so that when they are stretched apart all they want to do is snap back again. Hence the elasticity. It also carries a static electrical charge which means that the lips of bowls and saucers are attracted to it. The fear is that some of the plasticisers in the cling film are somehow transferred to fatty foods. It is always best to put food in a bowl or other container first, then put on a cling-film 'lid'.

CHAPTER 28

KITCHEN EQUIPMENT

Cooking can be one of the greatest pleasures in life, but it can also be rather a chore without the right equipment. The following listings probably don't enumerate every last gadget available in cookshops, but they will form a practical guide to things that are vital in every kitchen, others that are useful, and those unashamed 'luxuries' – pieces of equipment that you can manage quite well without, but which are good if you have the space for them, the money to spend on them and, in some cases, the specialist culinary knowledge and interest to use them.

The most basic needs are a good cooker, or oven and stove top, and a refrigerator, with or without a freezer. Water is important in the kitchen, and ideally the most efficient kitchen displays a logical sequence in storing, preparing, washing, cooking and serving of food.

MISCELLANEOUS HAND TOOLS

VITAL

- Can opener
- Bottle opener
- Corkscrew
- Wooden spoons of various sizes
- Perforated spoon
- Slotted metal fish slice
- Deep large ladle
- Long rolling pin
- Nutcracker
- Pepper mill

USEFUL

- Large plain metal spoon
- Tongs (scissor types are better)
- Small ladles
- Skimmers
- Wooden fork and spatula
- Flexible scrapers and rubber spatulas (a heavy duty one is good for making things like fondant)
- Pastry brush
- Salt mill
- Wire salad basket

LUXURY

- Marble slab
- Spaghetti tongs
- Ice cream scoop
- Steak hammer/tenderiser
- Pastry blender
- Pastry wheel or cutter (good for pasta too)
- Timer
- Sugar thermometer
- Fish scaler
- Piping bag and nozzles, plain or fancy
- Trussing needles; larding needles
- Jelly bag

MEASURING EQUIPMENT

VITAL

- A toughened glass measuring jug, with both metric and imperial.
- A set of scales showing both metric and imper-

301

ial – either the traditional balance scales with weights, or spring-balance scales.

- A set of measuring spoons, both metric and imperial.

LUXURY

- If you use American recipes, you could obtain a nest of measuring cups.

TOP OF THE STOVE EQUIPMENT

VITAL

- A good selection of saucepans, large, medium and small, with lids that fit well, heavy bottoms and heat-resistant handles and knobs. They should be straight-sided and fairly deep, but a small sloping-sided pan is good for some sauces, and a wide shallow pan for poaching and reducing. Saucepans are available in aluminium, cast iron, enamelled cast iron, stainless steel and copper. Many have non-stick coatings.
- Frying pans of 20–25cm (8–10in) in diameter are most useful. Some have lids. They should be fairly shallow with a thick base, and a long heat-resistant handle.
- A cast-iron ridged grill pan, for dry-frying/grilling, rectangular or round.
- A flameproof casserole, round or oval, which can be used on the stove top and in the oven.
- A strong two-handled colander (if the right size, this can double as a steamer over a saucepan).

USEFUL

- A deep-frying pan with a long-handled wire basket and a deep-frying thermometer.
- A double boiler or double saucepan.
- A steamer of some sort: a double pan with holes in the base of the upper pan; Chinese stacking bamboo baskets; an expandable metal basket which fits over a saucepan; or an improvised colander or drum sieve over a saucepan. See also page 15.
- A stockpot that is taller than it is wide, to prevent excess evaporation. It can be heavy, so should have two sturdy handles.

- A Chinese wok and its accessories.
- A flat heavy griddle or girdle.

LUXURY

- Asparagus pan
- Fish-kettle
- Crêpe or omelette pan
- Couscoussière
- Preserving pan

OVEN EQUIPMENT

VITAL

- A large strong casserole with a tight-fitting lid. The most useful are those which are flameproof as well, and can be brought to the table.
- A strong roasting tin with sides of about 5cm (2in) deep, which will fit comfortably in the oven (there must be room for air to circulate). This can double as a *bain-marie*.
- At least two baking sheets or trays, which will fit comfortably in the oven as above. Those with a dark finish are preferable, as they conduct heat more readily and evenly.
- Basic baking equipment: cake tins, round and square, of varying sizes (see page 124); loaf tins (500g/1lb and 1kg/2lb are most useful); flan rings or flan tins with removable bases; a bun or muffin tin (usually with 12 holes); shallow sponge or sandwich tins (see page 121). Those with a dull or black finish are preferable.

USEFUL

- An oven thermometer to check that your oven is performing as it should; a meat thermometer to register the internal temperature of meat or bird.
- Wire racks: one V-shaped for use in roasting, or some flat ones for cooling baked items.
- Shallow ovenproof baking dishes; pie dish.
- A straight-sided soufflé dish in glass or china; small soufflé dishes or ramekins.

LUXURY

- A terrine dish for pâté etc., preferably in cast iron; or hinged *pâté en croûte* moulds.
- Specialist baking tins such as brioche moulds – round with fluted sloping sides, available in

several sizes (they can double as decorative moulds for jellies and mousses); Swiss roll tins; springform cake tins, madeleine pans, charlotte moulds; fluted tube tins (for savarins etc.); barquette boat moulds.
- Blackbird pie funnel
- Clay pot or Römertopf for baking foods in their own juices.

CUTTING EQUIPMENT

VITAL

- A set of sturdy kitchen knives, with carbon steel or high carbon stainless-steel blades. The handles should be riveted to the blade, heat resistant, non-slip – and comfortable to hold. They will be expensive but a worthwhile investment.
- Strong kitchen scissors
- A cutting board; a bread board. Wood looks better than melanine or polyethylene, but is less hygienic. Wash and dry very thoroughly.
- A four-sided box grater with a choice of cutting edges and holes.
- A vegetable peeler: those with swivel-action blades are the best.

USEFUL

- A food processor. It will chop, mince, grind, shred, grate and slice.
- A Chinese cleaver
- A rotary grater
- Skewers of varying widths and lengths.

LUXURY

- A *mezzaluna* or *hachoir*, double-handled knife with a curving blade.
- Grapefruit knife; apple corer; citrus zester; cheese slicer; cherry stoner; melon baller; bean slicer; oyster knife; cheese knife.
- Nutmeg grater
- A mandoline (slicing implement)
- Poultry shears
- An electric carving knife (with a blade for cutting frozen foods).

MIXING AND MASHING EQUIPMENT

VITAL

- Some mixing bowls, available in varying sizes, in glass, glazed porcelain, earthenware or porcelain, stainless steel and copper. They must have flat bases, and rounded rather than straight sides. Pudding basins are smaller, with sloping sides and a lip; they are useful for much more than steamed puddings.
- A variety of sieves: a large round mesh one and a nylon one. (Conical strainers and drum sieves are rather more luxurious.)
- A variety of whisks: a wire balloon whisk; a hand-held rotary whisk or, better, an electric hand-held whisk.
- A masher for potatoes and other cooked vegetables.

USEFUL

- A food processor and blender or liquidiser will purée etc.; the former will also mix pastry and doughs, as will a food mixer.
- A hand-cranked *mouli-légumes* or food mill in stainless steel has a variety of cutting discs.
- A glass citrus juicer with a ridged dome in the centre.
- A garlic press. Most are fairly fiddly to clean, though, and often a little chopping board kept specifically for garlic and the flat of a knife will be more effective.
- A pestle and mortar.

LUXURY

- Various fitments and accessories for food processors or food mixers: spice grinders, coffee grinders etc.

MISCELLANEOUS LUXURIES

- An electric deep-fat fryer
- Pressure cooker
- Sorbetière or ice cream churn
- Barbecue, small or large, plus accessories.
- Pasta machine; pasta rolling pin.

CHAPTER 29

MENU PLANNING

Everyone who cooks can vouch for the maddening frequency with which the best dishes are turned out, not when we are entertaining or making a special effort, but here and there in everyday meals. The factors which contribute to this tantalising truth are not hard to fathom. Notably successful dishes are pretty sure to be based on fresh, seasonal ingredients, which have been cooked without hurry or distraction, and served as soon as they are ready.

The temptation when planning what to serve for any special occasion is to choose dishes which are over-elaborate, over-rich, and which over-stretch the cook in terms of the amount of last-minute preparation or cooking required. Learning the lessons to be found in those everyday triumphs involves making realistic plans that take into consideration the time required for shopping, preparation and cooking, and the adequacy of the cooking and storage facilities, as well as concocting a well-balanced menu.

Priorities for menus are as personal as taste, and as variable. Whether the occasion to be planned is a simple supper for two or an elaborate bash for fifty, the following checklist contains points to consider.

CHOOSING WHAT TO EAT

● Balance marks a good menu. Balance rich courses with light ones, and strong or complex tastes with fresh flavours.
● Consider appetising contrasts of texture and colour.
● Avoid repetition: too many rich sauces, several puréed vegetables, or soup followed by another wet dish such as a casserole. Olive oil in every course is a likelier hazard these days than the traditional pitfall of putting cream in every dish.
● Try to use ingredients which are in season because these are likely to taste best as well as being more reasonably priced than out-of-season delicacies.
● Make use of good food that needs minimal preparation. Easy first courses based on Parma style ham, smoked fish, or top quality bought terrines demand little further work.
● To avoid last-minute carving, consider birds such as partridge or poussin which can be dealt out one apiece, or dishes such as individual home-made pies.
● Cheese is a course that almost looks after itself. Consider offering one brilliant cheese rather than small pieces of several varieties. A whole Brie, or a mature truckle Cheddar surrounded by grapes or apples looks wholeheartedly generous.
● Make good use of dishes that can be cooked in advance. Most pâtés, terrines and mousses to be served cold benefit from a period of maturation in the refrigerator. Many main-course dishes such as casseroles of game or beef are even better when made in advance and reheated.

GETTING ORGANISED

● Remember that it is always much easier to use a recipe you have cooked at least once before.
● Check the menu against the pots, pans, burn-

ers, dishes and oven and refrigerator space that will be needed to produce it.

● Make a timetable, bearing in mind the extra time needed to prepare larger than usual quantities of ingredients, and any additional cooking time required.

● Scaling recipes up and down is not always only a matter of doubling or halving the ingredients. Sometimes proportions will need to be adjusted too. A large braise may need proportionately less liquid than a small one. Timings may alter for larger quantities. Liquid recipes cooked at or about the boiling point of water will take a little longer to come to the boil, but after that, the volume should make no difference to the cooking time. But large roasts or cakes will need longer in the oven than small ones, and will usually need to be cooked at lower temperatures if the heat is to penetrate the centre without bak-

ing the outside to a crisp.

● Putting several cold dishes into the oven at once to reheat will increase the time required to heat them thoroughly.

● Heating or reheating food taken straight from the refrigerator will take longer than cooking it from room temperature.

● To reheat food in the oven, use a moderate heat (180°C/350°F, gas mark 4).

● To keep food warm use a very cool oven (120°C/250°F, gas mark ½), or a double boiler. To keep several pans warm, improvise a multiple *bain-marie* by standing them in a roasting tin filled with hot water. Using one burner is also economical.

● Hot plates for hot dishes are even more important for large gatherings than for small ones if guests insist on waiting until everyone has been served.

CHAPTER 30

WEIGHTS AND MEASURES

No conversion system for the metric and Imperial weights and measures used in cookery is entirely satisfactory. All involve inelegant compromises. The pound illustrates the problem clearly. The commonsense metric equivalent is half a kilogram, or 500 grams, but a more accurate conversion is 450 grams. Butchers, greengrocers, fishmongers and older shoppers still operate in pounds and ounces. Although most pre-packed foodstuffs are labelled with both, many are now in standard metric sizes for which an Imperial conversion is given. The changeover from Imperial to metric is still incomplete.

This is why the system of conversion used in the recipes throughout this book is a rather literal one which allows the cook as much accuracy as possible when using recipes from many different sources.

Accurate measurement of ingredients is the one aspect of cooking over which we can have good control. We all use different pots and pans, and cookers, and make variable judgements about whether a sauce is thick or thin, or whether a piece of meat is cooked to medium rare or medium. Recipes, however carefully written, and however often they have been tested must, inevitably, give imprecise instructions about how long to cook things for. So precise measurement of ingredients provides a solid foundation.

A set of standard measuring spoons is indispensable. A tablespoon is *not* a huge serving spoon rescued from a canteen of Victorian cutlery. It is an accurate measure of volume which holds 15 millilitres or ½ fluid ounce. Spoon and cup measures are always level unless otherwise indicated in the recipe.

Old cookery books are now so sought-after by collectors that a number of the best have been reprinted in modern facsimile editions. Anyone wishing to cook recipes in books published before 1838, when the Imperial system of weights and measures was introduced, should note that prior to that date the pint in England was 16 fluid ounces, as it still is in America today. Other obsolete but useful measures of volume when cooking recipes from old cookery books are the dessertspoon, which holds 1½ teaspoons, the gill, which is 5 fluid ounces, and the old standard British cup, which is 10 fluid ounces.

The charts which follow show the metric and Imperial equivalents used throughout this book.

OVEN TEMPERATURES

very cool	= 110°C/225°F, gas mark ¼
	= 120°C/250°F, gas mark ½
cool	= 140°C/275°F, gas mark 1
	= 150°C/300°F, gas mark 2
moderate	= 160°C/325°F, gas mark 3
	= 180°C/350°F, gas mark 4
moderately hot	= 190°C/375°F, gas mark 5
	= 200°C/400°F, gas mark 6
hot	= 220°C/425°F, gas mark 7
	= 230°C/450°F, gas mark 8
very hot	= 240°C/475°F, gas mark 9

WEIGHTS

15 g = ½ oz	400 g = 14 oz
20 g = ¾ oz	425 g = 15 oz
30 g = 1 oz	450 g = 1 lb
55 g = 2 oz	500 g = 1 lb 2 oz
85 g = 3 oz	570 g = 1¼ lb
100 g = 3½ oz	680 g = 1½ lb
110 g = 4 oz	900 g = 2 lb
140 g = 5 oz	1 kg = 2 lb 3 oz
170 g = 6 oz	1.35 kg = 3 lb
200 g = 7 oz	1.8 kg = 4 lb
225 g = 8 oz	2.3 kg = 5 lb
255 g = 9 oz	2.7 kg = 6 lb
285 g = 10 oz	3.2 kg = 7 lb
310 g = 11 oz	3.4 kg = 8 lb
340 g = 12 oz	4 kg = 9 lb
370 g = 13 oz	4.5 kg = 10 lb

LIQUID MEASURES

1 teaspoon (5 ml) = 1 teaspoon
1 tablespoon (15 ml) = 1 tablespoon
120 ml = 4 fl oz
150 ml = ¼ pint = 5 fl oz
175 ml = 6 fl oz
200 ml = ⅓ pint = 7 fl oz
250 ml = 8 fl oz
300 ml = ½ pint = 10 fl oz
350 ml = 12 fl oz
400 ml = 14 fl oz
450 ml = ¾ pint = 15 fl oz
500 ml = 18 fl oz
600 ml = 1 pint = 20 fl oz
750 ml = 1¼ pints
900 ml = 1½ pints
1 litre = 1¾ pints
1.2 litres = 2 pints
1.25 litres = 2¼ pints
1.5 litres = 2½ pints
1.6 litres = 2¾ pints
1.75 litres = 3 pints
2 litres = 3½ pints
2.25 litres = 4 pints
2.5 litres = 4½ pints
2.75 litres = 5 pints

DIMENSIONS OF CUTTERS, TINS ETC.

3 mm = ⅛ inch
5 mm = ¼ inch
1 cm = ½ inch
2 cm = ¾ inch
2.5 cm = 1 inch
5 cm = 2 inches
6.5 cm = 2½ inches
7.5 cm = 3 inches
10 cm = 4 inches
15 cm = 6 inches
18 cm = 7 inches
20 cm = 8 inches
23 cm = 9 inches
25 cm = 10 inches
28 cm = 11 inches
30 cm = 12 inches
35 cm = 14 inches
40 cm = 16 inches

CAPACITY OF PANS, BOWLS, TINS ETC.

300 ml = ½ pint
450 ml = ¾ pint
600 ml = 1 pint
900 ml = 1½ pints
1 litre = 2 pints
1.25 litres = 2½ pints
1.5 litres = 3 pints
2 litres = 3½ pints
2.5 litres = 5 pints
3.5 litres = 7 pints

AMERICAN MEASURES

1 pint = 16 fl oz
1 cup = 8 fl oz

OLD FRENCH MEASURES

An assortment of everyday household vessels were pressed into service as measures in country kitchens. When recipes handed from mother to daughter came to be written down, the coffee cups and wine glasses that generations of cooks had actually used figured in the recipes. Remember when using these very approximate measurements that when great grand-mama was asked how much Cognac she put in the pot, her answer was no doubt accompanied by a gallic shrug.

I cuillère à café = I scant teaspoon
I cuillère à bouche = I tablespoon
I cuillère à soupe = I tablespoon
I verre à liqueur = I tablespoon
I cuillère à pot = 4 tablespoons
I tasse à café = 5 tablespoons
I verre à Bordeaux = 6 tablespoons
I verre = 7 fl oz

CONVERSION FORMULAS

To convert ounces into grams multiply the ounces by 28.35.

To convert grams into ounces, multiply the grams by .035.

To convert inches into centimetres, multiply the inches by 2.54.

To convert centimetres into inches, multiply the centimetres by .39.

To convert degrees Fahrenheit to Celsius, subtract 32, multiply by 5 and divide by 9.

To convert degrees Celsius to Fahrenheit, multiply by 9, divide by 5, and add 32.

GLOSSARY

Abalone A sea mollusc, called an ormer in Britain, and widely eaten in the US, China and Japan. Chinese cooking has many recipes for dried abalone called *pao yu*.

Acidulated water Cold water plus a spoonful of lemon juice or vinegar. Used to prevent the cut surfaces of raw fruit and vegetables from browning.

Agar-Agar A vegetable setting agent obtained from seaweed which can used instead of gelatine.

Aïoli A cold sauce of garlic and oil, similar to mayonnaise in texture, known as the butter of Provence.

à l'Américaine, and à l'Armoricaine The origins of the recipe for lobster *à l'Américaine* are disputed. Some claim it is a Breton invention and that it should be spelled 'armoricaine', after the ancient name of the region. Other say it was created by a chef in Provence to please an American client. Either way, it has a rich sauce including tomatoes, red peppers, wine, brandy and the uncooked tomalley or coral of the lobster.

Al dente A literal translation from Italian is 'to the tooth'. Used to describe the texture of cooked food that is still firm to the bite, particularly pasta and vegetables.

All-purpose flour In the US plain flour.

Amuse-gueules Translates loosely as 'tongue tickler'. Miniature savoury mouthfuls served with drinks before a meal.

Antipasti The dishes served to begin an Italian meal.

Aromatics Herbs, vegetables and spices used to scent and flavour foods.

Aspic A transparent savoury jelly made from clarified meat, fish, poultry, game or vegetable stock, used to glaze cold foods.

Bagna cauda In Italy, a dish of hot anchovy, garlic and olive oil sauce into which pieces of young, sweet vegetables are dipped at the table.

Barquette A small, boat-shaped pastry case or open tart.

Bain-marie A water bath. In the oven, a container of hot water, in which a dish that requires gentle heating is set to cook. On top of the stove, a double-saucepan, with hot water in the lower part, and the food to be heated gently in the top.

Ballotine A bird or joint of meat that is boned and re-formed round a stuffing, which is cooked, cooled and glazed with aspic to be served cold.

Bard To cover poultry, game or meat with a thin sheet of fat to keep it moist during roasting or grilling.

Baste To spoon fat, pan juices or another liquid over food during cooking to prevent drying.

Bavarois A custard-based pudding set with gelatine and enriched with whipped cream.

Béchamel A white sauce made by combining milk with a blond *roux* and seasonings. Used as it is, or with additions as the basis of other sauces.

Beignet French for a fritter.

Bell peppers Sweet, red and green vegetable peppers, as opposed to chillies, in American recipes.

Beurre manié Equal parts of plain flour and softened butter, beaten together, and used in small pieces to thicken sauces.

Bind To mix egg or another liquid with dry ingredients to make the mixture hold together, as in stuffings and fish cakes.

Bisque A rich, smooth fish soup, usually of crab or lobster.

Blanquette A rich, pale coloured stew, usually of veal or lamb.

Blanch To immerse briefly in boiling water. Used to prepare vegetables for freezing, to loosen the skins of tomatoes and other fruit before peeling, and to firm offal such as sweetbreads.

Borsch A family of very varied eastern European soups based on beetroot which is sometimes fermented.

Bouillon cubes Stock cubes in the US.

Bouquet garni A small bunch of herbs used to flavour stocks, soups, stews and braises.

Braise To brown food in fat and then cook it slowly in a closed pan with a small amount of liquid.

Bresaola Air-dried beef, a speciality of Lombardy in Italy, served thinly sliced with a dressing of olive oil, lemon juice and black pepper.

Brine A salt and water solution used to preserve or flavour vegetables, meat or fish.

Broil Currently in the US to grill, and in old English recipes.

Brown To sear the exterior of meat, poultry or game, to intensify the flavour before stewing, braising or pot-roasting. Also to finish a dish by setting it under a hot grill until the top surface colours.

Bruise To crush, but not pulverise, aromatic ingredients such as garlic or ginger, so that they give more of their flavour.

Bruschetta The Roman version of garlic bread. Slices of wholemeal *pane integrale* brushed with olive oil and garlic, and toasted.

Caramelise To turn sugar into caramel by heating it gently until it dissolves and then turns brown. Also to glaze vegetables, such as small onions, in a mixture of butter and sugar until the exterior is well coloured.

Carrageen Also known as Irish moss and pearl moss. A mucilaginous substance extracted from the seaweed and used to set puddings.

Cassareep A Caribbean flavouring sauce made from cassava root, and an essential ingredient for pepperpot stews.

Cassoulet A robust dish of dried haricot beans cooked with pork or lamb, sausages and *confit*, preserved goose or duck. A speciality of south-western France.

Catsup Tomato ketchup in the US.

Caul The web-like fatty membrane which surrounds a pig's intestines, and those of other animals. Also known as lace-fat. It is used to wrap skinless sausages, rissoles, faggots, French *crépinettes*, to hold their shape and lubricate them during cooking.

Ceviche or Seviche A South American way of preparing raw white fish by marinating it in lime or lemon juice which coagulates the proteins and 'cooks' it without heat.

Charcuterie Literally, the products of the pork butcher. The term now embraces hams, sausages, terrines, galantines, pâtés, pies and puddings, whether made from pork or other meats.

Chèvre Literally a goat in French, but also used as a blanket term for cheese made with goats' milk.

Chiffonade Leaves cut in fine ribbons.

Chine To saw through the junction between the spine and rib bones to make joints of meat easier to carve.

Chitterlings Can mean sausages made from bits of pig intestine and tripe, or the intestines themselves, which are prepared and cooked in milk with seasonings as for ox tripe. To butchers, chitterlings is the frilly part of the large intestine of the pig.

Chowder A stew, or soup, of fish and potatoes, especially in the US.

Civet A rich, dark game stew or casserole.

Clafoutis A French batter pudding, traditionally containing black cherries.

Clarify To remove solid particles from stocks or fats.

In the case of butter, milk solids are removed by heating until the oil and solids separate, then discarding the solids (see page 239).

Coeur à la crème A fresh soft cheese made in France and moulded in heart-shaped wicker baskets. Also a home-made dessert of fresh soft cheese and cream which is strained in individual heart-shaped moulds.

Compote Fresh or dried fruit stewed in a sweet syrup.

Confectioners' sugar Icing sugar in the US.

Confit Literally, 'preserved' in French. Most frequently used of goose or duck preserved in its own fat.

Consommé A clear soup based upon strong broth made from meat, poultry or game. Clarity and strength are the watchwords.

Cornstarch Cornflour in the US.

Corn syrup A heavy glucose syrup made from maize. A common ingredient in American recipes.

Coulis A purée of fruit or vegetables used as a sauce.

Court bouillon A poaching liquid for fish made with water, white wine or vinegar, herbs, vegetables and seasonings.

Cream To beat hard fat, usually butter or margarine, or a mixture of fat and sugar, until it is light and fluffy.

Crépinettes Any mixture of minced meat, but usually pork, wrapped in caul fat.

Crudités Small pieces of raw vegetables served as an appetiser, often with a mayonnaise-based dipping sauce.

Curd Coagulated proteins, usually of milk. The same word is used for the white flowering head of the cauliflower.

Curdle To separate into solid and liquid parts. Usually used of sauces, but also of creamed cake mixtures.

Cure To preserve foods, especially meat or fish, by salting, drying or smoking.

Darne A thick slice of fish which includes a section of the spine, as in a salmon steak.

Daube A French term for a rich stew of unbrowned meat and vegetables, moistened with wine and cooked in a covered pot.

Deglaze To add liquid to a pan in which food has been browned, to dissolve the residues and incorporate the pan juices as the basis for a gravy or sauce. (See also page 176.)

Degorge To use salt to extract some of the moisture from vegetables, such as aubergines or cucumber, prior to cooking or pickling.

Degrease To remove fat from the surface of a stock, soup or sauce.

Demi-glace Stock that has been reduced to the point where it begins to thicken, used as the basis for many sauces in the classic French repertoire.

Dhal The term in Indian cooking for pulses. Also for

spiced dishes of cooked pulses, often a purée of lentils.

Dice To cut into small cubes.

Dough Any soft, pasty mass, usually of flour, or meal, mixed with water.

Draw To remove the entrails of birds.

Drawn butter In the US, clarified butter. In Britain melted butter, or a melted butter sauce to which vinegar or water has been added.

Dredge To sprinkle liberally with sugar or flour.

Dress To prepare for cooking, or for eating. Of poultry and game birds, to pluck, clean and truss preparatory to cooking. Of crab and lobster, to remove the inedible parts, and prepare the cooked flesh for eating. Of salads, to mix with a sauce.

Dripping Domestically, the fat and meat juice residues of roasting. Commercially, rendered beef fat.

Dropping consistency A mixture which will adhere to a spoon which is held steady, but drop from it when the spoon is tapped smartly.

Dumpling A ball of dough, sweet or savoury, plain or enclosing a filling, and usually boiled.

Dutch oven A flameproof casserole in the US. But in old English cookery, a hood to reflect heat on to foods being cooked in front of an open fire.

Emulsify To create an emulsion, a mixture of two normally unmixable liquids, for example oil and water, by dispersing fine droplets of one throughout the other so that they are held in suspension.

En croûte Foods which are completely enclosed in a pastry crust are described as *en croûte*.

En papillote Foods which are cooked inside, and served from, packages made with oiled or buttered greaseproof paper.

Essence Any highly concentrated aromatic liquid used for flavouring.

Espresso Strong coffee made by forcing boiling water under pressure through finely ground roasted coffee.

Eviscerate To remove the viscera, or guts, of an animal, bird or fish.

Ferment To produce alcohol, acid or gases by controlled reactions between yeasts or bacteria with foodstuffs. The rising action of bread dough, the souring and thickening of milk in yogurt, and the transformation of grape juice into wine are examples of fermentation.

Filo A Greek and Middle Eastern pastry made in paper-thin sheets.

Fillet To separate flesh from bones.

Fines herbes A mixture of finely chopped fresh herbs that always includes parsley plus one or more other herbs such as chives, tarragon and chervil.

Flake Of fish, to separate the cooked or smoked flesh into small pieces with your fingers.

Fold in To combine two mixtures, at least one of which has been whisked, using a cutting, lifting and turning action to knock out as little of the air as possible. A large metal spoon is the best tool for the job.

Fritto misto Literally, fried mixture in Italian. Usually a deep-fried combination of meat with vegetables, or mixed fish, or mixed vegetables.

Fumet A stock, usually of fish, concentrated by reduction.

Galantine A dish of boned poultry or meat which is shaped and cooked in stock, to be served cold with an aspic glaze.

Garam masala In Indian cooking, a mixture of spices.

Ghee Clarified butter, or vegetable fat, used in Indian cooking.

Giblets The edible offal of poultry and feathered game.

Glace de viande Meat glaze. Stock which has been reduced until it sets in a thick, rubbery jelly.

Glaze To give foods a glossy finish. To paint pastry with egg before baking or to cover cold foods with aspic, for example.

Gluten A substance formed by the interaction of grain proteins with water. Wheat flour made from hard wheat contains the largest concentrations of the relevant proteins.

Gnocchi Small dumplings or lumps of pasta, usually shaped and ridged with a fork. They are often made at home from potato or semolina as well as with flour.

Granita A grainy, coarse-textured Italian water ice flavoured with coffee, fruit or wine.

Gratin A dish finished with a golden crust which is browned in the oven or under a grill. The crust is usually made with breadcrumbs or grated cheese.

Gravlax Also *gravad lax* in Sweden, and *gravlaks* in Norway, is raw salmon cured with salt and fresh dill. It is eaten raw usually with a sweet mustard sauce.

Grits Grain which has been partially refined and ground to a coarse meal, usually maize.

Gumbo A soup containing the vegetable okra.

Gut To remove the entrails, or viscera from birds, meat or fish.

Hang To mature the flavour and tenderise the flesh of meat, poultry and game by suspending the carcass in cool, airy conditions for a number of days.

Heavy cream Double cream in the US.

Hors d'oeuvre A small dish, or dishes, served at the beginning of a meal to whet the appetite.

Hull To remove the stalk, calyx and central core from soft fruits such as strawberries and raspberries.

Infuse To extract flavour from tea leaves, herbs and other foods by steeping them in hot liquid. The 311 flavoured liquid is then described as an infusion.

Julienne To cut vegetables into square-sectioned strips, usually about the thickness of matchsticks. Also, more finely cut strips of citrus zest.

Junket A pudding made with flavoured and sweetened milk which is set with rennet.

Kasha A Russian porridge or drier dish made from whole, husked buckwheat grains which are toasted before being cooked with water.

Kilocalorie A kilocalorie is the amount of heat required to raise the temperature of 1 litre of water by 1°C. By extension, it is used as a measure of the amount of energy food contains.

Kilojoule The kilojoule is a measure of energy, as distinct from the kilocalorie, which is a measure of heat. The kilojoule has been adopted internationally as the measure of the fuel value of food.

Kosher Food prepared according to orthodox Jewish dietary laws.

Knead To compress and stretch a dough repeatedly.

Lard To insert strips of fat into lean meat to lubricate it during cooking, and, by analogy, to insert strips of one foodstuff through another.

Also the descriptive name of rendered pork fat.

Liaison The French culinary term for a thickening for a sauce or soup. Any ingredient or combination of ingredients added to a liquid for the purpose of thickening it can be described as a liaison.

Liqueur A drink make from distilled alcohol flavoured with herbs, fruit, spices or other ingredients, and usually sweetened. Liqueurs are customarily drunk at the end of meals to aid digestion, and their alcoholic strength varies widely. In cooking they are used mainly to flavour puddings.

Lobster Thermidor Cooked lobster, returned to its shell, sauced and browned under a grill. The sauce variations are innumerable. André Simon, founder of the Wine and Food Society, described a white sauce flavoured with onion, cayenne, white wine, mushrooms, tomato and Parmesan.

Macerate To soften fruits by steeping them in syrup, spirits or liqueurs.

Macédoine A mixture of fruit or vegetables served hot or cold.

Manche à gigot A handle which is fixed to a leg of lamb or mutton so that the carver can keep a firm grip of the joint.

Mandoline A manually operated slicing machine used mainly for vegetables, which can produce plain or crinkle-cut slices of graduated thickness, fine julienne strips and thicker chips.

Marinate To soak raw foods, usually meat, fish, poultry or game, in a mixture of ingredients which lubricate, flavour and, in some instances, preserve or tenderise them. The marinating mixture is called a marinade.

Medallion Food, usually meat, cut in small, circular slices, and sometimes flattened.

Meringue An egg-white foam sweetened with sugar. In professional kitchens French meringue is made by whisking the egg whites and sugar cold. Swiss meringue is whisked over heat, and Italian meringue is sweetened with sugar syrup boiled to the soft ball stage.

Mesclun A mixture of young salad leaves. The word *mesclun* means 'mixture' in the Provençal language.

Millet A variety of grasses and small edible grains are known as millets. Most are eaten as porridges or unleavened breads, but millet can also be cooked in water or stock and served, like rice, as an accompaniment to stews and casseroles.

Mirepoix A flavouring mixture of chopped or finely diced vegetables, usually including carrot, onion and celery, and often, but not always, ham or bacon.

Mise en place The setting out, weighing and preparation of ingredients before cooking commences.

Molasses The liquid residue from refining cane sugar. The lowest grade is blackstrap molasses which has lost all the sugar that can be economically extracted. Baking molasses and treacle are much sweeter.

Mouli-légumes Literally a vegetable mill. A metal sieve through which food is forced by revolving blades. It purées food at the same time as sieving out pips, skin, bones etc.

Mousseline A light mixture of puréed raw fish or poultry, to which egg white and, usually, cream are added. The delicate *mousseline* is then poached or baked in small moulds in a *bain-marie* and is usually served with a well-flavoured sauce. Quenelles are made with fish *mousseline*.

Noodle Any dough shaped in strings or ribbons is described as a noodle. Oriental noodles are made with rice flour, mung bean starch, buckwheat flour and arrowroot as well as wheat flour.

Nuts Any large dry seed or fruit with a hard shell and an edible kernel is called a nut. Of the hundreds of varieties grown, only a few are important foodstuffs in this country and used in cooking. Most nuts are dried to improve their keeping qualities, but a few, including almonds and walnuts, can be bought green.

Nuts are an important protein source for vegetarians, and contain large amounts of carbohydrate, fat and, of course, calories. When buying nuts in the shell, choose those that are heavy for their size, but avoid any that are damp or show signs of mould. Despite their hard shells, nuts quickly dry and deteriorate in warm rooms, so buy them in small quantities and eat them sooner rather than later.

Many types of nuts can be bought already shelled and processed in various ways (see page 287).

Almonds, brazils, hazels, pecans, pistachios and walnuts are the most popular dessert nuts, to be shelled and eaten at table.

Fresh chestnuts must be cooked and are best of all roasted in front of the fire and peeled before being eaten with salt. They also need peeling before being boiled or steamed to make a purée, or for adding to stuffings. To skin fresh chestnuts make a small slit in the skin of each nut and boil or bake them in a moderate oven for about 5 minutes. Peel off the shells when they are cool enough to handle.

Fresh coconuts should feel heavy for their size and you should be able the hear the liquid sloshing inside them. To extract the clear juice, pierce two of the three 'eyes' in the top of the nut, and pour the liquid out of one of them. Then crack open the hard shell and remove the white flesh inside. To make the coconut milk called for in recipes, grate the flesh and cover with boiling water. Let it cool and strain off the milk, squeezing out as much as you can.

Oven-broil In the US, to cook in a little fat in a hot oven.

Pan-broil In the US, to pan-fry.

Pancetta Italy's version of streaky bacon includes spices in the cure.

Parboil To boil food for a short time so that it is partially cooked in preparation for cooking by another method. Potatoes can be parboiled before roasting.

Pâté A well-seasoned mixture of meat, poultry or game which is baked, lightly pressed, and served cold.

Pâte French for pastry and other doughs.

Pectin The naturally occuring gelling agent in fruit which causes jams and jellies to set. Fruits high in pectin include apples, gooseberries, quinces, lemons and Seville oranges.

Pickle To preserve in brine or vinegar.

Pilaf A dry dish of savoury rice, usually including meat or poultry, and often nuts and dried fruit. *Pilau* is the Indian equivalent.

Pit In the US, to stone fruit.

Pith In citrus fruits, the bitter-tasting white layer between the zest and and the flesh.

Pluck To remove the feathers from poultry and game. The same word is used for a sheep's stomach which is used for the casings of traditionally made haggis.

Poach To cook food gently by immersing it in simmering liquid.

Pot roast To cook a piece of browned meat gently in a closely covered pot with a little liquid.

Prosciutto The generic term for Italy's many dry-cured hams eaten raw in thin slices. The versions made in Parma and around Venice are particularly esteemed.

Purée Food which has a soft, smooth consistency as a result of being mashed and sieved, or passed through a food mill, or processed.

Quenelle See *Mousseline*.

Reduce To concentrate and/or thicken a liquid by evaporation.

Refresh To immerse freshly cooked vegetables in cold water to arrest the cooking process.

Render To melt animal or poultry fat slowly to a liquid, before straining off any residual solids. Beef dripping is produced by rendering beef fat.

Rennet A substance obtained from calves' stomachs which is used to coagulate milk to make junket and cheese.

Rissole Small savoury 'cake' made with leftover minced meats, vegetables or pulses. They are usually fried.

Roe The eggs and sperm of fish. Soft roe is from the male, grainy or hard roe from the female.

Romaine In the US, Cos lettuce.

Romano cheese In the US, the Italian cheese Pecorino Romano.

Roux A foundation for sauces made by cooking together flour and fat before adding liquid.

Salamander Traditionally, a metal plate which was heated and used to brown the top of foods. It has been superseded by the overhead grill.

Salmagundi A cold dish of chopped meat, anchovies, eggs and onions with oil and seasonings.

Salmi A dish of partly roasted game, which finishes cooking in a wine sauce.

Saltpetre The common name for potassium nitrate, used, in small quantities, in conjunction with common salt, as a preservative.

Satay Also *saté*. In Indonesian and Malay cooking, roasted peanuts, pounded to a paste, are the basis for satay, skewers of grilled meat in a peanut sauce.

Sauerkraut Finely sliced, salted and fermented white cabbage. It is a speciality in Germany, and in Alsace in France where it is known as *choucroûte*.

Sauté To cook in butter or fat until lightly browned.

Sear To brown the surface of meat very quickly on a high heat.

Serrano ham *Jamón serrano* is a dry-cured mountain ham from Spain. It is thinly sliced and eaten raw.

Shortening Cooking fat, especially in US baking.

Shuck To shell seafood such as oysters and clams.

Skillet In the US, a frying pan.

Skim To remove any froth, scum or fat from the top of a liquid.

313

Soufflé An airy confection lifted to extravagant heights with beaten egg white. Baked soufflés are eaten hot and are based on a sweet or savoury sauce or purée. Cold soufflés are set with gelatine.

Spatchcock To split small birds lengthways and to flatten them before cooking, usually by grilling.

Steep To soak in liquid.

Stir-fry A traditional oriental cooking method in which ingredients are simultaneously stirred and fried in a bowl-shaped wok over high heat.

Strain To remove solids from a liquid by passing it through a sieve.

Stock A broth flavoured with meat, poultry, game, fish or vegetables.

Superfine sugar In the US, caster sugar.

Suprême A boneless breast of poultry or game.

Sweet butter Unsalted butter made from fresh cream.

Sweet peppers The term sweet distinguishes large red, green and yellow peppers from hot chilli peppers. American recipes refer to them as bell peppers.

Swiss cheese In the US, Emmenthal cheese.

Syrup A solution of sugar and water.

Suet A layer of hard fat which encloses an animal's kidneys. It is usually bought already cleaned and shredded. A vegetarian fat which has been processed to behave like shredded suet is also sold.

Sushi A Japanese snack, made from rice flavoured with vinegar and garnished with seaweed, fish, egg, or other ingredients.

Tajine A deep earthenware dish with a conical lid which gives its name to the stews of the same name made in North Africa.

Tempura A Japanese dish of deep-fried fish, shellfish and vegetables in the lightest of batter coatings.

Tomalley The greenish coloured liver found in the thorax of lobster.

Truss To tie poultry and game birds into a compact and attractive shape before cooking, using a trussing needle and string, or skewers.

Variety meat In the US, offal.

Yeast Yeasts are microscopic single-cell fungi which occur naturally in great variety. Bakers' yeast is a strain evolved to raise bread dough by alcoholic fermentation. The alcohol produced during fermentation evaporates in the heat of the oven.

Zest The coloured, oily outer part of the skin of citrus fruits, used for flavouring.

Zucchini Courgettes in Italian and American recipes.

BIBLIOGRAPHY

Androuet, Pierre, *Guide du Fromage* (Aidan Ellis, revised edition, 1983).

Acton, Eliza, *The Best of Eliza Acton* (Penguin Books, 1st edition, 1974).

Ayrton, Elisabeth, *The Cookery of England* (Penguin Books, 1st edition, 1977).

Bissell, Frances, *Sainsbury's Book of Food* (Webster's Wine Price Guide, 1st edition, 1989).

Blanc, Raymond, *Recipes from Le Manoir aux Quat' Saisons* (Macdonald Orbis, 1st edition, 1988).

Boxer, Arabella, *Arabella Boxer's Book of English Food* (A John Curtis Book, Hodder & Stoughton, 1st edition, 1991).

David, Elizabeth, *English Bread and Yeast Cookery* (Allen Lane, 1st edition, 1977). *Spices, Salt and Aromatics in the English Kitchen* (Penguin Books, 1st edition, 1970). *A Book of Mediterranean Food* (Macdonald & Co., 2nd edition, 1958). *French Country Cooking* (Penguin Books, 2nd revised edition, 1966). *Summer Cooking* (Penguin Books, revised edition, 1965). *An Omelette and a Glass of Wine* (Jill Norman for Robert Hale, 1st edition, 1984). *Italian Food* (Penguin Books, 3rd edition, 1975).

Davidson, Alan, *Mediterranean Seafood* (Allen Lane, 2nd edition, 1981). *North Atlantic Seafood* (Macmillan, 1st edition, 1979).

Deighton, Len, *ABC of French Food* (Century Hutchinson, 1st edition, 1989).

Farmer, Fannie, *Fannie Farmer's Classic American Cookbook* (Papermac, 12th edition, 1981).

FitzGibbon, Theodora, *The Food of the Western World* (Hutchinson, 1st edition, 1976).

Forbes, Leslie, *A Table in Tuscany* (Webb & Bower, 1st edition, 1985). *A Table in Provence* (Webb & Bower, 1st edition, 1987).

Grigson, Jane, *Charcuterie and French Pork Cookery* (Penguin Books, 1st edition, 1970). *Good Things* (Michael Joseph, 1st edition, 1971). *Jane Grigson's Fruit Book* (Michael Joseph, 1st edition, 1982).

Hartley, Dorothy, *Food in England* (Futura, 2nd edition, 1985).

der Haroutunian, Arto, *North African Cookery*

(Century, 1st edition, 1985).

Hazan, Marcella, *The Classic Italian Cookbook* (Macmillan, revised edition, 1980). *The Second Classic Italian Cookbook* (Jill Norman & Hobhouse, revised edition, 1982).

Jaffrey, Madhur, *An Invitation to Indian Cooking* (Jonathan Cape, 1st edition, 1973). *Eastern Vegetarian Cooking* (Jonathan Cape, 1st edition, 1983).

Lambert Ortiz, Elisabeth, *Caribbean Cookery* (Penguin Books, revised edition, 1977). *The Book of Latin American Cooking* (Jill Norman for Robert Hale, 1st edition, 1984). *The Encyclopedia of Herbs, Spices and Flavourings* (Dorling Kindersley, 1st edition, 1992). *The Food of Spain and Portugal* (Lennard Publishing, 1st edition, 1989).

Leyel, Mrs C.F., and *Hartley*, Miss Olga, *The Gentle Art of Cookery* (Chatto & Windus, revised edition, 1974).

Lin, Hsiang Ju, and *Lin*, Tsuifeng, *Chinese Gastronomy* (Jill Norman & Hobhouse, 2nd edition, 1982).

Luard, Elisabeth, *European Peasant Cookery* (Bantam Press, 1st edition, 1986).

Mackie, Christine, *Life and Food in the Caribbean* (Weidenfeld and Nicolson, 1st edition, 1991).

Mackinlay, Caroline (editor), *The Preserving Book* (Pan Books, 1st edition, 1978).

McGee, Harold, *On Food and Cooking* (George Allen & Unwin, 1st UK edition, 1986). *The Curious Cook* (Harper Collins, 1st UK edition, 1992).

McNeill, F. Marian, *The Scots Kitchen* (Mayflower, 2nd edition, 1974).

Mosimann, Anton, *Cuisine à la Carte* (Northwood Books, 1st edition, 1981).

Nance Nordio, Jeanette, *Taste of Venice* (Webb & Bower, 1st edition, 1988).

National Association of Master Bakers, Confectioners and Caterers, *The Master Bakers' Book of Breadmaking* (Turret-Wheatland, 2nd edition, 1985).

Owen, Sri, *Indonesian Food and Cookery* (Prospect Books, 1st edition, 1980).

Pacioni, Giovanni, *The Macdonald Encylopedia of Mushrooms and Toadstools* (Macdonald, 1st English edition, 1985).

Phillips, Roger, *Mushrooms and Other Fungi of Great Britain and Europe* (Pan Books, 1st edition, 1981). *Wild Food* (Pan Books, 1st edition, 1983).

Roden, Claudia, *A Book of Middle Eastern Food* (Penguin Books, 1st edition, 1970).

Roux, Albert and Michel, *The Roux Brothers New Classic Cuisine* (Macdonald, 1st edition, 1983). *The Roux Brothers on Pâtisserie* (Macdonald, 1st edition, 1986).

Simon, André L., *A Concise Encyclopedia of Gastronomy* (Allen Lane, revised edition, 1983).

Stobart, Tom, *The Cook's Encyclopaedia* (Papermac, 1st edition, 1982).

Time-Life Books, *The Good Cook* (Time-Life Books, 1st editions, series published from 1978 to 1982).

Stewart, Katie, *Katie Stewart's Cookbook* (Victor Gollancz, 1st edition, 1983).

Willan, Anne, *French Regional Cooking* (Hutchinson, 1st edition, 1981).

INDEX